The Original Text-Wrestling Book

The Writing Program
University of Massachusetts Amherst

Marcia Curtis
Benjamin Balthaser
Michael Edwards
Zan Goncalves
Robert Hazard
Noria Jablonski
Brian Jordan
Shauna Seliy
with
Peggy Woods

KENDALL/HUNT PUBLISHING COMPANY
4050 Westmark Drive   Dubuque, Iowa 52002

*To Charlie Moran and Anne Herrington,
former Writing Program Directors,
without whom this program would not exist*

Cover photo of Sean Wooley wrestling is courtesy of David Wooley.

Contents

Alternate Contents

A List of Readings That Work Well Together

Rarely does any text stand on its own. Each is a part of a greater on-going conversation, and our understanding of one text is to a large extent determined—and deepened—by its relationship to another. Below each entry, we have suggested other entries in this book that comment on the first in intriguing ways and simultaneously open the conversation up to further commentary. When you write your own text-wrestling essay, if you don't feel you have enough to say about one reading, you may well have a lot to say about two. We have named just a few potential combinations and are sure other equally provocative pairings and links can be found.

Foreword

by Peter Elbow

And Jacob was left alone; and a man wrestled with him until the breaking of the day. When the man saw that he did not prevail against Jacob, he touched the hollow of his thigh; and Jacob's thigh was put out of joint as he wrestled with him. Then he said, "Let me go, for the day is breaking." But Jacob said, "I will not let you go, unless you bless me." And he said to him, "What is your name?" And he said, "Jacob." Then he said, "Your name shall no more be called Jacob, but Israel, for you have striven with God and with men, and have prevailed." And then he blessed him.

—Genesis 32. 24–29

"Text wrestling" might seem an odd name for a kind of essay. But with this metaphor, we are trying to suggest a way of writing about a published essay in which you engage or grapple with that essay. When people wrestle, they are struggling and yet embracing. One of the most famous stories from the Bible is one in which Jacob wrestles with an angel of God and refuses to stop until he wins a blessing. A text-wrestling essay insists on winning a blessing from the text it is writing about.

No doubt it is helpful if I turn now from metaphor and myth to a plain literal description of two common kinds of essay that we are trying to avoid by using the term "text wrestling":

- An essay in which you don't present your own thinking or opinions—instead devoting yourself entirely to explaining the essay you are writing *about*. (This kind of essay of pure explication *can* be useful, but it's not the idea here.)

- An essay in which you do present your thinking and opinion strongly, but don't really explore or engage with the essay you are supposedly writing about. Writers sometimes fail to do justice to the published essay in one of two ways. They say how much they agree with that essay but then just "pop in" quotes from it to "back up" and echo their own thinking. Or they say how much they disagree with the published essay, but develop only their *own* thinking and never really explore or enter into the thinking in the published essay.

It might seem as though the goals of a text-wrestling essay are paradoxical or contradictory. On the one hand, we ask you to put your attention outside yourself—to enter into someone else's point of view: to read more closely, accurately, fairly, and thoughtfully. Yet on the other hand, we ask you to take your own thinking and your own point of view more seriously than some assignments or teachers ask for. That is, we want you to learn to "speak up" or "speak out" when you write in response to the texts of authoritative authors—especially when those authors are writing in somewhat difficult or scholarly or academic language. The goal is to learn to bring your own thinking into a kind of dialogue of equals with the thinking of an important published author—to write with authority and agency.

In a sense we are asking you to be both objective and subjective—to play the "believing game" and the "doubting game." The common element here is respect: if you respect your own thinking, you will explore and develop your own train of thought and speak out vigorously; if you respect someone else's thinking, you will read closely and enter into their thinking and point of view.

We also have a practical teaching goal for this assignment. Because the whole class may work on the same texts, you will be in a better position to share your reading and interpretation and get feedback from your teacher and fellow students. And since you will probably write about just one or two essays, you will have an easier time getting on top of some scholarly practices that are essential for writing about texts: how to summarize fairly and clearly; how to fold quotations of the words of others comfortably into the flow of your own words; and how to use academic citations according to the appropriate conventions.

Exploring the Reading Process

What actually happens when people read? It's not so simple. Let's start by looking at the *writing* process. There's a common myth about writing as a hidden magical process—a myth that goes like this: some people are "good writers" because they have special talent and they can find good words and ideas in their heads. These people can sit down and write out perfect pieces of writing. But most of us—according to this myth—are poor writers or nonwriters because we don't seem to find good words and ideas when we sit down to write.

By now, I'm sure you realize that this myth is a very distorted picture of how writers actually function. You've had plenty of opportunity to experience the fact that writing is a gradual process of *constructing meanings*. You've been able to see concrete evidence of this gradual and often messy constructive process: early thoughts, notes or outlines or early drafts; middle drafts; revisions; final drafts. Almost all writers go through this process, and libraries often display drafts and revisions by famous writers (like Hemingway's twenty-some versions of a single passage). *Occasionally*, people get caught up into what feels almost like a trance state, and they can just pour down words that they find coming mysteriously to mind—and these words are good. It's tempting to speak of this as "inspiration"—that's what it feels like; it's probably happened to you. Freewriting can lead to this fortunate condition. And even when people write out only their *final* draft and don't seem to revise at all, they usually go through a process of constructing meanings as they pause again and again to decide which word to write next.

So let's compare the writing process to *reading*. Reading certainly seems more mysterious than writing—more *inner*. Reading usually happens faster—almost instantaneously: it looks as though you just pass your eyes over the words and the meanings pop into your head. It looks as though reading brings us back to that myth of mystery: good readers are people who come up automatically with the right meanings; bad readers are people who come up with wrong meanings or no meaning.

But in fact this is a myth for reading as much as it is for writing. If we look closely, we can see that reading, like writing, is a messy, active process of *constructing meanings*. It's just that in the case of reading, we have a harder time seeing this process. When we read, it *seems* as though we sit quietly and let the words print themselves on our retinas and thus pass inwards to our brains. But it's not that simple.

Consider what seems like an even simpler process—the process of vision. Consider the example of seeing a car down the road ahead of you. Cognitive psychologists have found out again and again, through complex experiments with high-speed cameras, that even vision is an active, exploratory process of creating meaning. It always occurs in stages through the passage of time, not instantaneously like an image passing through a lens. In the first stage of seeing, our mind receives the first pieces of information— the first trickles of electrical impulse—and quickly makes a guess or hypothesis about what we might be looking at. As we drive along, we instantaneously see a white car way down there ahead of us on the road. But the mind repeatedly checks this guess against further information, and we discover that it's actually a white boat being towed behind a car. In many situations, of course, our first guess is right—especially if the actual facts fit the context. A vehicle moving down the road is likely to be a car. For the story of perception is the story of how context and expectation are just as important as sensory data. Thus, when the actual facts don't fit the context, we often start out seeing "the wrong thing"—start out with a wrong hypothesis and then have to change it as new information comes in—until we finally "see" what's really there.

When we understand plain seeing as a time-bound, exploratory process—like hearing and all the rest of our sense perceptions—it's easy to understand how this constructive process goes on in the more complicated process of reading. We can take in the whole scene of the car on the road in just one glance—or rather that boat on the road. But we can't read a whole page of print at once—any more than we can *write* a page all at once. As we read a page, we can only read a few words at a time. As we understand them, our mind inevitably develops some guesses and hypotheses about what the rest of the sentence or paragraph or whole piece might be about. As we read further, we inevitably revise our guesses and hypotheses. This process of *guessing and revising* continues until gradually we construct larger meanings. Sometimes our larger meanings change radically on a second or third reading. In short, reading, like writing, is actually a process of "drafting" and "revising." When we look at something or start to read or hear words, we tend to *understand what we expect to understand*—till evidence forces us to revise our expectation. We expect cars on the road, not boats. Our first perceptions or hypotheses always grow out of what's already in our minds.

Difficulty in Reading

When we understand that reading is an active process of constructing meaning, we get a better picture of a widespread difficulty with reading. Some people mistakenly try to make themselves into good little cameras. They try to become perfectly passive photographic plates on which the meanings on the page *print themselves* with photographic accuracy. But since reading doesn't work that way, their reading suffers. "Hold still. Don't jiggle." This is good advice for using old cameras, but it's bad advice for reading. The more activity and moving around, the better. More hypothesis making, more checking, more activity. Even simple vision is impossible if our eye is completely stationary. Our eyes move constantly, and usually we move our heads to get slightly different views.

We can sum up this truth about reading by pointing to a simple fact: there are no meanings *in* words. If the words on the page were chocolate chips, you could eat them and they would *give* you energy. But words on the page *contain* nothing; they are just black marks. The only meanings you can get *out* of the word "cat" are the meanings you bring *to* those black marks—

or heard sounds. Since *you* brought the meanings to the word "cat" that you find there, they are *your* meanings; they are amalgams of all your past individual experiences with the word "cat." The only reason language works is that everyone more or less agrees to play the language game. We all seem tacitly to understand how convenient it is to use the same words for the same meanings: we try to give each other *more or less* similar experiences with, say, the word "cat." Babies and toddlers often use words differently, but we seem instinctively to try to get them to follow the rules of the game. Because of this unspoken agreement to play the language game cooperatively, researchers can write dictionaries that specify meanings. These dictionaries give the illusion that the meanings are *in* the words, but meanings really only exist in people's heads. And despite our best dictionaries, we have all had slightly *different* histories of experiences with the same word—sometimes very different histories. Have you noticed how often male and female readers—or young and old readers—have different reactions to the same event or movie or piece of reading? This is why it's so interesting and useful to compare the movies that play in your mind as you read or listen to words with the movies that play in other people's minds.

Notice, then, the social and cooperative dimension of reading and writing. Even if someone writes in a solitary hermit-like fashion (as Emily Dickinson is said to have done)—or reads alone without ever discussing a word—such people are cooperatively playing the language game with everyone else in their culture. If they weren't, they wouldn't be able to write or read meaningfully. And usually the collaborative dimension is much more outward and explicit. That is, most writers get some response from a friend or colleague on at least one draft before they give their writing to a wider audience. And those few brave souls who *finish* and publish a piece of writing without any discussion or sharing of a draft don't generally spend all their time alone in their room as Emily Dickinson supposedly did; usually they have talked productively with others about the topic of their writing. So, too, there's a pervasive social dimension with reading. Even though we usually sit silently as we read, we often discuss what we've read and try out our reactions and understandings with others to see what they think—just as we try out our writing on others for their reactions.

In what follows, you'll find a selection of texts, each one ready for reading, discussing, and wrestling. You'll also find a series of preparatory exercises and workshops. Each grows out of insights about the reading process just described. Each is also meant to help you engage with the writers and your fellow readers alike in both the solitary and social dimensions of reading and writing.

Peter Elbow, noted speaker and writer on composition, was director of the Writing Program at the University of Massachusetts Amherst from 1997 to 2000. More detailed descriptions of his ideas (such as his notions of the "believing game" and the "doubting game") may be found in his books *Writing without Teachers* (1973), *Writing with Power* (1981), and *Embracing Contraries: Explorations in Learning and Teaching* (1986). Peter Elbow also contributed the three workshop descriptions included in the Appendix of this volume and adapted in the Preparatory Exercises. Some of the material here draws from the first-year writing textbook he wrote with Pat Belanoff: *A Community of Writers: A Workshop Course in Writing*, 3rd edition, McGraw-Hill, 1999.

Acknowledgments

Though our editorial team began work on *The Original Text-Wrestling Book* in January 2001, the story of this volume goes back to 1997 when Peter Elbow, then director of the UMass Amherst Writing Program, introduced the text-wrestling essay into our First-Year Writing Program curriculum. The text-wrestling essay represented from the start an important and much needed addition to the Program syllabus. Many teachers embraced the concept, and its practice, enthusiastically. They sought out challenging short texts from every source available to them: literary and monthly magazines, essay collections, and other books. And the teachers photocopied their separate selections for use by individual classes aggregating some 3000 students annually.

Despite the real importance of the text-wrestling assignment, I was concerned about a lack of consistency in the students' reading, and therefore writing, experiences across such a large program as ours. More, though, I worried about the costs of our photocopying and about its legality. I feared we were asking our teachers—most of them graduate student instructors and all of them writers as well as teachers of writing—to bend, if not break, the very permission laws designed to protect them and the nascent writers in their classes.

So in fall 2000, when Peter retired and I began serving as the Writing Program's acting director, I asked for volunteers among our eighty or so staff members to work with me on this book project. Six graduate student instructors and one English Department faculty member quickly stepped forward. Over the next five months, we worked as a team, soliciting preparatory exercises, sample student essays, and text suggestions from other teachers; reading through the piles of materials we received and enduring the difficult process of selection; finally composing and editing the introductory and prefatory matter for our volume.

For five months, I was impressed and inspired by the level of thought as well as the level-headedness of discussion taking place among us eight editors. Therefore, before we express our team thanks to those helping us in our work, I want to thank these seven editorial team members—Benjamin Balthaser, Michael Edwards, Zan Goncalves, Robert Hazard, Noria Jablonski,

Brian Jordan, and Shauna Seliy. I only hope our students learn as much from this book as I have learned from working on it with this group of writers and editors.

—Marcia Curtis

+—• ⩻⬦⩼ •—+

As an editorial team, not only do we credit Peter Elbow for introducing text wrestling into our program, but we also thank him for generously donating the Foreword to this book and for contributing the three seminal workshops that appear in our Appendix for Teachers. Peter coined the term "text-wrestling essay" and established its place in our curriculum. Without him, this would not be *The Original Text-Wrestling Book*. Yet he should not be held accountable for the concept of a text-wrestling book or its remaining contents; those matters, and any mistakes attending them, are strictly our own.

We thank others who contributed to our project and whose work is represented here, too: Christine Cooper, Asheley Griffith, Margaret Price, Claire Schomp, Rochelle Vigurs, and Peggy Woods. And we thank the students whose own text-wrestling essays will serve as models for other students to learn from as well as enjoy: Kristi Cousins, Nadine Hanna, Michael Ianello, Matthew Libby, and Kristina Martino.

We also owe a debt of gratitude, however, to those whose presence is less visible on these pages: to the many, many teachers in the Program who suggested texts for inclusion in the volume; to the teachers whose particularized exercises and workshops appear on our Text-Wrestling Web Site rather than among the more generally applicable exercises printed here; and to all those first-year students whose excellent text-wrestling essays were submitted by their teachers. We chose readings, exercises, and sample student essays that we believed best fit together in this first edition of the book but fully appreciated every submission we received.

Finally, we sincerely thank Asheley Griffith for lending us her sharp editor's eye at the eleventh hour, when it really mattered.

—Editorial Team
(Benjamin Balthaser, Marcia Curtis, Michael Edwards, Zan Goncalves, Robert Hazard, Noria Jablonski, Brian Jordan, and Shauna Seliy)

The Original Text-Wrestling Book Web Site <http://writingprogram.hfa.umass.edu/otwb> contains additional preparatory workshops and exercises for the text-wrestling essay, supplementary information on the authors represented in this volume, and links to other useful sites. We invite all readers to visit this site and to join in furthering our project by sending suggested readings, exercises, and links to curtis@acad.umass.edu.

In first setting up this assignment for students, I pursued the metaphor and asked a wrestling coach to try to explain to me the basics of wrestling as he would teach them to a newcomer. What he pinpointed first was the *"fear of the mat,"* that is, not just the initial fear of trying it for the first few times, but also the sense that when you're out there, you're *"on your own."* It can be overwhelming to face the opponent with the awareness that it's just the two of you out there. I think this is the same initial problem most students have with text wrestling. The intimidation of the published text can reduce our best analysis efforts to mere summary or generalizing, total agreement, or total disagreement from a distance, when what is needed is close contact— *wrestling*!

So, what techniques does our coach recommend to his athletes to deal with this fear? First, you must realize that the opponent is someone just like you, with strengths, weaknesses, opinions and techniques. Confidence, practice, and knowledge of yourself are all keys to improving your chances of success. And when you're on the mat, you need a good understanding at all times of your placement and your opponent's: an awareness of balance and a visualization of where you are and where you are going next. A good wrestler will not only maintain a solid defense but will always be looking for chances to get a take-down. All of this is applicable to text wrestling. Focus, full understanding, and complete control of the information are all vital in successful text wrestling. Opponents will vary, and so will the teammates that a coach trains. But a match will always be good when the wrestlers take advantage of their strengths and remain in control of their position.

The key difference, of course, between the two types of wrestling is that text wrestling doesn't always have to be a *fight*. You may *agree* with the text and want to respond to *why* it is so successful. This is fine, as long as you maintain a close relationship with the text and refrain from simple summary or generalizations.

—Claire Schomp, *Wrestling with Texts*

Introduction

He that wrestles with us strengthens our nerves and sharpens
our skill. Our antagonist is our helper.
    —Edmund Burke, *Reflections on the Revolution in France*

You have engaged in conversations nearly all of your life—with friends, family, teachers, co-workers and occasionally strangers. Some of these conversations you began; some were already going on when you entered them. When you entered the university, you entered an on-going conversation among students and scholars, discourse that crosses the divides of time as well as geography. The conversation takes place in classrooms, in spoken discussions about the concepts central to every academic discipline individually and to intellectual life generally. More often, though, the conversation is a written one, conveyed in published texts, carried on in our reading of them, extended in the new texts produced in the form of essays, research papers, reports and eventually, perhaps, published articles.

As you undoubtedly know from your own experience, entering any conversation first calls for careful, attentive listening, not just to the main ideas, the gist, of what is being said but to all the details, nuances, and tone of their expression. In the sort of written conversation a text-wrestling essay represents, attentive listening means close, attentive reading of another person's essay, another person's text. It means making your own associations but withholding your own final judgments until you have studied carefully all the writer has to say and have analyzed the particular terms and tone, the metaphors and analogies, the logical reasoning and personal reasons at work within the text.

- Only by your own careful reading can you allow the writer to speak fully to you.
- Only when the writer has spoken fully to you can you represent the writer's ideas fairly in your written text.

And that fair, accurate representation of another writer's thoughts—in faithful summary, paraphrase, and quotation—is one hallmark of college writing and a successful text-wrestling essay.

True conversation also requires the active involvement of all participants and equal contributions from each one of them. Conversations are seldom satisfying if one participant feels too timid to speak up or is bullied by another into silence or simply repeats back what the other has said. So while you need to represent other writers' ideas fairly and fully in your text-wrestling essay, that is not all you need to do. You must respond to the other writer or writers whose texts you are reading with ideas of your own. Such responding requires your meeting the other writer as an equal, not always easy when facing a "professional" writer's published text. Careful reading and attention to the writer's reasoning as well as point of view will help remind you that every writer was probably once a student, just like you, and is certainly a human being, just like you—a human being deserving of your respectful listening but also your equally respectful and forceful response.

Finally, truly successful conversations are both collaborative and constructive. They do not bog down in passive agreement or lock up in uncompromising disagreement. True conversations find participants, as one writer has remarked, "drawing out each other's ideas, elaborating upon them, and building together a truth none could have constructed alone" (Clinchy 188). So in the text-wrestling essay, you may express agreement with some points a writer makes, disagreement with other points. But, more important, you will draw out that writer's ideas, perhaps by highlighting the terms or metaphors recurring throughout the text, or by comparing one writer's observations with observations made by another and examining both in the new light they shed on each other. You will elaborate upon the writer's thoughts, perhaps by applying them to different situations or by amplifying them with similar thoughts and experiences of your own. Together with writer and text you will construct "a truth" neither of you could have composed alone. And the "truth" you compose will be your text-wrestling essay, your own "text."

Why, then, do we call this written conversation the "text-*wrestling*" essay? The phrase *to wrestle with* means *to grapple with* or *to come to grips with,* and all three phrases—though denoting physical actions—are often used metaphorically to suggest profound intellectual or emotional activity. Through use of the term "text-wrestling essay," we mean to keep alive the physical, visceral sense of our metaphor as you, the reader, involve yourself fully in the act—the forceful and dynamic action—of reading. We also mean to call up the classical, even the mythical, vision of wrestlers, each battling yet simultaneously balancing the other in a close and highly controlled match between equals.

The "Text-Wrestling" Essay

Students who use this reader typically will write one or more text-wrestling essay, but what does that mean? What is a text-wrestling essay? What will it show you can do? Why is it valuable? How will you write it?

As you probably know, an essay may be defined as a person's thoughts—expressed in prose—on a particular subject or theme. Many of the selections in this book are essays, rather demanding ones. The texts presented are prose writings, each short enough to read at a single sitting, but intellectually, verbally, structurally or otherwise complex enough to reward several more re-readings. The essay you write will show you can address one or more of these difficult texts. Your completed text-wrestling essay will show that you can engage with sophisticated texts, discuss and understand them, quote from them by using accepted conventions of academic discourse, and emerge with your own well-articulated thoughts and judgments or conclusions in a text of your own making.

The purpose of this book includes but goes beyond informing, challenging, and exercising the mind. As a college or university student, you will be gradually positioning yourself within communities of other readers, writers, speaker, and thinkers, and engaging in conversation with them. The value of wrestling with rich texts of others, and with writing a responsive text of your own, is that doing so immerses you in an atmosphere of advanced thinking and communicating. The overall goal of text wrestling is to help bring your thoughts into dialogue with those of published writers, and to help you move toward writing with increased authority, agency, and standing.

Within this broad set of intentions are more specific objectives. Engaging with sophisticated texts and writing your text-wrestling essay will provide the following:

- Practice in reading as a demanding and constructive process
- Exposure to various approaches to analyzing and interpreting written texts
- Familiarity with selections from some accomplished authors addressing, in various styles, a range of subjects
- Opportunities for discussion and collaborative learning, since class members usually will be focusing on a limited number of texts explored together
- Practice in addressing complex material—material that cannot be reduced to a simple "sound-bite" or pro-or-con position

- Practice in analyzing, summarizing, and synthesizing information into a reasoned and coherent whole
- Exposure to and practice in techniques for integrating the words and thoughts of others into your own writing, and for crediting the sources of those words and thoughts ethically and accurately, and according to the conventions of MLA style.

The varied kinds of practice you receive will help you find what you think and have to say about the subject considered. As one teacher has stated about physical wrestling and wrestling with texts: "Confidence, practice, and knowledge of yourself are all keys to improving your chance for success" (Schomp).

Possibilities for Writing

How will you write the text-wrestling essay? To a considerable extent, that process and the particulars of your assignment will be shaped by individual teachers and classes. Of the numerous possibilities, here are just a few that have already been used effectively.

Wrestle with a single reading and produce a single multi-draft essay.

Address two or more related readings to widen the conversation and broaden your essay's content.

Draft beginnings of at least two essays on different readings—later completing or combining the most promising possibilities into one finished essay.

Wrestle not only with the readings but also with your classmates' commentary on the readings or with a sample student essay in this book.

Regardless of the overall approach taken, composition of text-wrestling essays needs to come after engagement with one or more complex texts, and to be guided by the goals and objectives set off with bullets above. The essays will be well-developed and carefully crafted prose compositions, documented according to conventions of MLA style.

The Readings

The diversity and range of the essays contained in this volume may give you an idea of the difficulty we had in choosing them: there's a broad scope of philosophies, topics, ideas and styles represented here, because we wanted this book to be as open, inclusive, and approachable as possible. We tried, as well, to include essays that would represent a corresponding diversity in their authors' backgrounds—from working class to professional academic, from activist to aesthete, from disabled to traditionally athletic, from Anglo to African-American, from new and emerging writers to writers firmly entrenched in the canon to writers engaged in breaking down notions of canonicity. Some of these authors represent traditional, even conservative, values; some challenge these notions. Some authors may be like you; others, very different. And while some of these differences or similarities will reveal themselves upon an initial glance, others will not be made apparent without your closer examination. In important senses, all of these essays take part in conversations: they represent a range of diverse backgrounds and ways of thinking, and many of them take on special interest, special significance, when read as a pair in tandem or linked in a writing sequence, one essay casting new light on the other. Indeed, in one instance a pair of readings—selections by Rita Hardiman and Bailey Jackson, and Bobbie Harro—are presented as a single unit.

Despite the diversity of these readings, we imagine (if you choose to read beyond the essays your teacher assigns) you'll notice a number of commonalties among the texts, and those commonalties are much of what constituted our criteria for choosing the texts. The simplest criterion, perhaps, is that all of these texts are *essays*: they're short prose compositions that tend to analyze or reflect upon actual concerns. They're not fiction, not stories, although they often contain narrative elements. In fact, they're very much the same sorts of things that your teachers are asking you to write: and, just as you take different positions in relation to your writing in the different essays that you write, so do these writers take a wide variety of authorial stances. Some of these essays are very much in the genre of the personal narratives; some are more expository in nature, with the author seeming more distant from the text. In any case, though, the content of their writing—what these authors are saying—demands to be paid careful attention to, we hope in the same manner that you want your own ideas and opinions to be paid attention to.

These essays bite, and these are essays that the reader can bite back. These are essays that manifest coherence and energy at every level of thought, form, and language. They carry with them a sense of urgency, an engagement not so much with the headlines as with the social, historical, or personal emergencies that lie beyond the daily immediacies of headline news. These are essays that we readers can, indeed *must*, read and return to again. They are essays that yield multiple readings, essays that remain with a reader for longer than the length of a semester, that one might wrestle with for longer than the span of a paper.

The style of all these essays is polished, as well: these writers pay attention to the ways in which they choose their words, in the same ways that your teachers expect you to. *How* writers express their ideas often can tell one just as much as *what* they actually say. In doing such a sort of secondary reading—in paying as much attention to an author's style and form as you do to her or his content—you're getting a twice-mediated text, reading the author's reading of the world. You'll find these authors reading advertisements, reading signs in nature, reading popular culture, reading student essays for the future of academia, reading for meaning in the broken glass of a riot, even reading what it means to read. This is no accident—the act of interpretation, although commonly associated with the literary text, is something we hope that can be taken beyond these essays and out into the world. We of course expect that you perform your own interpretation of the world, as well: part of the "wrestling," then, might be in trying to figure out how the ways you read the world don't quite fit with the way these authors read the world. And we expect that there won't be a perfect fit between you and the text.

Our difficulty in choosing these texts was part of our reason for choosing them: they're hard to summarize; they're not easily condensed, or simple, or transparent. A big part of this writing assignment is understanding that *easy* does not always mean *better*. While each of the essays in this anthology can be read in a single sitting, they are not "quick" reads; that is to say, this is not the sort of material you read on airplanes or in waiting rooms. Many of them are built up out of abstract ideas that resist quick understanding and easy reduction. That doesn't mean, though, that we expect them to be impenetrable. We were interested in choosing texts that made us think rather than texts that made us argue: as such, these essays do reward a certain kind of reading. These texts ask you to read more slowly than many people are accustomed to reading, and they ask you to *re*-read. Don't expect that you can simply skim these essays one time and be done. On the other hand, you shouldn't simply defer to them; as the term "wrestling" indicates, we assume that you won't simply or easily agree with what they have to say, or how they say it, but rather will struggle to hold on to them, to work with their weight and understand where the points of leverage are. Our hope in choosing these readings is to help you get accustomed to the hard work of what you'll be asked to do in college—and that, in doing that sort of hard intellectual work, you'll find confidence and satisfaction in it.

Preparatory Exercises

Our first encounter with an essay can be overwhelming. We hold the essay in our hands and let our eyes skim the first page. We begin counting pages trying to calculate how long it will take us to read to the end. As we stare at the title and begin quickly reading the first paragraph, it seems we can focus on just three questions: How am I going to read all of this? How am I going to understand everything this author is saying? What am I going to write about?

Rather than trying to think about reading, writing, and understanding the essay all at once, it is best to break the process down into a series of steps. The exercises included in this book will enable you to do that. Think of these exercises as strategies, ways that will enable you to find a way into the essay, enter into the conversation with the author, wrestle with the ideas presented, and then move out into your own essay.

When we read an essay, or any text, two things happen. We *observe* the words the author has written and, in effect, hear the message those words convey. But our hearing isn't passive. As we listen <u>to</u> the text's message, we also listen <u>for</u> it and actively *interpret* it. We have our own reactions, make our own associations, and apply our own judgments to the text in front of us, each of us interpreting the author's original message according to our own unique background and point of view. By reading the text, then, we infuse it with our own thoughts and literally bring it to life. So in many ways, writing means nothing without reading. Writer and reader work together to construct the meaning of every text. And with every new reader—perhaps with every new read*ing*—that text takes on new meaning, new life: It becomes a new text.

As readers, we must use our power to construct meaning wisely. We must be responsible readers—responsible to the writer, to the text, and to ourselves. Wise and responsible exercise of our power involves distinguishing between what is in the text and what is outside the text, within us ourselves. It involves making sure our own thoughts are not utterly lost, our own voice altogether silenced, in the writer's powerful words. But it also involves taking care that our own inner voice doesn't overpower the writer's voice, that our reading doesn't become misreading.

The exercises presented in this book are intended to help you become increasingly self-conscious as a reader, mindful of your power as a reader, and as a writer, through the process we refer to as "close reading"—of the text, of your own reader-response, and of the interactions between the two. The exercises will focus on *observation*—asking you to pay close attention to the writers' words themselves, to the text itself, to what the writer says and the way the writer says it, to the form or "medium" as well as the "message." They will also focus on *interpretation*—asking you to pay special attention to your own feelings and reactions to the text. Finally, they will enable you to bring your powers of *observation* and *interpretation* together as you forward the conversation by contributing your own essay, your own text.

Sample Text-Wrestling Essays by Students

These sample text-wrestling essays were all written by first-year college students, like you. Their skills and talents as writers, though already obvious, are still developing. Nevertheless, they hold their own in conversation with such published essayists as John Berger, Annie Dillard, William Gass, and Walker Percy. And all these student writers contribute their own ideas to the on-going conversation of academic life.

While every one of the five students shows strength as a writer, each demonstrates that strength in a different form and style. In "Seeing Our Own Individuality," for instance, Michael Ianello provides what may be characterized as a traditionally "academic" analysis of three writers—Berger, Dillard, and Sontag—while demonstrating, by his own careful craftsmanship, the creative potential of this essay form. Kristina Martino's "Uncovering Reality," on the other hand, focuses an analytic lens on a single reading, Debra Seagal's "Tales from the Cutting-Room Floor," and in doing so teases new meaning from Seagal's published "diary." Matthew Libby's "Learning: The Uncommon Nature of a Common Experience" brings two classmates' writings into his own discussion of Walker Percy and William Gass, thereby demonstrating one important way fellow students can help you wrestle with published texts.

Nadine Hanna demonstrates something quite different. Having assimilated into her consciousness and conscience the notions of social justice put forth by Rita Hardiman and Bailey Jackson as well as Bobbie Harro, Hanna wrestles with herself. Her personal essay "I Am an Oppressor" reaches far beyond private confession, though, to teach and challenge many of us to join her in her struggle. Finally, like Hanna, Kristi Cousins grapples with her own prior learning experiences, her own past conditioning. "Notes on an Education: A Dialogue," however, takes a lighter tone. It represents in form as well as content a playful critique of both Walker Percy's "The Loss of the Creature" and Cousins's own standard academic writing.

Whether agreeing or disagreeing with the readings, all these student writers stand up to the published authors and stand well beside them. Proving themselves worthy wrestlers, they provide in this volume their own now-published texts with which you may wrestle.

A Short Introduction to MLA Documentation Style

Correct quotation, citation and documentation can be daunting. The task itself seems simple enough: determine the type of work you are quoting and strictly follow the relevant citation model provided in a handbook or style manual. For example, if you quote from an essay selection contained in an anthology like this one, you simply skim the models in your handbook until you locate the one for an essay selection contained in an anthology and follow the pattern given: Author's last name, first name. "Essay Title." *Anthology Title*. Ed. anthology editor's Firstname Lastname. City published: Publisher, copyright date. Pages between which the essay occurs.

It all seems easy until you begin to do it! Suddenly you realize your essay has two authors and the anthology has seven editors. The handbook you are looking through has twenty listed entries for in-text citations and nearly a hundred for works cited—and that represents just the MLA style. Three other handbook sections are devoted to model listings for APA, CBE, and Turabian. The range of choices and variety of options can be overwhelming.

In this book, we have kept our aims—and our citation listing—modest. "A Short Introduction to MLA Documentation Style with a Sampling of Common In-Text Citations and Works Cited Entries" is precisely what its long title says it is. We've included in this section a brief explanation of the *whys* and *hows* of quoting other authors and "citing" the "sources"—that is, identifying the books, essays or other media in which those quotations were found. You'll find explained and demonstrated two principal ways to format quotations, one for short quotations of just a few words or a sentence and the other—what is termed the *block quotation*— for long quotations. You'll learn about the extremely useful *signal phrase* to introduce quotations. You'll be given a modest number of model *in-text citations* (author and page identifiers following each quotation) and an equally modest number of matching *works cited* entries (publication details listed at the end of a paper).

Much of this information can be found in the typical handbook or style manual as well. What you'll find different here is that we have limited both the in-text citation and works cited models to those you may need for a text-wrestling essay: for example, models for anthology selections, Web sites, personal interviews, works of art, and videos. And we have limited our style to the MLA (Modern Language Association) Style, since this is the documentation style associated with most English departments and writing programs.

The reason we chose brevity and simplicity over fullness is this: The text-wrestling essay will let you start small, with just the most common methods of quotation and citation. Here you can focus your efforts, practice documentation techniques and hone your skills, undaunted by too much information and too many choices. You can see the same skills and techniques applied in the sample student text-wrestling essays contained in this book. And you can even try your skills on the practice work sheets provided in this section before applying them to text-wrestling essays of your own.

Appendix for Teachers:
Three Workshops by Peter Elbow

In the Appendix for Teachers, you will find Peter Elbow's complete description of three workshops he uses when teaching the text-wrestling essay: "A Laboratory in the Reading Process" (elsewhere referred to as "Movies of the Mind"), "A Voice Workshop," and "A Dialogue [with the Author] Workshop." These three workshops developed out of the theoretical insights about reading described in the Foreword to this book, and though the Appendix is addressed to teachers, many students will undoubtedly be intrigued to read Peter Elbow's thoughtful description of his own teaching practices and principles as well. The three workshops are adapted as exercises in the Preparatory Exercises section of this book.

Works Cited

Clinchy, Blythe McVicker. "The Development of Thoughtfulness in College Women: Integrating Reason and Care." *The Composition of Ourselves*. Ed. Marcia Curtis. 2nd ed. Dubuque: Kendall/Hunt, 2000. 182–193.

Schomp, Claire. "Wrestling with Texts." Instructional handout. 2000.

Readings

Jean Anyon

Social Class and the Hidden Curriculum of Work

Jean Anyon is a professor of education. In "Social Class and the Hidden Curriculum of Work" Anyon makes the point that the real function of school is to reproduce social class. Her article is drawn from a study she conducted of fifth graders from different economic backgrounds at five different schools. She concludes that work is defined differently at each of the schools, thus preparing students to do particular kinds of work in the world. As you read, think about the schooling you received as a fifth grader. How was work defined in your classroom? What has your education prepared or failed to prepare you to do?

Scholars in political economy and the sociology of knowledge have recently argued that public schools in complex industrial societies like our own make available different types of educational experience and curriculum knowledge to students in different social classes. Bowles and Gintis[1] for example, have argued that students in different social-class backgrounds are rewarded for classroom behaviors that correspond to personality traits allegedly rewarded in the different occupational strata—the working classes for docility and obedience, the managerial classes for initiative and personal assertiveness. Basil Bernstein, Pierre Bourdieu, and Michael W. Apple,[2] focusing on school knowledge, have argued that knowledge and skills leading to social power and regard (medical, legal, managerial) are made available to the advantaged social groups but are withheld from the working classes, to whom a more "practical" curriculum is offered (manual skills, clerical knowledge). While there has been considerable argumentation of these points regarding education in England, France, and North America, there has been little or no attempt to investigate these ideas empirically in elementary or secondary schools and classrooms in this country.[3]

From *Journal of Education*, Vol. 162, No. 1, pp. 67–92 by Jean Anyon. Reprinted by permission of the author.

This article offers tentative empirical support (and qualification) of the above arguments by providing illustrative examples of differences in student *work* in classrooms in contrasting social class communities. The examples were gathered as part of an ethnographical study of curricular, pedagogical, and pupil evaluation practices in five elementary schools. The article attempts a theoretical contribution as well and assesses student work in the light of a theoretical approach to social-class analysis.... It will be suggested that there is a "hidden curriculum" in schoolwork that has profound implications for the theory—and consequence—of everyday activity in education....

The Sample of Schools

...The social-class designation of each of the five schools will be identified, and the income, occupation, and other relevant available social characteristics of the students and their parents will be described. The first three schools are in a medium-sized city district in northern New Jersey, and the other two are in a nearby New Jersey suburb.

The first two schools I will call *working-class schools*. Most of the parents have blue-collar jobs. Less than a third of the fathers are skilled, while the majority are in unskilled or semiskilled jobs. During the period of the study (1978–1979), approximately 15 percent of the fathers were unemployed. The large majority (85 percent) of the families are white. The following occupations are typical: platform, storeroom, and stockroom workers; foundrymen, pipe welders, and boilermakers; semiskilled and unskilled assemblyline operatives; gas station attendants, auto mechanics, maintenance workers, and security guards. Less than 30 percent of the women work, some part-time and some full-time, on assembly lines, in storerooms and stockrooms, as waitresses, barmaids, or sales clerks. Of the fifth-grade parents, none of the wives of the skilled workers had jobs. Approximately 15 percent of the families in each school are at or below the federal "poverty" level;[4] most of the rest of the family incomes are at or below $12,000, except some of the skilled workers whose incomes are higher. The incomes of the majority of the families in these two schools (at or below $12,000) are typical of 38.6 percent of the families in the United States.[5]

The third school is called the *middle-class school*, although because of neighborhood residence patterns, the population is a mixture of several societal classes. The parents' occupations can be divided into three groups: a small group of blue-collar "rich," who are skilled, well-paid workers such as printers, carpenters, plumbers, and construction workers. The second group is composed of parents in working-class and middle-class white-collar jobs:

women in office jobs, technicians, supervisors in industry, and parents employed by the city (such as firemen, policemen, and several of the school's teachers). The third group is composed of occupations such as personnel directors in local firms, accountants, "middle management," and a few small capitalists (owners of shops in the area). The children of several local doctors attend this school. Most family incomes are between $13,000 and $25,000, with a few higher. This income range is typical of 38.9 percent of the families in the United States.[6]

The fourth school has a parent population that is at the upper income level of the upper middle class and is predominantly professional. This school will be called the *affluent professional school*. Typical jobs are: cardiologist, interior designer, corporate lawyer or engineer, executive in advertising or television. There are some families who are not as affluent as the majority (the family of the superintendent of the district's schools, and the one or two families in which the fathers are skilled workers). In addition, a few of the families are more affluent than the majority and can be classified in the capitalist class (a partner in a prestigious Wall Street stock brokerage firm). Approximately 90 percent of the children in this school are white. Most family incomes are between $40,000 and $80,000. This income span represents approximately 7 percent of the families in the United States.[7]

In the fifth school the majority of the families belong to the capitalist class. This school will be called the *executive elite school* because most of the fathers are top executives (for example, presidents and vice-presidents) in major United States-based multinational corporations—for example, AT&T, RCA, Citibank, American Express, U. S. Steel. A sizable group of fathers are top executives in financial firms on Wall Street. There are also a number of fathers who list their occupations as "general counsel" to a particular corporation, and these corporations are also among the large multi-nationals. Many of the mothers do volunteer work in the Junior League, Junior Fortnightly, or other service groups; some are intricately involved in town politics; and some are themselves in well-paid occupations. There are no minority children in the school. Almost all the family incomes are over $100,000, with some in the $500,000 range. The incomes in this school represent less than 1 percent of the families in the United States.[8]

Since each of the five schools is only one instance of elementary education in a particular social class context, I will not generalize beyond the sample. However, the examples of schoolwork which follow will suggest characteristics of education in each social setting that appear to have theoretical and social significance and to be worth investigation in a larger number of schools....

The Working-Class Schools

In the two working-class schools, work is following the steps of a procedure. The procedure is usually mechanical, involving rote behavior and very little decision making or choice. The teachers rarely explain why the work is being assigned, how it might connect to other assignments, or what the idea is that lies behind the procedure or gives it coherence and perhaps meaning or significance. Available textbooks are not always used, and the teachers often prepare their own dittos or put work examples on the board. Most of the rules regarding work are designations of what the children are to do; the rules are steps to follow. These steps are told to the children by the teachers and are often written on the board. The children are usually told to copy the steps as notes. These notes are to be studied. Work is often evaluated not according to whether it is right or wrong but according to whether the children followed the right steps.

The following examples illustrate these points. In math, when two-digit division was introduced, the teacher in one school gave a four-minute lecture on what the terms are called (which number is the divisor, dividend, quotient, and remainder). The children were told to copy these names in their notebooks. Then the teacher told them the steps to follow to do the problems, saying, "This is how you do them." The teacher listed the steps on the board, and they appeared several days later as a chart hung in the middle of the front wall: "Divide, Multiply, Subtract, Bring Down." The children often did examples of two-digit division. When the teacher went over the examples with them, he told them what the procedure was for each problem, rarely asking them to conceptualize or explain it themselves: "Three into twenty-two is seven; do your subtraction and one is left over." During the week that two-digit division was introduced (or at any other time), the investigator did not observe any discussion of the idea of grouping involved in division, any use of manipulables, or any attempt to relate two-digit division to any other mathematical process. Nor was there any attempt to relate the steps to an actual or possible thought process of the children. The observer did not hear the terms *dividend, quotient,* and so on, used again. The math teacher in the other working-class school followed similar procedures regarding two-digit division and at one point her class seemed confused. She said, "You're confusing yourselves. You're tensing up. Remember, when you do this, it's the same steps over and over again—and that's the way division always is." Several weeks later, after a test, a group of her children "still didn't get it," and she made no attempt to explain the concept of dividing things into groups or to give them manipulables for their own investigation. Rather, she went over the steps with them again and told them that they "needed more practice."

In other areas of math, work is also carrying out often unexplained frag-mented procedures. For example, one of the teachers led the children through a series of steps to make a 1-inch grid on their paper *without* telling them that they were making a 1-inch grid or that it would be used to study scale. She said, "Take your ruler. Put it across the top. Make a mark at every number. Then move your ruler down to the bottom. No, put it across the bottom. Now make a mark on top of every number. Now draw a line from…" At this point a girl said that she had a faster way to do it and the teacher said, "No, you don't; you don't even know what I'm making yet. Do it this way or it's wrong." After they had made the lines up and down and across, the teacher told them she wanted them to make a figure by connect-ing some dots and to measure that, using the scale of 1 inch equals 1 mile. Then they were to cut it out. She said, "Don't cut it until I check it."

In both working-class schools, work in language arts is mechanics of punctuation (commas, periods, question marks, exclamation points), capi-talization, and the four kinds of sentences. One teacher explained to me, "Simple punctuation is all they'll ever use." Regarding punctuation, either a teacher or a ditto stated the rules for where, for example, to put commas. The investigator heard no classroom discussion of the aural context of punc-tuation (which, of course, is what gives each mark its meaning). Nor did the investigator hear any statement or inference that placing a punctuation mark could be a decision-making process, depending, for example, on one's in-tended meaning. Rather, the children were told to follow the rules. Language arts did not involve creative writing. There were several writing assignments throughout the year, but in each instance the children were given a ditto, and they wrote answers to questions on the sheet. For example, they wrote their "autobiography" by answering such questions as "Where were you born?" "What is your favorite animal?" on a sheet entitled "All About Me."

In one of the working-class schools, the class had a science period several times a week. On the three occasions observed, the children were not called upon to set up experiments or to give explanations for facts or concepts. Rather, on each occasion the teacher told them in his own words what the book said. The children copied the teacher's sentences from the board. Each day that preceded the day they were to do a science experiment, the teacher told them to copy the directions from the book for the procedure they would carry out the next day and to study the list at home that night. The day after each experiment, the teacher went over what they had "found" (they did the experiments as a class, and each was actually a class demonstration led by the teacher). Then the teacher wrote what they "found" on the board, and the children copied that in their notebooks. Once or twice a year there are science projects. The project is chosen and assigned by the teacher from a box of 3-by-5-inch cards. On the card the teacher has written the question to be answered, the books to use, and how much to write. Explaining the cards to the observer, the teacher said, "It tells them exactly what to do, or they couldn't do it."

Social studies in the working-class schools is also largely mechanical, rote work that was given little explanation or connection to larger contexts. In one school, for example, although there was a book available, social studies work was to copy the teacher's notes from the board. Several times a week for a period of several months the children copied these notes. The fifth grades in the district were to study United States history. The teacher used a booklet she had purchased called "The Fabulous Fifty States." Each day she put information from the booklet in outline form on the board and the children copied it. The type of information did not vary: the name of the state, its abbreviation, state capital, nickname of the state, its main products, main business, and a "Fabulous Fact" ("Idaho grew twenty-seven billion potatoes in one year. That's enough potatoes for each man, woman, and…"). As the children finished copying the sentences, the teacher erased them and wrote more. Children would occasionally go to the front to pull down the wall map in order to locate the states they were copying, and the teacher did not dissuade them. But the observer never saw her refer to the map; nor did the observer ever hear her make other than perfunctory remarks concerning the information the children were copying. Occasionally the children colored in a ditto and cut it out to make a stand-up figure (representing, for example, a man roping a cow in the Southwest). These were referred to by the teacher as their social studies "projects."

Rote behavior was often called for in classroom work. When going over math and language arts skills sheets, for example, as the teacher asked for the answer to each problem, he fired the questions rapidly, staccato, and the scene reminded the observer of a sergeant drilling recruits: above all, the questions demanded that you stay at attention: "The next one? What do I put here? … Here? Give us the next." Or "How many commas in this sentence? Where do I put them… The next one?"

The four fifth-grade teachers observed in the working-class schools attempted to control classroom time and space by making decisions without consulting the children and without explaining the basis for their decisions. The teacher's control thus often seemed capricious. Teachers, for instance, very often ignored the bells to switch classes—deciding among themselves to keep the children after the period was officially over to continue with the work or for disciplinary reasons or so they (the teachers) could stand in the hall and talk. There were no clocks in the rooms in either school, and the children often asked, "What period is this?" "When do we go to gym?" The children had no access to materials. These were handed out by teachers and closely guarded. Things in the room "belonged" to the teacher: "Bob, bring me my garbage can." The teachers continually gave the children orders. Only three times did the investigator hear a teacher in either working-class school preface a directive with an unsarcastic "please," or "let's" or "would you." Instead, the teachers said, "Shut up," "Shut your mouth," "Open your books," "Throw your gum away—if you want to rot your teeth, do it on your own time." Teachers made every effort to control the movement of the children, and often shouted, "Why are you out of your seat??!!" If the children got permission to leave the room, they had to take a written pass with the date and time....

Middle-Class School

In the middle-class school, work is getting the right answer. If one accumulates enough right answers, one gets a good grade. One must follow the directions in order to get the right answers, but the directions often call for some figuring, some choice, some decision making. For example, the children must often figure out by themselves what the directions ask them to do and how to get the answer: what do you do first, second, and perhaps third? Answers are usually found in books or by listening to the teacher. Answers are usually words, sentences, numbers, or facts and dates; one writes them on paper, and one should be neat. Answers must be given in the right order, and one cannot make them up.

The following activities are illustrative. Math involves some choice: one may do two-digit division the long way or the short way, and there are some math problems that can be done "in your head." When the teacher explains how to do two-digit division, there is recognition that a cognitive process is involved; she gives you several ways and says, "I want to make sure you understand what you're doing—so you get it right"; and, when they go over the homework, she asks the *children* to tell how they did the problem and what answer they got.

In social studies the daily work is to read the assigned pages in the textbook and to answer the teacher's questions. The questions are almost always designed to check on whether the students have read the assignment and understood it: who did so-and-so; what happened after that; when did it happen, where, and sometimes, why did it happen? The answers are in the book and in one's understanding of the book; the teacher's hints when one doesn't know the answers are to "read it again" or to look at the picture or at the rest of the paragraph. One is to search for the answer in the "context," in what is given.

Language arts is "simple grammar, what they need for everyday life." The language arts teacher says, "They should learn to speak properly, to write business letters and thank-you letters, and to understand what nouns and verbs and simple subjects are." Here, as well, actual work is to choose the right answers, to understand what is given. The teacher often says, "Please read the next sentence and then I'll question you about it." One teacher said in some exasperation to a boy who was fooling around in class, "If you don't know the answers to the questions I ask, then you can't stay in this *class*! [pause] You *never* know the answers to the questions I ask, and it's not fair to me—and certainly not to you!"

Most lessons are based on the textbook. This does not involve a critical perspective on what is given there. For example, a critical perspective in social studies is perceived as dangerous by these teachers because it may lead to controversial topics; the parents might complain. The children, however, are often curious, especially in social studies. Their questions are tolerated and usually answered perfunctorily. But after a few minutes the teacher will say, "All right, we're not going any farther. Please open your social studies workbook." While the teachers spend a lot of time explaining and expanding on what the textbooks say, there is little attempt to analyze how or why things happen, or to give thought to how pieces of a culture or, say, a system of numbers or elements of a language fit together or can be analyzed. What has happened in the past and what exists now may not be equitable or fair, but (shrug) that is the way things are and one does not confront such matters in school. For example, in social studies after a child is called on to read a passage about the pilgrims, the teacher summarizes the paragraph and then says, "So you can see how strict they were about everything." A child asks, "Why?" "Well, because they felt that if you weren't busy you'd get into trouble." Another child asks, "Is it true that they burned women at the stake?" The teacher says, "Yes, if a woman did anything strange, they hanged them. [sic] What would a woman do, do you think, to make them burn them? [sic] See if you can come up with better answers than any other [social studies] class." Several children offer suggestions, to which the teacher nods but does not comment. Then she says, "Okay, good," and calls on the next child to read.

Work tasks do not usually request creativity. Serious attention is rarely given in school work on *how* the children develop or express their own feelings and ideas, either linguistically or in graphic form. On the occasions when creativity or self-expression is requested, it is peripheral to the main activity or it is "enrichment" or "for fun." During a lesson on what similes are, for example, the teacher explains what they are, puts several on the board, gives some other examples herself, and then asks the children if they can "make some up." She calls on three children who give similes, two of which are actually in the book they have open before them. The teacher does not comment on this and then asks several others to choose similes from the list of phrases in the book. Several do so correctly, and she says, "Oh good! You're picking them out! See how good we are?" Their homework is to pick out the rest of the similes from the list.

Creativity is not often requested in social studies and science projects, either. Social studies projects, for example, are given with directions to "find information on your topic" and write it up. The children are not supposed to copy but to "put it in your own words." Although a number of the projects subsequently went beyond the teacher's direction to find information and had quite expressive covers and inside illustrations, the teacher's evaluative comments had to do with the amount of information, whether they had "copied," and if their work was neat.

The style of control of the three fifth-grade teachers observed in this school varied from somewhat easygoing to strict, but in contrast to the working-class schools, the teachers' decisions were usually based on external rules and regulations—for example, on criteria that were known or available to the children. Thus, the teachers always honor the bells for changing classes, and they usually evaluate children's work by what is in the textbooks and answer booklets.

There is little excitement in schoolwork for the children, and the assignments are perceived as having little to do with their interests and feelings. As one child said, what you do is "store facts up in your head like cold storage—until you need it later for a test or your job." Thus, doing well is important because there are thought to be *other*, likely rewards: a good job or college.[9]

Affluent Professional School

In the affluent professional school, work is creative activity carried out independently. The students are continually asked to express and apply ideas and concepts. Work involves individual thought and expressiveness, expansion and illustration of ideas, and choice of appropriate method and material. (The class is not considered an open classroom, and the principal explained that because of the large number of discipline problems in the fifth grade this year they did not departmentalize. The teacher who agreed to take part in the study said she is "more structured" this year than she usually is.) The products of work in this class are often written stories, editorials and essays, or representations of ideas in mural, graph, or craft form. The products of work should not be like everybody else's and should show individuality. They should exhibit good design, and (this is important) they must also fit empirical reality. Moreover, one's work should attempt to interpret or "make sense" of reality. The relatively few rules to be followed regarding work are usually criteria for, or limits on, individual activity. One's product is usually evaluated for the quality of its expression and for the appropriateness of its conception to the task. In many cases, one's own satisfaction with the product is an important criterion for its evaluation. When right answers are called for, as in commercial materials like SRA (Science Research Associates) and math, it is important that the children decide on an answer as a result of thinking about the idea involved in what they're being asked to do. Teacher's hints are to "think about it some more."

The following activities are illustrative. The class takes home a sheet requesting each child's parents to fill in the number of cars they have, the number of television sets, refrigerators, games, or rooms in the house, and so on. Each child is to figure the average number of a type of possession owned by the fifth grade. Each child must compile the "data" from all the sheets. A calculator is available in the classroom to do the mechanics of finding the average. Some children decide to send sheets to the fourth-grade families for comparison. Their work should be "verified" by a classmate before it is handed in.

Each child and his or her family has made a geoboard. The teacher asks the class to get their geoboards from the side cabinet, to take a handful of rubber bands, and then to listen to what she would like them to do. She says, "I would like you to design a figure and then find the perimeter and area. When you have it, check with your neighbor. After you've done that, please transfer it to graph paper and tomorrow I'll ask you to make up a question about it for someone. When you hand it in, please let me know whose it is and who verified it. Then I have something else for you to do that's really fun. [pause] Find the average number of chocolate chips in three cookies. I'll give you three cookies, and you'll have to *eat* your way through, I'm afraid!" Then she goes around the room and gives help, suggestions, praise, and admonitions that they are getting noisy. They work sitting, or standing up at their desks, at benches in the back, or on the floor. A child hands the teacher his paper and she comments, "I'm not accepting this paper. Do a better design." To another child she says, "That's fantastic! But you'll never find the area. Why don't you draw a figure inside [the big one] and subtract to get the area?"

The school district requires the fifth grade to study ancient civilization (in particular, Egypt, Athens, and Sumer). In this classroom, the emphasis is on illustrating and re-creating the culture of the people of ancient times. The following are typical activities: the children made an 8mm film on Egypt, which one of the parents edited. A girl in the class wrote the script, and the class acted it out. They put the sound on themselves. They read stories of those days. They wrote essays and stories depicting the lives of the people and the societal and occupational divisions. They chose from a list of projects, all of which involved graphic representations of ideas: for example, "Make a mural depicting the division of labor in Egyptian society."

Each child wrote and exchanged a letter in hieroglyphics with a fifth grader in another class, and they also exchanged stories they wrote in cuneiform. They made a scroll and singed the edges so it looked authentic. They each chose an occupation and made an Egyptian plaque representing that occupation, simulating the appropriate Egyptian design. They carved their design on a cylinder of wax, pressed the wax into clay, and then baked the clay. Although one girl did not choose an occupation but carved instead a series of gods and slaves, the teacher said, "That's all right, Amber, it's beautiful." As they were working the teacher said, "Don't cut into your clay until you're satisfied with your design."

Social studies also involves almost daily presentation by the children of some event from the news. The teacher's questions ask the children to expand what they say, to give more details, and to be more specific. Occasionally she adds some remarks to help them see connections between events.

The emphasis on expressing and illustrating ideas in social studies is accompanied in language arts by an emphasis on creative writing. Each child wrote a rebus story for a first grader whom they had interviewed to see what kind of story the child liked best. They wrote editorials on pending decisions by the school board and radio plays, some of which were read over the school intercom from the office and one of which was performed in the auditorium. There is no language arts textbook because, the teacher said, "The principal wants us to be creative." There is not much grammar, but there is punctuation. One morning when the observer arrived, the class was doing a punctuation ditto. The teacher later apologized for using the ditto. "It's just for review," she said. "I don't teach punctuation that way. We use their language." The ditto had three unambiguous rules for where to put commas in a sentence. As the teacher was going around to help the children with the ditto, she repeated several times, "Where you put commas depends on how you say the sentence; it depends on the situation and what you want to say." Several weeks later the observer saw another punctuation activity. The teacher had printed a five-paragraph story on an oak tag and then cut it into phrases. She read the whole story to the class from the book, then passed out the phrases. The group had to decide how the phrases could best be put together again. (They arranged the phrases on the floor.) The point was not to replicate the story, although that was not irrelevant, but to "decide what you think the best way is." Punctuation marks on cardboard pieces were then handed out, and the children discussed and then decided what mark was best at each place they thought one was needed. At the end of each paragraph the teacher asked, "Are you satisfied with the way the paragraphs are now? Read it to yourself and see how it sounds." Then she read the original story again, and they compared the two.

Describing her goals in science to the investigator, the teacher said, "We use ESS (Elementary Science Study). It's very good because it gives a hands-on experience—so they can make *sense* out of it. It doesn't matter whether it [what they find] is right or wrong. I bring them together and there's value in discussing their ideas."

The products of work in this class are often highly valued by the children and the teacher. In fact, this was the only school in which the investigator was not allowed to take original pieces of the children's work for her files. If the work was small enough, however, and was on paper, the investigator could duplicate it on the copying machine in the office.

The teacher's attempt to control the class involves constant negotiation. She does not give direct orders unless she is angry because the children have been too noisy. Normally, she tries to get them to foresee the consequences of their actions and to decide accordingly. For example, lining them up to go see a play written by the sixth graders, she says, "I presume you're lined up by someone with whom you want to sit. I hope you're lined up by someone you won't get in trouble with."…

One of the few rules governing the children's movement is that no more than three children may be out of the room at once. There is a school rule that anyone can go to the library at any time to get a book. In the fifth grade I observed, they sign their name on the chalkboard and leave. There are no passes. Finally, the children have a fair amount of officially sanctioned say over what happens in the class. For example, they often negotiate what work is to be done. If the teacher wants to move on to the next subject, but the children say they are not ready, they want to work on their present projects some more, she very often lets them do it.

Executive Elite School

In the executive elite school, work is developing one's analytical intellectual powers. Children are continually asked to reason through a problem, to produce intellectual products that are both logically sound and of top academic quality. A primary goal of thought is to conceptualize rules by which elements may fit together in systems and then to apply these rules in solving a problem. Schoolwork helps one to achieve, to excel, to prepare for life.

The following are illustrative. The math teacher teaches area and perimeter by having the children derive formulas for each. First she helps them, through discussion at the board, to arrive at $A = W \times L$ as a formula (not *the* formula) for area. After discussing several, she says, "Can anyone make up a formula for perimeter? Can you figure that out yourselves? [pause] Knowing what we know, can we think of a formula?" She works out three children's suggestions at the board, saying to two, "Yes, that's a good one," and then asks the class if they can think of any more. No one volunteers. To prod them, she says, "If you use rules and good reasoning, you get many ways. Chris, can you think up a formula?"

She discusses two-digit division with the children as a decision-making process. Presenting a new type of problem to them, she asks, "What's the *first* decision you'd make if presented with this kind of example? What is the first thing you'd *think*? Craig?" Craig says, "To find my first partial quotient." She responds, "Yes, that would be your first decision. How would you do that?" Craig explains, and then the teacher says, "OK, we'll see how that works for you." The class tries his way. Subsequently, she comments on the merits and shortcomings of several other children's decisions. Later, she tells the investigator that her goals in math are to develop their reasoning and mathematical thinking and that, unfortunately, "there's no *time* for manipulables."

While right answers are important in math, they are not "given" by the book or by the teacher but may be challenged by the children. Going over some problems in late September the teacher says, "Raise your hand if you do not agree." A child says, "I don't agree with sixty-four." The teacher responds, "OK, there's a question about sixty-four. [to class] Please check it. Owen, they're disagreeing with you. Kristen, they're checking yours." The teacher emphasized this repeatedly during September and October with statements like "Don't be afraid to say you disagree. In the last [math] class, somebody disagreed, and they were right. Before you disagree, check yours, and if you still think we're wrong, then we'll check it out." By Thanksgiving, the children did not often speak in terms of right and wrong math problems but of whether they agreed with the answer that had been given.

There are complicated math mimeos with many word problems. Whenever they go over the examples, they discuss how each child has set up the problem. The children must explain it precisely. On one occasion the teacher said, "I'm more—just as interested in *how* you set up the problem as in what answer you find. If you set up a problem in a good way, the answer is *easy* to find."

Social studies work is most often reading and discussion of concepts and independent research. There are only occasional artistic, expressive, or illustrative projects. Ancient Athens and Sumer are, rather, societies to analyze. The following questions are typical of those that guide the children's independent research. "What mistakes did Pericles make after the war?" "What mistakes did the citizens of Athens make?" What are the elements of a civilization?" "How did Greece build an economic empire?" "Compare the way Athens chose its leaders with the way we choose ours." Occasionally the children are asked to make up sample questions for their social studies tests. On an occasion when the investigator was present, the social studies teacher rejected a child's question by saying, "That's just fact. If I asked you that question on a test, you'd complain it was just memory! Good questions ask for concepts."

In social studies—but also in reading, science, and health—the teachers initiate classroom discussions of current social issues and problems. These discussions occurred on every one of the investigator's visits, and a teacher told me, "These children's opinions are important—it's important that they learn to reason things through." The classroom discussions always struck the observer as quite realistic and analytical, dealing with concrete social issues like the following: "Why do workers strike?" "Is that right or wrong?" "Why do we have inflation, and what can be done to stop it?" "Why do companies put chemicals in food when the natural ingredients are available?" and so on. Usually the children did not have to be prodded to give their opinions. In fact, their statements and the interchanges between them struck the observer as quite sophisticated conceptually and verbally, and well-informed. Occasionally the teachers would prod with statements such as, "Even if you don't know [the answers], if you think logically about it, you can figure it out." And "I'm asking you [these] questions to help you think this through."

Language arts emphasizes language as a complex system, one that should be mastered. The children are asked to diagram sentences of complex grammatical construction, to memorize irregular verb conjugation (he lay, he has lain, and so on...), and to use the proper participles, conjunctions, and interjections in their speech. The teacher (the same one who teaches social studies) told them, "It is not enough to get these right on tests; you must use what you learn [in grammar classes] in your written and oral work. I will grade you on that."

Most writing assignments are either research reports and essays for social studies or experiment analyses and write-ups for science. There is only an occasional story or other "creative writing" assignment. On the occasion observed by the investigator (the writing of a Halloween story), the points the teacher stressed in preparing the children to write involved the structural aspects of a story rather than the expression of feelings or other ideas. The teacher showed them a filmstrip, "The Seven Parts of a Story," and lectured them on plot development, mood setting, character development, consistency, and the use of a logical or appropriate ending. The stories they subsequently wrote were, in fact, well-structured, but many were also personal and expressive. The teacher's evaluative comments, however, did not refer to the expressiveness or artistry but were all directed toward whether they had "developed" the story well.

Language arts work also involved a large amount of practice in presentation of the self and in managing situations where the child was expected to be in charge. For example, there was a series of assignments in which each child had to be a "student teacher." The child had to plan a lesson in grammar, outlining, punctuation, or other language arts topic and explain the concept to the class. Each child was to prepare a worksheet or game and a homework assignment as well. After each presentation, the teacher and other children gave a critical appraisal of the "student teacher's" performance. Their criteria were: whether the student spoke clearly, whether the lesson was interesting, whether the student made any mistakes, and whether he or she kept control of the class. On an occasion when a child did not maintain control, the teacher said, "When you're up there, you have authority and you have to use it. I'll back you up." ...

The executive elite school is the only school where bells do not demarcate the periods of time. The two fifth-grade teachers were very strict about changing classes on schedule, however, as specific plans for each sessions had been made. The teachers attempted to keep tight control over the children during lessons, and the children were sometimes flippant, boisterous, and occasionally rude. However, the children may be brought into line by reminding them that "It is up to you." "You must control yourself," "you are responsible for your work," you must "set your own priorities." One teacher told a child, "You are the only driver of your car—and only you can regulate your speed." A new teacher complained to the observer that she had thought "these children" would have more control.

While strict attention to the lesson at hand is required, the teachers make relatively little attempt to regulate the movement of the children at other times. For example, except for the kindergartners the children in this school do not have to wait for the bell to ring in the morning; they may go to their classroom when they arrive at school. Fifth graders often came early to read, to finish work, or to catch up. After the first two months of school, the fifth-grade teachers did not line the children up to change classes or to go to gym and so on, but, when the children were ready and quiet, they were simply permitted to leave on their own.

In the classroom, the children could get materials when they needed them and took what they needed from closets and from the teacher's desk. They were in charge of the office at lunchtime. During class they did not have to sign out or ask to leave the room; they just got up and left. Because of the pressure to get work done, however, they did not leave the room very often. The teachers were very polite to the children, and the investigator heard no sarcasm, no nasty remarks, and few direct orders. The teachers never called the children "honey" or "dear" but always called them by name. The teachers were expected to be available before school, after school, and for part of their lunchtime to provide extra help if needed....

The foregoing analysis of differences in schoolwork in contrasting social class contexts suggests the following conclusion: the "hidden curriculum" of schoolwork is tacit preparation for relating to the process of production in a particular way. Differing curricular, pedagogical, and pupil evaluation practices emphasize different cognitive and behavioral skills in each social setting and thus contribute to the development in the children of certain potential relationships to physical and symbolic capital, to authority, and to the process of work. School experience, in the sample of schools discussed here, differed qualitatively by social class. These differences may not only contribute to the development in the children in each social class of certain types of economically significant relationships and not others but would thereby help to *reproduce* this system of relations in society. In the contribution to the reproduction of unequal social relations lies a theoretical meaning and social consequence of classroom practice.

The identification of different emphases in classrooms in a sample of contrasting social class contexts implies that further research should be conducted in a large number of schools to investigate the types of work tasks and interactions in each to see if they differ in the ways discussed here and to see if similar potential relationships are uncovered. Such research could have as a product the further elucidation of complex but not readily apparent connections between everyday activity in schools and classrooms and the unequal structure of economic relationships in which we work and live.

Endnotes

1. S. Bowles and H. Gintis, *Schooling in Capitalist America: Educational Reform and the Contradictions of Economic Life* (New York: Basic Books, 1976).
2. B. Bernstein, *Class, Codes and Control, Vol. 3. Towards a Theory of Educational Transmission*, 2d ed. (London: Routledge & Kegan Paul, 1977); P. Bourdieu and J. Passeron, *Reproduction in Education, Society and Culture* (Beverly Hills, Calif.: Sage, 1977): M. W. Apple, *Ideology and Curriculum* (Boston: Routledge & Kegan Paul, 1979).
3. But see, in a related vein, M. W. Apple and N. King, "What Do Schools Teach?" *Curriculum Inquiry* 6 (1977): 341–58; R. C. Rist, *The Urban School: A Factory for Failure* (Cambridge, Mass.: MIT Press, 1973).
4. The U.S. Bureau of the Census defines *poverty* for a nonfarm family of four as a yearly income of $6,191 a year or less. U.S. Bureau of the Census, *Statistical Abstract of the United States: 1978* (Washington, D.C.: U.S. Government Printing Office, 1978), 465, table 754.

5. U.S. Bureau of the Census, "Money Income in 1977 of Families and Persons in the United States," *Current Population Reports* Series P-60, no. 118 (Washington, D.C.: U.S. Government Printing Office, 1979), p. 2, table A.
6. Ibid.
7. This figure is an estimate. According to the Bureau of the Census, only 2.6 percent of families in the United States have money income of $50,000 or over. U.S. Bureau of the Census, *Current Population Reports* Series P-60. For figures on income at these higher levels, see J. D. Smith and S. Franklin, "The Concentration of Personal Wealth, 1922–1969," *American Economic Review* 64 (1974): 162–67.
8. Smith and Franklin, "The Concentration of Personal Wealth"
9. A dominant feeling, expressed directly and indirectly by teachers in this school, was boredom with their work. They did, however, in contrast to the working-class schools, almost always carry out lessons during class times.

Gloria Anzaldúa
How to Tame a Wild Tongue

Gloria Anzaldúa, the Chicana child of immigrant Mexican parents, was born in 1942 in Jesus Maria of the Valley, Texas, and grew up in Hargill, Texas, on the Mexican border. Anzaldúa describes herself as "a border woman," and her book *Borderlands/La Frontera: The New Mestiza* (Spinsters/Aunt Lute, 1987), from which this essay comes, straddles the boundaries of genre and language as well as geography, ethnicity and sexuality. "How to Tame a Wild Tongue" is part autobiographical narrative, part poetry, part social history, and part cultural critique. In it, Anzaldúa simultaneously explains and enacts the unbreakable bond between ethnic identity and its "twin skin," linquistic identity. Throughout her analysis of her own experiences as a Chicano speaker in an Anglo world, she slides (abruptly? seamlessly?) among eight languages, two variations of English and six of Spanish, including Chicano, Tex-Mex, and Castilian. Anzaldúa offers no translation and no apology. And the effect on a non-bilingual speaker is to experience, if for just a moment, what it is like to grow up in a world where the dominant language is not one's own. So Anzaldúa challenges us—to persist patiently in our effortful reading, to identify with her in her struggle for linguistic survival, or to toss down this book in frustration and join with the censoring voices of authority who would tame, or "cut out," her wild tongue.

"We're going to have to control your tongue," the dentist says, pulling out all the metal from my mouth. Silver bits plop and tinkle into the basin. My mouth is a motherlode.

The dentist is cleaning out my roots. I get a whiff of the stench when I gasp. "I can't cap that tooth yet, you're still draining," he says.

"We're going to have to do something about your tongue," I hear the anger rising in his voice. My tongue keeps pushing out the wads of cotton, pushing back the drills, the long thin needles. "I've never seen anything as strong or as stubborn," he says. And I think, how do you tame a wild tongue, train it to be quiet, how do you bridle and saddle it? How do you make it lie down?

> Who is to say that robbing a people of its language
> is less violent than war?
>
> —Ray Gwyn Smith[1]

I remember being caught speaking Spanish at recess—that was good for three licks on the knuckles with a sharp ruler. I remember being sent to the corner of the classroom for "talking back" to the Anglo teacher when all I was trying to do was tell her how to pronounce my name. "If you want to be American, speak 'American.' If you don't like it, go back to Mexico where you belong."

"I want you to speak English. *Pa' hallar buen trabajo tienes que saber hablar el inglés bien. Qué vale toda tu educación si todavía hablas inglés con un* 'accent,'" my mother would say, mortified that I spoke English like a Mexican. At Pan American University, I and all Chicano students were required to take two speech classes. Their purpose: to get rid of our accents.

Attacks on one's form of expression with the intent to censor are a violation of the First Amendment. *El Anglo con cara de inocente nos arrancó la lengua.* Wild tongues can't be tamed, they can only be cut out.

Overcoming the Tradition of Silence

> *Ahogadas, escupimos el oscuro.*
> *Peleando con nuestra propia sombra*
> *el silencio nos sepulta.*

En boca cerrada no entran moscas. "Flies don't enter a closed mouth" is a saying I kept hearing when I was a child. *Ser habladora* was to be a gossip and a liar, to talk too much. *Muchachitas bien criadas*, well-bred girls don't answer back. *Es una falta de respeto* to talk back to one's mother or father. I remember one of the sins I'd recite to the priest in the confession box the few times I went to confession: talking back to my mother, *hablar pa' 'tras, repelar. Hocicona, repelona, chismosa*, having a big mouth, questioning, carrying tales are all signs of being *mal criada*. In my culture they are all words that are derogatory if applied to women—I've never heard them applied to men.

The first time I heard two women, a Puerto Rican and a Cuban, say the word *"nosotras,"* I was shocked. I had not known the word existed. Chicanas use *nosotros* whether wer're male or female. We are robbed of our female being by the masculine plural. Language is a male discourse.

> And our tongues have become
> dry   the wilderness has
> dried out our tongues   and
> we have forgotten speech.
>
> —Irena Klepfisz[2]

Even our own people, other Spanish speakers *nos quieren poner candados en la boca.* They would hold us back with their bag of *reglas de academia.*

Oyé como ladra: el lenguaje de la frontera

> *Quien tiene boca se equivoca.*
>
> —Mexican saying

"*Pocho*, cultural traitor, you're speaking the oppressor's language by speaking English, you're ruining the Spanish language," I have been accused by various Latinos and Latinas. Chicano Spanish is considered by the purist and by most Latinos deficient, a mutilation of Spanish.

But Chicano Spanish is a border tongue which developed naturally. Change, *evolución, enriquecimiento de palabras nuevas por invención o adopción* have created variants of Chicano Spanish, *un nuevo lenguaje. Un lenguaje que corresponde a un modo de vivir.* Chicano Spanish is not incorrect, it is a living language.

For a people who are neither Spanish nor live in a country in which Spanish is the first language; for a people who live in a country in which English is the reigning tongue but who are not Anglo; for a people who cannot entirely identify with either standard (formal, Castilian) Spanish nor standard English, what recourse is left to them but to create their own language? A language which they can connect their identity to, one capable of communicating the realities and values true to themselves—a language with terms that are neither *español ni inglés,* but both. We speak a patois, a forked tongue, a variation of two languages.

Chicano Spanish sprang out of the Chicanos' need to identify ourselves as a distinct people. We needed a language with which we could communicate with ourselves, a secret language. For some of us, language is a homeland closer than the Southwest—for many Chicanos today live in the Midwest and East. And because we are a complex, heterogeneous people, we speak many languages. Some of the languages we speak are

1. Standard English
2. Working class and slang English
3. Standard Spanish
4. Standard Mexican Spanish
5. North Mexican Spanish dialect
6. Chicano Spanish (Texas, New Mexico, Arizona, and California have regional variations)
7. Tex-Mex
8. *Pachuco* (called *caló*)

My "home" tongues are the languages I speak with my sister and brothers, with my friends. They are the last five listed, with 6 and 7 being closest to my heart. From school, the media, and job situations, I've picked up standard and working class English. From Mamagrande Locha and from reading Spanish and Mexican literature, I've picked up Standard Spanish and Standard Mexican Spanish. From *los recién llegados*, Mexican immigrants, and *braceros*, I learned the North Mexican dialect. With Mexicans I'll try to speak either Standard Mexican Spanish or the North Mexican dialect. From my parents and Chicanos living in the Valley, I picked up Chicano Texas Spanish, and I speak it with my mom, younger brother (who married a Mexican and who rarely mixes Spanish with English), aunts, and older relatives.

With Chicanas from *Nuevo Mexico* or *Arizona* I will speak Chicano Spanish a little, but often they don't understand what I'm saying. With most California Chicanas I speak entirely in English (unless I forget). When I first moved to San Francisco, I'd rattle off something in Spanish, unintentionally embarrassing them. Often it is only with another Chicana *tejano* that I can talk freely.

Words distorted by English are known as anglicisms or *pochismos*. The *pocho* is an anglicized Mexican or American of Mexican origin who speaks Spanish with an accent characteristic of North Americans and who distorts and reconstructs the language according to the influence of English.[3] Tex-Mex, or Spanglish, comes most naturally to me. I may switch back and forth from English to Spanish in the same sentence or in the same word. With my sister and my brother Nune and with Chicano *tejano* contemporaries I speak in Tex-Mex.

From kids and people my own age I picked up *Pachuco*. *Pachuco* (the language of the zoot suiters) is a language of rebellion, both against Standard Spanish and Standard English. It is a secret language. Adults of the culture and outsiders cannot understand it. It is made up of slang words from both English and Spanish. *Ruca* means girl or woman, *vato* means guy or dude, *chale* means no, *simón* means yes, *churro* is sure, talk is *periquiar*, *pigionear* means petting, *que gacho* means how nerdy, *ponte águila* means watch out, death is called *la pelona*. Through lack of practice and not having others who can speak it, I've lost most of the *Pachuco* tongue.

Chicano Spanish

Chicanos, after 250 years of Spanish/Anglo colonization, have developed significant differences in the Spanish we speak. We collapse two adjacent vowels into a single syllable and sometimes shift the stress in certain words such as *maíz/maiz, cohete/cuete*. We leave out certain consonants when they appear between vowels: *lado/lao, mojada/mojao*. Chicanos from South Texas pronounce *f* as *j* as in *jue* (*fue*). Chicanos use "archaisms," words that are no longer in the Spanish language, words that have been evolved out. We say *semos, truje, haiga, ansina*, and *naiden*. We retain the "archaic" *j*, as in *jalar*, that derives from an earlier *h* (the French *halar* or the Germanic *halon* which was lost to standard Spanish in the sixteenth century), but which is still found in several regional dialects such as the one spoken in South Texas. (Due to geography, Chicanos from the Valley of South Texas were cut off linguistically from other speakers. We tend to use words that the Spaniards brought over from Medieval Spain. The majority of the Spanish colonizers in Mexico and the Southwest came from Extremadura—Hernán Cortés was one of them—and Andalucía. Andalucians pronounce *ll* like a *y*, and their *d*'s tend to be absorbed by adjacent vowels: *tirado* becomes *tirao*. They brought *el lenguaje popular, dialectos y regionalismos*.)[4]

Chicanos and other Spanish speakers also shift *ll* to *y* and *z* to *s*.[5] We leave out initial syllables, saying *tar* for *estar*, *toy* for *estoy*, *hora* for *ahora* (*cubanos* and *puertorriqueños* also leave out initial letters of some words). We also leave out the final syllable such as *pa* for *para*. The intervocalic *y*, the *ll* as in *tortilla, ella, botella*, gets replaced by *tortia* or *tortiya, ea, botea*. We add an additional syllable at the beginning of certain words: *atocar* for *tocar*, *agastar* for *gastar*. Sometimes we'll say *lavaste las vacijas*, other times *lavates* (substituting the *ates* verb ending for the *aste*).

We used anglicisms, words borrowed from English: *bola* from ball, *carpeta* from carpet, *máchina de lavar* (instead of *lavadora*) from washing machine. Tex-Mex argot, created by adding a Spanish sound at the beginning or end of an English word such as *cookiar* for cook, *watchar* for watch, *parkiar* for park, and *rapiar* for rape, is the result of the pressures on Spanish speakers to adapt to English.

We don't use the word *vosotros/as* or its accompanying verb form. We don't say *claro* (to mean yes), *imagínate*, or *me emociona*, unless we picked up Spanish from Latinas, out of a book, or in a classroom. Other Spanish-speaking groups are going through the same, or similar, development in their Spanish.

Linguistic Terrorism

Deslenguadas. Somos los del español deficiente. We are your linquistic nightmare, your linquistic aberration, your linguistic *mestisaje*, the subject of your *burla*. Because we speak with tongues of fire we are culturally crucified. Racially, culturally, and linguistically *somos huérfanos*—we speak an orphan tongue.

Chicanas who grew up speaking Chicano Spanish have internalized the belief that we speak poor Spanish. It is illegitimate, a bastard language. And because we internalize how our language has been used against us by the dominant culture, we use our language differences against each other.

Chicana feminists often skirt around each other with suspicion and hesitation. For the longest time I couldn't figure it out. Then it dawned on me. To be close to another Chicana is like looking into the mirror. We are afraid of what we'll see there. *Pena.* Shame. Low estimation of self. In childhood we are told that our language is wrong. Repeated attacks on our native tongue diminish our sense of self. The attacks continue throughout our lives.

Chicanas feel uncomfortable talking in Spanish to Latinas, afraid of their censure. Their language was not outlawed in their countries. They had a whole lifetime of being immersed in their native tongue; generations, centuries in which Spanish was a first language, taught in school, heard on radio and TV, and read in the newspaper.

If a person, Chicana or Latina, has a low estimation of my native tongue, she also has a low estimation of me. Often with *mexicanas y latinas* we'll speak English as a neutral language. Even among Chicanas we tend to speak English at parties or conferences. Yet, at the same time, we're afraid the other will think we're *agringadas* because we don't speak Chicano Spanish. We oppress each other trying to out-Chicano each other, vying to be the "real" Chicanas, to speak like Chicanos. There is no one Chicano language just as there is no one Chicano experience. A monolingual Chicana whose first language is English or Spanish is just as much a Chicana as one who speaks several variants of Spanish. A Chicana from Michigan or Chicago or Detroit is just as much a Chicana as one from the Southwest. Chicano Spanish is as diverse linguistically as it is regionally.

By the end of this century, Spanish speakers will comprise the biggest minority group in the United States, a country where students in high schools and colleges are encouraged to take French classes because French is considered more "cultured." But for a language to remain alive it must be used.[6] By the end of this century English, and not Spanish, will be the mother tongue of most Chicanos and Latinos.

So, if you want to really hurt me, talk badly about my language. Ethnic identity is twin skin to linguistic identity—I am my language. Until I can take pride in my language, I cannot take pride in myself. Until I can accept as legitimate Chicano Texas Spanish, Tex-Mex, and all the other languages I speak, I cannot accept the legitimacy of myself. Until I am free to write bilingually and to switch codes without having always to translate, while I still have to speak English or Spanish when I would rather speak Spanglish, and as long as I have to accommodate the English speakers rather than having them accommodate me, my tongue will be illegitimate.

I will no longer be made to feel ashamed of existing. I will have my voice: Indian, Spanish, white. I will have my serpent's tongue—my woman's voice, my sexual voice, my poet's voice. I will overcome the tradition of silence.

> My fingers
> move sly against your palm
> Like women everywhere, we speak in code....
> —Melanie Kaye/Kantrowitz[7]

"Vistas," corridos, y comida: My Native Tongue

In the 1960s, I read my first Chicano novel. It was *City of Night* by John Rechy, a gay Texan, son of a Scottish father and a Mexican mother. For days I walked around in stunned amazement that a Chicano could write and could get published. When I read *I Am Joaquín*[8] I was surprised to see a bilingual book by a Chicano in print. When I saw poetry written in Tex-Mex for the first time, a feeling of pure joy flashed through me. I felt like we really existed as a people. In 1971, when I started teaching High School English to Chicano students, I tried to supplement the required texts with works by Chicanos, only to be reprimanded and forbidden to do so by the principal. He claimed that I was supposed to teach "American" and English literature. At the risk of being fired, I swore my students to secrecy and slipped in Chicano short stories, poems, a play. In graduate school, while working toward a Ph.D., I had to "argue" with one adviser after the other, semester after semester, before I was allowed to make Chicano literature an area of focus.

Even before I read books by Chicanos or Mexicans, it was the Mexican movies I saw at the drive-in—the Thursday night special of $1.00 a carload—that gave me a sense of belonging. "*Vámonos a las vistas*," my mother would call out and we'd all—grandmother, brothers, sister, and cousins—squeeze into the car. We'd wolf down cheese and bologna white bread sandwiches while watching Pedro Infante in melodramatic tearjerkers like *Nosotros los pobres*, the first "real" Mexican movie (that was not an imitation of European movies). I remember seeing *Cuando los hijos se van* and surmising that all Mexican movies played up the love a mother has for her children and what ungrateful sons and daughters suffer when they are not devoted to their mothers. I remember the singing-type "westerns" of Jorge Negrete and Miquel Aceves Mejía. When watching Mexican movies, I felt a sense of homecoming as well as alienation. People who were to amount to something didn't go to Mexican movies, or *bailes*, or tune their radios to *bolero, rancherita*, and *corrido* music.

The whole time I was growing up, there was *norteño* music sometimes called North Mexican border music, or Tex-Mex music, or Chicano music, or *cantina* (bar) music. I grew up listening to *conjuntos*, three- or four-piece bands made up of folk musicians playing guitar, *bajo sexto*, drums, and button accordion, which Chicanos had borrowed from the German immigrants who had come to Central Texas and Mexico to farm and build breweries. In the Rio Grande Valley, Steve Jordan and Little Joe Hernández were popular, and Flaco Jiménez was the accordion king. The rhythms of Tex-Mex music are those of the polka, also adapted from the Germans, who in turn had borrowed the polka from the Czechs and Bohemians.

I remember the hot, sultry evenings when *corridos*—songs of love and death on the Texas-Mexican borderlands—reverberated out of cheap amplifiers from the local *cantinas* and wafted in through my bedroom window.

Corridos first became widely used along the South Texas/Mexican border during the early conflict between Chicanos and Anglos. The *corridos* are usually about Mexican heroes who do valiant deeds against the Anglo oppressors. Pancho Villa's song, "*La cucaracha*," is the most famous one. *Corridos* of John F. Kennedy and his death are still very popular in the Valley. Older Chicanos remember Lydia Mendoza, one of the great border *corrido* singers who was called *la Gloria de Tejas*. Her *"El tango negro,"* sung during the Great Depression, made her a singer of the people. The ever-present *corridos* narrated one hundred years of border history, bringing news of events as well as entertaining. These folk musicians and folk songs are our chief cultural mythmakers, and they made our hard lives seem bearable.

I grew up feeling ambivalent about our music. Country-western and rock-and-roll had more status. In the fifties and sixties, for the slightly educated and *agringado* Chicanos, there existed a sense of shame at being caught listening to our music. Yet I couldn't stop my feet from thumping to the music, could not stop humming the words, nor hide from myself the exhilaration I felt when I heard it.

There are more subtle ways that we internalize identification, especially in the forms of images and emotions. For me food and certain smells are tied to my identity, to my homeland. Woodsmoke curling up to an immense blue sky; woodsmoke perfuming my grandmother's clothes, her skin. The stench of cow manure and the yellow patches on the ground; the crack of a .22 rifle and the reek of cordite. Homemade white cheese sizzling in a pan, melting inside a folded *tortilla*. My sister Hilda's hot, spicy *menudo, chile colorado* making it deep red, pieces of *panza* and hominy floating on top. My brother Carito barbequing *fajitas* in the backyard. Even now and 3,000 miles away, I can see my mother spicing the ground beef, pork, and venison with *chile*. My mouth salivates at the thought of the hot steaming *tamales* I would be eating if I were home.

Si le preguntas a mi mamá, "¿Qué eres?"

> Identity is the essential core of who
> we are as individuals, the conscious
> experience of the self inside.
> —Gershen Kaufman[9]

Nosotros los Chicanos straddle the borderlands. On one side of us, we are constantly exposed to the Spanish of the Mexicans; on the other side we hear the Anglos' incessant clamoring so that we forget our language. Among ourselves we don't say *nosotros los americanos, o nosotros los españoles, o nosotros los hispanos*. We say *nosotros los mexicanos* (by *mexicanos* we do not mean citizens of Mexico; we do not mean a national identity, but a racial one). We distinguish between *mexicanos del otro lado* and *mexicanos de este lado*. Deep in our hearts we believe that being Mexican has nothing to do with which country one lives in. Being Mexican is a state of soul—not one of mind, not one of citizenship. Neither eagle nor serpent, but both. And like the ocean, neither animal respects borders.

> *Dime con quien andas y te diré quien eres.*
> (Tell me who your friends are and I'll tell you who you are.)
> —Mexican saying

Si le preguntas a mi mamá, "¿Qué eres?" te dirá, "Soy mexicana." My brothers and sister say the same. I sometimes will answer *"soy mexicana"* and at others will say *"soy Chicana" o "soy tejana."* But I identified as *"Raza"* before I ever identified as *"mexicana"* or "Chicana."

As a culture, we call ourselves Spanish when referring to ourselves as a linguistic group and when copping out. It is then that we forget our predominant Indian genes. We are 70–80 percent Indian.[10] We call ourselves Hispanic[11] or Spanish-American or Latin American or Latin when linking ourselves to other Spanish-speaking peoples of the Western hemisphere and when copping out. We call ourselves Mexican-American[12] to signify we are neither Mexican nor American, but more the noun "American" than the adjective "Mexican" (and when copping out).

Chicanos and other people of color suffer economically for not acculturating. This voluntary (yet forced) alienation makes for psychological conflict, a kind of dual identity—we don't identify with the Anglo-American cultural values and we don't totally identify with the Mexican cultural values. We are a synergy of two cultures with various degrees of Mexicanness or Angloness. I have so internalized the borderland conflict that sometimes I feel like one cancels out the other and we are zero, nothing, no one. *A veces no soy nada ni nadie. Pero hasta cuando no lo soy, lo soy.*

When not copping out, when we know we are more than nothing, we call ourselves Mexican, referring to race and ancestry; *mestizo* when affirming both our Indian and Spanish (but we hardly ever own our Black) ancestry; Chicano when referring to a politically aware people born and/or raised in the United States; *Raza* when referring to Chicanos; *tejanos* when we are Chicanos from Texas.

Chicanos did not know we were a people until 1965 when Cesar Chavez and the farmworkers united and *I Am Joaquín* was published and *la Raza Unida* party was formed in Texas. With that recognition, we became a distinct people. Something momentous happened to the Chicano soul—we became aware of our reality and acquired a name and a lanquage (Chicano Spanish) that reflected that reality. Now that we had a name, some of the fragmented pieces began to fall together—who we were, what we were, how we had evolved. We began to get glimpses of what we might eventually become.

Yet the struggle of identities continues, the struggle of borders is our reality still. One day the inner struggle will cease and a true integration take place. In the meantime, *tenémos que hacer la lucha. ¿Quién está protegiendo los ranchos de mi gente? ¿Quién está tratando de cerrar la fisura entre la india y el blanco en nuestra sangre? El Chicano, si, el Chicano que anda como un ladrón en su propia casa.*

Los Chicanos, how patient we seem, how very patient. There is the quiet of the Indian about us.[13] We know how to survive. When other races have given up their tongue we've kept ours. We know what it is to live under the hammer blow of the dominant *norteamericano* culture. But more than we count the blows, we count the days the weeks the years the centuries the aeons until the white laws and commerce and customs will rot in the deserts they've created, lie bleached. *Humildes* yet proud, *quietos* yet wild, *nosotros los mexicanos-Chicanos* will walk by the crumbling ashes as we go about our business. Stubborn, persevering, impenetrable as stone, yet possessing a malleability that renders us unbreakable, we, the *mestizas* and *mestizos*, will remain.

Endnotes

1. Ray Gwyn Smith, *Moorland Is Cold Country*, unpublished book.
2. Irena Klepfisz, "*Di rayze aheym*/The Journey Home," in *The Tribe of Dina: A Jewish Women's Anthology*, Melanie Kaye/Kantrowitz and Irena Klepfisz, eds. (Montpelier, VT: Sinister Wisdom Books, 1986), 49.
3. R. C. Ortega, *Dialectología Del Barrio*, trans. Hortencia S. Alwan (Los Angeles, CA: R. C. Ortega Publisher & Bookseller, 1977), 132.
4. Eduardo Hernandéz-Chávez, Andrew D. Cohen, and Anthony F. Beltramo, *El Lenguaje de los Chicanos: Regional and Social Characteristics of Language Used by Mexican Americans* (Arlington, VA: Center for Applied Linguistics, 1975), 39.
5. Hernandéz-Chávez, xvii.
6. Irena Klepfisz, "Secular Jewish Identity: Yidishkayt in America," in *The Tribe of Dina*, Kaye/Kantrowitz and Klepfisz, eds., 43.
7. Melanie Kaye/Kantrowitz, "Sign," in *We Speak in Code: Poems and Other Writings* (Pittsburgh, PA: Motheroot Publications, Inc., 1980), 85.
8. Rodolfo Gonzales, *I Am Joaquín/Yo Soy Joaquín* (New York, NY: Bantam Books, 1972). It was first published in 1967.
9. Gershen Kaufman, *Shame: The Power of Caring* (Cambridge, MA: Schenkman Books, Inc., 1980), 68.
10. John R. Chávez, *The Lost Land: The Chicano Images of the Southwest* (Albuquerque, NM: University of New Mexico Press, 1984), 88–90.

11. "Hispanic" is derived from *Hispanis* (*España*, a name given to the Iberian Peninsula in ancient times when it was a part of the Roman Empire) and is a term designated by the U.S. government to make it easier to handle us on paper.
12. The treaty of Guadalupe Hidalgo created the Mexican-American in 1848.
13. Anglos, in order to alleviate their guilt for dispossessing the Chicano, stressed the Spanish part of us and perpetrated the myth of the Spanish Southwest. We have accepted the fiction that we are Hispanic, that is Spanish, in order to accommodate ourselves to the dominant culture and its abhorrence of Indians. Chávez, 88–91.

James Baldwin
Notes of a Native Son

Born in 1924, in Harlem, James Baldwin started as a boy preacher in his father's storefront church. As a young man he met the famous African-American novelist and political advocate Richard Wright. Already at work as a writer, Baldwin became an important spokesperson for the Civil Rights Movement and continued to write short stories, novels, plays, poems, and powerful essays—such as the one we have here—that often dealt with issues of race and civil rights. "Notes of a Native Son" appeared in *Harper's Magazine* in 1955, in obvious "conversation" with Wright's novel *Native Son*, one of the first American novels to examine explicitly and unapologetically the brutality of racism and class relations in the United States. Nineteen fifty-five may seem like a faraway time—but is it? Think about Baldwin's essay, and the stories it contains, in light of current discrimination or racial issues you've witnessed in your community, among the people around you, or in the news. "Notes of a Native Son" is also a record of the formation of Baldwin's identity—the story of how his character and inner life were shaped by place, by family, by history. Think about ways in which your life has been shaped by similar forces.

One

On the twenty-ninth of July, in 1943, my father died. On the same day, a few hours later, his last child was born. Over a month before this, while all our energies were concentrated in waiting for these events, there had been, in Detroit, one of the bloodiest riots of the century. A few hours after my father's funeral, while he lay in state in the undertaker's chapel, a race riot broke out in Harlem. On the morning of the third of August, we drove my father to the graveyard through a wilderness of smashed plate glass.

The day of my father's funeral had also been my nineteenth birthday. As we drove him to the graveyard, the spoils of injustice, anarchy, discontent, and hatred were all around us. It seemed to me that God himself had devised, to mark my father's end, the most sustained and brutally dissonant of codas. And it seemed to me, too, that the violence which rose all about us as my father left the world had been devised as a corrective for the pride of his eldest son. I had declined to believe in that apocalypse which had been central to my father's vision; very well, life seemed to be saying, here is something that will certainly pass for an apocalypse until the real thing comes along. I had inclined to be contemptuous of my father for the conditions of his life, for the conditions of our lives. When his life had ended I began to wonder about that life and also, in a new way, to be apprehensive about my own.

I had not known my father very well. We had got on badly, partly because we shared, in our different fashions, the vice of stubborn pride. When he was dead I realized that I had hardly ever spoken to him. When he had been dead a long time I began to wish I had. It seems to be typical of life in America, where opportunities, real and fancied, are thicker than anywhere else on the globe, that the second generation has no time to talk to the first. No one, including my father, seems to have known exactly how old he was, but his mother had been born during slavery. He was of the first generation of free men. He, along with thousands of other Negroes, came North after 1919 and I was part of that generation which had never seen the landscape of what Negroes sometimes call the Old Country.

He had been born in New Orleans and had been quite a young man there during the time that Louis Armstrong, a boy, was running errands for the dives and honky-tonks of what was always presented to me as one of the most wicked of cities—to this day, whenever I think of New Orleans, I also helplessly think of Sodom and Gomorrah. My father never mentioned Louis Armstrong, except to forbid us to play his records; but there was a picture of him on our wall for a long time. One of my father's strong-willed female relatives had placed it there and forbade my father to take it down. He never did, but he eventually maneuvered her out of the house and when, some years later, she was in trouble and near death, he refused to do anything to help her.

He was, I think, very handsome. I gather this from photographs and from my own memories of him, dressed in his Sunday best and on his way to preach a sermon somewhere, when I was little. Handsome, proud, and ingrown, "like a toenail," somebody said. But he looked to me, as I grew older, like pictures I had seen of African tribal chieftains: he really should have been naked, with warpaint on and barbaric mementos, standing among spears. He could be chilling in the pulpit and indescribably cruel in his personal life and he was certainly the most bitter man I have ever met; yet it must be said that there was something else in him, buried in him, which lent him his tremendous power and, even, a rather crushing charm. It had something to do with his blackness, I think—he was very black—with his blackness and his beauty, and with the fact that he knew that he was black but did not know that he was beautiful. He claimed to be proud of his blackness but it had also been the cause of much humiliation and it had fixed bleak boundaries to his life. He was not a young man when we were growing up and he had already suffered many kinds of ruin; in his outrageously demanding and protective way he loved his children, who were black like him and menaced, like him; and all these things sometimes showed in his face when he tried, never to my knowledge with any success, to establish contact with any of us. When he took one of his children on his knee to play, the child always became fretful and began to cry; when he tried to help one of us with our homework the absolutely unabating tension which emanated from him caused our minds and our tongues to become paralyzed, so that he, scarcely knowing why, flew into a rage and the child, not knowing why, was punished. If it ever entered his head to bring a surprise home for his children, it was, almost unfailingly, the wrong surprise and even the big watermelons he often brought home on his back in the summertime led to the most appalling scenes. I do not remember, in all those years, that one of his children was ever glad to see him come home. From what I was able to gather of his early life, it seemed that this inability to establish contact with other people had always marked him and had been one of the things which had driven him out of New Orleans. There was something in him, therefore, groping and tentative, which was never expressed and which was buried with him. One saw it most clearly when he was facing new people and hoping to impress them. But he never did, not for long. We went from church to smaller and more improbable church, he found himself in less and less demand as a minister, and by the time he died none of his friends had come to see him for a long time. He had lived and died in an intolerable bitterness of spirit and it frightened me, as we drove him to the graveyard through those unquiet, ruined streets, to see how powerful and overflowing this bitterness could be and to realize that this bitterness now was mine.

When he died I had been away from home for a little over a year. In that year I had had time to become aware of the meaning of all my father's bitter warnings, had discovered the secret of his proudly pursed lips and rigid carriage: I had discovered the weight of white people in the world. I saw that this had been for my ancestors and now would be for me an awful thing to live with and that the bitterness which had helped to kill my father could also kill me.

He had been ill a long time—in the mind, as we now realized, reliving instances of his fantastic intransigence in the new light of his affliction and endeavoring to feel a sorrow for him which never, quite, came true. We had not known that he was being eaten up by paranoia, and the discovery that his cruelty, to our bodies and our minds, had been one of the symptoms of his illness was not, then, enough to enable us to forgive him. The younger children felt, quite simply, relief that he would not be coming home anymore. My mother's observation that it was he, after all, who had kept them alive all these years meant nothing because the problems of keeping children alive are not real for children. The older children felt, with my father gone, that they could invite their friends to the house without fear that their friends would be insulted or, as had sometimes happened with me, being told that their friends were in league with the devil and intended to rob our family of everything we owned. (I didn't fail to wonder, and it made me hate him, what on earth we owned that anybody else would want.)

His illness was beyond all hope of healing before anyone realized that he was ill. He had always been so strange and had lived, like a prophet, in such unimaginably close communion with the Lord that his long silences which were punctuated by moans and hallelujahs and snatches of old songs while he sat at the living-room window never seemed odd to us. It was not until he refused to eat because, he said, his family was trying to poison him that my mother was forced to accept as a fact what had, until then, been only an unwilling suspicion. When he was committed, it was discovered that he had tuberculosis and, as it turned out, the disease of his mind allowed the disease of his body to destroy him. For the doctors could not force him to eat, either, and, though he was fed intravenously, it was clear from the beginning that there was no hope for him.

In my mind's eye I could see him, sitting at the window, locked up in his terrors; hating and fearing every living soul including his children who had betrayed him, too, by reaching toward the world which had despised him. There were nine of us. I began to wonder what it could have felt like for such a man to have had nine children whom he could barely feed. He used to make little jokes about our poverty, which never, of course, seemed very funny to us; they could not have seemed very funny to him, either, or else our all too feeble response to them would never have caused such rages. He spent great energy and achieved, to our chagrin, no small amount of success in keeping us away from the people who surrounded us, people who had all-night rent parties to which we listened when we should have been sleeping, people who cursed and drank and flashed razor blades on Lenox Avenue. He could not understand why, if they had so much energy to spare, they could not use it to make their lives better. He treated almost everybody on our block with a most uncharitable asperity and neither they, nor, of course, their children were slow to reciprocate.

The only white people who came to our house were welfare workers and bill collectors. It was almost always my mother who dealt with them, for my father's temper, which was at the mercy of his pride, was never to be trusted. It was clear that he felt their very presence in his home to be a violation: this was conveyed by his carriage, almost ludicrously stiff, and by his voice, harsh and vindictively polite. When I was around nine or ten I wrote a play which was directed by a young, white schoolteacher, a woman, who then took an interest in me, and gave me books to read and, in order to corroborate my theatrical bent, decided to take me to see what she somewhat tactlessly referred to as "real" plays. Theater-going was forbidden in our house, but, with the really cruel intuitiveness of a child, I suspected that the color of this woman's skin would carry the day for me. When, at school, she suggested taking me to the theater, I did not, as I might have done if she had been a Negro, find a way of discouraging her, but agreed that she should pick me up at my house one evening. I then, very cleverly, left all the rest to my mother, who suggested to my father, as I knew she would, that it would not be very nice to let such a kind woman make the trip for nothing. Also, since it was a schoolteacher, I imagine that my mother countered the idea of sin with the idea of "education," which word, even with my father, carried a kind of bitter weight.

Before the teacher came my father took me aside to ask *why* she was coming, what *interest* she could possibly have in our house, in a boy like me. I said I didn't know but I, too, suggested that it had something to do with education. And I understood that my father was waiting for me to say something—I didn't quite know what; perhaps that I wanted his protection against this teacher and her "education." I said none of these things and the teacher came and we went out. It was clear, during the brief interview in our living room, that my father was agreeing very much against his will and that he would have refused permission if he had dared. The fact that he did not dare caused me to despise him: I had no way of knowing that he was facing in that living room a wholly unprecedented and frightening situation.

Later, when my father had been laid off from his job, this woman became very important to us. She was really a very sweet and generous woman and went to a great deal of trouble to be of help to us, particularly during one awful winter. My mother called her by the highest name she knew: she said she was a "christian." My father could scarcely disagree but during the four or five years of our relatively close association he never trusted her and was always trying to surprise in her open, Midwestern face the genuine, cunningly hidden, and hideous motivation. In later years, particularly when it began to be clear that this "education" of mine was going to lead me to perdition, he became more explicit and warned me that my white friends in high school were not really my friends and that I would see, when I was older, how white people would do anything to keep a Negro down. Some of them could be nice, he admitted, but none of them were to be trusted and most of them were not even nice. The best thing was to have as little to do with them as possible. I did not feel this way and I was certain, in my innocence, that I never would.

But the year which preceded my father's death had made a great change in my life. I had been living in New Jersey, working in defense plants, working and living among southerners, white and black. I knew about the South, of course, and about how southerners treated Negroes and how they expected them to behave, but it had never entered my mind that anyone would look at me and expect *me* to behave that way. I learned in New Jersey that to be a Negro meant, precisely, that one was never looked at but was simply at the mercy of the reflexes the color of one's skin caused in other people. I acted in New Jersey as I had always acted, that is as though I thought a great deal of myself—I had to *act* that way—with results that were, simply, unbelievable. I had scarcely arrived before I had earned the enmity, which was extraordinarily ingenious, of all my superiors and nearly all my co-workers. In the beginning, to make matters worse, I simply did not know what was happening. I did not know what I had done, and I shortly began to wonder what *anyone* could possibly do, to bring about such unanimous, active, and unbearably vocal hostility. I knew about jim crow but I had never experienced it. I went to the same self-service restaurant three times and stood with all the Princeton boys before the counter, waiting for a hamburger and coffee; it was always an extraordinarily long time before anything was set before me; but it was not until the fourth visit that I learned that, in fact, nothing had ever been set before me: I had simply picked something up. Negroes were not served there, I was told, and they had been waiting for me to realize that I was always the only Negro present. Once I was told this, I determined to go there all the time. But now they were ready for me and, though some dreadful scenes were subsequently enacted in that restaurant, I never ate there again.

It was the same story all over New Jersey, in bars, bowling alleys, diners, places to live. I was always being forced to leave, silently, or with mutual imprecations. I very shortly became notorious and children giggled behind me when I passed and their elders whispered or shouted—they really believed that I was mad. And it did begin to work on my mind, of course; I began to be afraid to go anywhere and to compensate for this I went places to which I really should not have gone and where, God knows, I had no desire to be. My reputation in town naturally enhanced my reputation at work and my working day became one long series of acrobatics designed to keep me out of trouble. I cannot say that these acrobatics succeeded. It began to seem that the machinery of the organization I worked for was turning over, day and night, with but one aim: to eject me. I was fired once, and contrived, with the aid of a friend from New York, to get back on the payroll; was fired again, and bounced back again. It took a while to fire me for the third time, but the third time took. There were no loopholes anywhere. There was not even any way of getting back inside the gates.

That year in New Jersey lives in my mind as though it were the year during which, having an unsuspected predilection for it, I first contracted some dread, chronic disease, the unfailing symptom of which is a kind of blind fever, a pounding in the skull and fire in the bowels. Once this disease is contracted, one can never be really carefree again, for the fever, without an instant's warning, can recur at any moment. It can wreck more important things than race relations. There is not a Negro alive who does not have this rage in his blood—one has the choice, merely, of living with it consciously or surrendering to it. As for me, this fever has recurred in me, and does, and will until the day I die.

My last night in New Jersey, a white friend from New York took me to the nearest big town, Trenton, to go to the movies and have a few drinks. As it turned out, he also saved me from, at the very least, a violent whipping. Almost every detail of that night stands out very clearly in my memory. I even remember the name of the movie we saw because its title impressed me as being so patly ironical. It was a movie about the German occupation of France, starring Maureen O'Hara and Charles Laughton and called *This Land Is Mine*. I remember the name of the diner we walked into when the movie ended: it was the "American Diner." When we walked in the counterman asked what we wanted and I remember answering with the casual sharpness which had become my habit: "We want a hamburger and a cup of coffee, what do you think we want?" I do not know why, after a year of such rebuffs, I so completely failed to anticipate his answer, which was, of course, "we don't serve Negroes here." This reply failed to discompose me, at least for the moment. I made some sardonic comment about the name of the diner and we walked out into the streets.

This was the time of what was called the "brownout," when the lights in all American cities were very dim. When we reentered the streets something happened to me which had the force of an optical illusion, or a nightmare. The streets were very crowded and I was facing north. People were moving in every direction but it seemed to me, in that instant, that all of the people I could see, and many more than that, were moving toward me, against me, and that everyone was white. I remember how their faces gleamed. And I felt, like a physical sensation, a *click* at the nape of my neck as though some interior string connecting my head to my body had been cut. I began to walk. I heard my friend call after me, but I ignored him. Heaven only knows what was going on in his mind, but he had the good sense not to touch me—I don't know what would have happened if he had—and to keep me in sight. I don't know what was going on in my mind, either; I certainly had no conscious plan. I wanted to do something to crush these white faces, which were crushing me. I walked for perhaps a block or two until I came to an enormous, glittering, and fashionable restaurant in which I knew not even the intercession of the Virgin would cause me to be served. I pushed through the doors and took the first vacant seat I saw, at a table for two, and waited.

I do not know how long I waited and I rather wonder, until today, what I could possibly have looked like. Whatever I looked like, I frightened the waitress who shortly appeared, and the moment she appeared all of my fury flowed toward her. I hated her for her white face, and for her great, astounded, frightened eyes. I felt that if she found a black man so frightening I would make her fright worthwhile.

She did not ask me what I wanted, but repeated, as though she had learned it somewhere, "We don't serve Negroes here." She did not say it with the blunt, derisive hostility to which I had grown so accustomed, but, rather, with a note of apology in her voice, and fear. This made me colder and more murderous than ever. I felt I had to do something with my hands. I wanted her to come close enough for me to get her neck between my hands.

So I pretended not to have understood her, hoping to draw her closer. And she did step a very short step closer, with her pencil poised incongruously over her pad, and repeated the formula: "…don't serve Negroes here."

Somehow, with the repetition of that phrase, which was already ringing in my head like a thousand bells of a nightmare, I realized that she would never come any closer and that I would have to strike from a distance. There was nothing on the table but an ordinary watermug half full of water, and I picked this up and hurled it with all my strength at her. She ducked and it missed her and shattered against the mirror behind the bar. And, with that sound, my frozen blood abruptly thawed, I returned from wherever I had been, I *saw*, for the first time, the restaurant, the people with their mouths open, already, as it seemed to me, rising as one man, and I realized what I had done, and where I was, and I was frightened. I rose and began running for the door. A round, potbellied man grabbed me by the nape of the neck just as I reached the doors and began to beat me about the face. I kicked him and got loose and ran into the streets. My friend whispered *"Run!"* and I ran.

My friend stayed outside the restaurant long enough to misdirect my pursuers and the police, who arrived, he told me, at once. I do not know what I said to him when he came to my room that night. I could not have said much. I felt, in the oddest, most awful way, that I had somehow betrayed him. I lived it over and over and over again, the way one relives an automobile accident after it has happened and one finds oneself alone and safe. I could not get over two facts, both equally difficult for the imagination to grasp, and one was that I could have been murdered. But the other was that I had been ready to commit murder. I saw nothing very clearly but I did see this: that my life, my *real* life, was in danger, and not from anything other people might do but from the hatred I carried in my own heart.

Two

I had returned home around the second week in June—in great haste because it seemed that my father's death and my mother's confinement were both a matter of hours. In the case of my mother, it soon became clear that she had simply made a miscalculation. This had always been her tendency and I don't believe that a single one of us arrived in the world, or has since arrived anywhere else, on time. But none of us dawdled so intolerably about the business of being born as did my baby sister. We sometimes amused ourselves, during those endless, stifling weeks, by picturing the baby sitting within in the safe, warm dark, bitterly regretting the necessity of becoming a part of our chaos and stubbornly putting it off as long as possible. I understood her perfectly and congratulated her on showing such good sense so soon. Death, however, sat as purposefully at my father's bedside as life stirred within my mother's womb and it was harder to understand why he so lingered in that long shadow. It seemed that he had bent, and for a long time, too, all of his energies toward dying. Now death was ready for him but my father held back.

All of Harlem, indeed, seemed to be infected by waiting. I had never before known it to be so violently still. Racial tensions throughout this country were exacerbated during the early years of the war, partly because the labor market brought together hundreds of thousands of ill-prepared people and partly because Negro soldiers, regardless of where they were born, received their military training in the south. What happened in defense plants and army camps had repercussions, naturally, in every Negro ghetto. The situation in Harlem had grown bad enough for clergymen, policemen, educators, politicians, and social workers to assert in one breath that there was no "crime wave" and to offer, in the very next breath, suggestions as to how to combat it. These suggestions always seemed to involve playgrounds, despite the fact that racial skirmishes were occurring in the playgrounds, too. Playground or not, crime wave or not, the Harlem police force had been augmented in March, and the unrest grew—perhaps, in fact, partly as a result of the ghetto's instinctive hatred of policemen. Perhaps the most revealing news item, out of the steady parade of reports of muggings, stabbings, shootings, assaults, gang wars, and accusations of police brutality, is the item concerning six Negro girls who set upon a white girl in the subway because, as they all too accurately put it, she was stepping on their toes. Indeed she was, all over the nation.

I had never before been so aware of policemen, on foot, on horseback, on corners, everywhere, always two by two. Nor had I ever been so aware of small knots of people. They were on stoops and on corners and in doorways, and what was striking about them, I think, was that they did not seem to be talking. Never, when I passed these groups, did the usual sound of a curse or a laugh ring out and neither did there seem to be any hum of gossip. There was certainly, on the other hand, occurring between them communication extraordinarily intense. Another thing that was striking was the unexpected diversity of the people who made up these groups. Usually, for example, one would see a group of sharpies standing on the street corner, jiving the passing chicks; or a group of older men, usually, for some reason, in the vicinity of a barber shop, discussing baseball scores, or the numbers, or making rather chilling observations about women they had known. Women, in a general way, tended to be seen less often together—unless they were church women, or very young girls, or prostitutes met together for an unprofessional instant. But that summer I saw the strangest combinations: large, respectable, churchly matrons standing on the stoops or the corners with their hair tied up, together with a girl in sleazy satin whose face bore the marks of gin and the razor, or heavy-set, abrupt, no-nonsense older men, in company with the most disreputable and fanatical "race" men, or these same "race" men with the sharpies, or these sharpies with the churchly women. Seventh Day Adventists and Methodists and Spiritualists seemed to be hobnobbing with Holyrollers and they were all, alike, entangled with the most flagrant disbelievers; something heavy in their stance seemed to indicate that they had all, incredibly, seen a common vision, and on each face there seemed to be the same strange, bitter shadow.

The churchly women and the matter-of-fact, no-nonsense men had children in the Army. The sleazy girls they talked to had lovers there, the sharpies and the "race" men had friends and brothers there. It would have demanded an unquestioning patriotism, happily as uncommon in this country as it is undesirable, for these people not to have been disturbed by the bitter letters they received, by the newspaper stories they read, not to have been enraged by the posters, then to be found all over New York, which described the Japanese as "yellow-bellied Japs." It was only the "race" men, to be sure, who spoke ceaselessly of being revenged—how this vengeance was to be exacted was not clear—for the indignities and dangers suffered by Negro boys in uniform; but everybody felt a directionless, hopeless bitterness, as well as that panic which can scarcely be suppressed when one knows that a human being one loves is beyond one's reach, and in danger. This helplessness and this gnawing uneasiness does something, at length, to even the toughest mind. Perhaps the best way to sum all this up is to say that the people I knew felt, mainly, a peculiar kind of relief when they knew that their boys were being shipped out of the south, to do battle overseas. It was, perhaps, like feeling that the most dangerous part of a dangerous journey had been passed and that now, even if death should come, it would come with honor and without the complicity of their countrymen. Such a death would be, in short, a fact with which one could hope to live.

It was on the twenty-eighth of July, which I believe was a Wednesday, that I visited my father for the first time during his illness and for the last time in his life. The moment I saw him I knew why I had put off this visit so long. I had told my mother that I did not want to see him because I hated him. But this was not true. It was only that I *had* hated him and I wanted to hold on to this hatred. I did not want to look on him as a ruin: it was not a ruin I had hated. I imagine that one of the reasons people cling to their hates so stubbornly is because they sense, once hate is gone, that they will be forced to deal with pain.

We traveled out to him, his older sister and myself, to what seemed to be the very end of a very Long Island. It was hot and dusty and we wrangled, my aunt and I, all the way out, over the fact that I had recently begun to smoke and, as she said, to give myself airs. But I knew that she wrangled with me because she could not bear to face the fact of her brother's dying. Neither could I endure the reality of her despair, her unstated bafflement as to what had happened to her brother's life, and her own. So we wrangled and I smoked and from time to time she fell into a heavy reverie. Covertly, I watched her face, which was the face of an old woman; it had fallen in, the eyes were sunken and lightless; soon she would be dying, too.

In my childhood—it had not been so long ago—I had thought her beautiful. She had been quick-witted and quick-moving and very generous with all the children and each of her visits had been an event. At one time one of my brothers and myself had thought of running away to live with her. Now she could no longer produce out of her handbag some unexpected and yet familiar delight. She made me feel pity and revulsion and fear. It was awful to realize that she no longer caused me to feel affection. The closer we came to the hospital the more querulous she became and at the same time, naturally, grew more dependent on me. Between pity and guilt and fear I began to feel that there was another me trapped in my skull like a jack-in-the-box who might escape my control at any moment and fill the air with screaming.

She began to cry the moment we entered the room and she saw him lying there, all shriveled and still, like a little black monkey. The great, gleaming apparatus which fed him and would have compelled him to be still even if he had been able to move brought to mind, not beneficence, but torture; the tubes entering his arm made me think of pictures I had seen when a child, of Gulliver, tied down by the pygmies on that island. My aunt wept and wept, there was a whistling sound in my father's throat; nothing was said; he could not speak. I wanted to take his hand, to say something. But I do not know what I could have said, even if he could have heard me. He was not really in that room with us, he had at last really embarked on his journey; and though my aunt told me that he said he was going to meet Jesus, I did not hear anything except that whistling in his throat. The doctor came back and we left, into that unbearable train again, and home. In the morning came the telegram saying that he was dead. Then the house was suddenly full of relatives, friends, hysteria, and confusion and I quickly left my mother and the children to the care of those impressive women, who, in Negro communities at least, automatically appear at times of bereavement armed with lotions, proverbs, and patience, and an ability to cook. I went downtown. By the time I returned, later the same day, my mother had been carried to the hospital and the baby had been born.

Three

For my father's funeral I had nothing black to wear and this posed a nagging problem all day long. It was one of those problems, simple or impossible of solution, to which the mind insanely clings in order to avoid the mind's real trouble. I spent most of that day at the downtown apartment of a girl I knew, celebrating my birthday with whisky and wondering what to wear that night. When planning a birthday celebration one naturally does not expect that it will be up against competition from a funeral and this girl had anticipated taking me out that night, for a big dinner and a night club afterwards. Sometime during the course of that long day we decided that we would go out anyway, when my father's funeral service was over. I imagine I decided it, since, as the funeral hour approached, it became clearer and clearer to me that I would not know what to do with myself when it was over. The girl, stifling her very lively concerns as to the possible effects of the whisky on one of my father's chief mourners, concentrated on being conciliatory and practically helpful. She found a black shirt for me somewhere and ironed it and, dressed in the darkest pants and jacket I owned, and slightly drunk, I made my way to my father's funeral.

The chapel was full, but not packed, and very quiet. There were, mainly, my father's relatives, and his children, and here and there I saw faces I had not seen since childhood, the faces of my father's one-time friends. They were very dark and solemn now, seeming somehow to suggest that they had known all along that something like this would happen. Chief among the mourners was my aunt, who had quarreled with my father all his life; by which I do not mean to suggest that her mourning was insincere or that she had not loved him. I suppose that she was one of the few people in the world who had, and their incessant quarreling proved precisely the strength of the tie that bound them. The only other person in the world, as far as I knew, whose relationship to my father rivaled my aunt's in depth was my mother, who was not there.

It seemed to me, of course, that it was a very long funeral. But it was, if anything, a rather shorter funeral than most, nor, since there were no overwhelming, uncontrollable expressions of grief, could it be called—if I dare to use the word—successful. The minister who preached my father's funeral sermon was one of the few my father had still been seeing as he neared his end. He presented to us in his sermon a man whom none of us had ever seen—a man thoughtful, patient, and forbearing, a Christian inspiration to all who knew him, and a model for his children. And no doubt the children, in their disturbed and guilty state, were almost ready to believe this; he had been remote enough to be anything and, anyway, the shock of the incontrovertible, that it was really our father lying up there in that casket, prepared the mind for anything. His sister moaned and this grief-stricken moaning was taken as corroboration. The other faces held a dark, noncommittal thoughtfulness. This was not the man they had known, but they had scarcely expected to be confronted with *him*; this was, in a sense deeper than questions of fact, the man they had not known, and the man they had not known may have been the real one. The real man, whoever he had been, had suffered and now he was dead: this was all that was sure and all that mattered now. Every man in the chapel hoped that when his hour came he, too, would be eulogized, which is to say forgiven, and that all of his lapses, greeds, errors, and strayings from the truth would be invested with coherence and looked upon with charity. This was perhaps the last thing human beings could give each other and it was what they demanded, after all, of the Lord. Only the Lord saw the midnight tears, only He was present when one of His children, moaning and wringing hands, paced up and down the room. When one slapped one's child in anger the recoil in the heart reverberated through heaven and became part of the pain of the universe. And when the children were hungry and sullen and distrustful and one watched them, daily, growing wilder, and further away, and running headlong into danger, it was the Lord who knew what the charged heart endured as the strap was laid to the backside; the Lord alone who knew what one *would* have said if one had had, like the Lord, the gift of the living word. It was the Lord who knew of the impossibility every parent in that room faced: how to prepare the child for the day when the child would be despised and how to *create* in the child—by what means?—a stronger antidote to this poison than one had found for oneself. The avenues, side streets, bars, billiard halls, hospitals, police stations, and even the playgrounds of Harlem—not to mention the houses of correction, the jails, and the morgue—testified to the potency of the poison while remaining silent as to the efficacy of whatever antidote, irresistibly raising the question of whether or not such an antidote existed; raising, which was worse, the question of whether or not an antidote was desirable; perhaps poison should be fought with poison. With these several schisms in the mind and with more terrors in the heart than could be named, it was better not to judge the man who had gone down under an impossible burden. It was better to remember: *Thou knowest this man's fall; but thou knowest not his wrassling.*

While the preacher talked and I watched the children—years of changing their diapers, scrubbing them, slapping them, taking them to school, and scolding them had had the perhaps inevitable result of making me love them, though I am not sure I knew this then—my mind was busily breaking out with a rash of disconnected impressions. Snatches of popular songs, indecent jokes, bits of books I had read, movie sequences, faces, voices, political issues—I thought I was going mad; all these impressions suspended, as it were, in the solution of the faint nausea produced in me by the heat and liquor. For a moment I had the impression that my alcoholic breath, inefficiently disguised with chewing gum, filled the entire chapel. Then someone began singing one of my father's favorite songs and, abruptly, I was with him, sitting on his knee, in the hot, enormous, crowded church which was the first church we attended. It was the Abyssinian Baptist Church on 138th Street. We had not gone there long. With this image, a host of others came. I had forgotten, in the rage of my growing up, how proud my father had been of me when I was little. Apparently, I had had a voice and my father had liked to show me off before the members of the church. I had forgotten what he had looked like when he was pleased but now I remembered that he had always been grinning with pleasure when my solos ended. I even remembered certain expressions on his face when he teased my mother—had he loved her? I would never know. And when had it all begun to change? For now it seemed that he had not always been cruel. I remembered being taken for a haircut and scraping my knee on the footrest of the barber's chair and I remembered my father's face as he soothed my crying and applied the stinging iodine. Then I remembered our fights, fights which had been of the worst possible kind because my technique had been silence.

I remembered the one time in all our life together when we had really spoken to each other.

It was on a Sunday and it must have been shortly before I left home. We were walking, just the two of us, in our usual silence, to or from church. I was in high school and had been doing a lot of writing and I was, at about this time, the editor of the high school magazine. But I had also been a Young Minister and had been preaching from the pulpit. Lately, I had been taking fewer engagements and preached as rarely as possible. It was said in the church, quite truthfully, that I was "cooling off."

My father asked me abruptly, "You'd rather write than preach, wouldn't you?"

I was astonished at his question—because it was a real question. I answered, "Yes."

That was all we said. It was awful to remember that that was all we had *ever* said.

The casket now was opened and the mourners were being led up the aisle to look for the last time on the deceased. The assumption was that the family was too overcome with grief to be allowed to make this journey alone and I watched while my aunt was led to the casket and, muffled in black, and shaking, led back to her seat. I disapproved of forcing the children to look on their dead father, considering that the shock of his death, or, more truthfully, the shock of death as a reality, was already a little more than a child could bear, but my judgment in this matter had been overruled and there they were, bewildered and frightened and very small, being led, one by one, to the casket. But there is also something very gallant about children at such moments. It has something to do with their silence and gravity and with the fact that one cannot help them. Their legs, somehow, seem *exposed*, so that it is at once incredible and terribly clear that their legs are all they have to hold them up.

I had not wanted to go to the casket myself and I certainly had not wished to be led there, but there was no way of avoiding either of these forms. One of the deacons led me up and I looked on my father's face. I cannot say that it looked like him at all. His blackness had been equivocated by powder and there was no suggestion in that casket of what his power had or could have been. He was simply an old man dead, and it was hard to believe that he had ever given anyone either joy or pain. Yet, his life filled that room. Further up the avenue his wife was holding his newborn child. Life and death so close together, and love and hatred, and right and wrong, said something to me which I did not want to hear concerning man, concerning the life of man.

After the funeral, while I was downtown desperately celebrating my birthday, a Negro soldier, in the lobby of the Hotel Braddock, got into a fight with a white policeman over a Negro girl. Negro girls, white policemen, in or out of uniform, and Negro males—in or out of uniform—were part of the furniture of the lobby of the Hotel Braddock and this was certainly not the first time such an incident had occurred. It was destined, however, to receive an unprecedented publicity, for the fight between the policeman and the soldier ended with the shooting of the soldier. Rumor, flowing immediately to the streets outside, stated that the soldier had been shot in the back, an instantaneous and revealing invention, and that the soldier had died protecting a Negro woman. The facts were somewhat different—for example, the soldier had not been shot in the back, and was not dead, and the girl seems to have been as dubious a symbol of womanhood as her white counterpart in Georgia usually is, but no one was interested in the facts. They preferred the invention because this invention expressed and corroborated their hates and fears so perfectly. It is just as well to remember that people are always doing this. Perhaps many of those legends, including Christianity, to which the world clings began their conquest of the world with just some such concerted surrender to distortion. The effect, in Harlem, of this particular legend was like the effect of a lit match in a tin of gasoline. The mob gathered before the doors of the Hotel Braddock simply began to swell and to spread in every direction, and Harlem exploded.

The mob did not cross the ghetto lines. It would have been easy, for example, to have gone over Morningside Park on the west side or to have crossed the Grand Central railroad tracks at 125th Street on the east side, to wreak havoc in white neighborhoods. The mob seems to have been mainly interested in something more potent and real than the white face; that is, in white power, and the principal damage done during the riot of the summer of 1943 was to white business establishments in Harlem. It might have been a far bloodier story, of course, if, at the hour the riot began, these establishments had still been open. From the Hotel Braddock the mob fanned out, east and west along 125th Street, and for the entire length of Lenox, Seventh, and Eighth avenues. Along each of these avenues, and along each major side street—116th, 125th, and so on—bars, stores, pawnshops, restaurants, even little luncheonettes had been smashed open and entered and looted—looted, it might be added, with more haste than efficiency. The shelves really looked as though a bomb had struck them. Cans of beans and soup and dog food, along with toilet paper, corn flakes, sardines and milk tumbled every which way, and abandoned cash registers and cases of beer leaned crazily out of the splintered windows and were strewn along the avenues. Sheets, blankets, and clothing of every description formed a kind of path, as though people had dropped them while running. I truly had not realized that Harlem *had* so many stores until I saw them all smashed open; the first time the word *wealth* ever entered my mind in relation to Harlem was when I saw it scattered in the streets. But one's first, incongruous impression of plenty was countered immediately by an impression of waste. None of this was doing anybody any good. It would have been better to have left the plate glass as it had been and the goods lying in the stores.

It would have been better, but it would also have been intolerable, for Harlem had needed something to smash. To smash something is the ghetto's chronic need. Most of the time it is the members of the ghetto who smash each other, and themselves. But as long as the ghetto walls are standing there will always come a moment when these outlets do not work. That summer, for example, it was not enough to get into a fight on Lenox Avenue, or curse out one's cronies in the barber shops. If ever, indeed, the violence which fills Harlem's churches, pool halls, and bars erupts outward in a more direct fashion, Harlem and its citizens are likely to vanish in an apocalyptic flood. That this is not likely to happen is due to a great many reasons, most hidden and powerful among them the Negro's real relation to the white American. This relation prohibits, simply, anything as uncomplicated and satisfactory as pure hatred. In order really to hate white people, one has to blot so much out of the mind—and the heart—that this hatred itself becomes an exhausting and self-destructive pose. But this does not mean, on the other hand, that love comes easily: the white world is too powerful, too complacent, too ready with gratuitous humiliation, and, above all, too ignorant and too innocent for that. One is absolutely forced to make perpetual qualifications and one's own reactions are always canceling each other out. It is this, really, which has driven so many people mad, both white and black. One is always in the position of having to decide between amputation and gangrene. Amputation is swift but time may prove that the amputation was not necessary—or one may delay the amputation too long. Gangrene is slow, but it is impossible to be sure that one is reading one's symptoms right. The idea of going through life as a cripple is more than one can bear, and equally unbearable is the risk of swelling up slowly, in agony, with poison. And the trouble, finally, is that the risks are real even if the choices do not exist.

"But as for me and my house," my father had said, "we will serve the Lord." I wondered, as we drove him to his resting place, what this line had meant for him. I had heard him preach it many times. I had preached it once myself, proudly giving it an interpretation different from my father's. Now the whole thing came back to me, as though my father and I were on our way to Sunday school and I were memorizing the golden text: *And if it seem evil unto you to serve the Lord, choose you this day whom you will serve, whether the gods which your fathers served that were on the side of the flood, or the gods of the Amorites, in whose land ye dwell: but as for me and my house, we will serve the Lord.* I suspected in these familiar lines a meaning which had never been there for me before. All of my father's texts and songs, which I had decided were meaningless, were arranged before me at his death like empty bottles, waiting to hold the meaning which life would give them for me. This was his legacy: nothing is ever escaped. That bleakly memorable morning I hated the unbelievable streets and the Negroes and whites who had, equally, made them that way. But I knew that it was folly, as my father would have said, this bitterness was folly. It was necessary to hold on to the things that mattered. The dead man mattered, the new life mattered; blackness and whiteness did not matter; to believe that they did was to acquiesce in one's own destruction. Hatred, which could destroy so much, never failed to destroy the man who hated and this was an immutable law.

It began to seem that one would have to hold in the mind forever two ideas which seemed to be in opposition. The first idea was acceptance, the acceptance, totally without rancor, of life as it is, and men as they are: in the light of this idea, it goes without saying that injustice is a commonplace. But this did not mean that one could be complacent, for the second idea was of equal power: that one must never, in one's own life, accept these injustices as commonplace but must fight them with all one's strength. This fight begins, however, in the heart and it now had been laid to my charge to keep my own heart free of hatred and despair. This intimation made my heart heavy and, now that my father was irrecoverable, I wished that he had been beside me so that I could have searched his face for the answers which only the future would give me now.

John Berger

Ways of Seeing

Imagine yourself in front of a television or at your computer terminal. Across the screen streams a series of images: Mona Lisa, Venus de Milo, a photograph of Madonna, an advertisement for Calvin Klein underwear, a still life by Picasso, a snapshot of you smiling in a T-shirt with the Mona Lisa'a face on the front. Now imagine you are sitting among hundreds of other students in a darkened lecture hall as your Art 100 instructor, laser pointer directed at a ten-foot-high projection of Leonardo da Vinci's masterpiece, recounts various theories explaining the Mona Lisa's enigmatic smile. Finally, imagine yourself in the quiet of the Paris Louvre, standing before the 21" × 30" oil-on-wood original portrait of the wife of Francesco del Giocondo—the original *Mona Lisa*. The differences among these three experiences constitute the topic of John Berger's "Ways of Seeing."

Born in London in 1926, Berger has been an artist, poet and screenwriter as well as essayist, and is very much part of a conversation that includes writers in this volume such as Annie Dillard, Walker Percy, and Susan Sontag. As Berger himself acknowledges, however, the conversation began for him with German critic and philosopher Walter Benjamin, whose ideas deeply influenced Berger and Sontag, too. Born in 1892, Benjamin was the son of German Jews. He fled to France in 1933 with the rise of the Nazis, but when Germany invaded France, Benjamin was forced to flee again. While attempting to cross the Franco-Spanish border in September 1940, he was ordered back to France. Benjamin committed suicide that night.

Benjamin's essay "The Work of Art in the Age of Mechanical Reproduction," to which Berger refers at the close of his own essay, reflects Benjamin's horror at the Nazi party's efforts to "aestheticize" politics, war and genocide—that is, to turn them into art. Rather than rendering politics aesthetic, Benjamin called for politicizing art. In

"Ways of Seeing," Berger does just that. The age of technology, he claims, has freed art objects from the grip of the wealthy few and made them available, through reproduction, to all of us. Yet the "language of images," our experience of art, our appreciation of art, and, most important, our human history represented in art all remain in the grip of a new controlling minority of art specialists who define for the rest of us what we see. The result is to "mystify," rather than clarify, art and our relationship to it. Though thirty years old, Berger's call to liberate art—and us, its viewers—may be especially timely in the current age of computerized image-making and the World Wide Web.

Seeing comes before words. The child looks and recognizes before it can speak.

But there is also another sense in which seeing comes before words. It is seeing which establishes our place in the surrounding world; we explain that world with words, but words can never undo the fact that we are surrounded by it. The relation between what we see and what we know is never settled. Each evening we see the sun set. We *know* that the earth is turning away from it. Yet the knowledge, the explanation, never quite fits the sight. The Surrealist painter Magritte commented on this always-present gap between words and seeing in a painting called *The Key of Dreams*.

The way we see things is affected by what we know or what we believe. In the Middle Ages when men believed in the physical existence of Hell the sight of fire must have meant something different from what it means today. Nevertheless their idea of Hell owed a lot to the sight of fire consuming and the ashes remaining—as well as to their experience of the pain of burns.

When in love, the sight of the beloved has a completeness which no words and no embrace can match: a completeness which only the act of making love can temporarily accommodate.

Yet this seeing which comes before words, and can never be quite covered by them, is not a question of mechanically reacting to stimuli. (It can only be thought of in this way if one isolates the

THE KEY OF DREAMS BY MAGRITTE 1898–1967

small part of the process which concerns the eye's retina.) We only see what we look at. To look is an act of choice. As a result of this act, what we see is brought within our reach—though not necessarily within arm's reach. To touch something is to situate oneself in relation to it. (Close your eyes, move round the room and notice how the faculty of touch is like a static, limited form of sight.) We never look at just one thing: we are always looking at the relation between things and ourselves. Our vision is continually active, continually moving, continually holding things in a circle around itself, constituting what is present to us as we are.

Soon after we can see, we are aware that we can also be seen. The eye of the other combines with our own eye to make it fully credible that we are part of the visible world.

If we accept that we can see that hill over there, we propose that from that hill we can be seen. The reciprocal nature of vision is more fundamental than that of spoken dialogue. And often dialogue is an attempt to verbalize this—an attempt to explain how, either metaphorically or literally, "you see things," and an attempt to discover how "he sees things."

In the sense in which we use the word in this book, all images are manmade [see below]. An image is a sight which has been recreated or reproduced. It is an appearance, or a set of appearances, which has been detached from the place and time in which it first made its appearance and preserved—for a few moments or a few centuries. Every image embodies a way

of seeing. Even a photograph. For photographs are not, as is often assumed, a mechanical record. Every time we look at a photograph, we are aware, however slightly, of the photographer selecting that sight from an infinity of other possible sights. This is true even in the most casual family snapshot. The photographer's way of seeing is reflected in his choice of subject. The painter's way of seeing is reconstituted by the marks he makes on the canvas or paper. Yet, although every image embodies a way of seeing, our perception or appreciation of an image depends also upon our own way of seeing. (It may be, for example, that Sheila is one figure among twenty; but for our own reasons she is the one we have eyes for.)

Images were first made to conjure up the appearance of something that was absent. Gradually it became evident that an image could outlast what it represented; it then showed how something or somebody had once looked—and thus by implication how the subject had once been seen by other people. Later still the specific vision of the image-maker was also recognized as part of the record. An image became a record of how X had seen Y. This was the result of an increasing consciousness of individuality, accompanying an increasing awareness of history. It would be rash to try to date this last development precisely. But certainly in Europe such consciousness has existed since the beginning of the Renaissance.

No other kind of relic or text from the past can offer such a direct testimony about the world which surrounded other people at other times. In this respect images are more precise and richer than literature. To say this is not to deny the expressive or imaginative quality of art, treating it as mere documentary evidence; the more imaginative the work, the more profoundly it allows us to share the artist's experience of the visible.

Yet when an image is presented as a work of art, the way people look at it is affected by a whole series of learnt assumptions about art. Assumptions concerning:

Beauty
Truth
Genius
Civilization
Form
Status
Taste, etc.

Many of these assumptions no longer accord with the world as it is. (The world-as-it-is is more than pure objective fact, it includes consciousness.) Out of true with the present, these assumptions obscure the past. They mystify rather than clarify. The past is never there waiting to be discovered, to be recognized for exactly what it is. History always constitutes the relation between a present and its past. Consequently fear of the present leads to mystification of the past. The past is not for living in; it is a well of conclusions from which we draw in order to act. Cultural mystification of the past entails a double loss. Works of art are made unnecessarily remote. And the past offers us fewer conclusions to complete in action.

When we "see" a landscape, we situate ourselves in it. If we "saw" the art of the past, we would situate ourselves in history. When we are prevented from seeing it, we are being deprived of the history which belongs to us. Who benefits from this deprivation? In the end, the art of the past is being mystified because a privileged minority is striving to invent a history which can retrospectively justify the role of the ruling classes, and such a justification can no longer make sense in modern terms. And so, inevitably, it mystifies.

Let us consider a typical example of such mystification. A two-volume study was recently published on Frans Hals.[1] It is the authoritative work to date on this painter. As a book of specialized art history it is no better and no worse than the average.

The last two great paintings by Frans Hals portray the Governors and the Governesses of an Alms House for old paupers in the Dutch seventeenth-century city of Haarlem. They were officially commissioned portraits. Hals, an old man of over eighty, was destitute. Most of his life he had been in debt. During the winter of 1664, the year he began painting these pictures, he obtained three loads of peat on public charity, otherwise he would have frozen to death. Those who now sat for him were administrators of such public charity.

Regents of the Old Men's Alms House by Hals (1580–1666).

Regentesses of the Old Men's Alms House by Hals (1580–1666).

The author records these facts and then explicitly says that it would be incorrect to read into the paintings any criticism of the sitters. There is no evidence, he says, that Hals painted them in a spirit of bitterness. The author considers them, however, remarkable works of art and explains why. Here he writes of the Regentesses:

Each woman speaks to us of the human condition with equal importance. Each woman stands out with equal clarity against the *enormous* dark surface, yet they are linked by a firm rhythmical arrangement and the subdued diagonal pattern formed by their heads and hands. Subtle

modulations of the *deep*, glowing blacks contribute to the *harmonious fusion* of the whole and form an *unforgettable contrast* with the *powerful* whites and vivid flesh tones where the detached strokes reach *a peak of breadth and strength*. [Berger's italics]

The compositional unity of a painting contributes fundamentally to the power of its image. It is reasonable to consider a painting's composition. But here the composition is written about as though it were in itself the emotional charge of the painting. Terms like *harmonious fusion, unforgettable contrast,* reaching *a peak of breadth and strength* transfer the emotion provoked by the image from the plane of lived experience, to that of disinterested "art appreciation." All conflict disappears. One is left with the unchanging "human condition," and the painting considered as a marvellously made object.

Very little is known about Hals or the Regents who commissioned him. It is not possible to produce circumstancial evidence to establish what their relations were. But there is the evidence of the paintings themselves: the evidence of a group of men and a group of women as seen by another man, the painter. Study this evidence and judge for yourself.

The art historian fears such direct judgement:

As in so many other pictures by Hals, the penetrating characterizations almost seduce us into believing that we know the personality traits and even the habits of the men and women portrayed.

What is this "seduction" he writes of? It is nothing less than the paintings working upon us. They work upon us because we accept the way Hals saw his sitters. We do not accept this innocently. We accept it in so far as it corresponds to our own observation of people, gestures, faces, institutions. This is possible because we still live in a society of comparable social relations and moral values. And it is precisely this which gives the paintings their psychological and social urgency. It is this—not the painter's skill as a "seducer"—which convinces us that we *can* know the people portrayed.

The author continues:

In the case of some critics the seduction has been a total success. It has, for example, been asserted that the Regent in the tipped slouch hat, which hardly covers any of his long, lank hair, and whose curiously set eyes do not focus, was shown in a drunken state. [below]

This, he suggests, is a libel. He argues that it was a fashion at that time to wear hats on the side of the head. He cites medical opinion to prove that the Regent's expression could well be the result of a facial paralysis. He insists

that the painting would have been unacceptable to the Regents if one of
them had been portrayed drunk. One
might go on discussing each of these
points for pages. (Men in seventeenth-
century Holland wore their hats on the
side of their heads in order to be
thought of as adventurous and pleasure-
loving. Heavy drinking was an approved practice. Etcetera.) But such a
discussion would take us even farther
away from the only confrontation
which matters and which the author is
determined to evade.

In this confrontation the Regents
and Regentesses stare at Hals, a desti-
tute old painter who has lost his reputation and lives off public charity; he
examines them through the eyes of a pauper who must nevertheless try to
be objective; i.e., must try to surmount the way he sees as a pauper. This is
the drama of these paintings. A drama of an "unforgettable contrast."

Mystification has little to do with the vocabulary used. Mystification is
the process of explaining away what might otherwise be evident. Hals was
the first portraitist to paint the new characters and expressions created by
capitalism. He did in pictorial terms what Balzac did two centuries later in
literature. Yet the author of the authoritative work on these paintings sums
up the artist's achievement by referring to

> Hals's unwavering commitment to his personal vision, which enriches
> our consciousness of our fellow men and heightens our awe for the ever-
> increasing power of the mighty impulses that enabled him to give us a
> close view of life's vital forces.

That is mystification.

In order to avoid mystifying the past (which can equally well suffer
pseudo-Marxist mystification) let us now examine the particular relation
which now exists, so far as pictorial images are concerned, between the present and the past. If we can see the present clearly enough, we shall ask the
right questions of the past.

Today we see the art of the past as nobody saw it before. We actually perceive it in a different way.

This difference can be illustrated in terms of what was thought of as perspective. The convention of perspective, which is unique to European art and

which was first established in the early Renaissance, centres everything on the eye of the beholder. It is like a beam from a lighthouse—only instead of light travelling outwards, appearances travel in. The conventions called those appearances *reality*. Perspective makes the single eye the centre of the visible world. Everything converges on to the eye as to the vanishing point of infinity. The visible world is arranged for the spectator as the universe was once thought to be arranged for God.

According to the convention of perspective there is no visual reciprocity. There is no need for God to situate himself in relation to others: he is himself the situation. The inherent contradiction in perspective was that it structured all images of reality to address a single spectator who, unlike God, could only be in one place at a time.

After the invention of the camera this contradiction gradually became apparent.

> I'm an eye. A mechanical eye. I, the machine, show you a world the way only I can see it. I free myself for today and forever from human immobility. I'm in constant movement. I approach and pull away from objects. I creep under them. I move alongside a running horse's mouth. I fall and rise with the falling and rising bodies. This is I, the machine, manoeuvring in the chaotic movements, recording one movement after another in the most complex combinations.
>
> Freed from the boundaries of time and space, I coordinate any and all points of the universe, wherever I want them to be. My way leads towards the creation of a fresh perception of the world. Thus I explain in a new way the world unknown to you.[2]

The camera isolated momentary appearances and in so doing destroyed the idea that images were timeless. Or, to put it another way, the camera showed that the notion of time passing was inseparable from the experience of the visual (except in paintings). What you saw depended upon where you were when. What you saw was relative to your position in time and space. It was no longer possible to imagine everything converging on the human eye as on the vanishing point of infinity.

Still from *Man with a Movie Camera* by Vertov (1895–1954)

Still Life with Wicker Chair by Picasso (1881–1973)
Reunion des Musees Nationaux / Art Resource, NY

This is not to say that before the invention of the camera men believed that everyone could see everything. But perspective organized the visual field as though that were indeed the ideal. Every drawing or painting that used perspective proposed to the spectator that he was the unique centre of the world. The camera—and more particularly the movie camera—demonstrated that there was no centre.

The invention of the camera changed the way men saw. The visible came to mean something different to them. This was immediately reflected in painting.

For the Impressionists the visible no longer presented itself to man in order to be seen. On the contrary, the visible, in continued flux, became fugitive. For the Cubists the visible was no longer what confronted the single eye, but the totality of possible views taken from points all round the object (or person) being depicted.

The invention of the camera also changed the way in which men saw paintings painted long before the camera was invented. Originally paintings were an integral part of the building for which they were designed. Sometimes in an early Renaissance church or chapel one has the feeling that the images on the wall are records of the building's interior life, that together

Church of St. Francis of Assisi
Scala/Art Resource, NY

© Barnabas Bosshart/CORBIS

they make up the building's memory—so much are they part of the particularity of the building.

The uniqueness of every painting was once part of the uniqueness of the place where it resided. Sometimes the painting was transportable. But it could never be seen in two places at the same time. When the camera reproduces a painting, it destroys the uniqueness of its image. As a result its meaning changes. Or, more exactly, its meaning multiplies and fragments into many meanings.

This is vividly illustrated by what happens when a painting is shown on a television screen. The painting enters each viewer's house. There it is surrounded by his wallpaper, his furniture, his mementos. It enters the atmosphere or his family. It becomes their talking point. It lends its meaning to their meaning. At the same time it enters a million other houses and, in each of them, is seen in a different context. Because of the camera, the painting now travels to the spectator rather than the spectator to the painting. In its travels, its meaning is diversified.

One might argue that all reproductions more or less distort, and that therefore the original painting is still in a sense unique. Here is a reproduction of the *Virgin of the Rocks* by Leonardo da Vinci (page 61, left).

Having seen this reproduction, one can go to the National Gallery to look at the original and there discover what the reproduction lacks. Alternatively one can forget about the quality of the reproduction and simply be reminded, when one sees the original, that it is a famous painting of which somewhere one has already seen a reproduction. But in either case the uniqueness of the original now lies in it being *the original of a reproduction*. It is no longer what its image shows that strikes one as unique; its first meaning is no longer to be found in what it says, but in what it is.

This new status of the original work is the perfectly rational consequences of the new means of reproduction. But it is at this point that a

Virgin of the Rocks by Leonardo da Vinci
(1452–1519) Louvre Erich Lessing/Art Resource, NY

process of mystification again enters. The meaning of the original work no longer lies in what it uniquely says but in what it uniquely is. How is its unique existence evaluated and defined in our present culture? It is defined as an object whose value depends upon its rarity. This market is affirmed and gauged by the price it fetches on the market. But because it is nevertheless "a work of art"—and art is thought to be greater than commerce—its market price is said to be a reflection of its spiritual value. Yet the spiritual value of an object, as distinct from a message or an example, can only be explained in terms of magic or religion. And since in modern society neither of these is a living force, the art object, the "work of art," is enveloped in an atmosphere of entirely bogus religiosity. Works of art are discussed and presented as though they were holy relics: relics which are first and foremost evidence of their own survival. The past in which they originated is studied in order to prove their survival genuine. They are declared art when their line of descent can be certified.

Before the *Virgin of the Rocks* the visitor to the National Gallery would be encouraged by nearly everything he might have heard and read about the painting to feel something like this: "I am in front of it. I can see it. This painting by Leonardo is unlike any other in the world. The National Gallery has the real one. If I look at this painting hard enough, I should somehow be able to feel its authenticity. The *Virgin of the Rocks* by Leonardo da Vinci: it is authentic and therefore it is beautiful."

To dismiss such feelings as naive would be quite wrong. They accord perfectly with the sophisticated culture of art experts for whom the National Gallery catalogue is written. The entry on the *Virgin of the Rocks* is one of the longest entries. It consists of fourteen closely printed pages. They do not deal with the meaning of the image. They deal with who commissioned the painting, legal squabbles, who owned it, its likely date, the families of its owners. Behind this information lie years of research. The aim of the research is to prove beyond any shadow of doubt that the painting is a genuine Leonardo. The secondary aim is to prove that an almost identical painting in the Louvre (page 61, right) is a replica of the National Gallery version.

The Virgin and Child with St. Anne and St. John the Baptist by Leonardo da Vinci (1452–1519). © Bettmann/CORBIS

French art historians try to prove the opposite.

The National Gallery sells more reproductions of Leonardo's cartoon of *The Virgin and Child with St. Anne and St. John the Baptist* [above] than any other picture in their collection. A few years ago it was known only to scholars. It became famous because an American wanted to buy it for two and a half million pounds.

Now it hangs in a room by itself. The room is like a chapel. The drawing is behind bullet-proof perspex. It has acquired a new kind of impressiveness. Not because of what it shows—not because of the meaning of its image. It has become impressive, mysterious, because of its market value.

The bogus religiosity which now surrounds original works of art, and which is ultimately dependent upon their market value, has become the substitute for what paintings lost when the camera made them reproducible. Its function is nostalgic. It is the final empty claim for the continuing values of an oligarchic, undemocratic culture. If the image is no longer unique and exclusive, the art object, the thing, must be made mysteriously so.

The majority of the population do not visit art museums. The table on page 63 shows how closely an interest in art is related to privileged education.

National proportion of art museum visitors according to level of education: Percentage of each educational category who visit art museums

	Greece	Poland	France	Holland
With no educational qualification	0.02	0.12	0.15	—
Only primary education	0.30	1.50	0.45	0.50
Only secondary education	0.5	10.4	10	20
Further and higher education	11.5	11.7	12.5	17.3

Source: Pierre Bourdieu and Alain Darbel, *L'Amour de l'art*, Editions de Minuit, Paris 1969, Appendix 5, table 4

Of the places listed below, which does a museum remind you of most?

	Manual workers (%)	Skilled and white collar (%)	Professional and upper mgmt (%)
Church	66	45	30.5
Library	9	34	28
Lecture hall	—	4	4.5
Department store or entrance hall in public building	—	7	2
Church and library	9	2	4.5
Church and lecture hall	4	2	—
Library and lecture hall	—	—	2
None of these	4	2	19.5
No reply	8	4	9
	100 (n = 53)	100 (n = 98)	100 (n = 99)

Source: As above, Appendix 4, table 8

The majority take it as axiomatic that the museums are full of holy relics which refer to a mystery which excludes them: the mystery of unaccountable wealth. Or, to put this another way, they believe that original masterpieces belong to the preserve (both materially and spiritually) of the rich. Another table indicates what the idea of an art gallery suggests to each social class.

In the age of pictorial reproduction the meaning of paintings is no longer attached to them; their meaning becomes transmittable: that is to say it becomes information of a sort, and, like all information, it is either put to use or ignored; information carries no special authority within itself. When

Venus and Mars by Botticelli (1445–1510). © National Gallery Collection; by kind permission of the Trustees of the National Gallery, London/CORBIS

a painting is put to use, its meaning is either modified or totally changed. One should be quite clear about what this involves. It is not a question of reproduction failing to reproduce certain aspects of an image faithfully; it is a question of reproduction making it possible, even inevitable, that an image will be used for many different purposes and that the reproduced image, unlike an original work, can lend itself to them all. Let us examine some of the ways in which the reproduced image lends itself to such usage.

Reproduction isolates a detail of a painting from the whole. The detail is transformed. An allegorical figure becomes a portrait of a girl.

When a painting is reproduced by a film camera it inevitably becomes material for the film-maker's argument.

A film which reproduces images of a painting leads the spectator, through the painting, to the film-maker's own conclusions. The painting lends authority to the film-maker. This is because a film unfolds in time and a painting does not. In a film the way one image follows another, their succession, constructs an argument which becomes irreversible. In a painting all its elements are there to be seen simultaneously. The spectator may need time to examine each element of the painting but whenever he reaches a conclusion, the simultaneity of the whole painting is there to reverse or qualify his conclusion. The painting maintains its own authority.

Procession to Calvary by Breughel (1525—1569)

Paintings are often reproduced with words around them.

Wheatfield with Crows by Vincent Van Gogh (1853–1890). Art Resource, NY

This is a landscape of a cornfield with birds flying out of it. Look at it for a moment. Then see the painting below.

This is the last picture that Van Gogh painted before he killed himself.

It is hard to define exactly how the words have changed the image but undoubtedly they have. The image now illustrates the sentence.

In this essay each image reproduced has become part of an argument which has little or nothing to do with the painting's original independent meaning. The words have quoted the paintings to confirm their own verbal authority....

Reproduced paintings, like all information, have to hold their own against all the other information being continually transmitted.

Consequently a reproduction, as well as making its own references to the image of its original, becomes itself the reference point for other images. The meaning of an image is changed according to what one sees immediately beside it or what comes immediately after it. Such authority as it retains, is distributed over the whole context in which it appears.

Because works of art are reproducible, they can, theoretically, be used by anybody. Yet mostly—in art books, magazines, films, or within gilt frames in living-rooms—reproductions are still used to bolster the illusion that nothing has changed, that art, with its unique undiminished authority, justifies most other forms of authority, that art makes inequality seem noble and hierarchies seem thrilling. For example, the whole concept of the National Cultural Heritage exploits the authority of art to glorify the present social system and its priorities.

The means of reproduction are used politically and commercially to disguise or deny what their existence makes possible. But sometimes individuals use them differently.

Adults and children sometimes have boards in their bedrooms or living-rooms on which they pin pieces of paper: letters, snapshots, reproductions of paintings, newspaper cuttings, original drawings, postcards. On each board all the images belong to the same language and all are more or less equal within it, because they have been chosen in a highly personal way to match and express the experience of the room's inhabitant. Logically, these boards should replace museums.

What are we saying by that? Let us first be sure about what we are not saying.

We are not saying that there is nothing left to experience before original works of art except a sense of awe because they have survived. The way original works of art are usually approached—through museum catalogues, guides, hired cassettes, etc.—is not the only way they might be approached. When the art of the past ceases to be viewed nostalgically, the works will cease to be holy relics—although they will never re-become what they were before the age of reproduction. We are not saying original works of art are now useless.

Original paintings are silent and still in a sense that information never is. Even a reproduction hung on a wall is not comparable in this respect for in the original the silence and stillness permeate the actual material, the paint, in which one follows the traces of the painter's immediate gestures. This has the effect of closing the distance in time between the painting of the picture

Woman Pouring Milk by Vermeer (1632–1675).

and one's own act of looking at it. In this special sense all paintings are contemporary. Hence the immediacy of their testimony. Their historical moment is literally there before our eyes. Cézanne made a similar observation from the painter's point of view. "A minute in the world's life passes! To paint it in its reality, and forget everything for that! To become that minute, to be the sensitive plate…give the image of what we see, forgetting everything that has appeared before our time…" What we make of that painted moment when it is before our eyes depends upon what we expect of art, and that in turn depends today upon how we have already experienced the meaning of paintings through reproductions.

Nor are we saying that all art can be understood spontaneously. We are not claiming that to cut out a magazine reproduction of an archaic Greek head, because it is reminiscent of some personal experience, and to pin it to a board beside other disparate images, is to come to terms with the full meaning of that head.

The idea of innocence faces two ways. By refusing to enter a conspiracy, one remains innocent of that conspiracy. But to remain innocent may also be to remain ignorant. The issue is not between innocence and knowledge (or between the natural and the cultural) but between a total approach to art which attempts to relate it to every aspect of experience and the esoteric approach of a few specialized experts who are the clerks of the nostalgia of a ruling class in decline. (In decline, not before the proletariat, but before the new power of the corporation and the state.) The real question is: to whom does the meaning of the art of the past properly belong? To those who can apply it to their own lives, or to a cultural hierarchy of relic specialists?

The visual arts have always existed within a certain preserve; originally this preserve was magical or sacred. But it was also physical: it was the place, the cave, the building, in which, or for which, the work was made. The experience of art, which at first was the experience of ritual, was set apart from the rest of life—precisely in order to be able to exercise power over it. Later the preserve of art became a social one. It entered the culture of the ruling class, whilst physically it was set apart and isolated in their palaces and houses. During all this history the authority of art was inseparable from the particular authority of the preserve.

What the modern means of reproduction have done is to destroy the authority of art and to remove it—or, rather, to remove its images which they reproduce—from any preserve. For the first time ever, images of art have become ephemeral, ubiquitous, insubstantial, available, valueless, free. They surround us in the same way as a language surrounds us. They have entered the mainstream of life over which they no longer, in themselves, have power.

Yet very few people are aware of what has happened because the means of reproduction are used nearly all the time to promote the illusion that nothing has changed except that the masses, thanks to reproductions, can now begin to appreciate art as the cultured minority once did. Understandably, the masses remain uninterested and sceptical.

If the new language of images were used differently, it would, through its use, confer a new kind of power. Within it we could begin to define our experiences more precisely in areas where words are inadequate. (Seeing comes before words.) Not only personal experience, but also the essential historical experience of our relation to the past: that is to say the experience of seeking to give meaning to our lives, of trying to understand the history of which we can become the active agents.

The art of the past no longer exists as it once did. Its authority is lost. In its place there is a language of images. What matters now is who uses that language for what purpose. This touches upon questions of copyright for reproduction, the ownership of art presses and publishers, the total policy of public art galleries and museums. As usually presented, these are narrow professional matters. One of the aims of this essay has been to show that what is really at stake is much larger. A people or a class which is cut off from its own past is far less free to choose and to act as a people or class than one that has been able to situate itself in history. This is why—and this is the only reason why—the entire art of the past has now become a political issue.

Many of the ideas in the preceding essay have been taken from another, written over forty years ago * *by the German critic and philosopher Walter Benjamin.*

His essay was entitled The Work of Art in the Age of Mechanical Reproduction. *This essay is available in English in a collection called* Illuminations *(Cape, London, 1970).*

Endnotes

1. Seymour Slive, *Frans Hals* (Phaidon, London).

2. This quotation is from an article written in 1923 by Dziga Vertov, the revolutionary Soviet film director.

*Now over seventy years ago [eds.]

Eli Clare

The Mountain

Eli Clare is a genderqueer writer and activist, living in Michigan. Clare uses the terms *sie* (pronounced "see") and *hier* (pronounced "here") rather than s/he and his/her to refer to *hierself*; these pronouns were coined by some of those who identify as transgender or genderqueer to signify a gender identity other than male or female. Sie has an on-going love affair with trees, rocks, and the wind and is the author of the book *Exile and Pride: Disability, Queerness, and Liberation*. The essay below, "The Mountain, " is drawn from hier book. In it Clare describes hier experience with cerebral palsy and in the process interrogates the terms *normal, disabled, impaired*, and *ableism*. She forces us to examine what it means to be identified as a "supercrip, queer, freak, redneck."

Consider the labels you have used to identify other people and the ones that have been used to identify you. What happens when we take on these labels and internalize them? What happens when we question these internalized notions of ourselves?

I: A Metaphor

The mountain as metaphor looms large in the lives of marginalized people, people whose bones get crushed in the grind of capitalism, patriarchy, white supremacy. How many of us have struggled up the mountain, measured ourselves against it, failed up there, lived in its shadow? We've hit our heads on glass ceilings, tried to climb the class ladder, lost fights against assimilation, scrambled toward that phantom called normality.

We hear from the summit that the world is grand from up there, that we live down here at the bottom because we are lazy, stupid, weak, and ugly. We decide to climb that mountain, or make a pact that our children will climb it. The climbing turns out to be unimaginably difficult. We are afraid; every time we look ahead we can find nothing remotely familiar or comfortable. We lose the trail. Our wheelchairs get stuck. We speak the wrong languages with the wrong accents, wear the wrong clothes, carry our bodies the wrong ways, ask the wrong questions, love the wrong people. And it's goddamn lonely up there on the mountain. We decide to stop climbing and build a new house right where we are. Or we decide to climb back down to the people we love, where the food, the clothes, the dirt, the sidewalk, the steaming asphalt under our feet, our crutches, all feel right. Or we find the path again, decide to continue climbing only to have the very people who told us how wonderful life is at the summit booby-trap the trail. They burn the bridge over the impassable canyon. They redraw our topo maps so that we end up walking in circles. They send their goons—those working-class and poor people they employ as their official brutes—to push us over the edge. Maybe we get to the summit, but probably not. And the price we pay is huge.

Up there on the mountain, we confront the external forces, the power brokers who benefit so much from the status quo and their privileged position at the very summit. But just as vividly, we come face-to-face with our own bodies, all that we cherish and despise, all that lies imbedded there. This I know because I have caught myself lurching up the mountain.

II: A Supercrip Story

I am a gimp, a crip, disabled with cerebral palsy. The story of me lurching up the mountain begins not on the mountain, but with one of the dominant images of disabled people, the supercrip. A boy without hands bats .486 on his Little League team. A blind man hikes the Appalachian Trail from end to end. An adolescent girl with Down's syndrome learns to drive and has a boyfriend. A guy with one leg runs across Canada. The nondisabled world is saturated with these stories: stories about gimps who engage in activities as grand as walking 2,500 miles or as mundane as learning to drive. They focus on disabled people "overcoming" our disabilities. They reinforce the superiority of the nondisabled body and mind. They turn individual disabled people, who are simply leading their lives, into symbols of inspiration.

Supercrip stories never focus on the conditions that make it so difficult for people with Down's to have romantic partners, for blind people to have adventures, for disabled kids to play sports. I don't mean medical conditions. I mean material, social, legal conditions. I mean lack of access, lack of employment, lack of education, lack of personal attendant services. I mean stereotypes and attitudes. I mean oppression. The dominant story about disability should be about ableism, not the inspirational supercrip crap, the believe-it-or-not disability story.

I've been a supercrip in the mind's eye of nondisabled people more than once. Running cross-country and track in high school, I came in dead last in more races than I care to count. My tense, wiry body, right foot wandering out to the side as I grew tired, pushed against the miles, the stopwatch, the final back stretch, the last muddy hill. Sometimes I was lapped by the front runners in races as short as the mile. Sometimes I trailed everyone on a cross-country course by two, three, four minutes. I ran because I loved to run, and yet after every race, strangers came to thank me, cry over me, tell me what an inspiration I was. To them, I was not just another hopelessly slow, tenacious high school athlete, but supercrip, tragic brave girl with CP, courageous cripple. It sucked. The slogan on one of my favorite t-shirts, black cotton inked with big fluorescent pink letters, one word per line, reads PISS ON PITY.

⊷ ⊫◈⊨ ⊶

Me lurching up the mountain is another kind of supercrip story, a story about internalizing supercripdom, about becoming supercrip in my own mind's eye, a story about climbing Mount Adams last summer with my friend Adrianne. We had been planning this trip for years. Adrianne spent her childhood roaming New Hampshire's White Mountains and wanted to take me to her favorite haunts. Six times in six years, we set the trip up, and every time something fell through at the last minute. Finally, last summer everything stayed in place.

I love the mountains almost as much as I love the ocean, not a soft, romantic kind of love, but a deep down rumble in my bones. When Adrianne pulled out her trail guides and topo maps and asked me to choose one of the mountains we'd climb, I looked for a big mountain, for a long, hard hike, for a trail that would take us well above treeline. I picked Mount Adams. I think I asked Adrianne, "Can I handle this trail?" meaning, "Will I have to clamber across deep gulches on narrow log bridges without hand railings to get to the top of this mountain?" Without a moment's hesitation, she said, "No problem."

I have walked from Los Angeles to Washington, D.C., on a peace walk; backpacked solo in the southern Appalachians, along Lake Superior, on the beaches at Point Reyes; slogged my way over Cottonwood Pass and down South Manitou's dunes. Learning to walk took me longer than most kids— certainly most nondisabled kids. I was two and a half before I figured out how to stand on my own two feet, drop my heels to the ground, balance my weight on the whole long flat of each foot. I wore orthopedic shoes—clunky, unbending monsters—for several years, but never had to suffer through physical therapy or surgery. Today, I can and often do walk unending miles for the pure joy of walking. In the disability community I am called a walkie, someone who doesn't use a wheelchair, who walks rather than rolls. Adrianne and I have been hiking buddies for years. I never questioned her judgment. Of course, I could handle Mount Adams.

The night before our hike, it rained. In the morning we thought we might have to postpone. The weather reports from the summit still looked uncertain, but by 10 a.m. the clouds started to lift, later than we had planned to begin but still okay. The first mile of trail snaked through steep jumbles of rock, leaving me breathing hard, sweat drenching my cotton t-shirt, dripping into my eyes. I love this pull and stretch, quad and calves, lungs and heart, straining.

⊶ ⊨◊⊨ ⊷

The trail divides and divides again, steeper and rockier now, moving not around but over piles of craggy granite, mossy and a bit slick from the night's rain. I start having to watch where I put my feet. Balance has always been somewhat of a problem for me, my right foot less steady than my left. On uncertain ground, each step becomes a studied move, especially when my weight is balanced on my right foot. I take the trail slowly, bringing both feet together, solid on one stone, before leaning into my next step. This assures my balance, but I lose all the momentum gained from swinging into a step, touching ground, pushing off again in the same moment. There is no rhythm to my stop-and-go clamber. I know that going down will be worse, gravity underscoring my lack of balance. I watch Adrianne ahead of me hop from one rock to the next up this tumble trail of granite. I know that she's breathing hard, that this is no easy climb, but also that each step isn't a strategic game for her. I start getting scared as the trail steepens, then steepens again, the rocks not letting up. I can't think of how I will ever come down this mountain. Fear sets up a rumble right alongside the love in my bones. I keep climbing. Adrianne starts waiting for me every 50 yards or so. I finally tell her I'm scared.

She's never hiked this trail before so can't tell me if this is as steep as it gets. We study the topo map, do a time check. We have many hours of daylight ahead of us, but we're both thinking about how much time it might take me to climb down, using my hands and butt when I can't trust my feet. I want to continue up to treeline, the pines shorter and shorter, grown twisted and withered, giving way to scrub brush, then to lichen-covered granite, up to the sun-drenched cap where the mountains all tumble out toward the hazy blue horizon. I want to so badly, but fear rumbles next to love next to real lived physical limitations, and so we decide to turn around. I cry, maybe for the first time, over something I want to do, had many reasons to believe I could, but really can't. I cry hard, then get up and follow Adrianne back down the mountain. It's hard and slow, and I use my hands and butt often and wish I could use gravity as Adrianne does to bounce from one flat spot to another, down this jumbled pile of rocks.

⊷ ⚒ ⊶

I thought a lot coming down Mount Adams. Thought about bitterness. For as long as I can remember, I have avoided certain questions. Would I have been a good runner if I didn't have CP? Could I have been a surgeon or pianist, a dancer or gymnast? Tempting questions that have no answers. I refuse to enter the territory marked *bitterness*. I wondered about a friend who calls herself one of the last of the polio tribe, born just before the polio vaccine's discovery. Does she ever ask what her life might look like had she been born five years later? On a topo map, bitterness would be outlined in red.

I thought about the model of disability that separates impairment from disability. Disability theorist Michael Oliver defines impairment as "lacking part of or all of a limb, or having a defective limb, organism or mechanism of the body." I lack a fair amount of fine motor control. My hands shake. I can't play a piano, place my hands gently on a keyboard, or type even 15 words a minute. Whole paragraphs never cascade from my fingertips. My longhand is a slow scrawl. I have trouble picking up small objects, putting them down. Dicing onions with a sharp knife puts my hands at risk. A food processor is not a yuppie kitchen luxury in my house, but an adaptive device. My gross motor skills are better but not great. I can walk mile after mile, run and jump and skip and hop, but don't expect me to walk a balance beam. A tightrope would be murder; boulder hopping and rock climbing, not much better. I am not asking for pity. I am telling you about impairment.

Oliver defines disability as "the disadvantage or restriction of activity caused by a contemporary social organization which takes no or little account of people who have physical [and/or cognitive/developmental/mental] impairments and thus excludes them from the mainstream of society." I write slowly enough that cashiers get impatient as I sign my name to checks, stop talking to me, turn to my companions, hand them my receipts. I have failed timed tests, important tests, because teachers wouldn't allow me extra time to finish the sheer physical act of writing, wouldn't allow me to use a typewriter. I have been turned away from jobs because my potential employer believed my slow, slurred speech meant I was stupid. Everywhere I go people stare at me, in restaurants as I eat, in grocery stores as I fish coins out of my pocket to pay the cashier, in parks as I play with my dog. I am not asking for pity. I am telling you about disability.

In large part, disability oppression is about access. Simply being on Mount Adams, halfway up Air Line Trail, represents a whole lot of access. When access is measured by curb cuts, ramps, and whether they are kept clear of snow and ice in the winter; by the width of doors and height of counters; by the presence or absence of Braille, closed captions, ASL, and TDDs; my not being able to climb all the way to the very top of Mount Adams stops being about disability. I decided that turning around before reaching the summit was more about impairment than disability.

But even as I formed the thought, I could feel my resistance to it. To neatly divide disability from impairment doesn't feel right. My experience of living with CP has been so shaped by ableism—or to use Oliver's language, my experience of impairment has been so shaped by disability—that I have trouble separating the two. I understand the difference between failing a test because some stupid school rule won't give me more time and failing to summit Mount Adams because it's too steep and slippery for my feet. The first failure centers on a socially constructed limitation, the second on a physical one.

At the same time, both center on my body. The faster I try to write, the more my pen slides out of control, muscles spasm, then contract trying to stop the tremors, my shoulder and upper arm growing painfully tight. Even though this socially constructed limitation has a simple solution—access to a typewriter, computer, tape recorder, or person to take dictation—I experience the problem on a very physical level. In the case of the bodily limitation, my experience is similarly physical. My feet simply don't know the necessary balance. I lurch along from one rock to the next, catching myself repeatedly as I start to fall, quads quickly sore from exertion, tension, lack of momentum. These physical experiences, one caused by a social construction, the other by a bodily limitation, translate directly into frustration, making me want to crumple the test I can't finish, hurl the rocks I can't climb. This frustration knows no neat theoretical divide between disability and impairment. Neither does disappointment nor embarrassment. On good days, I can separate the anger I turn inward at my body from the anger that needs to be turned outward, directed at the daily ableist shit, but there is nothing simple or neat about kindling the latter while transforming the former. I decided that Oliver's model of disability makes theoretical and political sense but misses important emotional realities.

I thought of my nondisabled friends who don't care for camping, hiking, or backpacking. They would never spend a vacation sweat-drenched and breathing hard halfway up a mountain. I started to list their names, told Adrianne what I was doing. She reminded me of other friends who enjoy easy day hikes on smooth, well-maintained trails. Many of them would never even attempt the tumbled trail of rock I climbed for an hour and a half before turning around. We added their names to my list. It turned into a long roster. I decided that if part of what happened to me up there was about impairment, another part was about desire, my desire to climb mountains.

I thought about supercrips. Some of us—the boy who bats .486, the man who through-hikes the A.T.—accomplish something truly extraordinary and become supercrips. Others of us—the teenager with Down's who has a boyfriend, the kid with CP who runs track and cross-country—lead entirely ordinary lives and still become supercrips. Nothing about having a boyfriend or running cross-country is particularly noteworthy. Bat .486 or have a boyfriend, it doesn't matter; either way we are astonishing. In the creation of supercrip stories, nondisabled people don't celebrate any particular achievement, however extraordinary or mundane. Rather, these stories rely upon the perception that disability and achievement contradict each other and that any disabled person who overcomes this contradiction is heroic.

To believe that achievement contradicts disability is to pair helplessness with disability, a pairing for which crips pay an awful price. The nondisabled world locks us away in nursing homes. It deprives us the resources to live independently. It physically and sexually abuses us in astoundingly high numbers. It refuses to give us jobs because even when a workplace is accessible, the speech impediment, the limp, the ventilator, the seeing-eye dog are read as signs of inability. The price is incredibly high.

⚊⚊ ⚊◆⚌ ⚊⚊

And here, supercrip turns complicated. On the other side of supercripdom lies pity, tragedy, and the nursing home. Disabled people know this, and in our process of knowing, some of us internalize the crap. We make supercrip our own, particularly the type that pushes into the extraordinary, cracks into our physical limitation. We use supercripdom as a shield, a protection, as if this individual internalization could defend us against disability oppression.

I climbed Mount Adams for an hour and half scared, not sure I'd ever be able to climb down, knowing that on the next rock my balance could give out, and yet I climbed. Climbed surely because I wanted the summit, because of the love rumbling in my bones. But climbed also because I want to say, "Yes, I have CP, but see. See, watch me. I can climb mountains too." I wanted to prove myself once again. I wanted to overcome my CP.

Overcoming has a powerful grip. Back home, my friends told me, "But you can walk any of us under the table." My sister, a serious mountain climber who spends many a weekend high up in the North Cascades, told me, "I bet with the right gear and enough practice you *could* climb Mount Adams." A woman who doesn't know me told Adrianne, "Tell your friend not to give up. She can do anything she wants. She just has to want it hard enough." I told myself as Adrianne and I started talking about another trip to the Whites, "If I used a walking stick, and we picked a dry day and a different trail, maybe I could make it up to the top of Adams." I never once heard, "You made the right choice when you turned around." The mountain just won't let go.

III: Home

I will never find home on the mountain. This I know. Rather home starts here in my body, in all that lies imbedded beneath my skin. My disabled body: born prematurely in the backwoods of Oregon, I was first diagnosed as "mentally retarded," and then later as having CP. I grew up to the words *cripple, retard, monkey, defect,* took all the staring into me and learned to shut it out.

My body violated: early on my father started raping me, physically abusing me in ways that can only be described as torture, and sharing my body with other people, mostly men, who did the same. I abandoned that body, decided to be a hermit, to be done with humans, to live among the trees, with the salmon, to ride the south wind bareback.

My white body: the only person of color in my hometown was an African-American boy, adopted by a white family. I grew up to persistent rumors of a lynching tree way back in the hills, of the sheriff running people out of the county. For a long time after moving to the city, college scholarship in hand, all I could do was gawk at the multitude of humans: homeless people, their shopping carts and bedrolls, Black people, Chinese people, Chicanos, drag queens and punks, vets down on Portland's Burnside Avenue, white men in their wool suits, limos shined to sparkle. I watched them all sucking in the thick weave of Spanish, Cantonese, street talk, English. This is how I became aware of my whiteness.

My queer body: I spent my childhood, a tomboy not sure of my girlness, queer without a name for my queerness. I cut firewood on clearcuts, swam in the river, ran the beaches at Battle Rock and Cape Blanco. When I found dykes, fell in love for the first time, came into a political queer community, I felt as if I had found home again.

The body as home, but only if it is understood that bodies are never singular, but rather haunted, strengthened, underscored by countless other bodies. My alcoholic, Libertarian father and his father, the gravedigger, from whom my father learned his violence. I still dream about them sometimes, ugly dreams that leave me panting with fear in the middle of the night. One day I will be done with them. The white, working-class loggers, fishermen, and ranchers I grew up among: Les Smith, John Black, Walt Maya. Their ways of dressing, moving, talking helped shape my sense of self. Today when I hear queer activists say the word *redneck* like a cuss word, I think of those men, backs of their necks turning red in the summertime from long days of work outside, felling trees, pulling fishnets, baling hay. I think of my butchness, grounded there, overlaid by a queer, urban sensibility. A body of white, rural, working-class values. I still feel an allegiance to this body, even as I reject the virulent racism, the unexamined destruction of forest and river. How could I possibly call my body home without the bodies of trees that repeatedly provided me refuge? Without queer bodies? Without crip bodies? Without transgendered and transsexual bodies? Without the history of disabled people who worked as freaks in the freak show, displaying their bodies: Charles Stratton posed as General Tom Thumb, Hiriam and Barney Davis billed as the "Wild Men from Borneo"? The answer is simple. I couldn't.

The body as home, but only if it is understood that place and community and culture burrow deep into our bones. My earliest and most enduring sense of place is in the backwoods of Oregon, where I grew up but no longer live, in a logging and fishing town of a thousand that hangs on to the most western edge of the continental United States. To the west stretches the Pacific Ocean; to the east the Siskiyou Mountains rise, not tall enough to be mountains but too steep to be hills. Portland is a seven-hour drive north; San Francisco, a twelve-hour drive south. Home for me is marked by Douglas fir and chinook salmon, south wind whipping the ocean into a fury of waves and surf. Marked by the aching knowledge of environmental destruction, the sad truth of that town founded on the genocide of Native peoples, the Tuni and Coquille, Talkemas and Latgawas. In writing about the backwoods and the rural, white, working-class culture found there, I am not being nostalgic, reaching backward toward a re-creation of the past. Rather I am reaching toward my bones. When I write about losing that place, about living in exile, I am putting words to a loss which also grasps at my bones.

The body as home, but only if it is understood that language too lives under the skin. I think of the words *crip, queer, freak, redneck.* None of these are easy words. They mark the jagged edge between self-hatred and pride, the chasm between how the dominant culture views marginalized peoples and how we view ourselves, the razor between finding home, finding our bodies, and living in exile, living on the metaphoric mountain. Whatever our relationships with these words—whether we embrace them or hate them, feel them draw blood as they hit our skin or find them entirely fitting, refuse to say them or simply feel uncomfortable in their presence—we deal with their power every day. I hear these words all the time. They are whispered in the mirror as I dress to go out, as I straighten my tie and shrug into my suit jacket; on the streets as folks gawk at my trembling hands, stare trying to figure out whether I'm a woman or man; in half the rhetoric I hear from environmentalists and queer activists, rhetoric where rural working-class people get cast as clods and bigots. At the same time, I use some, but not all, of these words to call out my pride, to strengthen my resistance, to place myself within community. *Crip, queer, freak, redneck* burrowed into my body.

The body as home, but only if it is understood that bodies can be stolen, fed lies and poison, torn away from us. They rise up around me—bodies stolen by hunger, war, breast cancer, AIDS, rape; the daily grind of factory, sweatshop, cannery, sawmill; the lynching rope; the freezing streets; the nursing home and prison. African-American drag performer Leonard/Lynn Vines, walking through his Baltimore neighborhood, called a "drag queen faggot bitch" and shot six times. Matt Sheppard—gay, white, young—tied to a fence post in Wyoming and beaten to death. Some bodies are taken for good; other bodies live on, numb, abandoned, full of self-hate. Both have been stolen. Disabled people cast as supercrips and tragedies; lesbian/gay/bisexual/trans people told over and over again that we are twisted and unnatural; poor people made responsible for their own poverty. Stereotypes and lies lodge in our bodies as surely as bullets. They live and fester there, stealing the body.

The body as home, but only if it is understood that the stolen body can be reclaimed. The bodies irrevocably taken from us: we can memorialize them in quilts, granite walls, candlelight vigils; remember and mourn them; use their deaths to strengthen our will. And as for the lies and false images, we need to name them, transform them, create something entirely new in their place, something that comes close and finally true to the bone, entering our bodies as liberation, joy, fury, hope, a will to refigure the world. The body as home.

***

The mountain will never be home, and still I have to remember it grips me. Supercrip lives inside my body, ready and willing to push the physical limitations, to try the "extraordinary," because down at the base of the mountain waits a nursing home. I hang on to a vision. Someday after the revolution, disabled people will live ordinary lives, neither heroic nor tragic. *Crip, queer, freak, redneck* will be mere words describing human difference. Supercrip will be dead; the nursing home, burnt down; the metaphoric mountain, collapsed in volcanic splendor. Post-revolution I expect there will still be literal mountains I want to climb and can't, but I'll be able to say without doubt, without hesitation, "Let's turn around here. This one is too steep, too slippery for my feet."

Annie Dillard

Seeing

Annie Dillard's "Seeing" asks us to keep our eyes open, to read carefully both the tiny and the enormous, the enduring and the fleeting. Dillard is a writer, naturalist, and religious philosopher who has spent much time observing nature and contemplating the spiritual in the natural world. Influenced by Henry David Thoreau, she spent four seasons living near Tinker Creek, Virginia, observing and writing about nature. Dillard's book *Pilgrim at Tinker Creek*, from which "Seeing" is excerpted, won the 1975 Pulitzer Prize. In this essay she explores the nature of sight as it relates to light and the absence of light, how it is that "darkness appalls and light dazzles" us. Drawing from her own visual experiences and stories of formerly blind people who regain sight, she forms conclusions about what we can and cannot understand in the act of seeing. She carefully explores the meaning of space, light, and distance in the lives of the sighted and the blind. Note, too, ways in which Dillard reads nature closely as well as responsively.

When I was six or seven years old, growing up in Pittsburgh, I used to take a precious penny of my own and hide it for someone else to find. It was a curious compulsion; sadly, I've never been seized by it since. For some reason I always "hid" the penny along the same stretch of sidewalk up the street. I would cradle it at the roots of a sycamore, say, or in a hole left by a chipped-off piece of sidewalk. Then I would take a piece of chalk, and, starting at either end of the block, draw huge arrows leading up to the penny from both directions. After I learned to write I labeled the arrows: SURPRISE AHEAD or MONEY THIS WAY. I was greatly excited, during all this arrow-drawing, at the thought of the first lucky passer-by who would receive in this way, regardless of merit, a free gift from the universe. But I never lurked about. I would go straight home and not give the matter another thought, until, some months later, I would be gripped again by the impulse to hide another penny.

It is still the first week in January, and I've got great plans. I've been thinking about seeing. There are lots of things to see, unwrapped gifts and free surprises. The world is fairly studded and strewn with pennies cast broadside from a generous hand. But—and this is the point—who gets excited by a mere penny? If you follow one arrow, if you crouch motionless on a bank to watch a tremulous ripple thrill on the water and are rewarded by the sight of a muskrat kit paddling from its den, will you count that sight a chip of copper only, and go your rueful way? It is dire poverty indeed when a man is so malnourished and fatigued that he won't stoop to pick up a penny. But if you cultivate a healthy poverty and simplicity, so that finding a penny will literally make your day, then, since the world is in fact planted in pennies, you have with your poverty bought a lifetime of days. It is that simple. What you see is what you get.

I used to be able to see flying insects in the air. I'd look ahead and see, not the row of hemlocks across the road, but the air in front of it. My eyes would focus along that column of air, picking out flying insects. But I lost interest, I guess, for I dropped the habit. Now I can see birds. Probably some people can look at the grass at their feet and discover all the crawling creatures. I would like to know grasses and sedges—and care. Then my least journey into the world would be a field trip, a series of happy recognitions. Thoreau, in an expansive mood, exulted, "What a rich book might be made about buds, including, perhaps, sprouts!" It would be nice to think so. I cherish mental images I have of three perfectly happy people. One collects stones. Another—an Englishman, say—watches clouds. The third lives on a coast and collects drops of seawater which he examines microscopically and mounts. But I don't see what the specialist sees, and so I cut myself off, not only from the total picture, but from the various forms of happiness.

Unfortunately, nature is very much a now-you-see-it, now-you-don't affair. A fish flashes, then dissolves in the water before my eyes like so much salt. Deer apparently ascend bodily into heaven; the brightest oriole fades into leaves. These disappearances stun me into stillness and concentration; they say of nature that it conceals with a grand nonchalance, and they say of vision that it is a deliberate gift, the revelation of a dancer who for my eyes only flings away her seven veils. For nature does reveal as well as conceal: now-you-don't-see-it, now-you-do. For a week last September migrating red-winged blackbirds were feeding heavily down by the creek at the back of the house. One day I went out to investigate the racket; I walked up to a tree, an Osage orange, and a hundred birds flew away. They simply materialized out of the tree. I saw a tree, then a whisk of color, then a tree again. I walked closer and another hundred blackbirds took flight. Not a branch, not a twig budged: The birds were apparently weightless as well as invisible. Or, it was as if the leaves of the Osage orange had been freed from a spell in the form of red-winged blackbirds; they flew from the tree, caught my eye in the sky, and vanished. When I looked again at the tree the leaves had reassembled as if nothing had happened. Finally I walked directly to the trunk of the tree and a final hundred, the real diehards, appeared, spread, and vanished. How could so many hide in the tree without my seeing them? The Osage orange, unruffled, looked just as it had looked from the house, when three hundred red-winged blackbirds cried from its crown. I looked downstream where they flew, and they were gone. Searching, I couldn't spot one. I wandered downstream to force them to play their hand, but they'd crossed the creek and scattered. One show to a customer. These appearances catch at my throat; they are the free gifts, the bright coppers at the roots of trees.

It's all a matter of keeping my eyes open. Nature is like one of those line drawings of a tree that are puzzles for children: Can you find hidden in the leaves a duck, a house, a boy, a bucket, a zebra, and a boot? Specialists can find the most incredibly well-hidden things. A book I read when I was young recommended an easy way to find caterpillars to rear: You simply find some fresh caterpillar droppings, look up, and there's your caterpillar. More recently an author advised me to set my mind at ease about those piles of cut stems on the ground in grassy fields. Field mice make them; they cut the grass down by degrees to reach the seeds at the head. It seems that when the grass is tightly packed, as in a field of ripe grain, the blade won't topple at a single cut through the stem; instead, the cut stem simply drops vertically, held in the crush of grain. The mouse severs the bottom again and again, the stem keeps dropping an inch at a time, and finally the head is low enough for the mouse to reach the seeds. Meanwhile, the mouse is positively littering the field with its little piles of cut stems into which, presumably, the author of the book is constantly stumbling.

If I can't see these minutiae, I still try to keep my eyes open. I'm always on the lookout for antlion traps in sandy soil, monarch pupae near milkweed, skipper larvae in locust leaves. These things are utterly common, and I've not seen one. I bang on hollow trees near water, but so far no flying squirrels have appeared. In flat country I watch every sunset in hopes of seeing the green ray. The green ray is a seldom-seen streak of light that rises from the sun like a spurting fountain at the moment of sunset; it throbs into the sky for two seconds and disappears. One more reason to keep my eyes open. A photography professor at the University of Florida just happened to see a bird die in midflight; it jerked, died, dropped, and smashed on the ground. I squint at the wind because I read Stewart Edward White: "I have always maintained that if you looked closely enough you could *see* the wind—the dim, hardly-made-out, fine debris fleeing high in the air." White was an excellent observer, and devoted an entire chapter of *The Mountains* to the subject of seeing deer: "As soon as you can forget the naturally obvious and construct an artificial obvious, then you too will see deer."

But the artificial obvious is hard to see. My eyes account for less than one percent of the weight of my head; I'm bony and dense; I see what I expect. I once spent a full three minutes looking at a bullfrog that was so unexpectedly large I couldn't see it even though a dozen enthusiastic campers were shouting directions. Finally I asked, "What color am I looking for?" and a fellow said, "Green." When at last I picked out the frog, I saw what painters are up against: The thing wasn't green at all, but the color of wet hickory bark.

The lover can see, and the knowledgeable. I visited an aunt and uncle at a quarter-horse ranch in Cody, Wyoming. I couldn't do much of anything useful, but I could, I thought, draw. So, as we all sat around the kitchen table after supper, I produced a sheet of paper and drew a horse. "That's one lame horse," my aunt volunteered. The rest of the family joined in: "Only place to saddle that one is his neck"; "Looks like we better shoot the poor thing, on account of those terrible growths." Meekly, I slid the pencil and paper down the table. Everyone in that family, including my three young cousins, could draw a horse. Beautifully. When the paper came back it looked as though five shining, real quarter horses had been corraled by mistake with a papier-mâché moose; the real horses seemed to gaze at the monster with a steady, puzzled air. I stay away from horses now, but I can do a creditable goldfish. The point is that I just don't know what the lover knows; I just can't see the artificial obvious that those in the know construct. The herpetologist asks the native, "Are there snakes in that ravine?" "Nosir." And the herpetologist comes home with, yessir, three bags full. Are there butterflies on that mountain? Are the bluets in bloom, are there arrowheads here, or fossil shells in the shale?

Peeping through my keyhole I see within the range of only about thirty percent of the light that comes from the sun; the rest is infrared and some little ultraviolet, perfectly apparent to many animals, but invisible to me. A nightmare network of ganglia, charged and firing without my knowledge, cuts and splices what I do see, editing it for my brain. Donald E. Carr points out that the sense impressions of one-celled animals are *not* edited for the brain: "This is philosophically interesting in a rather mournful way, since it means that only the simplest animals perceive the universe as it is."

A fog that won't burn away drifts and flows across my field of vision. When you see fog move against a backdrop of deep pines, you don't see the fog itself, but streaks of clearness floating across the air in dark shreds. So I see only tatters of clearness through a pervading obscurity. I can't distinguish the fog from the overcast sky; I can't be sure if the light is direct or reflected. Everywhere darkness and the presence of the unseen appalls. We estimate now that only one atom dances alone in every cubic meter of intergalactic space. I blink and squint. What planet or power yanks Halley's Comet out of orbit? We haven't seen that force yet; it's a question of distance, density, and the pallor of reflected light. We rock, cradled in the swaddling band of darkness. Even the simple darkness of night whispers suggestions to the mind. Last summer, in August, I stayed at the creek too late.

Where Tinker Creek flows under the sycamore log bridge to the tearshaped island, it is slow and shallow, fringed thinly in cattail marsh. At this spot an astonishing bloom of life supports vast breeding populations of insects, fish, reptiles, birds, and mammals. On windless summer evenings I stalk along the creek bank or straddle the sycamore log in absolute stillness, watching for muskrats. The night I stayed too late I was hunched on the log staring spellbound at spreading, reflected stains of lilac on the water. A cloud in the sky suddenly lighted as if turned on by a switch; its reflection just as suddenly materialized on the water upstream, flat and floating, so that I couldn't see the creek bottom, or life in the water under the cloud. Downstream, away from the cloud on the water, water turtles smooth as beans were gliding down with the current in a series of easy, weightless push-offs, as men bound on the moon. I didn't know whether to trace the progress of one turtle I was sure of, risking sticking my face in one of the bridge's spider webs made invisible by the gathering dark, or take a chance on seeing the carp, or scan the mudbank in hope of seeing a muskrat, or follow the last of the swallows who caught at my heart and trailed it after them like streamers as they appeared from directly below, under the log, flying upstream with the tails forked, so fast.

But shadows spread, and deepened, and stayed. After thousands of years we're still strangers to darkness, fearful aliens in an enemy camp with our arms crossed over our chests. I stirred. A land turtle on the bank, startled, hissed the air from its lungs and withdrew into its shell. An uneasy pink here, an unfathomable blue there, gave great suggestion of lurking beings. Things were going on. I couldn't see whether that sere rustle I heard was a distant rattlesnake, slit-eyed, or a nearby sparrow kicking in the dry flood debris slung at the foot of a willow. Tremendous action roiled the water everywhere I looked, big action, inexplicable. A tremor welled up beside a gaping muskrat burrow in the bank and I caught my breath, but no muskrat appeared. The ripples continued to fan upstream with a steady, powerful thrust. Night was knitting over my face an eyeless mask, and I still sat transfixed. A distant airplane, a delta wing out of nightmare, made a gliding shadow on the creek's bottom that looked like a stingray cruising upstream. At once a black fin slit the pink cloud on the water, shearing it in two. The two halves merged together and seemed to dissolve before my eyes. Darkness pooled in the cleft of the creek and rose, as water collects in a well. Untamed, dreaming lights flickered over the sky. I saw hints of hulking underwater shadows, two pale splashes out of the water, and round ripples rolling close together from a blackened center.

At last I stared upstream where only the deepest violet remained of the cloud, a cloud so high its underbelly still glowed feeble color reflected from a hidden sky lighted in turn by a sun halfway to China. And out of that violet, a sudden enormous black body arced over the water. I saw only a cylindrical sleekness. Head and tail, if there was a head and tail, were both submerged in cloud. I saw only one ebony fling, a headlong dive to darkness; then the waters closed, and the lights went out.

I walked home in a shivering daze, up hill and down. Later I lay open-mouthed in bed, my arms flung wide at my sides to steady the whirling darkness. At this latitude I'm spinning 836 miles an hour round the earth's axis; I often fancy I feel my sweeping fall as a break-neck arc like the dive of dolphins, and the hollow rushing of wind raises hair on my neck and the side of my face. In orbit around the sun I'm moving 64,800 miles an hour. The solar system as a whole, like a merry-go-round unhinged, spins, bobs, and blinks at the speed of 43,200 miles an hour along a course set east of Hercules. Someone has piped, and we are dancing a tarantella until the sweat pours. I open my eyes and I see dark, muscled forms curl out of water, with flapping gills and flattened eyes. I close my eyes and I see stars, deep stars giving way to deeper stars, deeper stars bowing to deepest stars at the crown of an infinite cone.

"Still," wrote van Gogh in a letter, "a great deal of light falls on everything." If we are blinded by darkness, we are also blinded by light. When too much light falls on everything, a special terror results. Peter Freuchen describes the notorious kayak sickness to which Greenland Eskimos are prone. "The Greenland fjords are peculiar for the spells of completely quiet weather, when there is not enough wind to blow out a match and the water is like a sheet of glass. The kayak hunter must sit in his boat without stirring a finger so as not to scare the shy seals away…. The sun, low in the sky, sends a glare into his eyes, and the landscape around moves into the realm of the unreal. The reflex from the mirrorlike water hypnotizes him, he seems to be unable to move, and all of a sudden it is as if he were floating in a bottomless void, sinking, sinking, and sinking…. Horror-stricken, he tries to stir, to cry out, but he cannot, he is completely paralyzed, he just falls and falls." Some hunters are especially cursed with this panic, and bring ruin and sometimes starvation to their families.

Sometimes here in Virginia at sunset low clouds on the southern or northern horizon are completely invisible in the lighted sky. I only know one is there because I can see its reflection in still water. The first time I discovered this mystery I looked from cloud to no-cloud in bewilderment, checking my bearings over and over, thinking maybe the ark of the covenant was just passing by south of Dead Man Mountain. Only much later did I read the explanation: Polarized light from the sky is very much weakened by reflection, but the light in clouds isn't polarized. So invisible clouds pass among visible clouds, till all slide over the mountains; so a greater light extinguishes a lesser as though it didn't exist.

In the great meteor shower of August, the Perseid, I wail all day for the shooting stars I miss. They're out there showering down, committing hara-kiri in a flame of fatal attraction, and hissing perhaps at last into the ocean. But at dawn what looks like a blue dome clamps down over me like a lid on a pot. The stars and planets could smash and I'd never know. Only a piece of ashen moon occasionally climbs up or down the inside of the dome, and our local star without surcease explodes on our heads. We have really only that one light, one source for all power, and yet we must turn away from it by universal decree. Nobody here on the planet seems aware of this strange, powerful taboo, that we all walk about carefully averting our faces, this way and that, lest our eyes be blasted forever.

Darkness appalls and light dazzles; the scrap of visible light that doesn't hurt my eyes hurts my brain. What I see sets me swaying. Size and distance and the sudden swelling of meanings confuse me, bowl me over. I straddle the sycamore log bridge over Tinker Creek in the summer. I look at the lighted creek bottom: Snail tracks tunnel the mud in quavering curves. A crayfish jerks, but by the time I absorb what has happened, he's gone in a billowing smokescreen of silt. I look at the water: minnows and shiners. If I'm thinking minnows, a carp will fill my brain till I scream. I look at the water's surface: skaters, bubbles, and leaves sliding down. Suddenly, my own face, reflected, startles me witless. Those snails have been tracking my face! Finally, with a shuddering wrench of the will, I see clouds, cirrus clouds. I'm dizzy, I fall in. This looking business is risky.

Once I stood on a humped rock on nearby Purgatory Mountain, watching through binoculars the great autumn hawk migration below, until I discovered that I was in danger of joining the hawks on a vertical migration of my own. I was used to binoculars, but not, apparently, to balancing on humped rocks while looking through them. I staggered. Everything advanced and receded by turns; the world was full of unexplained foreshortenings and depths. A distant huge tan object, a hawk the size of an elephant, turned out to be the browned bough of a nearby loblolly pine. I followed a sharp-shinned hawk against a featureless sky, rotating my head unawares as it flew, and when I lowered the glass a glimpse of my own looming shoulder sent me staggering. What prevents the men on Palomar from falling, voiceless and blinded, from their tiny, vaulted chairs?

I reel in confusion; I don't understand what I see. With the naked eye I can see two million light-years to the Andromeda galaxy. Often I slop some creek water in a jar and when I get home I dump it in a white china bowl. After the silt settles I return and see tracings of minute snails on the bottom, a planarian or two winding round the rim of water, roundworms shimmying frantically, and finally, when my eyes have adjusted to these dimensions, amoebae. At first the amoebae look like muscae volitantes, those curled moving spots you seem to see in your eyes when you stare at a distant wall. Then I see the amoebae as drops of water congealed, bluish, translucent, like chips of sky in the bowl. At length I choose one individual and give myself over to its idea of an evening. I see it dribble a grainy foot before it on its wet, unfathomable way. Do its unedited sense impressions include the fierce focus of my eyes? Shall I take it outside and show it Andromeda, and blow its little endoplasm? I stir the water with a finger, in case it's running out of oxygen. Maybe I should get a tropical aquarium with motorized bubblers and lights, and keep this one for a pet. Yes, it would tell its fissioned descendants, the universe is two feet by five, and if you listen closely you can hear the buzzing music of the spheres.

Oh, it's mysterious lamplit evenings, here in the galaxy, one after the other. It's one of those nights when I wander from window to window, looking for a sign. But I can't see. Terror and a beauty insoluble are a ribband of blue woven into the fringes of garments of things both great and small. No culture explains, no bivouac offers real haven or rest. But it could be that we are not seeing something. Galileo thought comets were an optical illusion. This is fertile ground: Since we are certain that they're not, we can look at what our scientists have been saying with fresh hope. What if there are *really* gleaming, castellated cities hung upside-down over the desert sand? What limpid lakes and cool date palms have our caravans always passed untried? Until, one by one, by the blindest of leaps, we light on the road to these places, we must stumble in darkness and hunger. I turn from the window. I'm blind as a bat, sensing only from every direction the echo of my own thin cries.

I chanced on a wonderful book by Marius von Senden, called *Space and Light*. When Western surgeons discovered how to perform safe cataract operations, they ranged across Europe and America operating on dozens of men and women of all ages who had been blinded by cataracts since birth. Von Senden collected accounts of such cases; the histories are fascinating. Many doctors had tested their patients' sense perceptions and ideas of space both before and after the operations. The vast majority of patients, of both sexes and all ages, had, in von Senden's opinion, no idea of space whatsoever. Form, distance, and size were so many meaningless syllables. A patient "had no idea of depth, confusing it with roundness." Before the operation a doctor would give a blind patient a cube and a sphere; the patient would tongue it or feel it with his hands, and name it correctly. After the operation the doctor would show the same objects to the patient without letting him touch them; now he had no clue whatsoever what he was seeing. One patient called lemonade "square" because it pricked on his tongue as a square shape pricked on the touch of his hands. Of another postoperative patient, the doctor writes, "I have found in her no notion of size, for example, not even within the narrow limits which she might have encompassed with the aid of touch. Thus when I asked her to show me how big her mother was, she did not stretch out her hands, but set her two index-fingers a few inches apart." Other doctors reported their patients' own statements to similar effect. "The room he was in…he knew to be but part of the house, yet he could not conceive that the whole house could look bigger"; "Those who are blind from birth…have no real conception of height or distance. A house that is a mile away is thought of as nearby, but requiring the taking of a lot of steps…. The elevator that whizzes him up and down gives no more sense of vertical distance than does the train of horizontal."

For the newly sighted, vision is pure sensation unencumbered by meaning: "The girl went through the experience that we all go through and forget, the moment we are born. She saw, but it did not mean anything but a lot of different kinds of brightness." Again, "I asked the patient what he could see; he answered that he saw an extensive field of light, in which everything appeared dull, confused, and in motion. He could not distinguish objects." Another patient saw "nothing but a confusion of forms and colours." When a newly sighted girl saw photographs and paintings, she asked, "'Why do they put those dark marks all over them?' 'Those aren't dark marks,' her mother explained, 'those are shadows. That is one of the ways the eye knows that things have shape. If it were not for shadows many things would look flat.' 'Well, that's how things do look,' Joan answered. 'Everything looks flat with dark patches.'"

But it is the patients' concepts of space that are most revealing. One patient, according to his doctor, "practiced his vision in a strange fashion; thus he takes off one of his boots, throws it some way off in front of him, and then attempts to gauge the distance at which it lies; he takes a few steps toward the boot and tries to grasp it; on failing to reach it, he moves on a step or two and gropes for the boot until he finally gets hold of it." "But even at this stage, after three weeks' experience of seeing," von Senden goes on, "'space,' as he conceives it, ends with visual space, i.e., with color-patches that happen to bound his view. He does not yet have the notion that a larger object (a chair) can mask a smaller one (a dog), or that the latter can still be present even though it is not directly seen."

In general the newly sighted see the world as a dazzle of color-patches. They are pleased by the sensation of color, and learn quickly to name the colors, but the rest of seeing is tormentingly difficult. Soon after his operation a patient "generally bumps into one of these color-patches and observes them to be substantial, since they resist him as tactual objects do. In walking about it also strikes him—or can if he pays attention—that he is continually passing in between the colors he sees, that he can go past a visual object, that a part of it then steadily disappears from view; and that in spite of this, however he twists and turns—whether entering the room from the door, for example, or returning back to it—he always has a visual space in front of him. Thus he gradually comes to realize that there is also a space behind him, which he does not see."

The mental effort involved in these reasonings proves overwhelming for many patients. It oppresses them to realize, if they ever do at all, the tremendous size of the world, which they had previously conceived of as something touchingly manageable. It oppresses them to realize that they have been visible to people all along, perhaps unattractively so, without their knowledge or consent. A disheartening number of them refuse to use their new vision, continuing to go over objects with their tongues, and lapsing into apathy and despair. "The child can see, but will not make use of his sight. Only when pressed can he with difficulty be brought to look at objects in his neighborhood; but more than a foot away it is impossible to bestir him to the necessary effort." Of a twenty-one-year-old girl, the doctor relates, "Her unfortunate father, who had hoped for so much from this operation, wrote that his daughter carefully shuts her eyes whenever she wishes to go about the house, especially when she comes to a staircase, and that she is never happier or more at ease than when, by closing her eyelids, she relapses into her former state of total blindness." A fifteen-year-old boy, who was also in love with a girl at the asylum for the blind, finally blurted out, "No, really, I can't stand it any more; I want to be sent back to the asylum again. If things aren't altered, I'll tear my eyes out."

Some do learn to see, especially the young ones. But it changes their lives. One doctor comments on "the rapid and complete loss of that striking and wonderful serenity which is characteristic only of those who have never yet seen." A blind man who learns to see is ashamed of his old habits. He dresses up, grooms himself, and tries to make a good impression. While he was blind he was indifferent to objects unless they were edible; now, "a sifting of values sets in…his thoughts and wishes are mightily stirred and some few of the patients are thereby led into dissimulation, envy, theft and fraud."

On the other hand, many newly sighted people speak well of the world, and teach us how dull is our own vision. To one patient, a human hand, unrecognized, is "something bright and then holes." Shown a bunch of grapes, a boy calls out, "It is dark, blue and shiny…. It isn't smooth, it has bumps and hollows." A little girl visits a garden. "She is greatly astonished, and can scarcely be persuaded to answer, stands speechless in front of the tree, which she only names on taking hold of it, and then as 'the tree with the lights in it.'" Some delight in their sight and give themselves over to the visual world. Of a patient just after her bandages were removed, her doctor writes, "The first things to attract her attention were her own hands; she looked at them very closely, moved them repeatedly to and fro, bent and stretched the fingers, and seemed greatly astonished at the sight." One girl was eager to tell her blind friend that "men do not really look like trees at all," and astounded to discover that her every visitor had an utterly different face. Finally, a twenty-two-year-old girl was dazzled by the world's brightness and kept her eyes shut for two weeks. When at the end of that time she opened her eyes again, she did not recognize any objects, but, "the more she now directed her gaze upon everything about her, the more it could be seen how an expression of gratification and astonishment overspread her features; she repeatedly exclaimed: 'Oh God! How beautiful!'"

I saw color-patches for weeks after I read this wonderful book. It was summer; the peaches were ripe in the valley orchards. When I woke in the morning, color-patches wrapped round my eyes, intricately, leaving not one unfilled spot. All day long I walked among shifting color-patches that parted before me like the Red Sea and closed again in silence, transfigured, wherever I looked back. Some patches swelled and loomed, while others vanished utterly, and dark marks flitted at random over the whole dazzling sweep. But I couldn't sustain the illusion of flatness. I've been around for too long. Form is condemned to an eternal danse macabre with meaning: I couldn't unpeach the peaches. Nor can I remember ever having seen without understanding: the color-patches of infancy are lost. My brain then must have been smooth as any balloon. I'm told I reached for the moon; many babies do. But the color-patches of infancy swelled as meaning filled them; they arrayed themselves in solemn ranks down distance which unrolled and stretched before me like a plain. The moon rocketed away. I live now in a world of shadows that shape and distance color, a world where space makes a kind of terrible sense. What gnosticism is this, and what physics? The fluttering patch I saw in my nursery window—silver and green and shape-shifting blue—is gone; a row of Lombardy poplars takes its place, mute, across the distant lawn. That humming oblong creature pale as light that stole along the walls of my room at night, stretching exhilaratingly around the corners, is gone, too, gone the night I ate of the bittersweet fruit, put two and two together and puckered forever my brain. Martin Buber tells this tale: "Rabbi Mendel once boasted to his teacher Rabbi Elimelekh that evenings he saw the angel who rolls away the light before the darkness, and mornings the angel who rolls away the darkness before the light. 'Yes,' said Rabbi Elimelekh, 'in my youth I saw that too. Later on you don't see these things any more.'"

Why didn't someone hand those newly sighted people paints and brushes from the start, when they still didn't know what anything was? Then maybe we all could see color-patches too, the world unraveled from reason, Eden before Adam gave names. The scales would drop from my eyes; I'd see trees like men walking; I'd run down the road against all orders, hallooing and leaping.

Seeing is of course very much a matter of verbalization. Unless I call my attention to what passes before my eyes, I simply won't see it. It is, as Ruskin says, "not merely unnoticed, but in the full, clear sense of the word, unseen." My eyes alone can't solve analogy tests using figures, the ones which show, with increasing elaborations, a big square, then a small square in a big square, then a big triangle, and expect me to find a small triangle in a big triangle. I have to say the words, describe what I'm seeing. If Tinker Mountain erupted, I'd be likely to notice. But if I want to notice the lesser cataclysms of valley life, I have to maintain in my head a running description of the present. It's not that I'm observant; it's just that I talk too much. Otherwise, especially in a strange place, I'll never know what's happening. Like a blind man at the ball game, I need a radio.

When I see this way I analyze and pry. I hurl over logs and roll away stones; I study the bank a square foot at a time, probing and tilting my head. Some days when a mist covers the mountains, when the muskrats won't show and the microscope's mirror shatters, I want to climb up the blank blue dome as a man would storm the inside of a circus tent, wildly, dangling, and with a steel knife claw a rent in the top, peep, and, if I must, fall.

But there is another kind of seeing that involves a letting go. When I see this way I sway transfixed and emptied. The difference between the two ways of seeing is the diffrerence between walking with and without a camera. When I walk with a camera I walk from shot to shot, reading the light on a calibrated meter. When I walk without a camera, my own shutter opens, and the moment's light prints on my own silver gut. When I see this second way I am above all an unscrupulous observer.

It was sunny one evening last summer at Tinker Creek; the sun was low in the sky, upstream. I was sitting on the sycamore log bridge with the sunset at my back, watching the shiners the size of minnows who were feeding over the muddy sand in skittery schools. Again and again, one fish, then another, turned for a split second across the current and flash! the sun shot out from its silver side. I couldn't watch for it. It was always just happening somewhere else, and it drew my vision just as it disappeared: flash, like a sudden dazzle of the thinnest blade, a sparking over a dun and olive ground at chance intervals from every direction. Then I noticed white specks, some sort of pale petals, small, floating from under my feet on the creek's surface, very slow and steady. So I blurred my eyes and gazed toward the brim of my hat and saw a new world. I saw the pale white circles roll up, roll up, like the world's turning, mute and perfect, and I saw the linear flashes, gleaming silver, like stars being born at random down a rolling scroll of time. Something broke and something opened. I filled up like a new wineskin. I breathed an air like light; I saw a light like water. I was the lip of a fountain the creek filled forever; I was ether, the leaf in the zephyr; I was flesh-flake, feather, bone.

When I see this way I see truly. As Thoreau says, I return to my senses. I am the man who watches the baseball game in silence in an empty stadium. I see the game purely; I'm abstracted and dazed. When it's all over and the white-suited players lope off the green field to their shadowed dugouts, I leap to my feet; I cheer and cheer.

But I can't go out and try to see this way. I'll fail, I'll go mad. All I can do is try to gag the commentator, to hush the noise of useless interior babble that keeps me from seeing just as surely as a newspaper dangled before my eyes. The effort is really a discipline requiring a lifetime of dedicated struggle; it marks the literature of saints and monks of every order East and West, under every rule and no rule, discalced and shod. The world's spiritual geniuses seem to discover universally that the mind's muddy river, this ceaseless flow of trivia and trash, cannot be dammed, and that trying to dam it is a waste of effort that might lead to madness. Instead you must allow the muddy river to flow unheeded in the dim channels of consciousness; you raise your sights; you look along it, mildly, acknowledging its presence without interest and gazing beyond it into the realm of the real where subjects and objects act and rest purely, without utterance. "Launch into the deep," says Jacques Ellul, "and you shall see."

The secret of seeing is, then, the pearl of great price. If I thought he could teach me to find it and keep it forever I would stagger barefoot across a hundred deserts after any lunatic at all. But although the pearl may be found, it may not be sought. The literature of illumination reveals this above all: Although it comes to those who wait for it, it is always, even to the most practiced and adept, a gift and a total surprise. I return from one walk knowing where the killdeer nests in the field by the creek and the hour the laurel blooms. I return from the same walk a day later scarcely knowing my own name. Litanies hum in my ears; my tongue flaps in my mouth Ailinon, alleluia! I cannot cause light; the most I can do is try to put myself in the path of its beam. It is possible, in deep space, to sail on solar wind. Light, be it particle or wave, has force: you rig a giant sail and go. The secret of seeing is to sail on solar wind. Hone and spread your spirit till you yourself are a sail, whetted, translucent, broadside to the merest puff.

When her doctor took her bandages off and led her into the garden, the girl who was no longer blind saw "the tree with the lights in it." It was for this tree I searched through the peach orchards of summer, in the forests of fall and down winter and spring for years. Then one day I was walking along Tinker Creek thinking of nothing at all and I saw the tree with the lights in it. I saw the backyard cedar where the mourning doves roost charged and transfigured, each cell buzzing with flame. I stood on the grass with the lights in it, grass that was wholly fire, utterly focused and utterly dreamed. It was less like seeing than like being for the first time seen, knocked breathless by a powerful glance. The flood of fire abated, but I'm still spending the power. Gradually the lights went out in the cedar, the colors died, the cells unflamed and disappeared. I was still ringing. I had been my whole life a bell, and never knew it until at that moment I was lifted and struck. I have since only very rarely seen the tree with the lights in it. The vision comes and goes, mostly goes, but I live for it, for the moment when the mountains open and a new light roars in spate through the crack, and the mountains slam.

Mark Edmundson

On the Uses of a
Liberal Education

Mark Edmundson teaches English at the University of Virginia and serves as a contributing editor to *Harper's Magazine*. His "On the Uses of a Liberal Education" examines the collusion between college professors unwilling to challenge the "cool consumer worldview" of their students and students accustomed to education as entertainment. He describes a safe, placid classroom discourse in which both sides seem unable "to see intellectual work as a *confrontation* between two people, student and author, where stakes matter." This example of risk-free classroom exchange highlights the risks that come with a failure to text-wrestle: how taking on demanding thinkers and writers is needed to challenge "established ways of seeing" and to understand "how malleable the present is and how promising and fraught with danger is the future."

I. As Lite Entertainment for
Bored College Students

Today is evaluation day in my Freud class, and everything has changed. The class meets twice a week, late in the afternoon, and the clientele, about fifty undergraduates, tends to drag in and slump, looking disconsolate and a little lost, waiting for a jump start. To get the discussion moving, they usually require a joke, an anecdote, an off-the-wall question—When you were a kid, were your Halloween getups ego costumes, id costumes, or supergo costumes? That sort of thing. But today, as soon as I flourish the forms, a buzz rises in the room. Today they write their assessments of the course, their as-sessments of *me*, and they are without a doubt wide-awake. "What is your evaluation of the instructor?" asks question number eight, entreating them to circle a number between five (excellent) and one (poor, poor). Whatever interpretive subtlety they've acquired during the term is now out the win-dow. Edmundson: one to five, stand and shoot.

And they do. As I retreat through the door—I never stay around for this phase of the ritual—I look over my shoulder and see them toiling away like the devil's auditors. They're pitched into high writing gear, even the ones who struggle to squeeze out their journal entries word by word, stoked on a procedure they have by now supremely mastered. They're playing the in-formed consumer, letting the provider know where he's come through and where he's not quite up to snuff.

But why am I so distressed, bolting like a refugee out of my own class-room, where I usually hold easy sway? Chances are the evaluations will be much like what they've been in the past—they'll be just fine. It's likely that I'll be commended for being "interesting" (and I am commended, many times over), that I'll be cited for my relaxed and tolerant ways (that happens, too), that my sense of humor and capacity to connect the arcana of the sub-ject matter with current culture will come in for some praise (yup). I've been hassled this term, finishing a manuscript, and so haven't given their jour-nals the attention I should have, and for that I'm called—quite civilly, though—to account. Overall, I get off pretty well.

Yet I have to admit that I do not much like the image of myself that emerges from these forms, the image of knowledgeable, humorous detach-ment and bland tolerance. I do not like the forms themselves, with their number ratings, reminiscent of the sheets circulated after the TV pilot has just played to its sample audience in Burbank. Most of all I dislike the atti-tude of calm consumer expertise that pervades the responses. I'm disturbed by the serene belief that my function—and, more important, Freud's, or Shakespeare's, or Blake's—is to divert, entertain, and interest. Observes one respondent, not at all unrepresentative: "Edmundson has done a fantastic job of presenting this difficult, important & controversial material in an en-joyable and approachable way."

Thanks but no thanks. I don't teach to amuse, to divert, or even, for that matter, to be merely interesting. When someone says she "enjoyed" the course—and that word crops up again and again in my evaluations—some-where at the edge of my immediate complacency I feel encroaching self-dislike. That is not at all what I had in mind. The off-the-wall questions and the sidebar jokes are meant as lead-ins to stronger stuff—in the case of the Freud course, to a complexly tragic view of life. But the affability and the one-liners often seem to be all that land with the students; their journals and evaluations leave me little doubt.

I want some of them to say that they've been changed by the course. I want them to measure themselves against what they've read. It's said that some time ago a Columbia University instructor used to issue a harsh two-part question. One: What book did you most dislike in the course? Two: What intellectual or characterological flaws in you does that dislike point to? The hand that framed that question was surely heavy. But at least it compels one to see intellectual work as a confrontation between two people, student and author, where the stakes matter. Those Columbia students were being asked to relate the quality of an *encounter*, not rate the action as though it had unfolded on the big screen.

Why are my students describing the Oedipus complex and the death drive as being interesting and enjoyable to contemplate? And why am I coming across as an urbane, mildly ironic, endlessly affable guide to this intellectual territory, operating without intensity, generous, funny, and loose?

Because that's what works. On evaluation day, I reap the rewards of my partial compliance with the culture of my students and, too, with the culture of the university as it now operates. It's a culture that's gotten little exploration. Current critics tend to think that liberal-arts education is in crisis because universities have been invaded by professors with peculiar ideas: deconstruction, Lacanianism, feminism, queer theory. They believe that genius and tradition are out and that P.C., multiculturalism, and identity politics are in because of an invasion by tribes of tenured radicals, the late millennial equivalents of the Visigoth hordes that cracked Rome's walls.

But mulling over my evaluations and then trying to take a hard, extended look at campus life both here at the University of Virginia and around the country eventually led me to some different conclusions. To me, liberal-arts education is as ineffective as it is now not chiefly because there are a lot of strange theories in the air. (Used well, those theories *can* be illuminating.) Rather, it's that university culture, like American culture writ large, is, to put it crudely, ever more devoted to consumption and entertainment, to the using and using up of goods and images. For someone growing up in America now, there are few available alternatives to the cool consumer worldview. My students didn't ask for that view, much less create it, but they bring a consumer weltanschauung to school, where it exerts a powerful, and largely unacknowledged, influence. If we want to understand current universities, with their multiple woes, we might try leaving the realms of expert debate and fine ideas and turning to the classrooms and campuses, where a new kind of weather is gathering.

From time to time I bump into a colleague in the corridor and we have what I've come to think of as a Joon Lee fest. Joon Lee is one of the best students I've taught. He's endlessly curious, has read a small library's worth, seen every movie, and knows all about showbiz and entertainment. For a class of mine he wrote an essay using Nietzsche's Apollo and Dionysus to analyze the pop group The Supremes. A trite, cultural-studies bonbon? Not at all. He said striking things about conceptions of race in America and about how they shape our ideas of beauty. When I talk with one of his other teachers, we run on about the general splendors of his work and presence. But what inevitably follows a JL fest is a mournful reprise about the divide that separates him and a few other remarkable students from their contemporaries. It's not that some aren't nearly as bright—in terms of intellectual ability, my students are all that I could ask for. Instead, it's that Joon Lee has decided to follow his inter (inter)ests and let them make him into a singular and rather eccentric man; in his charming way, he doesn't mind being at odds with most anyone.

It's his capacity for enthusiasm that sets Joon apart from what I've come to think of as the reigning generational style. Whether the students are sorority/fraternity types, grunge aficionados, piercer/tattooers, black or white, rich or middle class (alas, I teach almost no students from truly poor backgrounds), they are, nearly across the board, very, very self-contained. On good days they display a light, appealing glow; on bad days, shuffling disgruntlement. But there's little fire, little passion to be found.

This point came home to me a few weeks ago when I was wandering across the university grounds. There, beneath a classically cast portico, were two students, male and female, having a rip-roaring argument. They were incensed, bellowing at each other, headstrong, confident, and wild. It struck me how rarely I see this kind of full-out feeling in students anymore. Strong emotional display is forbidden. When conflicts arise, it's generally understood that one of the parties will say something sarcastically propitiating ("whatever" often does it) and slouch away.

How did my students reach this peculiar state in which all passion seems to be spent? I think that many of them have imbibed their sense of self from consumer culture in general and from the tube in particular. They're the progeny of 100 cable channels and omnipresent Blockbuster outlets. TV, Marshall McLuhan famously said, is a cool medium. Those who play best on it are low-key and nonassertive; they blend in. Enthusiasm, à la Joon Lee, quickly looks absurd. The form of character that's most appealing on TV is calmly self-interested though never greedy, attuned to the conventions, and ironic. Judicious timing is preferred to sudden self-assertion. The TV medium is inhospitable to inspiration, improvization, failures, slipups. All must run perfectly.

Naturally, a cool youth culture is a marketing bonanza for producers of the right products, who do all they can to enlarge the culture and keep it grinding. The Internet, TV, and magazines now teem with what I call persona ads, ads for Nikes and Reeboks and Jeeps and Blazers that don't so much endorse the capacities of the product *per se* as show you what sort of person you will be once you've acquired it. The Jeep ad that features hip, outdoorsy kids whipping a Frisbee from mountaintop to mountaintop isn't so much about what Jeeps can do as it is about the kind of people who own them. Buy a Jeep and be one with them. The ad is of little consequence in itself, but expand its message exponentially and you have the central thrust of current consumer culture—buy in order to be.

Most of my students seem desperate to blend in, to look right, not to make a spectacle of themselves. (Do I have to tell you that those two students having the argument under the portico turned out to be acting in a role-playing game?) The specter of the uncool creates a subtle tyranny. It's apparently an easy standard to subscribe to, this Letterman-like, Tarantino-like cool, but once committed to it, you discover that matters are rather different. You're inhibited, except on ordained occasions, from showing emotion, stifled from trying to achieve anything original. You're made to feel that even the slightest departure from the reigning code will get you genially ostracized. This is a culture tensely committed to a laid-back norm.

Am I coming off like something of a crank here? Maybe. Oscar Wilde, who is almost never wrong, suggested that it is perilous to promiscuously contradict people who are much younger than yourself. Point taken. But one of the lessons that consumer hype tries to insinuate is that we must never rebel against the new, never even question it. If it's new—a new need, a new product, a new show, a new style, a new generation—it must be good. So maybe, even at the risk of winning the withered, brown laurels of crankdom, it pays to resist newness-worship and cast a colder eye.

Praise for my students? I have some of that too. What my students are, at their best, is decent. They are potent believers in equality. They help out at the soup kitchen and volunteer to tutor poor kids to get a stripe on their résumés, sure. But they also want other people to have a fair shot. And in their commitment to fairness they are discerning; there you see them at their intellectual best. If I were on trial and innocent, I'd want them on the jury.

What they will not generally do, though, is indict the current system. They won't talk about how the exigencies of capitalism lead to a reserve army of the unemployed and nearly inevitable misery. That would be getting too loud, too brash. For the pervading view is the cool consumer perspective, where passion and strong admiration are forbidden. "To stand in awe of nothing, Numicus, is perhaps the one and only thing that can make a man happy and keep him so," says Horace in the *Epistles*, and I fear that his lines ought to hang as a motto over the university in this era of high consumer capitalism.

It's easy to mount one's high horse and blame the students for this state of affairs. But they didn't create the present culture of consumption. (It was largely my own generation, that of the Sixties, that let the counterculture search for pleasure devolve into a quest for commodities.) And they weren't the ones responsible, when they were six and seven and eight years old, for unplugging the TV set from time to time or for hauling off and kicking a hole through it. It's my generation of parents who sheltered these students, kept them away from the hard knocks of everyday life, making them cautious and overfragile, who demanded that their teachers, from grade school on, flatter them endlessly so that the kids are shocked if their college profs don't reflexively suck up to them.

Of course, the current generational style isn't simply derived from culture and environment. It's also about dollars. Students worry that taking too many chances with their educations will sabotage their future prospects. They're aware of the fact that a drop that looks more and more like one wall of the Grand Canyon separates the top economic tenth from the rest of the population. There's a sentiment currently abroad that if you step aside for a moment, to write, to travel, to fall too hard in love, you might lose position permanently. We may be on a conveyor belt, but it's worse down there on the filth-strewn floor. So don't sound off, don't blow your chance.

But wait. I teach at the famously conservative University of Virginia. Can I extend my view from Charlottesville to encompass the whole country, a whole generation of college students? I can only say that I hear comparable stories about classroom life from colleagues everywhere in America. When I visit other schools to lecture, I see a similar scene unfolding. There are, of course, terrific students everywhere. And they're all the better for the way they've had to strive against the existing conformity. At some of the small liberal-arts colleges, the tradition of strong engagement persists. But overall, the students strike me as being sweet and sad, hovering in a nearly suspended animation.

Too often now the pedagogical challenge is to make a lot from a little. Teaching Wordsworth's "Tintern Abbey," you ask for comments. No one responds. So you call on Stephen. Stephen: "The sound, this poem really flows." You: "Stephen seems interested in the music of the poem. We might extend his comment to ask if this poem's music coheres with its argument. Are they consistent? Or is there an emotional pain submerged here that's contrary to the poem's appealing melody?" All right, it's not usually that bad. But close. One friend describes it as rebound teaching: they proffer a weightless comment, you hit it back for all you're worth, then it comes dribbling out again. Occasionally a professor will try to explain away this intellectual timidity by describing the students as perpetrators of postmodern irony, a highly sophisticated mode. Everything's a slick counterfeit, a simulacrum, so by no means should any phenomenon be taken seriously. But the students don't have the urbane, Oscar Wilde–type demeanor that should go with this view. Oscar was cheerful, funny, confident, strange. (Wilde, mortally ill, living in a Paris flophouse: "My wallpaper and I are fighting a duel to the death. One or the other of us has to go.") This generation's style is considerate, easy to please, and a touch depressed.

Granted, you might say, the kids come to school immersed in a consumer mentality—they're good Americans, after all—but then the university and the professors do everything in their power to fight that dreary mind-set in the interest of higher ideals, right? So it should be. But let us look at what is actually coming to pass.

Over the past few years, the physical layout of my university has been changing. To put it a little indecorously, the place is looking more and more like a retirement spread for the young. Our funds go to construction, into new dorms, into renovating the student union. We have a new aquatics center and ever-improving gyms, stocked with StairMasters and Nautilus machines. Engraved on the wall in the gleaming aquatics building is a line by our founder, Thomas Jefferson, declaring that everyone ought to get about two hours' exercise a day. Clearly even the author of the Declaration of Independence endorses the turning of his university into a sports-and-fitness emporium.

But such improvements shouldn't be surprising. Universities need to attract the best (that is, the smartest *and* the richest) students in order to survive in an ever more competitive market. Schools want kids whose parents can pay the full freight, not the ones who need scholarships or want to bargain down the tuition costs. If the marketing surveys say that the kids require sports centers, then, trustees willing, they shall have them. In fact, as I began looking around, I came to see that more and more of what's going on in the university is customer driven. The consumer pressures that beset me on evaluation day are only a part of an overall trend.

From the start, the contemporary university's relationship with students has a solicitous, nearly servile tone. As soon as someone enters his junior year in high school, and especially if he's living in a prosperous zip code, the informational material—the advertising—comes flooding in. Pictures, testimonials, videocassettes, and CD ROMs (some bidden, some not) arrive at the door from colleges across the country, all trying to capture the student and his tuition cash. The freshman-to-be sees photos of well-appointed dorm rooms; of elaborate phys-ed facilities; of fine dining rooms; of expertly kept sports fields; of orchestras and drama troupes; of students working alone (no overbearing grown-ups in range), peering with high seriousness into computers and microscopes; or of students arrayed outdoors in attractive conversational garlands.

Occasionally—but only occasionally, for we usually photograph rather badly; in appearance we tend at best to be styleless—there's a professor teaching a class. (The college catalogues I received, by my request only, in the late Sixties were austere affairs full of professors' credentials and course descriptions; it was clear on whose terms the enterprise was going to unfold.) A college financial officer recently put matters to me in concise, if slightly melodramatic, terms: "Colleges don't have admissions offices anymore, they have marketing departments." Is it surprising that someone who has been approached with photos and tapes, bells and whistles, might come in thinking that the Freud and Shakespeare she had signed up to study were also going to be agreeable treats?

How did we reach this point? In part the answer is a matter of demographics and (surprise) of money. Aided by the G.I. bill, the college-going population in America dramatically increased after the Second World War. Then came the baby boomers, and to accommodate them, schools continued to grow. Universities expand easily enough, but with tenure locking faculty in for lifetime jobs, and with the general reluctance of administrators to eliminate their own slots, it's not easy for a university to contract. So after the baby boomers had passed through—like a fat meal digested by a boa constrictor—the college turned to energetic promotional strategies to fill the empty chairs. And suddenly college became a buyer's market. What students and their parents wanted had to be taken more and more into account. That usually meant creating more comfortable, less challenging environments, places where almost no one failed, everything was enjoyable, and everyone was nice.

Just as universities must compete with one another for students, so must the individual departments. At a time of rank economic anxiety, the English and history majors have to contend for students against the more success-insuring branches, such as the sciences and the commerce school. In 1968, more than 21 percent of all the bachelor's degrees conferred in America were in the humanities; by 1993, that number had fallen to about 13 percent. The humanities now must struggle to attract students, many of whose parents devoutly wish they would study something else.

One of the ways we've tried to stay attractive is by loosening up. We grade much more softly than our colleagues in science. In English, we don't give many Ds, or Cs for that matter. (The rigors of Chem 101 create almost as many English majors per year as do the splendors of Shakespeare.) A professor at Stanford recently explained grade inflation in the humanities by observing that the undergraduates were getting smarter every year; the higher grades simply recorded how much better they were than their predecessors. Sure.

Along with softening the grades, many humanities departments have relaxed major requirements. There are some good reasons for introducing more choice into curricula and requiring fewer standard courses. But the move, like many others in the university now, jibes with a tendency to serve—and not challenge—the students. Students can also float in and out of classes during the first two weeks of each term without making any commitment. The common name for this time span—shopping period—speaks volumes about the consumer mentality that's now in play. Usually, too, the kids can drop courses up until the last month with only an innocuous "W" on their transcripts. Does a course look too challenging? No problem. Take it pass-fail. A happy consumer is, by definition, one with multiple options, one who can always have what he wants. And since a course is something the students and their parents have bought and paid for, why can't they do with it pretty much as they please?

A sure result of the university's widening elective leeway is to give students more power over their teachers. Those who don't like you can simply avoid you. If the clientele dislikes you *en masse*, you can be left without students, period. My first term teaching I walked into my introduction to poetry course and found it inhabited by one student, the gloriously named Bambi Lynn Dean. Bambi and I chatted amiably awhile, but for all that she and the pleasure of her name could offer, I was fast on the way to meltdown. It was all a mistake, luckily, a problem with the scheduling book. Everyone was waiting for me next door. But in a dozen years of teaching I haven't forgotten that feeling of being ignominiously marooned. For it happens to others, and not always because of scheduling glitches. I've seen older colleagues go through hot embarrassment at not having enough students sign up for their courses: they graded too hard, demanded too much, had beliefs too far out of keeping with the existing disposition. It takes only a few such instances to draw other members of the professoriat further into line.

And if what's called tenure reform—which generally just means the abolition of tenure—is broadly enacted, professors will be yet more vulnerable to the whims of their customer-students. Teach what pulls the kids in, or walk. What about entire departments that don't deliver? If the kids say no to Latin and Greek, is it time to dissolve classics? Such questions are being entertained more and more seriously by university administrators.

How does one prosper with the present clientele? Many of the most successful professors now are the ones who have "decentered" their classrooms. There's a new emphasis on group projects and on computer-generated exchanges among the students. What they seem to want most is to talk to one another. A classroom now is frequently an "environment," a place highly conducive to the exchange of existing ideas, the students' ideas. Listening to one another, students sometimes change their opinions. But what they generally can't do is acquire a new vocabulary, a new perspective, that will cast issues in a fresh light.

The Socratic method—the animated, sometimes impolite give-and-take between student and teacher—seems too jagged for current sensibilities. Students frequently come to my office to tell me how intimidated they feel in class; the thought of being embarrassed in front of the group fills them with dread. I remember a student telling me how humiliating it was to be corrected by the teacher, by me. So I asked the logical question: "Should I let a major factual error go by so as to save discomfort?" The student—a good student, smart and earnest—said that was a tough question. He'd need to think about it.

Disturbing? Sure. But I wonder, are we really getting students ready for Socratic exchange with professors when we push them off into vast lecture rooms, two and three hundred to a class, sometimes face them with only grad students until their third year, and signal in our myriad professorial ways that we often have much better things to do than sit in our offices and talk with them? How bad will the student-faculty ratios have to become, how teeming the lecture courses, before we hear students righteously complaining, as they did thirty years ago, about the impersonality of their schools, about their decline into knowledge factories? "This is a firm," said Mario Savio at Berkeley during the Free Speech protests of the Sixties, "and if the Board of Regents are the board of directors, …then…the faculty are a bunch of employees and we're the raw material. But we're a bunch of raw material that don't mean…to be made into any product."

Teachers who really do confront students, who provide significant challenges to what they believe, *can* be very successful, granted. But sometimes such professors generate more than a little trouble for themselves. A controversial teacher can send students hurrying to the deans and the counselors, claiming to have been offended. ("Offensive" is the preferred term of repugnance today, just as "enjoyable" is the summit of praise.) Colleges have brought in hordes of counselors and deans to make sure that everything is smooth, serene, unflustered, that everyone has a good time. To the counselor, to the dean, and to the university legal squad, that which is normal, healthy, and prudent is best.

An air of caution and deference is everywhere. When my students come to talk with me in my office, they often exhibit a Franciscan humility. "Do you have a moment?" "I know you're busy. I won't take up much of your time." Their presences tend to be very light; they almost never change the temperature of the room. The dress is nondescript: clothes are in earth tones; shoes are practical—cross-trainers, hiking boots, work shoes. Dr. Martens, with now and then a stylish pair of raised-sole boots on one of the young women. Many, male and female both, peep from beneath the bills of monogrammed baseball caps. Quite a few wear sports, or even corporate, logos, sometimes on one piece of clothing but occasionally (and disconcertingly) on more. The walk is slow; speech is careful, sweet, a bit weary, and without strong inflection. (After the first lively week of the term, most seem far in debt to sleep.) They are almost unfailingly polite. They don't want to offend me; I could hurt them, savage their grades.

Naturally, there are exceptions, kids I chat animatedly with, who offer a joke, or go on about this or that new CD (almost never a book, no). But most of the traffic is genially sleepwalking. I have to admit that I'm a touch wary, too. I tend to hold back. An unguarded remark, a joke that's taken to be off-color, or simply an uncomprehended comment can lead to difficulties. I keep it literal. They scare me a little, these kind and melancholy students, who themselves seem rather frightened of their own lives.

Before they arrive, we ply the students with luscious ads, guaranteeing them a cross between summer camp and lotusland. When they get here, flattery and nonstop entertainment are available, if that's what they want. And when they leave? How do we send our students out into the world? More and more, our administrators call the booking agents and line up one or another celebrity to usher the graduates into the millennium. This past spring, Kermit the Frog won himself an honorary degree at Southampton College on Long Island; Bruce Willis and Yogi Berra took credentials away at Montclair State; Arnold Schwarzenegger scored at the University of Wisconsin-Superior. At Wellesley, Oprah Winfrey gave the commencement address. (*Wellesley*—one of the most rigorous academic colleges in the nation.) At the University of Vermont, Whoopi Goldberg laid down the word. But why should a worthy administrator contract the likes of Susan Sontag, Christopher Hitchens, or Robert Hughes—someone who might actually say something, something disturbing, something "offensive"—when he can get what the parents and kids apparently want and what the newspapers will softly commend—more lite entertainment, more TV?

Is it a surprise, then, that this generation of students—steeped in consumer culture before going off to school, treated as potent customers by the university well before their date of arrival, then pandered to from day one until the morning of the final kiss-off from Kermit or one of his kin—are inclined to see the books they read as a string of entertainment to be placidly enjoyed or languidly cast down? Given the way universities are now administered (which is more and more to say, given the way that they are currently marketed), is it a shock that the kids don't come to school hot to learn, unable to bear their own ignorance? For some measure of self-dislike, or self-discontent—which is much different than simple depression—seems to me to be a prerequisite for getting an education that matters. My students, alas, usually lack the confidence to acknowledge what would be their most precious asset for learning: their ignorance.

Not long ago, I asked my Freud class a question that, however hoary, never fails to solicit intriguing responses: Who are your heroes? Whom do you admire? After one remarkable answer, featuring T. S. Eliot as hero, a series of generic replies rolled in, one gray wave after the next: my father, my best friend, a doctor who lives in our town, my high school history teacher. Virtually all the heroes were people my students had known personally, people who had done something local, specific, and practical, and had done it for them. They were good people, unselfish people, these heroes, but most of all they were people who had delivered the goods.

My students' answers didn't exhibit any philosophical resistance to the idea of greatness. It's not that they had been primed by their professors with complex arguments to combat genius. For the truth is that these students don't need debunking theories. Long before college, skepticism became their habitual mode. They are the progeny of Bart Simpson and David Letterman, and the hyper-cool ethos of the box. It's inane to say that theorizing professors have created them, as many conservative critics like to do. Rather, they have substantially created a university environment in which facile skepticism can thrive without being substantially contested.

Skeptical approaches have *potential* value. If you have no all-encompassing religious faith, no faith in historical destiny, the future of the West, or anything comparably grand, you need to acquire your vision of the world somewhere. If it's from literature, then the various visions literature offers have to be inquired into skeptically. Surely it matters that women are denigrated in Milton and in Pope, that some novelistic voices assume an overbearing godlike authority, that the poor are, in this or that writer, inevitably cast as clowns. You can't buy all of literature wholesale if it's going to help draw your patterns of belief.

But demystifying theories are now overused, applied mechanically. It's all logocentrism, patriarchy, ideology. And in this the student environment—laid-back, skeptical, knowing—is, I believe, central. Full-out debunking is what plays with this clientele. Some have been doing it nearly as long as, if more crudely than, their deconstructionist teachers. In the context of the contemporary university, and cool consumer culture, a useful intellectual skepticism has become exaggerated into a fundamentalist caricature of itself. The teachers have buckled to their students' views.

At its best, multiculturalism can be attractive as well-deployed theory. What could be more valuable than encountering the best work of far-flung cultures and becoming a citizen of the world? But in the current consumer environment, where flattery plays so well, the urge to encounter the other can devolve into the urge to find others who embody and celebrate the right ethnic origins. So we put aside the African novelist Chinua Achebe's abrasive, troubling *Things Fall Apart* and gravitate toward hymns on Africa, cradle of all civilizations.

What about the phenomenon called political correctness? Raising the standard of civility and tolerance in the university has been—who can deny it?—a very good thing. Yet this admirable impulse has expanded to the point where one is enjoined to speak well—and only well—of women, blacks, gays, the disabled, in fact of virtually everyone. And we can owe this expansion in many ways to the student culture. Students now do not wish to be criticized, not in any form. (The culture of consumption never criticizes them, at least not *overtly*.) In the current university, the movement for urbane tolerance has devolved into an imperative against critical reaction, turning much of the intellectual life into a dreary Sargasso Sea. At a certain point, professors stopped being usefully sensitive and became more like careful retailers who have it as a cardinal point of doctrine never to piss the customers off.

To some professors, the solution lies in the movement called cultural studies. What students need, they believe, is to form a critical perspective on pop culture. It's a fine idea, no doubt. Students should be able to run a critical commentary against the stream of consumer stimulations in which they're immersed. But cultural-studies programs rarely work, because no matter what you propose by way of analysis, things tend to bolt downhill toward an uncritical discussion of students' tastes, into what they like and don't like. If you want to do a Frankfurt School-style analysis of *Braveheart*, you can be pretty sure that by mid-class Adorno and Horkeimer will be consigned to the junk heap of history and you'll be collectively weighing the charms of Mel Gibson. One sometimes wonders if cultural studies hasn't prospered because, under the guise of serious intellectual analysis, it gives the customers what they most want—easy pleasure, more TV. Cultural studies becomes nothing better than what its detractors claim it is—Madonna studies—when students kick loose from the critical perspective and groove to the product, and that, in my experience teaching film and pop culture, happens plenty.

On the issue of genius, as on multiculturalism and political correctness, we professors of the humanities have, I think, also failed to press back against our students' consumer tastes. Here we tend to nurse a pair of—to put it charitably—disparate views. In one mode, we're inclined to a programmatic debunking criticism. We call the concept of genius into question. But in our professional lives per se, we aren't usually disposed against the idea of distinguished achievement. We argue animatedly about the caliber of potential colleagues. We support a star system, in which some professors are far better paid, teach less, and under better conditions than the rest. In our own profession, we are creating a system that is the mirror image of the one we're dismantling in the curriculum. Ask a professor what she thinks of the work of Stephen Greenblatt, a leading critic of Shakespeare, and you'll hear it for an hour. Ask her what her views are on Shakespeare's genius and she's likely to begin questioning the term along with the whole "discourse of evaluation." This dual sensibility may be intellectually incoherent. But in its awareness of what plays with students, it's conducive to good classroom evaluations and, in its awareness of where and how the professional bread is buttered, to self-advancement as well.

My overall point is this: It's not that a left-wing professorial coup has taken over the university. It's that at American universities, left-liberal politics have collided with the ethos of consumerism. The consumer ethos is winning.

Then how do those who at least occasionally promote genius and high literary ideals look to current students? How do we appear, those of us who take teaching to be something of a performance art and who imagine that if you give yourself over completely to your subject you'll be rewarded with insight beyond what you individually command?

I'm reminded of an old piece of newsreel footage I saw once. The speaker (perhaps it was Lenin, maybe Trotsky) was haranguing a large crowd. He was expostulating, arm waving, carrying on. Whether it was flawed technology or the man himself, I'm not sure, but the orator looked like an intricate mechanical device that had sprung into fast-forward. To my students, who mistrust enthusiasm in every form, that's me when I start riffing about Freud or Blake. But more and more, as my evaluations showed, I've been replacing enthusiasm and intellectual animation with stand-up routines, keeping it all at arms length, praising under the cover of irony.

It's too bad that the idea of genius has been denigrated so far, because it actually offers a live alternative to the demoralizing culture of hip in which most of my students are mired. By embracing the works and lives of extraordinary people, you can adapt new ideals to revise those that came courtesy of your parents, your neighborhood, your clan—or the tube. The aim of a good liberal-arts education was once, to adapt an observation by the scholar Walter Jackson Bate, to see that "we need not be the passive victims of what we deterministically call 'circumstances' (social, cultural, or reductively psychological-personal), but that by linking ourselves through what Keats calls an 'immortal free-masonry' with the great we can become freer— freer to be ourselves, to be what we most want and value."

But genius isn't just a personal standard; genius can also have political effect. To me, one of the best things about democratic thinking is the conviction that genius can spring up anywhere. Walt Whitman is born into the working class and thirty-six years later we have a poetic image of America that gives a passionate dimension to the legalistic brilliance of the Constitution. A democracy needs to constantly develop, and to do so it requires the most powerful visionary minds to interpret the present and to propose possible shapes for the future. By continuing to notice and praise genius, we create a culture in which the kind of poetic gamble that Whitman made—a gamble in which failure would have entailed rank humiliation, depression, maybe suicide—still takes place. By rebelling against established ways of seeing and saying things, genius helps us to apprehend how malleable the present is and how promising and fraught with danger is the future. If we teachers do not endorse genius and self-overcoming, can we be surprised when our students find their ideal images in TV's latest persona ads?

A world uninterested in genius is a despondent place, whose sad denizens drift from coffee bar to Prozac dispensary, unfired by ideals, by the glowing image of the self that one might become. As Northrop Frye says in a beautiful and now dramatically unfashionable sentence, "The artist who uses the same energy and genius that Homer and Isaiah had will find that he not only lives in the same palace of art as Homer and Isaiah, but lives in it at the same time." We ought not to deny the existence of such a place simply because we, or those we care for, find the demands it makes intimidating, the rent too high.

What happens if we keep trudging along this bleak course? What happens if our most intelligent students never learn to strive to overcome what they are? What if genius, and the imitation of genius, become silly, outmoded ideas? What you're likely to get are more and more one-dimensional men and women. These will be people who live for easy pleasures, for comfort and prosperity, who think of money first, then second, and third, who hug the status quo; people who believe in God as a sort of insurance policy (cover your bets); people who are never surprised. They will be people so pleased with themselves (when they're not in despair at the general pointlessness of their lives) that they cannot imagine humanity could do better. They'll think it their highest duty to clone themselves as frequently as possible. They'll claim to be happy, and they'll live a long time.

It is probably time now to offer a spate of inspiring solutions. Here ought to come a list of reforms, with due notations about a core curriculum and various requirements. What the traditionalists who offer such solutions miss is that no matter what our current students are given to read, many of them will simply translate it into melodrama, with flat characters and predictable morals. (The unabated capitalist culture that conservative critics so often endorse has put students in a position to do little else.) One can't simply wave a curricular wand and reverse acculturation.

Perhaps it would be a good idea to try firing the counselors and sending half the deans back into their classrooms, dismantling the football team and making the stadium into a playground for local kids, emptying the fraternities, and boarding up the student-activities office. Such measures would convey the message that American colleges are not northern outposts of Club Med. A willingness on the part of the faculty to defy student conviction and affront them occasionally—to be usefully offensive—also might not be a bad thing. We professors talk a lot about subversion, which generally means subverting the views of people who never hear us talk or read our work. But to subvert the views of our students, our customers, that would be something else again.

Ultimately, though, it is up to individuals—and individual students in particular—to make their own way against the current sludgy tide. There's still the library, still the museum, there's still the occasional teacher who lives to find things greater than herself to admire. There are still fellow students who have not been cowed. Universities are inefficient, cluttered, archaic places, with many unguarded corners where one can open a book or gaze out onto the larger world and construe it freely. Those who do as much, trusting themselves against the weight of current opinion, will have contributed something to bringing this sad dispensation to an end. As for myself, I'm canning my low-key one-liners; when the kids' TV-based tastes come to the fore, I'll aim and shoot. And when it's time to praise genius, I'll try to do it in the right style, full-out, with faith that finer artistic spirits (maybe not Homer and Isaiah quite, but close, close), still alive somewhere in the ether, will help me out when my invention flags, the students doze, or the dean mutters into the phone. I'm getting back to a more exuberant style; I'll be expostulating and arm waving straight into the millenium, yes I will.

Thomas Frank
Why Johnny Can't Dissent

Thomas Frank is the editor-in-chief of *The Baffler*, a journal designed
to confront and challenge a world equipped with "an ad on every
surface, a demographic on every face, and a A&R man in every avant-
garde." His essay for this collection, "Why Johnny Can't Dissent," asks
the simple question: what do you do when big business wants to look
like a rebel and the rebels are wearing brand name logos? According
to Frank, the world of business is no longer one of rigid "lifestyle con-
servatism": blue-suits, graphs, gated communities, board rooms
stocked with copies of the *Wall Street Journal* and *Harvard Business
Week*. No longer does corporate America dream of itself driving the
quiet, tree-shaded lanes in Dad's Oldsmobile; it roars down the highway on a Harley, a dog-eared copy of *On the Road* in hand, and a
wild ear-shattering *whoop* just audible over the rock n' roll on the
stereo. Corporate America, according to Frank, wants to be with-it,
hip, and above all rebellious as the punks of yesteryear. Frank asks us:
is this rebellion? *Can* corporate America strut like James Dean? *Can*
power rap with the masses? *Can* Coke really be *It*? Frank's essay res-
onates well with Mark Crispin Miller's "Deride & Conquer," as both
discuss ways in which consumer capitalism, through television and
advertising, alters and influences the way we understand the world.

> The public be damned! I work for my stockholders.
> —William H. Vanderbilt, 1879

> Break the rules. Stand apart. Keep your head. Go
> with your heart.
> —TV commercial for Vanderbilt perfume, 1994

Capitalism is changing, obviously and drastically. From the moneyed pages
of the *Wall Street Journal* to TV commercials for airlines and photocopiers

we hear every day about the new order's globe-spanning, cyber-accumulating ways. But our notion about what's wrong with American life and how the figures responsible are to be confronted haven't changed much in thirty years. Call it, for convenience, the "countercultural idea." It holds that the paramount ailment of our society is conformity, a malady that has variously been described as over-organization, bureaucracy, homogeneity, hierarchy, logocentrism, technocracy, the Combine, the Apollonian. We all know what it is and what it does. It transforms humanity into "organization man," into "the man in the gray flannel suit." It is "Moloch whose mind is pure machinery," the "incomprehensible prison" that consumes "brains and imagination." It is artifice, starched shirts, tailfins, carefully mowed lawns, and always, always, the consciousness of impending nuclear destruction. It is a stiff, militaristic order that seeks to suppress instinct, to forbid sex and pleasure, to deny basic human impulses and individuality, to enforce through a rigid uniformity a meaningless plastic consumerism.

As this half of the countercultural idea originated during the 1950s, it is appropriate that the evils of conformity are most conveniently summarized with images of 1950s suburban correctness. You know, that land of sedate music, sexual repression, deference to authority, Red Scares, and smiling white people standing politely in line to go to church. Constantly appearing as a symbol of arch-backwardness in advertising and movies, it is an image we find easy to evoke.

The ways in which this system are to be resisted are equally well understood and agreed-upon. The Establishment demands homogeneity; we revolt by embracing diverse, individual lifestyles. It demands self-denial and rigid adherence to convention; we revolt through immediate gratification, instinct uninhibited, and liberation of the libido and the appetites. Few have put it more bluntly than Jerry Rubin did in 1970: "Amerika says: Don't! The yippies say: Do It!" The countercultural idea is hostile to any law and every establishment. "Whenever we see a rule, we must break it," Rubin continued. "Only by breaking rules do we discover who we are." Above all rebellion consists of a sort of Nietzschean antinomianism, an automatic questioning of rules, a rejection of whatever social prescriptions we've happened to inherit. Just Do It is the whole of the law.

The patron saints of the countercultural idea are, of course, the Beats, whose frenzied style and merry alienation still maintain a powerful grip on the American imagination. Even forty years after the publication of *On the Road*, the works of Kerouac, Ginsberg, and Burroughs remain the *sine qua non* of dissidence, the model for aspiring poets, rock stars, or indeed anyone who feels vaguely artistic or alienated. That frenzied sensibility of pure experience, life on the edge, immediate gratification, and total freedom from moral restraint, which the Beats first propounded back in those heady days when suddenly everyone could have their own TV and powerful V-8, has stuck with us through all the intervening years and become something of a permanent American Style. Go to any poetry reading and you can see a string of junior Kerouacs go through the routine, upsetting cultural hierarchies by pushing themselves to the limit, straining for that gorgeous moment of original vice when Allen Ginsberg first read "Howl" in 1955 and the patriarchs of our fantasies recoiled in shock. The Gap may have since claimed Ginsberg and *USA Today* may run feature stories about the brilliance of the beloved Kerouac, but the rebel race continues today regardless, with ever-heightening shit-references calculated to scare Jesse Helms, talk about sex and smack that is supposed to bring the electricity of real life, and ever-more determined defiance of the repressive rules and mores of the American 1950s—rules and mores that by now we know only from movies.

But one hardly has to go to a poetry reading to see the countercultural idea acted out. Its frenzied ecstasies have long since become an official aesthetic of consumer society, a monotheme of mass as well as adversarial culture. Turn on the TV and there it is instantly: the unending drama of consumer unbound and in search of an ever-heightened good time, the inescapable rock 'n' roll soundtrack, dreadlocks and ponytails bounding into Taco Bells, a drunken, swinging-camera epiphany of tennis shoes, outlaw soda pops, and mind-bending dandruff shampoos. Corporate America, it turns out, no longer speaks in the voice of oppressive order that it did when Ginsberg moaned in 1956 that *Time* magazine was

> always telling me about responsibility. Business-
> men are serious. Movie producers are serious.
> Everybody's serious but me.

Nobody wants you to think they're serious today, least of all Time Warner. On the contrary: the Culture Trust is now our leader in the Ginsbergian search for kicks upon kicks. Corporate America is not an oppressor but a sponsor of fun, provider of lifestyle accoutrements, facilitator of carnival, our slang-speaking partner in the quest for that ever-more apocalyptic orgasm. The countercultural idea has become capitalist orthodoxy, its hunger for transgression upon transgression now perfectly suited to an economic-cultural regime that runs on ever-faster cyclings of the new; its taste for self-fulfillment and its intolerance for the confines of tradition now permitting vast latitude in consuming practices and lifestyle experimentation.

Consumerism is no longer about "conformity" but about "difference." Advertising teaches us not in the ways of puritanical self-denial (a bizarre notion on the face of it), but in orgiastic, never-ending self-fulfillment. It counsels not rigid adherence to the tastes of the herd but vigilant and constantly updated individualism. We consume not to fit in, but to prove, on the surface at least, that we are rock 'n' roll rebels, each one of us as rule-breaking and hierarchy-defying as our heroes of the 60s, who now pitch cars, shoes, and beer. This imperative of endless difference is today the genius at the heart of American capitalism, and eternal fleeing from "sameness" that satiates our thirst for the New with such achievements of civilization as the infinite brands of identical cola, the myriad colors and irrepressible variety of the cigarette rack at 7-Eleven.

As existential rebellion has become a more or less official style of Information Age capitalism, so has the countercultural notion of a static, repressive Establishment grown hopelessly obsolete. However the basic impulses of the countercultural idea may have disturbed a nation lost in Cold War darkness, they are today in fundamental agreement with the basic tenets of Information Age business theory. So close are they, in fact, that it has become difficult to understand the countercultural idea as anything more than the self-justifying ideology of the new bourgeoisie that has arisen since the 1960s, the cultural means by which this group has proven itself ever so much better skilled than its slow-moving, security-minded forebears at adapting to the accelerated, always-changing consumerism of today. The anointed cultural opponents of capitalism are now capitalism's ideologues.

The two come together in perfect synchronization in a figure like Camille Paglia, whose ravings are grounded in the absolutely noncontroversial ideas of the golden sixties. According to Paglia, American business is still exactly what it was believed to have been in that beloved decade, that is, "puritanical and desensualized." Its great opponents are, of course, liberated figures like "the beatniks," Bob Dylan, and the Beatles. Culture is, quite simply, a binary battle between the repressive Apollonian order of capitalism and the Dionysian impulses of the counterculture. Rebellion makes no sense without repression; we must remain forever convinced of capitalism's fundamental hostility to pleasure in order to consume capitalism's rebel products as avidly as we do. It comes as little surprise when, after criticizing the "Apollonian capitalist machine" (in her book, *Vamps & Tramps*), Paglia applauds American mass culture (in *Utne Reader*), the preeminent product of the "capitalist machine," as a "third great eruption" of a Dionysian "paganism." For her, as for most other designated dissidents, there is no contradiction between replaying the standard critique of capitalist conformity and repressiveness and then endorsing its rebel products—for Paglia the car culture and Madonna—as the obvious solution: the Culture Trust offers both Establishment and Resistance in one convenient package. The only question that remains is why Paglia has not yet landed an endorsement contract from a soda pop or automobile manufacturer.

Other legendary exponents of the countercultural idea have been more fortunate—William S. Burroughs, for example, who appears in a television spot for the Nike corporation. But so openly does the commercial flaunt the confluence of capital and counterculture that it has brought considerable criticism down on the head of the aging beat. Writing in the *Village Voice*, Leslie Savan marvels at the contradiction between Burroughs' writings and the faceless corporate entity for which he is now pushing product. "Now the realization that *nothing* threatens the system has freed advertising to exploit even the most marginal element of society, " Savan observes. "In fact, being hip is no longer quite enough—better the pitchman be 'underground.'" Meanwhile Burroughs' manager insists, as all future Cultural Studies treatments of the ad will no doubt also insist, that Burroughs' presence actually makes the commercial "deeply subversive"—"I hate to repeat the usual mantra, but you know, homosexual drug addict, manslaughter, accidental homicide." But Savan wonders whether, in fact, it is Burroughs who has been assimilated by corporate America. "The problem comes, " she writes, "in how easily any idea, deed, or image can become part of the sponsored world."

The most startling revelation to emerge from the Burroughs/Nike partnership is not that corporate America has overwhelmed its cultural foes or that Burroughs can somehow remain "subversive" through it all, but the complete lack of dissonance between the two sides. Of course Burroughs is not "subversive," but neither has he "sold out": His ravings are no longer appreciably different from the official folklore of American capitalism. What's changed is not Burroughs, but business itself. As expertly as Burroughs once bayoneted American proprieties, as stridently as he once proclaimed himself beyond the laws of man and God, he is today a respected ideologue of the Information Age, occupying roughly the position in the pantheon of corporate-cultural thought once reserved strictly for Notre Dame football coaches and positive-thinking Methodist ministers. His inspirational writings are boardroom favorites, his dark nihilistic burpings the happy homilies of the new corporate faith.

For with the assumption of power by Drucker's and Reich's new class has come an entirely new ideology of business, a way of justifying and exercising power that has little to do with the "conformity" and the "establishment" so vilified by the countercultural idea. The management theorists and "leadership" charlatans of the Information Age don't waste their time prattling about hierarchy and regulation, but about disorder, chaos, and the meaninglessness of convention. With its reorganization around information, capitalism has developed a new mythology, a sort of corporate antinomianism according to which the breaking of rules and the elimination of rigid corporate structure have become the central article of faith for millions of aspiring executives.

Dropping *Naked Lunch* and picking up *Thriving on Chaos*, the ground-breaking 1987 management text by Tom Peters, the most popular business writer of the past decade, one finds more philosophical similarities than one would expect from two manifestos of, respectively, dissident culture and business culture. If anything, Peters' celebration of disorder is, by virtue of its hard statistics, bleaker and more nightmarish than Burroughs'. For this popular lecturer on such once-blithe topics as competitiveness and pop psychology there is nothing, absolutely nothing, that is certain. His world is one in which the corporate wisdom of the past is meaningless, established customs are ridiculous, and "rules" are some sort of curse, a remnant of the foolish fifties that exist to be defied, not obeyed. We live in what Peters calls "A World Turned Upside Down," in which whirl is king and, in order to survive, businesses must eventually embrace Peters' universal solution: "Revolution!" "To meet the demands of the fast-changing competitive scene," he counsels, "we must simply learn to love change as much as we have hated it in the past." He advises businessmen to become Robespierres of routine, to demand of their underlings, "'What have you changed lately?' 'How fast are you changing?' and 'Are you pursuing bold enough change goals?'" "Revolution," of course, means for Peters the same thing it did to Burroughs and Ginsberg, Presley and the Stones in their heyday: breaking rules, pissing off the suits, shocking the bean-counters: "Actively and publicly hail defiance of the rules, many of which you doubtless labored mightily to construct in the first place." Peters even suggests that his readers implement this hostility to logocentrism in a carnivalesque celebration, drinking beer out in "the woods" and destroying "all the forms and rules and discontinued reports" and, "if you've got real nerve," a photocopier as well.

Today corporate antinomianism is the emphatic message of nearly every new business text, continually escalating the corporate insurrection begun by Peters. Capitalism, at least as it is envisioned by the best-selling management handbooks, is no longer about enforcing Order, but destroying it. "Revolution," once the totemic catchphrase of the counterculture, has become the totemic catchphrase of boomer-as-capitalist. The Information Age businessman holds inherited ideas and traditional practices not in reverence, but in high suspicion. Even reason itself is now found to be an enemy of true competitiveness, an out-of-date faculty to be scrupulously avoided by conscientious managers. A 1990 book by Charles Handy entitled *The Age of Unreason* agrees with Peters that we inhabit a time in which "there can be no certainty" and suggests that readers engage in full-fledged epistemological revolution: "Thinking Upside Down," using new ways of "learning which can…be seen as disrespectful if not downright rebellious," methods of approaching problems that have "never been popular with the upholders of continuity and of the status quo." Three years later the authors of *Reengineering the Corporation* ("A Manifesto for Business Revolution," as its subtitle declares) are ready to push this doctrine even farther. Not only should we be suspicious of traditional practices, but we should cast out virtually everything learned over the past two centuries!

> Business reengineering means putting aside much of the received wisdom of two hundred years of industrial management. It means forgetting how work was done in the age of the mass market and deciding how it can best be done now. In business reengineering, old job titles and old organizational arrangements—departments, divisions, groups, and so on—cease to matter. They are artifacts of another age.

As countercultural rebellion becomes corporate ideology, even the beloved Buddhism of the Beats wins a place on the executive bookshelf. In *The Leader as Martial Artist* (1993), Arnold Mindell advises men of commerce in the ways of the Tao, mastery of which he likens, of course, to surfing. For Mindell's Zen businessman, as for the followers of Tom Peters, the world is a wildly chaotic place of opportunity, navigable only to an enlightened "leader" who can discern the "timespirits" at work behind the scenes. In terms Peters himself might use were he a more meditative sort of inspiration professional, Mindell explains that "the wise facilitator" doesn't seek to prevent the inevitable and random clashes between "conflicting field spirits," but to anticipate such bouts of disorder and profit thereby.

Contemporary corporate fantasy imagines a world of ceaseless, turbulent change, of centers that ecstatically fail to hold, of joyous extinction for the craven gray-flannel creature of the past. Businessmen today decorate the walls of their offices not with portraits of President Eisenhower and emblems of suburban order, but with images of extreme athletic daring, with sayings about "diversity" and "empowerment" and "thinking outside the box." They theorize their world not in the bar car of the commuter train, but in weepy corporate retreats at which they beat their tom-toms and envision themselves as part of the great avant-garde tradition of edge-livers, risk-takers, and ass-kickers. Their world is a place not of sublimation and conformity, but of "leadership" and bold talk about defying the herd. And there is nothing this new enlightened species of businessman despises more than "rules" and "reason." The prominent culture-warriors of the right may believe that the counterculture was capitalism's undoing, but the antinomian businessmen know better. "One of the t-shirt slogans of the sixties read, 'Question authority,'" the authors of *Reengineering the Corporation* write. "Process owners might buy their reengineering team members the nineties version: 'Question assumptions.'"

The new businessman quite naturally gravitates to the slogans and sensibilities of the rebel sixties to express his understanding of the new Information World. He is led in what one magazine calls "the business revolution" by office-park subversives it hails as "business activists," "change agents," and "corporate radicals." He speaks to his comrades through commercials like the one for "Warp," a type of IBM computer operating system, in which an electric guitar soundtrack and psychedelic video effects surround hip executives with earrings and hairdos who are visibly stunned by the product's gnarly 'tude (It's a "totally cool way to run your computer," read the product's print ads). He understands the world through *Fast Company*, a successful new magazine whose editors take their inspiration from Hunter S. Thompson and whose stories describe such things as a "dis-organization" that inhabits an "anti-office" where "all vestiges of hierarchy have disappeared" or a computer scientist who is also "a rabble rouser, an agent provocateur, a product of the 1960s who never lost his activist fire or democratic values." He is what sociologists Paul Leinberger and Bruce Tucker have called "The New Individualist," the new and improved manager whose arty worldview and creative hip derive directly from his formative sixties days. The one thing this new executive is definitely *not* is Organization Man, the hyper-rational counter of beans, attender of church, and wearer of stiff hats.

In television commercials, through which the new American businessman presents his visions and self-understanding to the public, perpetual revolution and the gospel of rule-breaking are the orthodoxy of the day. You only need to watch for a few minutes before you see one of these slogans and understand the grip of antinomianism over the corporate mind:

Sometimes You Gotta Break the Rules	—*Burger King*
If You Don't Like the Rules, Change Them	—*WXRT-FM*
The Rules Have Changed	—*Dodge*
The Art of Changing	—*Swatch*
There's no one way to do it.	—*Levi's*
This is different. Different is good.	—*Arby's*
Just Different From the Rest	—*Special Export beer*
The Line Has Been Crossed: The Revolutionary New Supra	—*Toyota*
Resist the Usual —*the slogan of both Clash Clear Malt and Young & Rubicam*	
Innovate Don't Imitate	—*Hugo Boss*
Chart Your Own Course	—*Navigator Cologne*
It separates you from the crowd	—*Vision Cologne*

In most, the commercial message is driven home with the vanguard iconography of the rebel: screaming guitars, whirling cameras, and startled old timers who, we predict, will become an increasingly indispensable prop as consumers require ever-greater assurances that, Yes! You *are* a rebel! Just look at how offended they are!

Our businessmen imagine themselves rebels, and our rebels sound more and more like ideologists of business. Henry Rollins, for example, the maker of loutish, overbearing music and composer of high-school-grade poetry, straddles both worlds unproblematically. Rollins' writing and lyrics strike all the standard alienated literary poses: He rails against overcivilization and yearns to "disconnect." He veers back and forth between vague threats toward "weak" people who "bring me down" and blustery declarations of his weightlifting ability and physical prowess. As a result he ruled for several years as the preeminent darling of *Details* magazine, a periodical handbook for the young executive on the rise, where rebellion has achieved a perfect synthesis with corporate ideology. In 1992 *Details* named Rollins a "rock 'n' roll samurai," an "emblem...of a new masculinity" whose "enlightened honesty" is "a way of being that seems to flesh out many of the ideas expressed in contemporary culture and fashion." In 1994 the magazine consummated its relationship with Rollins by naming him "Man of the Year," printing a fawning story about his muscular worldview and decorating its cover with a photo in which Rollins displays his tattoos and rubs his chin in a thoughtful manner.

Details found Rollins to be such an appropriate role model for the struggling young businessman not only because of his music-product, but because of his excellent "self-styled identity," which the magazine describes in terms normally reserved for the breast-beating and soul-searching variety of motivational seminars. Although he derives it from the quality-maximizing wisdom of the East rather than the unfashionable doctrines of Calvin, Rollins' rebel posture is identical to that fabled ethic of the small capitalist whose regimen of positive thinking and hard work will one day pay off. *Details* describes one of Rollins' songs, quite seriously, as "a self-motivational superforce, an anthem of empowerment," teaching lessons that any aspiring middle-manager must internalize. Elsewhere, Iggy Pop, that great chronicler of the ambitionless life, praises Rollins as a "high achiever" who "wants to go somewhere." Rollins himself even seems to invite such an interpretation. His recent spoken-word accounts of touring with Black Flag, delivered in an unrelenting two-hour drill-instructor staccato, begins with the timeless bourgeois story of opportunity taken, of young Henry leaving the security of a "straight job," enlisting with a group of visionaries who were "the hardest working people I have ever seen," and learning "what hard work is all about." In the liner notes he speaks proudly of his Deming-esque dedication to quality, of how his bandmates "Delivered under pressure at incredible odds." When describing his relationship with his parents for the readers of *Details*, Rollins quickly cuts to the critical matter, the results that

such dedication has brought: "Mom, Dad, I outgross both of you put together," a happy observation he repeats in his interview with the *New York
Times Magazine.*

Despite the extreme hostility of punk rockers with which Rollins had to
contend all through the 1980s, it is he who has been chosen by the commercial media as the godfather of rock 'n' roll revolt. It is not difficult to see
why. For Rollins the punk rock decade was but a lengthy seminar on leadership skills, thriving on chaos, and total quality management. Rollins'
much-celebrated anger is indistinguishable from the anger of the frustrated
junior executive who finds obstacles on the way to the top. His discipline
and determination are the automatic catechism of any small entrepreneur
who's just finished brainwashing himself with the latest leadership and positive-thinking tracts; his poetry is the inspired verse of *21 Days to Unlimited
Power* or *Let's Get Results, Not Excuses.* Henry Rollins is no more a threat to
established power in America than was Dale Carnegie. And yet Rollins as
king of the rebels—peerless and ultimate—is the message hammered home
wherever photos of his growling visage appear. If you're unhappy with your
lot, the Culture Trust tells us with each new tale of Rollins, if you feel you
must rebel, take your cue from this most disgruntled guy of all: Lift weights!
Work hard! Meditate in your back yard! Root out the weaknesses deep down
inside yourself! But whatever you do, *don't* think about who controls power
or how it is wielded.

The structure and thinking of American business have changed enormously
in the years since our popular conceptions of its problems and abuses were
formulated. In the meantime the mad frothings and jolly apolitical revolt
of Beat, despite their vast popularity and insurgent air, have become powerless against a new regime that, one suspects, few of Beat's present-day ad-
mirers and practitioners feel any need to study or understand. Today that
beautiful countercultural idea, endorsed now by everyone from the surviving
Beats to shampoo manufacturers, is more the official doctrine of corporate
America than it is a program of resistance. What we understand as "dissent"
does not subvert, does not challenge, does not even question the cultural
faiths of Western business. What David Rieff wrote of the revolutionary pre-
tensions of multiculturalism is equally true of the countercultural idea: "The
more one reads in academic multiculturalist journals and in business publications, and the more one contrasts the speeches of CEOs and the speeches of noted multiculturalist academics, the more one is struck by the
similarities in the way they view the world." What's happened is not co-op-
tation or appropriation, but a simple and direct confluence of interest.

The problem with cultural dissent in America isn't that it's been co-opted, absorbed, or ripped-off. Of course it's been all of these things. But it has proven so hopelessly susceptible to such assaults for the same reason it has become so harmless in the first place, so toothless even before Mr. Geffen's boys discover it angsting away in some bar in Lawrence, Kansas: It is no longer any different from the official culture it's supposed to be subverting. The basic impulses of the countercultural idea, as descended from the holy Beats, are about as threatening to the new breed of antinomian businessmen as Anthony Robbins, selling success & how to achieve it on a late-night infomercial.

The people who staff the Combine aren't like Nurse Ratched. They aren't Frank Burns, they aren't the Church Lady, they aren't Dean Wormer from *Animal House*, they aren't those repressed old folks in the commercials who want to ban Tropicana Fruit Twisters. They're hipper than you can ever hope to be because *hip is their official ideology*, and they're always going to be there at the poetry reading to encourage your "rebellion" with a hearty "right on, man!" before you even know they're in the auditorium. You can't outrun them, or even stay ahead of them for very long: it's their racetrack, and that's them waiting at the finish line to congratulate you on how *outrageous* your new style is, on how you *shocked* those stuffy prudes out in the heartland.

William Gass

On Reading to Oneself

William Gass is a fiction writer, translator of poetry, and essayist. Interestingly enough, the academic discipline he teaches in is not English, but philosophy. With that in mind, it might be productive to start reading this essay by considering how its concerns move beyond the merely literary or critical: is Gass saying something about the way we live and act? In the middle of this essay, he characterizes Gertrude Stein's writing as having "no gist, no simple translation, no key concept." For Gass, this is a quality to be valued: at the beginning of the very next paragraph, he quotes a sentence from Stein—his favorite, he says—that serves as both a stumbling block and anchoring point, from which his essay expands in a number of directions. The sentence is a difficult sentence, resisting interpretation in the same way that the essay itself may seem to. So why would William Gass write an essay about reading that itself is hard to read? For the first few pages, it seems as though he's talking about the glories of speed-reading, but then—at times—you'll catch yourself noticing that he's actually writing about precisely the things that you're doing at the moment that you read his words. In responding to Gass, you may want to consider why he would use such a strategy, and what he would call the variety or varieties of reading strategies (he describes several, one of which relates to speed reading, and another to the Gertrude Stein sentence) he seems to want you to use. Can the essay be read as a set of operating instructions for itself?

I was never much of an athlete, but I was once a member of a team. Indeed, I was its star, and we were champions. I belonged to a squad of speed readers, although I was never awarded a letter for it. Still, we took on the top teams in our territory, and read as rapidly as possible every time we were challenged to a match, hoping to finish in front of our opponents: that towheaded punk from Canton, the tomato-cheeked girl from Marietta, or that silent pair of sisters, all spectacles and squints, who looked tough as German script, and who hailed from Shaker Heights, Ohio, a region noted for its swift, mean raveners of text. We called ourselves "The Speeders." Of course. Everybody did. There were the Sharon Speeders, the Steubenville Speeders, the Sperryville Speeders, and the Niles Nouns. The Niles Nouns never won. How could they—with that name. Nouns are always at rest.

I lost a match once to a kid from a forgettable small town, but I do remember he had green teeth. And that's the way, I'm afraid, we always appeared to others: as creeps with squints, bad posture, unclean complexions, unscrubbed teeth, unremediably tousled hair. We never had dates, only memorized them; and when any real team went on the road to represent the school, we carried the socks, the Tootsie Rolls, the towels. My nemesis had a head of thin red hair like rust on a saw; he screwed a suggestive little finger into his large fungiform ears. He was made of rust, moss, and wax, and I had lost to him…lost…and the shame of that defeat still rushes to my face whenever I remember it. Nevertheless, although our team had no sweaters, we never earned a letter, and our exploits never made the papers, I still possess a substantial gold-colored medallion on which one sunbeaming eye seems hung above a book like a spider. Both book and eye are open—wide. I take that open, streaming eye to have been a symbol and an omen.

Our reading life has its salad days, its autumnal times. At first, of course, we do it badly, scarcely keeping our balance, toddling along behind our finger, so intent on remembering what each word is supposed to mean that the sentence is no longer a path, and we arrive at its end without having gone anywhere. Thus it is with all the things we learn, for at first they passively oppose us; they lie outside us like mist or the laws of nature; we have to issue orders to our eyes, our limbs, our understanding: lift this, shift that, thumb the space bar, lean more to one side, let up on the clutch—and take it easy, or you'll strip the gears—and don't forget to modify the verb, or remember what an escudo's worth. After a while, though, we find we like standing up, riding a bike, singing *Don Giovanni*, making puff paste or puppy love, building model planes. Then we are indeed like the adolescent in our eager green enthusiasms: they are plentiful as leaves. Every page is a pasture, and we are let out to graze like hungry herds.

Do you remember the magic the word 'thigh' could work on you, showing up suddenly in the middle of a passage like a whiff of cologne in a theater? I admit it: the widening of the upper thigh remains a miracle, and, honestly, many of us once read the word 'thigh' as if we were exploring Africa, seeking the source of the Nile. No volume was too hefty, then, no style too verbal; the weight of a big book was more comforting than Christmas candy; though you have to be lucky, strike the right text at the right time, because the special excitement which Thomas Wolfe provides, for instance, can be felt only in the teens; and when, again, will any of us possess the energy, the patience, the inner sympathy for volcanic bombast, to read—to enjoy—Carlyle?

Rereading —repeating—was automatic. Who needed the lessons taught by Gertrude Stein? I must have rushed through a pleasant little baseball book called *The Crimson Pennant* at least a dozen times, consuming a cake I had already cut into crumbs, yet that big base hit which always came when matters were most crucial was never more satisfying than on the final occasion when its hero and I ran round those bases, and shyly lifted our caps toward the crowd.

I said who needed the lessons taught by Gertrude Stein, but one of the best books for beginners remains her magical *First Reader*. Here are the opening lines of "Lesson One":

> A dog said that he was going to learn to read. The other dogs said he could learn to bark but he could not learn to read. They did not know that dog, if he said he was going to learn to read, he would learn to read. He might be drowned dead in water but if he said that he was going to read he was going to learn to read.
>
> He never was drowned in water not dead drowned and he never did learn to read. Are there any children like that. One two three. Are there any children like that. Four five six. Are there any children like that. Seven eight nine are there any children like that.

There turn out to be ten, each with a dog who says he is going to learn to read, and shortly the story gets very exciting.

Back in the days of "once upon a time," no one threatened to warm our behinds if we didn't read another Nancy Drew by Tuesday; no sour-faced virgin browbeat us with *The Blithedale Romance* or held out *The Cloister and the Hearth* like a cold plate of "it's good for you" food. We were on our own. I read Swinburne and the *Adventures of the Shadow*. I read Havelock Ellis and Tom Swift and *The Idylls of the King*. I read whatever came to hand, and what came to hand were a lot of naughty French novels, some by Émile Zola, detective stories, medical adventures, books about bees, biographies of Napoleon, and *Thus Spake Zarathustra* like a bolt of lightning. I read them all, whatever they were, with an ease that defies the goat's digestion, and with an ease which is now so easily forgotten, just as we forget the wild wobble in the wheels, or the humiliating falls we took, when we began our life on spokes. That wind I felt, when I finally stayed upright around the block, continuously reaffirmed the basic joy of cycling . It told me not merely that I was moving, but that I was moving *under my own power*; just as later, when

I'd passed my driver's test, I would feel another sort of exhilaration—an intense, addictive, dangerous one—that of command: of my ability to control the energy produced by another thing or person, to direct the life contained in another creature. Yes, in those early word-drunk years, I would down a book or two a day as though they were gins. I read for adventure, excitement, to sample the exotic and the strange, for climax and resolution, to participate in otherwise unknown and forbidden passions. I forgot what it was to be *under my own power, under my own steam.* I knew that Shakespeare came after Sophocles, but I forgot that I went back and forth between them as though they were towns. In my passion for time, I forgot their geography. All books occupy the same space. Dante and Dickens: they cheek by jowl. And although books begin their life in the world at different times, these dates rarely determine the days they begin in yours and mine. We forget simple things like that: that we are built of books. I forgot the Coke I was drinking, the chair, the chill in the air. I was, like so many adolescents, as eager to leap from my ordinary life as the salmon are to get upstream. I sought a replacement for the world. With a surreptitious lamp lit, I stayed awake to dream. I grew reckless. I read for speed.

When you read for speed you do not read recursively, looping along the line like a sewing machine, stitching something together—say the panel of a bodice to a sleeve—linking a pair of terms, the contents of a clause, closing a seam by following the internal directions of the sentence (not when you read for speed), so that the word 'you' is first fastened to the word 'read,' and then the phrase 'for speed' is attached to both in order that the entire expression can be finally fronted by a grandly capitalized 'When...' (but not when you read for speed), while all of that, in turn, is gathered up to await the completion of the later segment which begins 'you do not read recursively' (certainly not when you read for speed). You can hear how long it seems to take—this patient process—and how confusing it can become. Nor do you linger over language, repeating (not when you read for speed) some especially pleasant little passage, in the enjoyment, perhaps, of a modest rhyme (for example, the small clause 'when you read for speed'), or a particularly apt turn of phrase (an image, for instance, such as the one which dealt with my difficult opponent's green teeth and thin red hair—like rust on a saw), (none of that, when you read for speed). Nor, naturally, do you move your lips as you read the word 'read' or the words 'moving your lips,' so that the poor fellow next to you in the reading room has to watch intently to see what your lips are saying: are you asking him out? for the loan of his *Plutarch's Lives*? and of course the poor fellow is flummoxed to find that you are moving your lips to say 'moving your lips.' What can that mean? The lip-mover—Oh, such a person is low on our skill scale. We are taught to have scorn for her, for him.

On the other hand, the speeding reader drops diagonally down across the page, on a slant like a skier; cuts across the text the way a butcher prefers to slice sausage, so that a small round can be made to yield a misleadingly larger, oval piece. The speeding reader is after the kernel, the heart, the gist. Paragraphs become a country the eye flies over looking for landmarks, reference points, airports, restrooms, passages of sex. The speeding reader guts a book the way the skillful clean fish. The gills are gone, the tail, the scales, the fins; then the fillet slides away swiftly as though fed to a seal; and only the slow reader, one whom those with green teeth chew through like furious worms; only the reader whose finger falters in front of long words, who moves the lips, who dances the text, will notice the odd crowd of images—flier, skier, butcher, seal—which have gathered to comment on the aims and activities of the speeding reader, perhaps like gossips at a wedding. To the speeding reader, this jostle of images, this crazy collision of ideals—of landing strip, kernel, heart, guts, sex—will not be felt or even recognized, because these readers are after what they regard as the inner core of meaning; it is the gist they want, the heart of the matter; they want what can equally well be said in their own, other, and always fewer words; so that the gist of this passage could be said to be: readers who read rapidly read only for the most generalized and stereotyped significances. For them, meaning floats over the page like fluffy clouds. Cliché is forever in fashion. They read, as we say, synonymously, seeking sameness; and, indeed, it is all the same to them if they are said in one moment to be greedy as seals, and in another moment likened to descalers of fish. They…you, I…we get the idea.

Most writing and most reading proceeds, not in terms of specific words and phrases, although specific ones must be used, but in terms of loose general sets or gatherings of synonyms. Synonymous writing is relatively easy to read, provided one doesn't drowse, because it lives in the approximate; it survives wide tolerances; its standards of relevance resemble those of a streetwalker, and its pleasures are of the same kind.

If any of us read, "When Jack put his hand in the till, he got his fingers burned, so that now he's all washed up at the Bank," we might smile at this silly collision of commonplaces, but we would also "get the drift," the melody, the gist. The gist is that Jack was caught with his hand in the cookie jar and consequently was given a sack he can't put his cookies in. Well, the stupid mother cut his own throat just to get his necktie red. Jack—man—wow!—I mean, he fucked up for sure—and now he's screwed—man—like a wet place—he's been wiped up! Punctuation dissolves into dashes; it contracts, shrinks, disappears entirely. Fred did the CRIME, got CAUGHT, now feels the PAIN. These three general ideas, like cartoon balloons, drift above the surface of the sentence, and are read as easily as Al Capp.

Precise writing becomes difficult, and slow, precisely because it requires that we read it precisely—take it all in. Most of us put words on a page the way kids throw snow at a wall. Only the general white splat matters anyhow.

When I participated in them, speed-reading matches had two halves like a game of football. The first consisted of the rapid reading itself, through which, of course, I whizzzzed, all the while making the sound of turning pages and closing covers in order to disconcert Green Teeth or the Silent Shaker Heights Sisters, who were to think I had completed my reading already. I didn't wear glasses then, but I carried a case to every match, and always dropped it at a pertinent moment, along with a few coins.

Next we were required to answer questions about what we claimed we'd covered, and quickness, here, was again essential. The questions, however, soon disclosed their biases. They had a structure, their own gist; and it became possible, after some experience, to guess what would be asked about a text almost before it had been begun. Is it Goldilocks we're skimming? Then what is the favorite breakfast food of the three bears? How does Goldilocks escape from the house? Why weren't the three bears at home when Goldilocks came calling? The multiple answers we were offered also had their tired tilt, and, like the questions, quickly gave themselves away. The favorite breakfast foods, for instance, were: (a) Quaker Oats (who, we can imagine, are paying for the prizes this year, and in this sly fashion get their name in); (b) Just Rite (written like a brand name); (c) porridge (usually misspelled); (d) sugar-coated curds and whey. No one ever wondered whether Goldilocks was suffering from sibling rivalry; why she had become a teenie trasher; or why mother bear's bowl of porridge was cold when baby bear's smaller bowl was still warm, and Just Rite. There were many other mysteries, but not for these quiz masters who didn't even want to know the sexual significance of Cinderella's slipper, or why it had to be made of glass (the better to drink from, of course). I won my championship medal by ignoring the text entirely (it was a section from Vol. II of Oswald Spengler's *The Decline of the West*, the part which begins "Regard the flowers at eventide as, one after the other, they close in the setting sun…" but then, of course, you remember that perhaps overfamiliar passage). I skipped the questions as well, and simply encircled the gloomiest alternatives offered. Won in record time. No one's got through Spengler with such dispatch since.

What did these matches, with their quizzes for comprehension, their love of literal learning, tell me? They told me that time was money (a speed reader's dearest idea); they told me what the world wanted me to read when I read, eat when I ate, see when I saw. Like the glutton, I was to get everything in and out of the store in a hurry. Turnover was topmost. What the world wanted me to get was the gist, but the gist was nothing but an idea of trade—an idea so drearily uniform and emaciated that it might have modeled dresses.

We are expected to get on with our life, to pass over it so swiftly we needn't notice its lack of quality, the mismatch of theory with thing, the gap between program and practice. We must live as we read; listen as we live. Please: only the melody…shards of "golden oldies," foreplays of what's "just about out" and "all the rage," of what's "brand new." We've grown accustomed to the slum our consciousness has become. It tastes like the spit in our own mouth, not the spit from the mouth of another.

This trail of clichés, sorry commonplaces, dreary stereotypes, boring slogans, loud adverts and brutal simplifications, titles, trademarks, tags, *typiques*, our mind leaves behind like the slime of a slug—the sameness we excrete—is democratic: one stool's no better than another to the normally undiscerning eye and impatient bowel. 'To be all washed up' is not a kingly expression which 'over the hill' or 'past his prime' must serve like a slave. Each cliché is a varlet and a churl, but there's no master. Each one refers us, with a vague wave of its hand, to the entire unkempt class. The meaning we impute to our expressions is never fixed; our thought (and *there* is a self-important term), our thought moves aimlessly from one form of words to another, scarcely touching any, like a bee in God's garden. The fact is that Jack has had it. We all know *that*. He's run the course. And now he's been zapped. Why go on about it?

There are three other ways of reading that I'd like to recommend. They are slow, old-fashioned, not easy either, rarely practiced. They must be learned. Together with the speeder they describe the proper way to write as well as read, and can serve as a partial emblem for the right life.

That seems unlikely, yet they apply to all our needs, our habits: thinking, seeing, eating, drinking. We can gulp our glass of wine if we please. To get the gist. And the gist is the level of alcohol in the blood, the pixilated breath one blows into the test balloon. It makes appropriate the expression: have a belt. It makes dangerous the expression: one for the road. We can toss down a text, a time of life, a love affair, that walk in the park which gets us from here to there. We can chug-a-lug them. You have, perhaps, had to travel sometime with a person whose passion was that simple: it was *getting there*. You have no doubt encountered people who impatiently wait for the payoff; they urge you to come to the point; at dinner, the early courses merely delay dessert; they don't go to the games, only bet on them; they look solely at the bottom line (that obscene phrase whose further meaning synonymous readers never notice); they are persons consumed by consequences; they want to climax without the bother of buildup or crescendo.

But we can read and walk and write and look in quite a different way. It *is* possible. I was saved from sameness by philosophy and Immanuel Kant, by Gertrude Stein and her seeming repetitions. You can't speed read *Process and Reality* or *The Critique of Pure Reason*. You can't speed read Wallace Stevens or Mallarmé. There is no gist, no simple translation, no key concept which will unlock these works; actually, there is no lock, no door, no wall, no room, no house, no world…

One of my favorite sentences is by Gertrude Stein. It goes: "It looked like a garden, but he had hurt himself by accident." Our example is actually two sentences: "It looked like a garden" and "He had hurt himself by accident." Separately, and apart, each is a perfectly ordinary, ignorable element of proletarian prose; but when they are brought together in this unusual way, they force us to consider their real, complete, and peculiar natures. The injury, we may decide, although it looked self-inflicted, planned, kept up, was actually the result of an accident. How much better we feel when we know that Gertrude Stein's sentence has a gloss, because now we can forget it. The fellow was actually *not* trying to defraud his insurance company, although at first it looked like it.

Alas for the security of our comfort, her sentence is not equivalent to its synonymous reading—this consoling interpretation. It cannot be replaced by another. It cannot be translated without a *complete loss of its very special effect*. It was composed—this sentence—with a fine esthetic feel for "difference," for clean and clear distinctions, for the true weight and full use of the word. If, when we say we understand something someone's said, we mean that we can rephrase the matter, put it in other words (and we frequently do mean this), then Gertrude Stein's critics may be right: you can't *understand* such a sentence; and it has no value *as a medium of exchange*.

We can attempt to understand the sentences in another way. We can point out the elements and relations which, together, produce its special effect. For instance, we can call attention to the juxtaposition of an event which normally happens in a moment (an accident) with a condition which is achieved over a long period of time (a garden); or cite the contrasts between care and carelessness, the desirable and undesirable, between appearance and reality, chance and design, which the two sentences set up; and note the pivotal shift of pronouns ("It looked…but he had…"). We might furthermore comment on the particular kind of surprise the entire sentence provides, because after reading "It looked like a garden, but…" we certainly expect something like "but the plants had all sprung up like weeds."

The isolation of analytical functions in the sentence is accomplished by comparing the actual sentence with its possible variations. What is the force of the phrase, "by accident"? We can find out by removing it.

It looked like a garden, but he had hurt himself with a hammer.

We replace 'hurt' with 'injured' in order to feel the difference a little alliteration makes; what the new meter does; and to understand to what degree, exactly, 'hurt' is a more intimate and warmer word, less physical in its implications, yet also benignly general and vague in a way 'wounded,' for instance, is not.

We can try being specific:

It looked like a rose garden, but he had hurt himself by slipping on the ice.

We can also see, if we look, how lengthening the second sentence segment spoils the effect of the whole:

It looked like a garden; but he had nevertheless managed to hurt himself quite by accident.

The onset of the surprise must be swift, otherwise everything is ruined. Suppose we extend our example's other arm:

It looked, as well as I could make it out through the early morning mist, like a garden, but he had hurt himself by accident.

We can make other substitutions, sometimes rather wild ones, in order to measure the distances between resemblances:

It looked like a flower box, but he had hurt himself by accident.
It looked like a Dali, but he had hurt himself by accident.

It looked like a garden, but he had dug himself up by accident.
It looked like a garden, but he had hurt himself by post.

It is important that we keep our sentence's most "normal" form in front of us, namely: "It looked very intentional, but he had hurt himself by accident." By now, through repetition, and by dint of analysis, the sentence has lost its ability to shock or surprise, and like a religious chant has surrendered whatever meaning it might have had. On the other hand, in a month's time, out of the blue, the sentence will return to consciousness with the force of a revelation.

What we've done, in short, is to reenact the idealized method of its conscious composition. We have made explicit the nature of its verbal choices by examining some of those which might have been made instead, as if we were translating English into English.

If synonymous reading is to be contrasted with antonymical reading, which stresses untranslatability, difference, and uniqueness; then analytical reading, which looks at the way words are put together to achieve certain effects, should be contrasted with synthetical reading, which concentrates on the quality and character of the effect itself. Synthetical reading integrates every element and *responds*.

Imagine for a moment a consummate Brunswick stew. In such a perfect dish, not only must the carrot contribute its bit, but *this* carrot must contribute *its*. As we sample the stew, we first of all must realize we are eating just that: stew. This knowledge gives our tongue its orientation; it tells us what to look for, what values count, what belongs, and what (like bubble gum) does not; it informs us about the *method* of its preparation. We assure ourselves it is stew we are eating by comparing our present experience with others (or we ask the waitress, who tells us what the chef says). That is, this stew has a general character (look, smell, texture, flavor)—a "gist"—which we then may match with others of its sort. So far we are engaged in synonymous eating (as disgusting as that sounds). One bite of stew, one bowl of chili, one flattened hamburger patty, is like another patty, bowl, or bite. Clearly, for the rapid eater or the speed reader, consciousness will not register much difference, and the difference that does appear will be, of course, in *content*. I've eaten this bowl of porridge, so that bowl must be another one.

But the educated and careful tongue will taste and discriminate this particular stew from every other. Tasting is a dialectical process in which one proceeds from general to specific similarities, but this can be accomplished only through a series of differentiations. Antonymical tasting (which also sounds disgusting) ultimately "identifies" this dish, not only as pure stew, but as Brunswick stew, and knows whether it was done in Creole style or not, and then finally it recognizes, in this plate's present version of the recipe, that the squirrels were fat and gray and came from Mississippi where they fed on elderberries and acorns of the swamp oak. One grasps an act, an object, an idea, a sentence synthetically, simply by feeling or receiving its full effect—in the case of the stew that means its complete, unique taste. I need not be able to name the ingredients; I need not be able to describe how the dish was prepared; but I should be a paragon of appreciation. This quality, because it is the experience of differentiation within a context of comparison, cannot be captured in concepts, cannot be expressed in words. Analytical tasting has a different aim. It desires to discover what went into the dish; it reconstructs the recipe, and recreates the method of its preparation. It moves from effects to causes.

Reading is a complicated, profound, silent, still, very personal, very private, a very solitary, yet civilizing activity. Nothing is more social than speech—we are bound together by our common sounds more securely than even by our laws—nevertheless, no one is more aware of the isolated self than the reader; for a reader communes with the word heard immaterially in that hollow of the head made only for hearing, a room nowhere in the body in any ordinary sense. On the bus, every one of us may be deep in something different. Sitting next to a priest, I can still enjoy my pornography, although I may keep a thumb discreetly on top of the title: *The Cancan Girls Celebrate Christmas*. It doesn't matter to me that Father McIvie is reading about investments, or that the kid with rusty hair in the seat ahead is devouring a book about handicapping horses. Yet while all of us, in our verbal recreations, are full of respect for the privacy of our neighbors, the placards advertising perfume or footware invade the public space like a visual smell; Muzak fills every unstopped ear the way the static of the street does. The movies, radio, TV, theater, orchestra: all run on at their own rate, and the listener or the viewer must attend, keep up, or lose out; but not the reader. The reader is free. The reader is in charge, and pedals the cycle. It is easy for a reader to announce that his present run of Proust has been postponed until the holidays.

Reading, that is, is not a public imposition. Of course, when we read, many of us squirm and fidget. One of the closest friends of my youth would sensuously wind and unwind on his forefinger the long blond strands of his hair. How he read: that is how I remember him. Yes, our postures are often provocative, perverse. Yet these outward movements of the body really testify to the importance of the inner movements of the mind; and even those rapid flickers of the eye, as we shift from word to word, phrase to phrase, and clause to clause, hoping to keep our head afloat on a flood of Faulkner or Proust or Joyce or James, are registers of reason: for reading is reasoning, figuring things out through thoughts, making arrangements out of arrangements until we've understood a text so fully it is nothing but feeling and pure responses; until its conceptual turns are like the reversals of mood in a marriage: petty, sad, ecstatic, commonplace, foreseeable, amazing.

In order to have this experience, however, one must learn to perform the text, say, sing, shout the words to oneself, give them, with *our minds, their body*; otherwise the eye skates over every syllable like the speeder. There can be no doubt that often what we read should be skimmed, as what we are frequently asked to drink should be spilled; but the speeding reader is alone in another, less satisfactory way, one quite different from that of the reader who says the words to herself, because as we read we divide into a theater: there is the performer who shapes these silent sounds, moving the muscles of the larynx almost invisibly; and there is the listener who hears them said, and who responds to their passion or their wisdom.

Such a reader sees every text as unique; greets every work as a familiar stranger. Such a reader is willing to allow another's words to become hers, his.

In the next moment, let us read a wine, so as to show how many things may be read which have not been written. We have prepared for the occasion, of course. The bottle has been allowed to breathe. Books need to breathe, too. They should be opened properly, hefted, thumbed. Their covers part like pairs of supplicating palms. The paper, print, layout should be appreciated. But now we decant the text into our wide-open and welcoming eyes. We warm the wine in the bowl of the glass with our hand. We let its bouquet collect above it like the red of red roses seems to stain the air. We wade—shoeless, to be sure—through the color it has liquefied. We roll a bit of it about in our mouths. We sip. We savor. We say some sentences of that great master Sir Thomas Browne: "We tearme sleepe a death, and yet it is waking that kills us, and destroyes those spirits which are the house of life. Tis indeed a part of life that best expresseth death, for every man truely lives so long as hee acts his nature, or someway makes good the faculties of himself…" Are these words not from a fine field, in a splendid year? There is, of course, a sameness in all these words: life/death, man/nature; we get the drift. But the differences! the differences make all the difference, the way nose and eyes and cheekbones form a face; the way a muscle makes emotion pass across it. It is the differences we read. Differences are not only identifiable, distinct; they are epidemic: the wine is light, perhaps, spicy, slow to release its grip upon itself, the upper thigh is widening wonderfully, the night air has hands, words fly out of our mouths like birds: "but who knows the fate of his bones," Browne says, "or how often he is to be buried"; yet as I say his soul out loud, he lives again; he has risen up in me, and I can be, for him, that temporary savior that every real reader is, putting his words in my mouth; not nervously, notice, as though they were pieces of chewed gum, but in that way which is necessary if the heart is to hear them; and though they are his words, and his soul, then, which returns through me, I am in charge; he has asked nothing of me; his words move because I move them. It is like cycling, reading is. Can you feel the air, the pure passage of the spirit past the exposed skin?

So this reading will be like living, then; the living each of you will be off in a moment to be busy with; not always speedily, I hope, or in the continuous anxiety of consequence, the sullenness of inattention, the annoying static of distraction. But it will be only a semblance of living—this living—nevertheless, the way unspoken reading is a semblance, unless, from time to time, you perform the outer world and let it live within; because only in that manner can it deliver itself to us. As Rainer Maria Rilke once commanded: "dance the taste of the fruit you have been tasting. Dance the orange." I should like to multiply that charge, even past all possibility. Speak the street to yourself sometimes, hear the horns in the forest, read the breeze aloud, and make that inner wind yours, because, whether Nature, Man, or God has given us the text, we independently possess the ability to read, to read really well, and to move our own mind freely in tune to the moving world.

Malcolm Gladwell

The Sports Taboo

Why blacks are like boys and whites are like girls

Malcolm Gladwell was born in England and grew up in Canada. A former reporter for *The Washington Post*, he has also been a columnist at *The New Yorker*. In "The Sports Taboo," he asks: "So why aren't we allowed to say that there might be athletically significant differences between blacks and whites?' To make his point, he uses the example of standardized tests, and the ways in which performance on these tests varies according to gender, similar to ways that race affects athletic ability: "...blacks are like boys and whites are like girls." Gladwell is not saying any race or gender is better, only that there are differences, and he goes on to explore these differences in terms of nature (genetic variability), nurture (learned helplessness), and one's own desire.

The education of any athlete begins, in part, with an education in the racial taxonomy of his chosen sport—in the subtle, unwritten rules about what whites are supposed to be good at and what blacks are supposed to be good at. In football, whites play quarterback and blacks play running back; in baseball whites pitch and blacks play the outfield. I grew up in Canada, where my brother Geoffrey and I ran high-school track, and in Canada the rule of running was that anything under the quarter-mile belonged to the West Indians. This didn't mean that white people didn't run the sprints. But the expectation was that they would never win, and, sure enough, they rarely did. There was just a handful of West Indian immigrants in Ontario at that point—clustered in and around Toronto—but they *owned* Canadian sprinting, setting up under the stands at every major championship, cranking up the reggae on their boom boxes, and then humiliating everyone else on the track. My brother and I weren't from Toronto, so we weren't part of that scene. But our West Indian heritage meant that we got to share in the swagger. Geoffrey was a magnificent runner, with powerful legs and a barrel chest, and when he was warming up he used to do that exaggerated, slow-motion jog that the white guys would try to do and never quite pull off. I was a miler, which was a little outside the West Indian range. But, the way I figured it, the rules meant that no one should ever outkick me over the final two hundred metres of any race. And in the golden summer of my fourteenth year, when my running career prematurely peaked, no one ever did

When I started running, there was a quarter-miler just a few years older than I was by the name of Arnold Stotz. He was a bulldog of a runner, hugely talented, and each year that he moved through the sprinting ranks he invariably broke the existing four-hundred-metre record in his age class. Stotz was white, though, and every time I saw the results of a big track meet I'd keep an eye out for his name, because I was convinced that he could not keep winning. It was as if I saw his whiteness as a degenerative disease, which would eventually claim and cripple him. I never asked him whether he felt the same anxiety, but I can't imagine that he didn't. There was only so long that anyone could defy the rules. One day, at the provincial championships, I looked up at the results board and Stotz was gone.

Talking openly about the racial dimension of sports in this way, of course, is considered unseemly. It's all right to say that blacks dominate sports because they lack opportunities elsewhere. That's the "Hoop Dreams" line, which says whites are allowed to acknowledge black athletic success as long as they feel guilty about it. What you're not supposed to say is what we were saying in my track days—that we were better *because* we were black, because of something intrinsic to being black. Nobody said anything like that publicly last month when Tiger Woods won the Masters or when, a week later, African men claimed thirteen out of the top twenty places in the Boston Marathon. Nor is it likely to come up this month, when African-Americans will make up eighty per cent of the players on the floor for the N.B.A. playoffs. When the popular television sports commentator Jimmy (the Greek) Snyder did break this taboo, in 1988—infamously ruminating on the size and significance of black thighs—one prominent N.A.A.C.P. official said that his remarks "could set race relations back a hundred years." The assumption is that the whole project of trying to get us to treat each other the same will be undermined if we don't all agree that under the skin we actually are the same.

The point of this, presumably, is to put our discussion of sports on a par with legal notions of racial equality, which would be a fine idea except that civil-rights law governs matters like housing and employment and the sports taboo covers matters like what can be said about someone's jump shot. In his much heralded new book *Darwin's Athletes*, the University of Texas scholar John Hoberman tries to argue that these two things are the same, that it's impossible to speak of black physical superiority without implying intellectual inferiority. But it isn't long before the argument starts to get ridiculous. "The spectacle of black athleticism," he writes, inevitably turns into "a highly public image of black retardation." Oh, really? What, exactly, about Tiger Woods's victory in the Masters resembled "a highly public image of black retardation"? Today's black athletes are multimillion-dollar corporate pitchmen, with talk shows and sneaker deals and publicity machines and almost daily media opportunities to share their thoughts with the world, and it's very hard to see how all this contrives to make them look stupid. Hoberman spends a lot of time trying to inflate the significance of sports, arguing that how we talk about events on the baseball diamond or the track has grave consequences for how we talk about race in general. Here he is, for example, on Jackie Robinson:

> The sheer volume of sentimental and intellectual energy that has been invested in the mythic saga of Jackie Robinson has discouraged further thinking about what his career did and did not accomplish....Black America has paid a high and largely unacknowledged price for the extraordinary prominence given the black athlete rather than other black men of action (such as military pilots and astronauts), who represent modern aptitudes in ways that athletes cannot.

Please. Black America has paid a high and largely unacknowledged price for a long list of things, and having great athletes is far from the top of the list. Sometimes a baseball player is just a baseball player, and sometimes an observation about racial difference is just an observation about racial difference. Few object when medical scientists talk about the significant epidemiological differences between blacks and whites—the fact that blacks have a higher incidence of hypertension than whites and twice as many black males die of diabetes and prostate cancer as white males, that breast tumors appear to grow faster in black women than in white women, that black girls show signs of puberty sooner than white girls. So why aren't we allowed to say that there might be athletically significant differences between blacks and whites?

According to the medical evidence, African-Americans seem to have, on the average, greater bone mass than do white Americans—a difference that suggests greater muscle mass. Black men have slightly higher circulating levels of testosterone and human-growth hormone than their white counterparts, and blacks over all tend to have proportionally slimmer hips, wider shoulders, and longer legs. In one study, the Swedish physiologist Bengt Saltin compared a group of Kenyan distance runners with a group of Swedish distance runners and found interesting differences in muscle composition: Saltin reported that the Africans appeared to have more blood-carrying capillaries and more mitochondria (the body's cellular power plant) in the fibers of their quadriceps. Another study found that, while black South African distance runners ran at the same speed as white South African runners, they were able to use more oxygen—eighty-nine per cent versus eighty-one per cent—over extended periods: somehow, they were able to exert themselves more. Such evidence suggested that there were physical differences in black athletes which have a bearing on activities like running and jumping, which should hardly come as a surprise to anyone who follows competitive sports.

To use track as an example—since track is probably the purest measure of athletic ability—Africans recorded fifteen out of the twenty fastest times last year in the men's ten-thousand-metre event. In the five thousand metres, eighteen out of the twenty fastest times were recorded by Africans. In the fifteen hundred metres, thriteen out of the twenty fastest times were African, and in the sprints, in the men's hundred metres, you have to go all the way down to the twenty-third place in the world rankings—to Geir Moen, of Norway—before you find a white face. There is a point at which it becomes foolish to deny the fact of black athletic prowess, and even more foolish to banish speculation on the topic. Clearly, something is going on. The question is what.

⊷ ⚎⚭⚎ ⊶

If we are to decide what to make of the differences between blacks and whites, we first have to decide what to make of the word "difference," which can mean any number of things. A useful case study is to compare the ability of men and women in math. If you give a large, representative sample of male and female students a standardized math test, their mean scores will come out pretty much the same. But if you look at the margins, at the very best and the very worst students, sharp differences emerge. In the math portion of an achievement test conducted by Project Talent—a nationwide survey of fifteen-year-olds—there were 1.3 boys for every girl in the top ten per cent, 1.5 boys for every girl in the top five per cent, and seven boys for every girl in the top one per cent. In the fifty-six-year history of the Putnam Mathematical Competition, which has been described as the Olympics of college math, all but one of the winners have been male. Conversely, if you look at people with the very lowest math ability, you'll find more boys than girls there, too. In other words, although the average math ability of boys and girls is the same, the distribution isn't: there are more males than females at the bottom of the pile, more males than females at the top of the pile, and fewer males than females in the middle. Statisticians refer to this as a difference in variability.

This pattern, as it turns out, is repeated in almost every conceivable area of gender difference. Boys are more variable than girls on the College Board entrance exam and in routine elementary-school spelling tests. Male mortality patterns are more variable than female patterns; that is, many more men die in early and middle age than women, who tend to die in more of a concentrated clump toward the end of life. The problem is that variability differences are regularly confused with average differences. If men had higher average math scores than women, you could say they were better at the subject. But because they are only more variable the word "better" seems inappropriate.

The same holds true for differences between the races. A racist stereotype is the assertion of average difference—it's the claim that the typical white is superior to the typical black. It allows a white man to assume that the black man he passes on the street is stupider than he is. By contrast, if what racists believed was that black intelligence was simply more variable than white intelligence, then it would be impossible for them to construct a stereotype about black intelligence at all. They wouldn't be able to generalize. If they wanted to believe that there were a lot of blacks dumber than whites, they would also have to believe that there were a lot of blacks smarter than they were. This distinction is critical to understanding the relation between race and athletic performance. What are we seeing when we remark black domination of élite sporting events—an average difference between the races or merely a difference in variability?

This question has been explored by geneticists and physical anthropologists, and some of the most notable work has been conducted over the past few years by Kenneth Kidd, at Yale. Kidd and his colleagues have been taking DNA samples from two African Pygmy tribes in Zaire and the Central African Republic and comparing them with DNA samples taken from populations all over the world. What they have been looking for is variants—subtle differences between the DNA of one person and another—and what they have found is fascinating. "I would say, without a doubt, that in almost any single African population—a tribe or however you want to define it—there is more genetic variation than in all the rest of the world put together," Kidd told me. In a sample of fifty Pygmies, for example, you might find nine variants in one stretch of DNA. In a sample of hundreds of people from around the rest of the world, you might find only a total of six variants in that same stretch of DNA—and probably every one of those six variants would also be found in the Pygmies. If everyone in the world was wiped out except Africans, in other words, almost all the human genetic diversity would be preserved.

The likelihood is that these results reflect Africa's status as the homeland of *Homo sapiens*: since every human population outside Africa is essentially a subset of the original African population, it makes sense that everyone in such a population would be a genetic subset of Africans, too. So you can expect groups of Africans to be more variable in respect to almost anything that has a genetic component. If, for example, your genes control how you react to aspirin, you'd expect to see more Africans than whites for whom one aspirin stops a bad headache, more for whom no amount of aspirin works, more who are allergic to aspirin, and more who need to take, say, four aspirin at a time to get any benefit—but far fewer Africans for whom the standard two-aspirin dose would work well. And to the extent that running is influenced by genetic factors you would expect to see more really fast blacks—and more really slow blacks—than whites but far fewer Africans of merely average speed. Blacks are like boys. Whites are like girls.

There is nothing particulary scary about this fact, and certainly nothing to warrant the kind of gag order on talk of racial differences which is now in place. What it means is that comparing élite athletes of different races tells you very little about the races themselves. A few years ago, for example, a prominent scientist argued for black athletic supremacy by pointing out there had never been a white Michael Jordan. True. But, as the Yale anthropologist Jonathan Marks has noted, until recently there was no black Michael Jordan, either. Michael Jordan, like Tiger Woods or Wayne Gretzky or Cal Ripken, is one of the best players in his sport not because he's like the other members of his own ethnic group but precisely because he's not like them—or like anyone else, for that matter. Élite athletes are élite athletes because, in some sense, they are on the fringes of genetic variability. As it happens, African populations seem to create more of these genetic outliers than white populations do, and this is what underpins the claim that blacks are better athletes than whites. But that's all the claim amounts to. It doesn't say anything at all about the rest of us, of all races, muddling around in the genetic middle.

There is a second consideration to keep in mind when we compare blacks and whites. Take the men's hundred-metre final at the Atlanta Olympics. Every runner in that race was of either Western African or Southern African descent, as you would expect if Africans had some genetic affinity for sprinting. But suppose we forget about skin color and look just at country of origin. The eight-man final was made up of two African-Americans, two Africans (one from Namibia and one from Nigeria), a Trinidadian, a Canadian of Jamaican descent, an Englishman of Jamaican descent, and a Jamaican. The race was won by the Jamaican-Canadian, in world-record time, with the Namibian coming in second and the Trinidadian third. The sprint relay—the 4 × 100—was won by a team from Canada, consisting of the Jamaican-Canadian from the final, a Haitian-Canadian, a Trinidadian-

Canadian, and another Jamaican-Canadian. Now it appears that African heritage is important as an initial determinant of sprinting ability, but also that the most important advantage of all is some kind of cultural or environmental factor associated with the Caribbean.

Or consider, in a completely different realm, the problem of hypertension. Black Americans have a higher incidence of hypertension than white Americans, even after you control for every conceivable variable, including income, diet, and weight, so it's tempting to conclude that there is something about being of African descent that makes blacks prone to hypertension. But it turns out that although some Caribbean countries have a problem with hypertension, others—Jamaica, St. Kitts, and the Bahamas—don't. It also turns out that people in Liberia and Nigeria—two countries where many New World slaves came from—have similar and perhaps even lower blood-pressure rates than white North Americans, while studies of Zulus, Indians, and whites in Durban, South Africa, showed that urban white males had the highest hypertension rates and urban white females had the lowest. So it's likely that the disease has nothing at all to do with Africanness.

The same is true for the distinctive muscle characteristic observed when Kenyans were compared with Swedes. Saltin, the Swedish physiologist, subsequently found many of the same characteristics in Nordic skiers who train at high altitudes and Nordic runners who train in very hilly regions—conditions, in other words, that resemble the mountainous regions of Kenya's Rift Valley, where so many of the country's distance runners come from. The key factor seems to be Kenya, not genes.

Lots of things that seem to be genetic in origin, then, actually aren't. Similarly, lots of things that we wouldn't normally think might affect athletic ability actually do. Once again, the social-science literature on male and female math achievement is instructive. Psychologists argue that when it comes to subjects like math, boys tend to engage in what's known as ability attribution. A boy who is doing well will attribute his success to the fact that he's good at math, and if he's doing badly he'll blame his teacher or his own lack of motivation—anything but his ability. That makes it easy for him to bounce back from failure or disappointment, and gives him a lot of confidence in the face of a tough new challenge. After all, if you think you do well in math because you're good at math, what's stopping you from being good at, say, algebra, or advanced calculus? On the other hand, if you ask a girl why she is doing well in math she will say, more often than not, that she succeeds because she works hard. If she's doing poorly, she'll say she isn't smart enough. This, as should be obvious, is a self-defeating attitude. Psychologists call it "learned helplessness"—the state in which failure is perceived as insurmountable. Girls who engage in effort attribution learn helplessness because in the face of a more difficult task like algebra or advanced calculus they can conceive of no solution. They're convinced that they can't work harder, because they think they're working as hard as they can, and that they can't rely on their intelligence, because they never thought they were that smart to begin with. In fact, one of the fascinating findings of attribution research is that the smarter girls are, the more likely they are to fall into this trap. High achievers are sometimes the most helpless. Here, surely, is part of the explanation for greater math variability among males. The female math whizzes, the ones who should be competing in the top one and two per cent with their male counterparts, are the ones most often paralyzed by a lack of confidence in their own aptitude. They think they belong only in the intellectual middle.

The striking thing about these descriptions of male and female stereotyping in math, though, is how similar they are to black and white stereotyping in athletics—to the unwritten rules holding that blacks achieve through natural ability and whites through effort. Here's how *Sports Illustrated* described, in a recent article, the white basketball player Steve Kerr, who plays alongside Michael Jordan for the Chicago Bulls. According to the magazine, Kerr is a "hard-working overachiever," distinguished by his "work ethic and heady play" and by a shooting style "born of a million practice shots." Bear in mind that Kerr is one of the best shooters in basketball today, and a key player on what is arguably one of the finest basketball teams in history. Bear in mind, too, that there is no evidence that Kerr works any harder than his teammates, least of all Jordan himself, whose work habits are legendary. But you'd never guess that from the article. It concludes, "All over America, whenever quicker, stronger gym rats see Kerr in action, they must wonder, How can that guy be out there instead of me?"

There are real consequences to this stereotyping. As the psychologists Carol Dweck and Barbara Licht write of high-achieving schoolgirls, "[They] may view themselves as so motivated and well disciplined that they cannot entertain the possibility that they did poorly on an academic task because of insufficient effort. Since blaming the teacher would also be out of character, blaming their abilities when they confront difficulty may seem like the most reasonable option." If you substitute the words "white athletes" for "girls" and "coach" for "teacher," I think you have part of the reason that so many white athletes are underrepresented at the highest levels of professional sports. Whites have been saddled with the athletic equivalent of learned helplessness—the idea that it is all but fruitless to try and compete at the highest levels, because they have only effort on their side. The causes of athletic and gender discrimination may be diverse, but its effects are not. Once again, blacks are like boys, and whites are like girls.

When I was in college, I once met an old acquaintance from my high-school running days. Both of us had long since quit track, and we talked about a recurrent fantasy we found we'd both had for getting back into shape. It was that we would go away somewhere remote for a year and do nothing but train, so that when the year was up we might finally know how good we were. Neither of us had any intention of doing this, though, which is why it was a fantasy. In adolescence, athletic excess has a certain appeal— during high school, I happily spent Sunday afternoons running up and down snow-covered sandhills—but with most of us that obsessiveness soon begins to fade. Athletic success depends on having the right genes and on a self-reinforcing belief in one's own ability. But it also depends on a rare form of tunnel vision. To be a great athlete, you have to *care*, and what was obvious to us both was that neither of us cared anymore. This is the last piece of the puzzle about what we mean when we say one group is better at something than another: sometimes different groups care about different things. Of the seven hundred men who play major-league baseball, for example, eighty-six come from either the Dominican Republic or Puerto Rico, even though those two islands have a combined population of only eleven million. But then baseball is something Dominicans and Puerto Ricans care about—and you can say the same thing about African-Americans and basketball, West Indians and sprinting, Canadians and hockey, and Russians and chess. Desire is the great intangible in performance, and unlike genes or psychological affect we can't measure it and trace its implications. This is the problem, in the end, with the question of whether blacks are better at sports than whites. It's not that it's offensive, or that it leads to discrimination. It's that, in some sense, it's not a terribly interesting question; "better" promises a tidier explanation than can ever be provided.

I quit competitive running when I was sixteen—just after the summer I had qualified for the Ontario track team in my age class. Late that August, we had traveled to St. John's, Newfoundland, for the Canadian championships. In those days, I was whippet-thin, as milers often are, five feet six and not much more than a hundred pounds, and I could skim along the ground so lightly that I barely needed to catch my breath. I had two white friends on that team, both distance runners, too, and both, improbably, even smaller and lighter than I was. Every morning, the three of us would run through the streets of St. John's, charging up the hills and flying down the other side. One of these friend went on to have a distinguished college running career, the other became a world-class miler; that summer, I myself was the Canadian record holder in the fifteen hundred metres for my age class. We were almost terrifyingly competitive, without a shred of doubt in our ability, and as we raced along we never stopped talking and joking, just to prove how absurdly easy we found running to be. I thought of us all as equals. Then, on the last day of our stay in St. John's, we ran to the bottom of Signal Hill, which is the town's principal geographical landmark—an abrupt outcrop as steep as anything in San Francisco. We stopped at the base, and the two of them turned to me and announced that we were all going to run straight up Signal Hill *backward*. I don't know whether I had more running ability than those two or whether my Africanness gave me any genetic advantage over their whiteness. What I do know is that such questions were irrelevant, because, as I realized, they were willing to go to far greater lengths to develop their talent. They ran up the hill backward. I ran home.

Lucy Grealy

Mirrorings

"Mirrorings" is the seed that eventually became Lucy Grealy's book *Autobiography of a Face*. In this essay, Grealy describes her childhood experience with cancer and the resulting deformity of her face, and how her appearance shaped her identity and self-worth. She vacillates between the knowledge that the image of her face is "a surface...not related to any true, deep definition of the self," and at the same time,"...it is only through appearances that we experience and make decisions about the everyday world." Consider ways that appearance is a kind of text that is read and interpreted, or "wrestled" with.

There was a long period of time, almost a year, during which I never looked in a mirror. It wasn't easy, for I'd never suspected just how omnipresent are our own images. I began by merely avoiding mirrors, but by the end of the year I found myself with an acute knowledge of the reflected image, its numerous tricks and wiles, how it can spring up at any moment: a glass table-top, a well-polished door handle, a darkened window, a pair of sunglasses, a restaurant's otherwise magnificent brass-plated coffee machine sitting innocently by the cash register.

At the time, I had just moved, alone, to Scotland and was surviving on the dole, as Britain's social security benefits are called. I didn't know anyone and had no idea how I was going to live, yet I went anyway because by happenstance I'd met a plastic surgeon there who said he could help me. I had been living in London working temp jobs. While in London, I'd received more nasty comments about my face than I had in the previous three years, living in Iowa, New York, and Germany. These comments, all from men and all odiously sexual, hurt and disoriented me. I also had journeyed to Scotland because after more than a dozen operations in the States my insurance had run out, along with my hope that further operations could make any *real* difference. Here, however, was a surgeon who had some new techniques,

145

and here, amazingly enough, was a government willing to foot the bill: I didn't feel I could pass up yet another change to "fix" my face, which I confusedly thought concurrent with "fixing" my self, my soul, my life.

Twenty years ago, when I was nine and living in America, I came home from school one day with a toothache. Several weeks and misdiagnoses later, surgeons removed most of the right side of my jaw in an attempt to prevent the cancer they found there from spreading. No one properly explained the operation to me, and I awoke in a cocoon of pain that prevented me from moving or speaking. Tubes ran in and out of my body, and because I was temporarily unable to speak after the surgery and could not ask questions, I made up my own explanations for the tubes' existence. I remember the mysterious manner the adults displayed toward me. They asked me to do things: lie still for x-rays, not cry for needles, and so on, tasks that, although not easy, never seemed equal to the praise I received in return. Reinforced to me again and again was how I was "a brave girl" for not crying, "a good girl" for not complaining, and soon I began defining myself this way, equating strength with silence.

Then the chemotherapy began. In the seventies chemo was even cruder than it is now, the basic premise being to poison patients right up to the very brink of their own death. Until this point I almost never cried and almost always received praise in return. Thus I got what I considered the better part of the deal. But now it was like a practical joke that had gotten out of hand. Chemotherapy was a nightmare and I wanted it to stop; I didn't want to be brave anymore. Yet I had grown so used to defining myself as "brave"—i.e., *silent*—that the thought of losing this sense of myself was even more terifying. I was certain that if I broke down I would be despicable in the eyes of both my parents and the doctors.

The task of taking me into the city for the chemo injections fell mostly on my mother, though sometimes my father made the trip. Overwhelmed by the sight of the vomiting and weeping, my father developed the routine of "going to get the car," meaning that he left the doctor's office before the injection was administered, on the premise that then he could have the car ready and waiting when it was all over. Ashamed of my suffering, I felt relief when he was finally out of the room. When my mother took me, she stayed in the room, yet this only made the distance between us even more tangible. She explained that it was wrong to cry *before* the needle went in; afterward was one thing, but before, that was mere fear, and hadn't I demonstrated my bravery earlier? Every Friday for two and a half years I climbed up onto that big doctor table and told myself not to cry, and every week I failed. The two large syringes were filled with chemicals so caustic to the vein that each had to be administered very slowly. The whole process took about four minutes; I had to remain utterly still. Dry retching began in the first fifteen seconds, then the throb behind my eyes gave everything a yellow-green aura, and the bone-deep pain alternating extreme hot and cold flashes made me tremble. But still I had to sit motionless and not move my arm. No one spoke to me—not the doctor, who was a paradigm of the cold-physician; not the nurse, who told my mother I reacted much more violently than many of "the other children"; and not my mother, who, surely overwhelmed by the sight of her child's suffering, thought the best thing to do was remind me to be brave, to try not to cry. All the while I hated myself for having wept before the needle went in, convinced that the nurse and my mother were right, that I was "overdoing it," that the throwing up was psychosomatic, that my mother was angry with me for not being good and brave enough.

Yet each week, two or three days after the injection, there came the first flicker of feeling better, the always forgotten and gratefully rediscovered understanding that to simply be well in my body was the greatest thing I could ask for. I thought other people felt appreciation and physical joy all the time, and I felt cheated because I was able to feel it only once a week.

Because I'd lost my hair, I wore a hat constantly, but this fooled no one, least of all myself. During this time, my mother worked in a nursing home in a Hasidic community. Hasidic law dictates that married women cover their hair, and most commonly this is done with a wig. My mother's friends were now all too willing to donate their discarded wigs, and soon the house seemed filled with them. I never wore one, for they frightened me even when my mother insisted I looked better in one of the few that actually fit. Yet I didn't know how to say no to the women who kept graciously offering their wigs. The cats enjoyed sleeping on them and the dogs playing with them, and we grew used to having to pick a wig up off a chair we wanted to sit in. It never struck us as odd until one day a visitor commented wryly as he cleared a chair for himself, and suddenly a great wave of shame overcame me. I had nightmares about wigs and flushed if I even heard the word, and one night I put myself out of my misery by getting up after everyone was asleep and gathering all the wigs except for one the dogs were fond of and that they had chewed up anyway. I hid all the rest in an old chest.

When you are only ten, which is when the chemotherapy began, two and a half years seem like your whole life, yet it did finally end, for the cancer was gone. I remember the last day of treatment clearly because it was the only day on which I succeeded in not crying, and because later, in private, I cried harder than I had in years; I thought now I would no longer be "special," that without the arena of chemotherapy in which to prove myself no one would ever love me, that I would fade unnoticed into the background. But this idea about *not being different* didn't last very long. Before, I foolishly believed that people stared at me because I was bald. After my hair eventually grew in, it didn't take long before I understood that I looked different for another reason. My face. People stared at me in stores, and other children made fun of me to the point that I came to expect such re-actions constantly, wherever I went. School became a battleground.

Halloween, that night of frights, became my favorite holiday because I could put on a mask and walk among the blessed for a few brief, sweet hours. Such freedom I felt, walking down the street, my face hidden! Through the imperfect oval holes I could peer out at other faces, masked or painted or not, and see on those faces nothing but the normal faces of childhood looking back at me, faces I mistakenly thought were the faces everyone else but me saw all the time, faces that were simply curious and ready for fun, not the faces I usually braced myself for, the cruel, lonely, vicious ones I spent every day other than Halloween waiting to see around each corner. As I breathed in the condensed, plastic-scented air under the mask, I somehow thought that I was breathing in normality, that this joy and weightlessness were what the world was composed of, and that it was only my face that kept me from it, my face that was my own mask that kept me from knowing the joy I was sure everyone but me lived with intimate-ly. How could the other children not know it? Not know that to be free of the fear of taunts and the burden of knowing no one would ever love you was all that anyone could ever ask for? I was a pauper walking for a short while in the clothes of the prince, and when the day ended I gave up my disguise with dismay.

I was living in an extreme situation, and because I did not particularly care for the world I was in, I lived in others, and because the world I did live in was dangerous now, I incorporated this danger into my secret life. I imag-ined myself to be an Indian. Walking down the streets, I stepped through the forest, my body ready for any opportunity to fight or flee one of the big cats that I knew stalked me. Vietnam and Cambodia, in the news then as scenes of catastrophic horror, were other places I walked through daily. I made my way down the school hall, knowing a land mine or a sniper might give themselves away at any moment with the subtle metal click I'd read about. Compared with a land mine, a mere insult about my face seemed a frivolous thing.

In those years, not yet a teenager, I secretly read—knowing it was some-how inappropriate—works by Primo Levi and Elie Wiesel, and every book by a survivor I could find by myself without asking the librarian. Auschwitz, Birkenau: I felt the blows of the capos and somehow knew that because at any moment we might be called upon to live for a week on one loaf of bread and some water called soup, the peanut-butter sandwich I found on my plate was nothing less than a miracle, an utter and sheer miracle capable of making me literally weep with joy.

I decided to become a "deep" person. I wasn't exactly sure what this would entail, but I believed that if I could just find the right philosophy, think the right thoughts, my suffering would end. To try to understand the world I was in, I undertook to find out what was "real," and I quickly began seeing reality as existing in the lowest common denominator, that suffering was the one and only dependable thing. But rather than spend all of my time despairing, though certainly I did plenty of that, I developed a form of defensive egomania: I felt I was the only one walking about in the world who understood what was really important. I looked upon people complaining about the most mundane things—nothing on TV, traffic jams, the price of new clothes—and felt joy because I knew how unimportant those things really were and felt unenlightened superiority because other people didn't. Because in my fantasy life I had learned to be thankful for each cold, blanketless night that I survived on the cramped wooden bunks, my pain and despair were a stroll through the country in comparison. I was often miserable, but I knew that to feel warm instead of cold was its own kind of joy, that to eat was a reenactment of the grace of some god whom I could only dimly define, and that to simply be alive was a rare, ephemeral gift.

As I became a teenager, my isolation began. My nonidentical twin sister started going out with boys, and I started—my most tragic mistake of all—to listen to and believe the taunts thrown at me daily by the very boys she and the other girls were interested in. I was a dog, a monster, the ugliest girl they had ever seen. Of all the remarks, the most damaging wasn't even directed at me but was really an insult to "Jerry," a boy I never saw because every day between fourth and fifth periods, when I was cornered by a particular group of kids, I was too ashamed to lift my eyes off the floor. "Hey, look, it's Jerry's girlfriend!" they shrieked when they saw me, and I felt such shame, knowing that this was the deepest insult to Jerry that they could imagine.

When pressed to it, one makes compensations. I came to love winter, when I could wrap up the disfigured lower half of my face in a scarf: I could speak to people and they would have no idea to whom and to what they were really speaking. I developed the bad habits of letting my long hair hang in my face and of always covering my chin and mouth with my hand, hoping it might be mistaken as a thoughtful, accidental gesture. I also became interested in horses and got a job at a rundown local stable. Having those horses to go to each day after school saved my life; I spent all of my time either with them or thinking about them. Completely and utterly repressed by the time I was sixteen, I was convinced that I would never want a boyfriend, not ever, and wasn't it convenient for me, even a blessing, that none would ever want me. I told myself I was free to concentrate on the "true reality" of life, whatever that was. My sister and her friends put on blue eye shadow, blow-dried their hair, and spent interminable hours in the local mall, and I looked down on them for this, knew they were misleading themselves and being overly occupied with the "mere surface" of living. I'd had thoughts like this when I was younger, ten or twelve, but now my philosophy was haunted by desires so frightening I was unable even to admit they existed.

Throughout all of this, I was undergoing reconstructive surgery in an attempt to rebuild my jaw. It started when I was fifteen, two years after chemo ended. I had known for years I would have operations to fix my face, and at night I fantasized about how good my life would finally be then. One day I got a clue that maybe it wouldn't be so easy. An older plastic surgeon explained the process of "pedestals" to me, and told me it would take *ten years* to fix my face. Ten years? Why even bother, I thought; I'll be ancient by then. I went to a medical library and looked up the "pedestals" he talked about. There were gruesome pictures of people with grotesque tubes of their own skin growing out of their bodies, tubes of skin that were harvested like some kind of crop and then rearranged, with results that did not look at all normal or acceptable to my eye. But then I met a younger surgeon, who was working on a new way of grafting that did not involve pedestals, and I became more hopeful and once again began to await the fixing of my face, the day when I would be whole, content, loved.

   Long-term plastic surgery is not like in the movies. There is no one single operation that will change everything, and there is certainly no slow unwrapping of the gauze in order to view the final, remarkable result. There is always swelling, sometimes to a grotesque degree, there are often bruises, and always there are scars. After each operation, too frightened to simply go look in the mirror, I developed an oblique method, with several stages. First, I tried to catch my reflection in an overhead lamp: the roundness of the metal distorted my image just enough to obscure details and give no true sense of size or proportion. Then I slowly worked my way up to looking at the reflection in someone's eyeglasses, and from there I went to walking as briskly as possible by a mirror, glancing only quickly. I repeated this as many times as it would take me, passing the mirror slightly more slowly each time until finally I was able to stand still and confront myself.

   The theory behind most reconstructive surgery is to take large chunks of muscle, skin, and bone and slap them into the roughly appropriate place, then, slowly begin to carve this mess into some sort of shape. It involves long, major operations, countless lesser ones, a lot of pain, and many, many years. And also, it does not always work. With my young surgeon in New York, who with each passing year was becoming not so young, I had two or three soft-tissue grafts, two skin grafts, a bone graft, and some dozen other operations to "revise" my face, yet when I left graduate school at the age of twenty-five I was still more or less in the same position I had started in: a deep hole in the right side of my face and a rapidly shrinking left side and chin, a result of the radiation I'd had as a child and the stress placed upon the bone by the the other operations. I was caught in a cycle of having a big operation, one that would force me to look monstrous from the swelling for many months, then having the subsequent revision operations that improved my looks tremendously, and then slowly, over the period of a few months or a year, watching the graft reabsorb back into my body, slowly shrinking down and leaving me with nothing but the scarred donor site the graft had originally come from.

It wasn't until I was in college that I finally allowed that maybe, just maybe, it might be nice to have a boyfriend. I went to a small, liberal, predominantly female school and suddenly, after years of alienation in high school, discovered that there were other people I could enjoy talking to who thought me intelligent and talented. I was, however, still operating on the assumption that no one, not ever, would be physically attracted to me, and in a curious way this shaped my personality. I became forthright and honest in the way that only the truly self-confident are, who do not expect to be rejected, and in the way of those like me, who do not even dare to ask acceptance from others and therefore expect no rejection. I had come to know myself as a person, but I would be in graduate school before I was literally, physically able to use my name and the word "woman" in the same sentence.

Now my friends repeated for me endlessly that most of it was in my mind, that, granted, I did not look like everyone else, but that didn't mean I looked bad. I am sure now that they were right some of the time. But with the constant surgery I was in a perpetual state of transfiguration. I rarely looked the same for more than six months at a time. So ashamed of my face, I was unable even to admit that this constant change affected me; I let everyone who wanted to know that it was only what was inside that mattered, that I had "grown used to" the surgery, that none of it bothered me at all. Just as I had done in childhood, I pretended nothing was wrong, and this was constantly mistaken by others for bravery. I spent a great deal of time looking in the mirror in private, positioning my head to show off my eyes and nose, which were not only normal but quite pretty, as my friends told me often. But I could not bring myself to see them for more than a moment. I looked in the mirror and saw not the normal upper half of my face but only the disfigured lower half.

People still teased me. Not daily, as when I was younger, but in ways that caused me more pain than ever before. Children stared at me, and I learned to cross the street to avoid them; this bothered me, but not as much as the insults I got from men. Their taunts came at me not because I was disfigured but because I was a disfigured *woman*. They came from boys, sometimes men, and almost always from a group of them. I had long, blond hair, and I also had a thin figure. Sometimes, from a distance, men would see a thin blonde and whistle, something I dreaded more than anything else because I knew that as they got closer, their tune, so to speak, would inevitably change; they would stare openly or, worse, turn away quickly in shame or repulsion. I decided to cut my hair to avoid any misconception that anyone, however briefly, might have about my being attractive. Only two or three times have I ever been teased by a single person, and I can think of only one time when I was ever teased by a woman. Had I been a man, would I have had to walk down the street while a group of young women followed and denigrated my sexual worth?

Not surprisingly, then, I viewed sex as my salvation. I was sure that if only I could get someone to sleep with me, it would mean I wasn't ugly, that I was attractive, even lovable. This line of reasoning led me into the beds of several manipulative men who liked themselves even less than they liked me, and I in turn left each short-term affair hating myself, obscenely sure that if only I had been prettier it would have worked—he would have loved me and it would have been like those other love affairs that I was certain "normal" women had all the time. Gradually, I became unable to say "I'm depressed" but could say only "I'm ugly," because the two had become inextricably linked in my mind. Into that universal lie, that sad equation of "if only…" that we are all prey to, I was sure that if only I had a normal face, then I would be happy.

The new surgeon in Scotland, Oliver Fenton, recommended that I undergo a procedure involving something called a tissue expander, followed by a bone graft. A tissue expander is a small balloon placed under the skin and then slowly blown up over the course of several months, the object being to stretch out the skin and create room and cover for the new bone. It's a bizarre, nightmarish thing to do to your face, yet I was hopeful about the end results and I was also able to spend the three months that the expansion took in the hospital. I've always felt safe in hospitals: they're the one place I feel free from the need to explain the way I look. For this reason the first tissue expander was bearable—just —and the bone graft that followed it was a success; it did not melt away like the previous ones.

The surgical stress this put upon what remained of my original jaw instigated the deterioration of that bone, however, and it became unhappily apparent that I was going to need the same operation I'd just had on the right side done to the left. I remember my surgeon telling me this at an outpatient clinic. I planned to be traveling down to London that same night on an overnight train, and I barely made it to the station on time, such a fumbling state of despair was I in.

I could not imagine going through it *again*, and just as I had done all my life, I searched and searched through my intellect for a way to make it okay, make it bearable, for a way to *do* it. I lay awake all night on that train, feeling the tracks slip beneath me with odd eroticism, when I remembered an afternoon from my three months in the hospital. Boredom was a big problem those long afternoons, the days marked by meals and television programs. Waiting for the afternoon tea to come, wondering desperately how I could make time pass, it had suddenly occurred to me that I didn't have to make time pass, that it would do it of its own accord, that I simply had to relax and take no action. Lying on the train, remembering that, I realized I had no obligation to improve my situation, that I didn't have to explain or understand it, that I could just simply let it happen. By the time the train pulled into King's Cross station, I felt able to bear it yet again, not entirely sure what other choice I had.

But there was an element I didn't yet know about. When I returned to Scotland to set up a date to have the tissue expander inserted, I was told quite casually that I'd be in the hospital only three or four days. Wasn't I going to spend the whole expansion time in the hospital? I asked in a whisper. What's the point of that? came the answer. You can just come in every day to the outpatient ward to have it expanded. Horrified by this, I was speechless. I would have to live and move about in the outside world with a giant balloon inside the tissue of my face? I can't remember what I did for the next few days before I went into the hospital, but I vaguely recall that these days involved a great deal of drinking alone in bars and at home.

I had the operation and went home at the end of the week. The only things that gave me any comfort during the months I lived with my tissue expander were my writing and Franz Kafka. I started a novel and completely absorbed myself in it, writing for hours each day. The only way I could walk down the street, could stand the stares I received, was to think to myself, "I'll bet none of them are writing a novel." It was that strange, old, familiar form of egomania, directly related to my dismissive, conceited thoughts of adolescence. As for Kafka, who had always been one of my favorite writers, he helped me in that I felt permission to feel alienated, and to have that alienation be okay, bearable, noble even. In the same way that imagining I lived in Cambodia helped me as a child, I walked the streets of my dark little Scottish city by the sea and knew without doubt that I was living in a story Kafka would have been proud to write.

The one good thing about a tissue expander is that you look so bad with it in that no matter what you look like once it's finally removed, your face has to look better. I had my bone graft and my fifth soft-tissue graft and, yes, even I had to admit I looked better. But it didn't look like me. Something was wrong: was *this* the face I had waited through eighteen years and almost thirty operations for? I somehow just couldn't make what I saw in the mirror correspond to the person I thought I was. It wasn't only that I continued to feel ugly; I simply could not conceive of the image as belonging to me. My own image was the image of a stranger, and rather than try to understand this, I simply stopped looking in the mirror. I perfected the technique of brushing my teeth without a mirror, grew my hair in such a way that it would require only a quick, simple brush, and wore clothes that were simply and easily put on, no complex layers or lines that might require even the most minor of visual adjustments.

On one level I understood that the image of my face was merely that, an image, a surface that was not directly related to any true, deep definition of the self. But I also knew that it is only through appearances that we experience and make decisions about the everyday world, and I was not always able to gather the strength to prefer the deeper world to the shallower one. I looked for ways to find a bridge that would allow me access to both, rather than riding out the constant swings between peace and anguish. The only direction I had to go in to achieve this was to strive for a state of awareness and self-honesty that sometimes, to this day, occasionally rewards me. I have found, I believe, that our whole lives are dominated, though it is not always so clearly translatable, by the question "How do I look?" Take all the many nouns in our lives—car, house, job, family, love, friends—and substitute the personal pronoun "I." It is not that we are all so self-obsessed; it is that all things eventually relate back to ourselves, and it is our own sense of how we appear to the world by which we chart our lives, how we navigate our personalities, which would otherwise be adrift in the ocean of *other* people's obsessions.

One evening toward the end of my year-long separation from the mirror, I was sitting in a café talking to someone—an attractive man, as it happened—and we were having a lovely, engaging conversation. For some reason I suddenly wondered what I looked like to him. What was he *actually* seeing when he saw me? So many times I've asked this of myself, and always the answer is this: a warm, smart woman, yes, but an unattractive one. I sat there in the café and asked myself this old question, and startlingly, for the first time in my life, I had no answer readily prepared. I had not looked in a mirror for so long that I quite simply had no clue as to what I looked like. I studied the man as he spoke; my entire life I had seen my ugliness reflected back to me. But now, as reluctant as I was to admit it, the only indication in my companion's behavior was positive.

And then, that evening in that café, I experienced a moment of the freedom I'd been practicing for behind my Halloween mask all those years ago. But whereas as a child I expected my liberation to come as a result of gaining something, a new face, it came to me now as the result of shedding something, of shedding my image. I once thought that truth was eternal, that when you understood something it was with you forever. I know now that this isn't so, that most truths are inherently unretainable, that we have to work hard all our lives to remember the most basic things. Society is no help; it tells us again and again that we can most be ourselves by looking like someone else, leaving our own faces behind to turn into ghosts that will inevitably resent and haunt us. It is no mistake that in movies and literature the dead sometimes know they are dead only after they can no longer see themselves in the mirror; and as I sat there feeling the warmth of the cup against my palm, this small observation seemed like a great revelation to me. I wanted to tell the man I was with about it, but he was involved in his own topic and I did not want to interrupt him, so instead I looked with curiosity toward the window behind him, its night-darkened glass reflecting the whole café, to see if I could, now, recognize myself.

Rita Hardiman & Bailey Jackson

Conceptual Foundations for Social Justice Courses

Bobbie Harro

The Cycle of Socialization

The two following essays—this one, by Rita Hardiman and Bailey Jackson, and the next one, "The Cycle of Socialization" by Bobbie Harro—have been grouped together to be used as a unit, though they also function quite well independently of each other. Those who have approached them as a unit generally recommend reading Harro's essay first, then Hardiman and Jackson's.

The authors of both essays are all associated with the University of Massachusetts in one way or another: Bobbie Harro received her Ed.D. from the University and currently teaches in the School of Human Services at Springfield College, while Bailey Jackson is a professor and former Dean of the University of Massachusetts School of Education, and Rita Hardiman sometimes teaches at the University as well, and is the co-founder of New Perspectives, Inc., "a research, training, and consulting organization that specializes in social justice and social diversity in organizations." All three authors are interested and actively involved with, in one way or another, education and social justice. Bobbie Harro examines the construction of our beliefs concerning identity, making visible the often invisible forces at work. By exposing the workings of the cycle of identity construction, Harro leads the reader to examine the construction of her own identity, and raises a number of challenging questions about education and identity. Hardiman and Jackson follow up on some of these questions, particularly in terms of the relationship of identity to oppression: they believe that oppression is learned by both the oppressor and the oppressed, and they maintain that it can therefore be unlearned, step by step. In their essay, they introduce the social identity development model that describes five stages of consciousness for both oppressor and oppressed as each moves toward a "liberated social identity in an oppressive environment."

Conceptual Foundations for Social Justice Courses

Our conceptual model includes a definition of oppression in which individuals play a variety of roles in a multilayered and dynamic script. The model includes the dominant and subordinate social roles, as oppressor and oppressed (or agent and target of oppression), in interaction with the structural characteristics that hold the overall script in place. We present a generic model of social identity development based on our earlier work on black identity development (Jackson, 1976a,b) and white identity development (Hardiman, 1979, 1982) in order to understand and anticipate how these roles may interact with each other and change over time in relation to a person's various social group memberships.

During the late 1970s and early 1980s we used the identity development models in courses on racism, cultural bias, and counseling from a racial perspective. Our interactions with colleagues and students engaged in the women's, gay liberation, and disability rights movements, and workshops focusing on antisemitism and classism, led us to see striking parallels and commonalities in the manifestations of different forms of oppression. We also explored the applicability of social identity development for other peoples of color (Kim, 1981) biracial people (Wijeyesinghe, 1992), and women and members of other social identity groups within the contexts of racism, sexism, antisemitism, heterosexism, ableism, and classism. We then extended the racial identity models to a generic model that examines how members of agent and target groups experiece internalized domination or internalized subordination and change their sense of relationship to other members of their target or agent group at various stages of consciousness.

Our starting point is that once systems of oppression are in place, they are self-perpetuating. We want to understand the structures of self-perpetuation, the roles people play in the system of oppression and how these roles interact. Eventually our generic model of social identity development came to be subsumed within the general model of oppression.

According to our model, *social oppression* exists when one social group, whether knowingly or unconsciously, exploits another social group for its own benefit. Social oppression is distinct from a situation of simple brute force in that it is an interlocking system that involves ideological control as well as domination and control of the social institutions and resources of the society, resulting in a condition of privilege for the agent group relative to the disenfranchisement and exploitation of the target group.

Oppression is not simply an ideology or set of beliefs that assert one group's superiority over another, nor is it random violence, harassment, or discrimination toward members of target groups. A condition of social oppression exists when the following key elements are in place:

- The agent group has the power to define and name reality and determine what is "normal," "real," or "correct."

- Harassment, discrimination, exploitation, marginalization, and other forms of differential and unequal treatment are institutionalized and systematic. These acts often do not require the conscious thought or effort of individual members of the agent group but are rather part of business as usual that become embedded in social structures over time.

- Psychological colonization of the target group occurs through socializing the oppressed to internalize their oppressed condition and collude with the oppressor's ideology and social system. This is what Freire refers to as the oppressed playing "host" to the oppressor (1970).

- The target group's culture, language, and history are misrepresented, discounted, or eradicated and the dominant group's culture is imposed.

Social oppression then involves a relationship between an agent group and a target group that keeps the system of domination in place. Recognizing the importance of collusion to the system of oppression does not mean that targets share equal responsibility for their situation with agents, or that they collude willingly. Rather, the collusion of targets is the result of agents taking control over time of the institutions of a society, as well as the minds, ideology, language, culture, and history of the targets.

Part of the method of establishing dominance in the system of oppression is the naming of the target group by the agent group. The ability to name reflects who has power. Agent groups establish their dominance by controlling how targets are named. The eradication or chipping away of a group's identity is not always a visible or conscious process. Rather it happens gradually, and in many respects, unconsciously. Over an extended period of time, a system of domination becomes institutionalized so that conscious intent is no longer necessary to keep power and privilege in the hands of the agent group.

While oppression is reproduced in the institutions and structures of society, individual people also play a role in its operation and maintenance. Some groups and individuals are victims or targets of injustice and oppression and other groups and individuals are agents who reap the benefits of illegitimate privilege by virture of their social group membership(s).

⊷ ⊵◈⊰ ⊶

Social Identity Development Theory

The generic social identity development theory is an adaptation of black identity development theory (Jackson, 1976) and white identity development theory (Hardiman, 1982). Social identity development theory has also been influenced by other theorists and applications to other social groups (Cross, 1971, 1978, 1991; Helms, 1990; Kim, 1981; Schapiro, 1985). Social identity development theory describes attributes that are common to the identity development process for members of all target and agent groups.

We present the stages, for purposes of conceptual clarity, as if a person were to move neatly from one stage to the next. In reality most people experience several stages simultaneously, holding complex perspectives on a range of issues and living a mixture of social identities. This developmental model can be helpful in understanding student perspectives and selecting instructional strategies, but we caution against using it simplistically to label people.

Stage I—Naive/No Social Consciousness

At birth and during early childhood, agents and targets are unaware of the complex codes of appropriate behavior for members of their social group. They naively operate from their own needs, interests, and curiosity about social group differences and break rules and push against the boundaries of social identity group membership. Through these boundary violations they

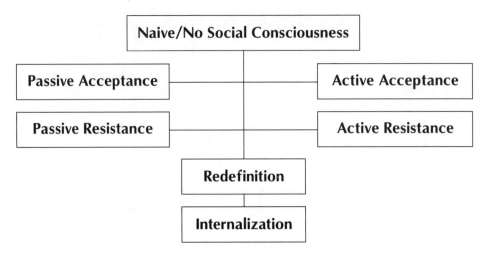

Stages of Social Identity Development (Hardiman & Jackson, 1992)

begin to learn lessons about what it means to be a member of their social identity group—agent or a target.

In the transition from Naive to Acceptance consciousness, agents and targets become aware of the differences between themselves and members of other social groups. While they may not feel completely comfortable with people who are different, they generally don't feel fearful, hostile, superior, or inferior. Children at this stage display an interest in understanding the differences between people and often ask questions that embarrass or threaten adults, such as "Why do people have different skin color?" or "Can two women get married?" This stage is brief and covers the period between birth and three to four years of age.

The events that transform children from a naive or unsocialized stage to a stage of acceptance of their social dominance or subordination are numerous. The most significant socializers appear to be parents, who are role models of attitudes and behaviors, and who convey important messages through their words and silences, actions and inactions; the formal education system, including teachers, and the formal and informal curriculum; peers, who set the standards for appropriate and inappropriate behavior; religious organizations; the mass media; and the larger community with its norms, laws, social structures, and cultures that set the limits, formal and informal, for the behavior of citizens.

Two related changes take place as the young agent or target moves into the Acceptance stage. One, they begin to learn and adopt an ideology or belief system about their own and other social identity groups. Another is they begin to learn that the world has rules, laws, institutions, and authority figures that permit certain behaviors and prohibit others, even if these rules do not make sense, and violate other principles such as freedom, equality, and axioms such as "do unto others." Both types of learning are immensely powerful, pervasive, and consistent, so much so that the acceptance of this socialization to some degree seems inevitable. This socialization process results in the second stage of identity development, Acceptance.

Stage II—Acceptance

The stage of Acceptance represents some degree of internalization, whether conscious or unconscious, of the dominant culture's logic system. People at this stage have "accepted" the messages about the nature of their group identity, the superiority of agents (Whites, heterosexuals, men, Christians), and the inferiority of targets (people of color, gays, lesbians, bisexuals, women, Jews). The Acceptance stage has two manifestations, passive and active, which refer to the relative consciousness and intentionality with which a person holds to the dominant belief system.

Agent in Acceptance

As agents in the Passive Acceptance stage have learned and to some degree internalized codes of appropriate behavior, conscious effort is no longer required to remind them of what to do and how to think. Dominant beliefs and actions are part of their everyday life, as when a white store clerk carefully watches black customers to see if they are shoplifting, or a Christian manager sets a date for an important meeting on a Jewish holiday. Questions that arose during the naive stage have been submerged and repressed such that individuals are able to live their lives without doubt. When questions occasionally arise, there is a built-in system of rationalization to fall back on and provide answers.

For those raised in the Active Acceptance stage, instruction about the inadequacies, weaknesses, deviance, and basic inferiority of targeted people occurs in a very direct manner. They are told in many ways "that's how those people are"—Mexicans are lazy, Jews control the banks, women are dumb, gays are sinners, and the disabled are objects of pity. People raised in a Passive Acceptance environment learn to blame the victim for the effect of oppression (Ryan, 1971). The key difference between Active and Passive messages is whether they are overt or covert.

Agents of oppression who have adopted an Acceptance consciousness are generally unaware that they have privileges as dominant group members of an oppressive society. They are usually unaware that they think of themselves and other agents as superior. More subtle is the assumption that the agent's experience is normative or "the way things are done." Therefore men should of course be heterosexual and masculine and those who deviate are sick or abnormal. Passive Acceptance of the agent's perspective as normative is more subtle than outright belief in superiority, but in practice it has many of the same negative effects as Active Acceptance.

Agents of oppression who move from the Naive stage into the entry and adoption phase of Active Acceptance tend to express their superiority more directly. In the extreme form, agents in Active Acceptance may join organizations (KKK, Christian Identity) that are designed to promote supremacy. Many agents who are in the Active Acceptance stage devote their lives to maintaining their dominant perspective and privilege.

Most agents are well into their adult years before encountering events or circumstances which begin the transition to the Resistance stage. This transition marks a confusing and often painful period. Information or experiences that contradict the Acceptance world view have been initially ignored or passed off as isolated or exceptional. Gradually as the individual begins to encounter more conflicting information these isolated incidents form a discernible pattern. The contradictions that initiate the transition period can occur in the form of a personal connection or friendship with a target, or through significant social events or information presented in books, media, and formal education.

Agents begin to experience difficult emotions during this exit phase and entry into Resistance consciousness. Their accepted identity as White, male, Christian, or heterosexual comes under scrutiny and they are often afraid and uncertain what the implications of this self-examination will be. The questioning that begins during this exit phase of Acceptance builds into the stage of Resistance.

Targets in Acceptance

Targets in the Acceptance stage have learned and accepted messages about the inferiority of targets and target culture. Often these negative/oppressive messages are held simultaneously and in contradiction to more positive messages about their social group conveyed by same-group adults or social peers. Typically, the person lives with and rationalizes varying degrees of cognitive dissonance on a daily basis.

Some targets operate at a Passive Acceptance consciousness, unaware of the degree to which their thoughts, feelings and behaviors reflect the dominant group ideology. Some women prefer to work for men or to purchase services from male doctors, dentists, and lawyers because of an ingrained belief that women are not smart or capable enough to handle these jobs.

Targets in the Active Acceptance stage more consciously identify with the dominant group and its ideology. For example, some people of color are opposed to civil rights laws and affirmative action because they believe that people of color are less successful due to their own laziness and pathological culture.

Socialization of targets into the dominant world view is essentially an invisible process that is difficult to unlearn. Targets who retain this world view for life successfully rationalize efforts on the part of others to change their consciousness. Even targets who experience an urge to question their current status may find themselves seduced into remaining in place by the rewards offered by agents.

Targets who reach the exit phase of an Acceptance world view begin to acknowledge the collusive and harmful effects of the learned logic system and behavior patterns. Sometimes external events are so blatant that the person is hard-pressed not to recognize the existence of oppression. Other times an individual may encounter someone of their own group who is a powerful role model, as when a lesbian in Acceptance encounters an "out" lesbian who spurs her to reject internalized homophobia, and a closeted existence.

Stage III—Resistance

The Resistance stage is one of increased awareness of the existence of oppression and its impact on agents and targets.

Agents in Resistance

As a result of experiences and information that challenge the accepted ideology and self-definition, agents entering Resistance reject earlier social positions and begin formulating a new world view. This is a dramatic paradigm shift from an ideology that blames the victims for their condition to an ideology that names one's own agent group as the source of oppression as agents become aware that oppression exists and causes the disparity between agent and target groups. Furthermore, agents begin investigating their own role in perpetuating oppression. For example, a white person may become aware for the first time of white privilege in employment, recreation, travel, or schooling.

Anger is a prevalent feeling at this stage—anger toward other agents and the nature of the agent's social group identity. Some agents wish they weren't members of their dominant group and distance themselves from other agents who don't share their new consciousness. Some zealously confront other agents for their group's oppressive actions and attitudes. Others are ostracized because their behaviors and attitudes threaten other agents who are in the Acceptance stage.

Agents in Resistance begin to develop a systemic view of how their identity has been shaped by social factors beyond their control as they re-examine the roles agents play in supporting oppression. This occurs particularly for liberal agents who have been involved in helping targets assimilate into the agent's culture and society. When the problem is redefined as an agent problem, the strategies for addressing it change. This new understanding helps some move beyond guilt and feeling overwhelmed by personal responsibility. Having negotiated the conflict between their own values and societal definitions of appropriate behavior for their group, they begin to move towards a new identity. At Resistance agents develop an awareness of their social identity, but one which is not necessarily positive. The task of Redefinition then is to engage in a process of renaming and developing a social identity that is positive and affirming.

Targets in Resistance

Acknowledgment and questioning of the cumulative experiences of oppression and their negative effects lead targets to the Resistance stage. Targets generally begin by questioning previously accepted "truths" about the way things are, for example, that men are superior, or that any person of color who works hard enough can realize their dreams. Gradually target group members become more skilled at identifying the oppressive premises woven into the fabric of all aspects of their social experience. They may also begin to feel intensified hostility toward agents, and other targets who collude with agents.

The overt expression of hostile reactions to oppression marks the transition from the entry to the adoption phase of Resistance. At this point the target group member has fully internalized the antithesis of the earlier Acceptance consciousness, and may experience increased and sometimes overwhelming anger, pain, hurt, and rage. The combination of these powerful emotions and the intellectual understanding of how oppression works may feel all-consuming. At this stage members of the target group often adopt a posture as anti-agent, for example anti-White, anti-male, anti-straight. Identity is defined in opposition to the oppressor.

Some targets may find that the Resistance stage results in losing benefits acquired when they colluded with the Acceptance consciousness and may choose a path of Passive Resistance, in hopes that they will be able to stay in favor with agents, while rejecting oppression. This strategy typically proves too frustating and contradictory to sustain.

For most targeted people at Resistance the primary task is to end the pattern of collusion and cleanse their internalized oppressive beliefs and attitudes. During the course of the Resistance stage, targets often discover that they have become proactive and do have some power, even if not of the same type and quantity available to members of agent groups. Also, the targets begin to recognize that a considerable amount of energy has been put into "Who I am not." As they move toward the new question "Who am I?" they exit Resistance and enter Redefinition.

Stage IV—Redefinition

The focus of the Redefinition stage is on creating an identity that is independent of an oppressive system based on hierarchical superiority and inferiority.

Agents in Redefinition

At this stage agents begin to redefine the social group identity in a way that is independent of social oppression and stereotyping of targeted group(s). In prior stages agents have not been concerned with their own social identity but focused on targeted people and *their* problems (Acceptance). Or they have *reacted* to the social issue of oppression (Resistance). The experiences in Resistance leave agents feeling negatively about their social group membership, confused about their role in dealing with oppression, and isolated from many other members of their social group. Developing a positive definition of their social identity and identifying aspects of their culture and group that are affirming are necessary parts of this stage. Men who form groups to examine their socialization and critically assess the definition of masculinity that they have internalized illustrate agents at this stage.

In contrast to the negative feelings about their social group identity in Resistance, people in Redefinition develop pride in their group and a sense of personal esteem. There is a recognition that all groups have unique and different values that enrich human life, but that no culture or social group is better than another. The transition from Redefinition to Internalization emanates from the need to integrate and internalize this new social identity within one's total identity. Having established a sense of pride in themselves and their group, they are now ready to act more spontaneously on their values in everyday life.

Targets in Redefinition

In the Redefinition stage targeted people are primarily concerned with defining themselves in terms that are independent of the perceived strengths and/or weaknesses of the agent and the agent's culture. The Redefinition stage is particularly significant for targets because it is at this juncture that they shift their attention and energy away from a concern for their interactions with agents toward a concern for primary contact with members of their own social group who are at the same stage of consciousness. This type of behavior tends to be viewed negatively in an oppressive society and is often seen as counterproductive by liberal agents who view themselves as kind and benevolent. Members of targeted groups who are in Redefinition are generally labeled troublemakers or separatists. Agents who have worked to get subordinates into dominant social institutions will be particularly confused and/or put off by this apparent "self-segregating" and ungrateful behavior by targeted people. Targets in Redefinition, however, do not see interaction with agents as useful in their quest for a positive or nurturing identity.

Renaming is one primary concern in this stage as targets search for paradigms that facilitate this task. This search often begins with the formation of a new reference group consisting of other targeted people with a Redefinition consciousness. Targeted people who are still embedded in the Acceptance or Resistance stages of consciousness are not likely to share the same concerns and personal needs as those experiencing Redefinition, and they are generally not supportive of the issues that Redefining people are attempting to address. Many targets form support groups and networks of like-minded people to focus on issues of self-definition.

The search for a social identity often involves reclaiming one's group heritage. Through revisiting or exploring one's heritage/culture, targets in Redefinition often find values, traditions, customs, philosophical assumptions, and concepts of time-work-family that are appealing and nurturing. They rediscover many aspects of their heritage that have been handed down through the generations and still affect their way of life today. They become clearer about the uniqueness of their group and come to realize they are considerably more than merely the victims of oppression. As they experience their group identity in a way that engenders pride, they may adopt a new name such as disabled rather than handicapped, or Black or African American rather than Negro. When people in Redefinition begin to contemplate the implications that this new sense of self has for all aspects of life, they exit Redefinition and enter Internalization.

Stage V—Internalization

In the Internalization stage, the main task is to incorporate the identity developed in the Redefinition stage into all aspects of everyday life. Even though targets have internalized consciousness, they are still likely to revisit or encounter situations that trigger earlier world views. For example, a Jew may feel that other Jews are acting "too Jewish" in a corporate setting and suddenly realize how he or she has bought into antisemitic stereotypes. The process of refining identity can be ongoing as new sources of history or past feelings and thoughts characteristic of earlier stages reemerge. As long as people live in an oppressive society, the process of uncovering previously unrecognized areas of Acceptance and Resistance will be ongoing even though their predominant consciousness may be in Redefinition or Internalization.

Agents in Internalization

Agents at this stage, aware of their past and concerned about creating a more equal future, try to apply and integrate their new social identity into other facets of their overall identity, since change in one dimension will undoubtedly affect all others. Implicit in the term Internalization is the assumption that the new aspects become a natural part of behavior so that people act unconsciously, without external controls, and without having to consciously think about what they are doing. The new behavior becomes spontaneous.

Targets in Internalization

At this stage targeted people are engaged in the process of integrating and internalizing their newly developed consciousness and group pride. They realize that the process of redefining identity is a valuable learning and consciousness-expanding experience. It is now time to test this new sense of self in a wider context than the supportive reference group focused on in the Redefinition stage and to determine what effects this new social identity will have on the many social roles that people play. Targets at the Internalization stage begin by interacting and often renegotiating with the significant people in their lives for the purpose of establishing the type of social interactions that will serve their new social identity. Even in situations where their perspective is not valued and renegotiation does not succeed, they find that their new self-esteem and self-concept can provide the necessary sustenance to prevail.

Another significant aspect of Internalization consciousness is the appreciation of the plight of all targets of any form of oppression. Having moved through the liberation process for their own experience of oppression, it becomes easier for the person with an Internalization consciousness to have empathy for members of other targeted groups in relation to whom they are agents (for example, a heterosexual Latino who can now acknowledge and explore Christian or heterosexual privilege). It is less likely that a target in Resistance or Redefinition consciousness will be able to acknowledge coexistent agent identities. Furthermore, those who find themselves victims of more than one form of oppression (for example, black women or disabled Jews) find that their developmental process in one area of their social identity may be useful in dealing with other of their targeted identities as well. There is essentially no exit phase for this stage; the ongoing task is one of lifelong exploration and nurturance.

References

Cross, W. E. Jr. (1971). The Negro-to-Black Conversion Experience: Toward a Psychology of Black Liberation. *Black World*, 20 (9), 13–27.

____. (1978). Models of Psychological Nigrescence: A Literature Review. *Journal of Black Psychology*, 5 (1), 13–31.

____. (1991). Shades of Black: Diversity in African-American Identity. Philadelphia: Temple University Press.

Freire, P. (1970). *Pedagogy of the Oppressed.* NY: Seabury.

Hardiman, R. (1979). White Identity Development Theory. University of Massachusetts, Amherst. Unpublished manuscript.

____. (1982). White Identity Development: A Process Oriented Model for Describing the Racial Consciousness of White Americans. Dissertation Abstracts International, A 43/01, p. 104 (University Microfilms No. AAC 8210330).

Helms, J. E. (1990). *Black and White Identity: Theory, Research and Practice.* Westport, CT: Greenwood Press.

Jackson, B. (1976a). The Function of Black Identity Development Theory in Achieving Relevance in Education for Black Students. Dissertation Abstracts International, A 37/09, 5667 (University Microfilms No. ACC 7706381).

____. (1976b). Black Identity Development. In L. Golubschick and B. Persky (Eds.), *Urban Social and Educational Issues.* Dubuque, IA: Kendall/Hunt.

Kim, J. (1981). Processes of Asian American Identity Development: A Study of Japanese American Women's Perceptions of Their Struggles to Achieve Positive Identities as Americans of Asian Ancestry. Dissertation Abstracts International, A 42/04, p. 1551 (University Microfilms No. AAC 8118010).

Ryan, W. (1971). *Blaming the Victim.* NY: Pantheon.

Schapiro, S. A. (1985). Changing Men: The Rationale, Theory, and Design of a Men's Consciousness Raising Program. Dissertation Abstracts International, A 46/09, p. 2549 (University Microfilms AAC 8517150).

Wijeyesinghe, C. (1992). Towards an Understanding of The Racial Identity of Bi-Racial People: The Experience of Racial Self-Identification of African-American/Euro-American Adults and the Factors Affecting Their Choices of Racial Identity. Dissertation Abstracts International, A 53/11, p. 3803 (University Microfilms AAC 9305915).

The Cycle of Socialization

Socialization and Context

Often, when people begin to study the phenomenon of oppression, they start with recognizing that human beings are different from each other in many ways based upon gender, ethnicity, skin color, first language, age, ability status, religion, sexual orientation, and economic class. The obvious first leap that people make is the assumption that if we just began to *appreciate differences*, and *treat each other with respect*, then everything would be all right, and there would be no oppression. This view is represented beautifully by the now famous quote from Rodney King in response to the riots following his beating and the release of the police officers who were filmed beating him: "Why can't we all just get along?" It should be that simple, but it isn't.

Instead, we are each born into a specific set of *social identities*, related to the categories of difference mentioned above, and these social identities predispose us to unequal *roles* in the dynamic system of oppression. We are then socialized by powerful sources in our worlds to play the roles prescribed by an inequitable social system (Hardiman and Jackson 1997). This socialization process is *pervasive* (coming from all sides and sources), *consistent* (patterned and predictable), *circular* (self-supporting), *self-perpetuating* (intradependent) and often *invisible* (unconscious and unnamed) (Bell 1997). All of these characteristics will be clarified in the description of the *cycle of socialization* that follows.

In struggling to understand what roles we have been socialized to play, how we are affected by issues of oppression in our lives, and how we participate in maintaining them, we must begin by making an inventory of our own social identities with relationship to each issue of oppression. An excellent first learning activity is to make a personal inventory of our various social identities relating to the categories listed above—gender, race, age, sexual orientation, religion, economic class, and ability/disability status. The results of this inventory make up the mosaic of social identities (our *social identity profile*) that shape(s) our socialization (Harro 1986, Griffin 1997).

Cycle of Socialization

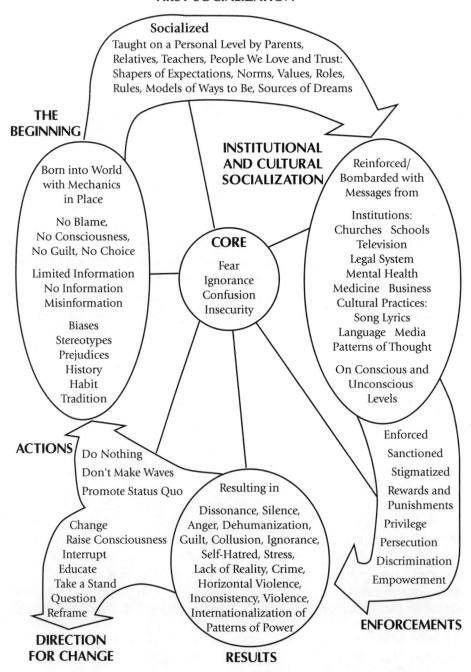

FIRST SOCIALIZATION

Socialized
Taught on a Personal Level by Parents,
Relatives, Teachers, People We Love and Trust:
Shapers of Expectations, Norms, Values, Roles,
Rules, Models of Ways to Be, Sources of Dreams

THE BEGINNING

INSTITUTIONAL AND CULTURAL SOCIALIZATION

Born into World
with Mechanics
in Place

No Blame,
No Consciousness,
No Guilt, No Choice

Limited Information
No Information
Misinformation

Biases
Stereotypes
Prejudices
History
Habit
Tradition

CORE
Fear
Ignorance
Confusion
Insecurity

Reinforced/
Bombarded with
Messages from

Institutions:
Churches   Schools
Television
Legal System
Mental Health
Medicine   Business
Cultural Practices:
Song Lyrics
Language   Media
Patterns of Thought

On Conscious and
Unconscious
Levels

ACTIONS

Do Nothing
Don't Make Waves
Promote Status Quo

Change
Raise Consciousness
Interrupt
Educate
Take a Stand
Question
Reframe

Resulting in

Dissonance, Silence,
Anger, Dehumanization,
Guilt, Collusion, Ignorance,
Self-Hatred, Stress,
Lack of Reality, Crime,
Horizontal Violence,
Inconsistency, Violence,
Internationalization of
Patterns of Power

Enforced
Sanctioned
Stigmatized
Rewards and
Punishments
Privilege
Persecution
Discrimination
Empowerment

ENFORCEMENTS

DIRECTION FOR CHANGE

RESULTS

We get systematic training in "how to be" each of our social identities throughout our lives. The cycle of socialization that follows is one way of representing how the socialization process happens, from what sources it comes, how it affects our lives, and how it perpetuates itself. The "Directions for Change" that conclude this chapter suggest ways for interrupting the cycle of socialization and taking charge of our own lives. For purposes of learning, it is often useful to choose only *one* of our social identities, and trace it through the cycle of socialization, since it can be quite overwhelming to explore seven identities at once.

The Beginning (Circle no. 1)

Our socialization begins before we are born, with no choice on our part. No one brings us a survey, in the womb, inquiring into which gender, class, religion, sexual orientation, cultural group, ability status, or age we might want to be born. These identities are ascribed to us at birth through no effort or decision or choice of our own; there is, therefore, no reason to blame each other or hold each other responsible for the identities we have. This first step in the socialization process is outside our control. In addition to having no choice, we also have no initial consciousness about who we are. We don't question our identities at this point. We just *are* who we are.

On top of these givens, we are born into a world where all of the mechanics, assumptions, rules, and structures of oppression are already in place and functioning; we have had nothing to do with constructing them. There is no reason for any of us to feel guilty or responsible for the world into which we are born. We are innocents, falling into an already established system.

The characteristics of this system were built long before we existed, based upon history, habit, tradition, patterns of belief, prejudices, stereotypes, and myths. *Dominant* or *agent* groups are considered the "norm" around which assumptions are built, and these groups receive attention and recognition. Agents have relatively more social power, and can "name" others. They are privileged at birth, and ascribed access to options and opportunities, often without realizing it. We are "lucky" to be born into these groups and rarely question it. Agent groups include men, white people, middle- and upper-class people, abled people, middle-aged people, heterosexuals, and gentiles.

On the other hand, there are many social identity groups about which little or nothing is known because they have not been considered important enough to study. These are referred to as *subordinate* groups or *target* groups. Some target groups are virtually invisible while others are defined by misinformation or very limited information. Targets are disenfranchised, exploited, and victimized by prejudice, discrimination, and other structural obstacles. Target groups include women; racially oppressed groups; gay, lesbian, bisexual and transgendered people; disabled people; Jews; elders; youth; and people living in poverty (Baker-Miller 1976; Hardiman and Jackson 1997). We are "unlucky" to be born into target groups and therefore devalued by the existing society. Both groups are dehumanized by being socialized into prescribed roles without consciousness or permission.

First Socialization (Arrow no. 1)

Immediately upon our births we begin to be socialized by the people we love and trust the most, our families or the adults who are raising us. They shape our self-concepts and self-perceptions, the norms and rules we must follow, the roles we are taught to play, our expectations for the future, and our dreams. These people serve as role models for us, and they teach us how to behave. This socialization happens both intrapersonally (how we think about ourselves) and interpersonally (how we relate to others). We are told things like, "Boys don't cry"; "You shouldn't trust white people"; "They're better than we are. Stay in your place"; "Don't worry if you break the toy. We can always buy another one"; "Christianity is the true religion"; "Children should be seen and not heard"; "Don't tell anyone that your aunt is mentally retarded. It's embarrassing"; and "Don't kiss other girls. You're supposed to like boys." These messages are an automatic part of our early socialization, and we don't initially question them. We are too dependent on our parents or those raising us, and we haven't yet developed the ability to think for ourselves, so we unconsciously conform to their views.

It is important to observe that they, too, are not to be blamed. They are doing the best they can to raise us, and they have only their own backgrounds from which to draw. They may not have thought critically about what they are teaching us, and may be unconsciously passing on what was taught to them. Some of us may have been raised by parents who *have* thought critically about the messages that they are giving us, but they are still not in the majority. This could be good or bad, as well, depending on what their views are. A consciously racist parent may intentionally pass on racist beliefs to his children, and a consciously feminist parent may intentionally pass on non-stereotypical roles to her children, so it can go either way.

Regardless of the content of the teaching, we have been exposed, without initial question, to a strong set of rules, roles, and assumptions that cannot but shape our sense of ourselves and the world. They influence what we take with us when we venture out of our protected family units into the larger world of other institutions.

A powerful way to check out the accuracy of these assertions is to choose one of our social identities and write down at least ten examples of what we learned about being that identity. It's helpful to consider whether we chose an agent or a target identity. We may find that we have thought more about our target identities, and therefore they are easier to inventory. Gender rules are sometimes the easiest, so we might start there. We might also consider doing it for an agent group identity, like males, white people, heterosexuals, gentiles, adults, middle-class people, able-bodied or able-minded people. Most likely, we will find it easier to list learnings for targeted groups than for agent groups.

Institutional and Cultural Socialization (Circle no. 2)

Once we begin to attend school, go to a place of worship, visit a medical facility, play on a sports team, work with a social worker, seek services or products from a business, or learn about laws and the legal system, our socialization sources are rapidly multiplied based on how many institutions with which we have contact. Most of the messages we receive about how to be, whom to "look up to" and "look down on," what rules to follow, what roles to play, what assumptions to make, what to believe, and what to think will probably reinforce or contradict what we have learned at home.

We might learn at school that girls shouldn't be interested in a woodworking shop class, that only white students go out for the tennis team, that kids who learn differently or think independently get put in special education, that it's okay for wealthy kids to miss classes for a family vacation, that it's okay to harass the boy who walks and talks like a girl, that most of the kids who drop out are from the south side of town, that "jocks" don't have to do the same work that "nerds" do to pass, or that kids who belong to another religious group are "weird." We learn who gets preferential treatment and who gets picked on. We are exposed to rules, roles, and assumptions that are not fair to everyone.

If we are members of the groups that benefit from the rules, we may not notice that they aren't fair. If we are members of the groups that are penalized by the rules, we may have a constant feeling of discomfort. We learn that these rules, roles, and assumptions are part of a structure that is larger than just our families. We get consistent similar messages from religion, the family doctor, the social worker, the local store, or the police officer, and so it is hard to not believe what we are learning. We learn that black people are more likely to steal, so store detectives follow them in stores. Boys are expected to fight and use violence, so they are encouraged to learn how. We shouldn't stare at or ask questions about disabled people; it isn't polite. Gay and lesbian people are sick and perverted. Kids who live in certain sections of town are probably on welfare, taking our hard-earned tax dollars. Money talks. White means good; black means bad. Girls are responsible for birth control. It's a man's world. Jews are cheap. Arabs are terrorists. And so on.

We are inundated with unquestioned and stereotypical messages that shape how we think and what we believe about ourselves and others. What makes this "brainwashing" even more insidious is the fact that it is woven into every structural thread of the fabric of our culture. The media (television, the Internet, advertising, newspapers, and radio), our language patterns, the lyrics to songs, our cultural practices and holidays, and the very assumptions on which our society is built all contribute to the reinforcement of the biased messages and stereotypes we receive. Think about Howard Stern, Jerry Springer, *Married with Children*, beer and car advertising, talk radio, *girl* vs. *man*, Christmas vacation, the Rolling Stones' "Under My Thumb," the "old boys' network," and websites that foster hate. We could identify thousands of examples to illustrate the oppressive messages that bombard us daily from various institutions and aspects of our culture, reinforcing our divisions and "justifying" discrimination and prejudice.

Enforcements (Arrow no. 2)

It might seem logical to ask why people don't just begin to think independently if they don't like what they are seeing around them. Why don't we ignore these messages if we are uncomfortable with them, or if they are hurting us? Largely, we don't ignore the messages, rules, roles, structures, and assumptions because there are enforcements in place to maintain them. People who try to contradict the "norm" pay a price for their independent thinking, and people who conform (consciously or unconsciously) minimally receive the benefit of being left alone for not making waves, such as acceptance in their designated roles, being considered normal or "a team player," or being allowed to stay in their places. Maximally, they receive rewards and privileges for maintaining the status quo such as access to higher places; attention and recognition for having "made it" or being the model member of their group; or the privilege that brings them money, connections, or power.

People who go against the grain of conventional societal messages are accused of being troublemakers, of making waves, or of being "the cause of the problem." If they are members of target groups, they are held up as examples of why this group is inferior to the agent group. Examples of this include the significantly higher numbers of people of color who are targeted by the criminal justice system. Although the number of white people who are committing crimes is just as high, those whites are much less likely to be arrested, charged, tried, convicted, or sentenced to jail than are people of color. Do different laws apply depending on a person's skin color?

Battering statistics are rising as more women assert their equal rights with men, and the number one suspect for the murder of women in the United States is the husband or boyfriend. Should women who try to be equal with men be killed? The rationale given by some racists for the burning of black churches was that "they were getting too strong." Does religious freedom and the freedom to assemble apply only to white citizens? Two men walking together in a southeastern U.S. city were beaten, and one died, because "they were walking so close, they must be gay." Are two men who refuse to abide by the "keep your distance" rule for men so threatening that they must be attacked and killed? These examples of differential punishment being given to members or *perceived* members of target groups are only half of the picture.

If members of agent groups break the rules, they too are punished. White people who support their colleagues of color may be called "n———-lover." Heterosexual men who take on primary child-care responsibilities, cry easily, or hug their male friends are accused of being dominated by their spouses, of being "sissies," or being gay. Middle-class people who work as advocates on economic issues are accused of being do-gooders or self-righteous liberals. Heterosexuals who work for the rights of gay, lesbian, bisexual, or transgendered people are immediately suspected of being "in the closet" themselves.

Results (Circle no. 3)

It is not surprising that the results of this systematic learning are devastating to all involved. If we are examining our target identities, we may experience anger, a sense of being silenced, dissonance between what the United States stands for and what we experience, low self-esteem, high levels of stress, a sense of hopelessness and disempowerment that can lead to crime and self-destructive behavior, frustration, mistrust, and dehumanization. By participating in our roles as targets we reinforce stereotypes, collude in our own demise, and perpetuate the system of oppression. This learned helplessness is often called *internalized oppression* because we have learned to become our own oppressors from within.

If we are examining our agent identities, we may experience guilt from unearned privilege or oppressive acts, fear of payback, tendency to collude in the system to be self-protective, high levels of stress, ignorance of and loss of contact with the target groups, a sense of distorted reality about how the world is, fear of rising crime and violence levels, limited worldview, obliviousness to the damage we do, and dehumanization. By participating in our roles as agents, and remaining unconscious of or being unwilling to interrupt the cycle, we perpetuate the system of oppression.

These results are often cited as the problems facing our society today: high drop-out rates, crime, poverty, drugs, and so on. Ironically, the root causes of them are inherent in the very assumptions on which the society is built: dualism, hierarchy, competition, individualism, domination, colonialism, and the scarcity principle. To the extent that we fail to interrupt this cycle we keep the assumptions, the problems, and the oppression alive.

A way that we might personally explore this model is to take one of the societal problems and trace its root causes back through the cycle to the core belief systems or patterns in U.S. society that feed and play host to it. It is not a coincidence that the United States is suffering from these results today; rather, it is a logical outcome of our embracing the status quo, without thinking or challenging.

Actions (Arrow no. 3)

When we arrive at the results of this terrible cycle, we face the decision of what to do next. It is easiest to do nothing, and simply to allow the perpetuation of the status quo. We may choose not to make waves, to stay in our familiar patterns. We may say, "Oh well, it's been that way for hundreds of years. What can I do to change it? It is a huge phenomenon, and my small efforts won't count for much." Many of us choose to do nothing because it is (for a while) easier to stay with what is familiar. Besides, it is frightening to try to interrupt something so large. "What does it have to do with me, anyway?" say many agents. "This isn't my problem. I am above this." We fail to realize that we have become participants just by doing nothing. This cycle has a life of its own. It doesn't need our active support because it has its own centrifugal force. It goes on, and unless we choose to interrupt it, it will continue to go on. Our silence is consent. Until our discomfort becomes larger than our comfort, we will probably stay in this cycle.

Some of us who are targets have been so beaten down by the relentless messages of the cycle that we have given up and resigned ourselves to survive it or to self-destruct. We are the victims of the cycle, and are playing our roles as victims to keep the cycle alive. We will probably go around a few more times before we die. It hurts too much to fight such a big cycle. We need the help of our brothers and sisters and our agent allies to try for change.

The Core at the Center of the Cycle

We are blocked from action by the fear and insecurity that we have been taught. We have been kept ignorant and confused by the myths and misinformation that we have been fed, and we lack a core of confidence and vision to guide us. We don't know how to take action against a system so powerful and pervasive. As long as our core is filled with these negative elements, we will be paralyzed and will re-create the same cycle again.

Somehow, however, change and hope still find their way to the surface. Perhaps someone's discomfort or pain becomes larger than her complacency. Perhaps strength, encouragement, determination, love, hope, or connection to other people begins to grow in someone's core, and he decides to take a different direction, and to interrupt this cycle.

Direction for Change

Some of us who are targets try to interrupt the cycle, because for us the discomfort *has* gotten larger than the comfort. If we try this alone, or without organization, we may be kicked back down to our powerless positions. If we begin a new direction, and even work with our agent allies, however, we can create our own hope.

Some of us who are agents may decide to use our power and privilege to try to make change—out of either guilt, moral values, or vision. If our motivation is guilt, we are doomed to fail, but if we operate from a strong moral base and vision, and if we work together with our targeted brothers and sisters, we create hope. We become allies with our target groups, and build coalitions for success.

When groups begin to empower themselves—by learning more about each other, by unlearning old myths and stereotypes, by challenging the status quo—we make the difficult decision to interrupt the cycle of socialization. We begin to question the givens, the assumptions of the society, the norms, the values, the rules, the roles, and even the structures. As we attempt this, it becomes obvious that we cannot do it alone. We must build coalitions with people who are like us and people who are different from us. We will not be the minority if we work in coalitions. We will gain the necessary vision and power to reconstruct new rules that truly are equal, roles that complement each other instead of competing, assumptions that value all groups instead of ascribing value to some and devaluing others, and structures that promote cooperation and shared power instead of power over each other.

For this new direction of action to work, we need education for critical consciousness for all groups. We need to take a stand, reframe our understandings, question the status quo, and begin a critical transformation that can break down this cycle of socialization and start a new cycle leading to liberation for all. This is possible. We *can* change the world.

References

Baker-Miller, J. (1976). *Toward a New Psychology of Women*. Boston: Beacon Press.

Bell, L. A. (1997). Theoretical foundations for social justice education. In M. Adams, L. A. Bell, and P. Griffin, eds., *Teaching for Diversity and Social Justice: A Sourcebook*. New York: Routledge.

Griffin, P. (1997). Introductory module for the single issue courses. In M. Adams, L. A. Bell, and P. Griffin, eds., *Teaching for Diversity and Social Justice: A Sourcebook*. New York: Routledge.

Harro, R. L. (1986). *Teaching about Heterosexism: A Psychological Education Design Project*. University of Massachusetts, Amherst; unpublished manuscript.

Hardiman, R. and B. W. Jackson. (1997). Conceptual Foundations for Social Justice Courses. In M. Adams, L. A. Bell, and P. Griffin, eds., *Teaching for Diversity and Social Justice: A Sourcebook*. New York: Routledge.

Geeta Kothari

If You Are What You Eat, Then What Am I?

Geeta Kothari graduated from Smith College, and in addition to being a writer of fiction and nonfiction, she teaches English and directs the Writing Center at the University of Pittsburgh. In another essay, "Where Are You From?" she describes her experiences of people stereotyping her as a foreigner (she's from New York) and an outsider because of her Indian appearance. She argues "those who belong must conform to the ways of the community, censoring their actions and words, either consciously or unconsciously." A similar difficulty is at the heart of this essay, which was included in *The Best American Essays 2000*: how does one adapt to a culture without losing one's heritage?

As you read, pay attention to the different positions the people in Kothari's essay take: where does she locate herself? Her husband? Her parents? Her sister? The "codes" described in the introductory quotation from Ignatieff are layered and shifting in the experiences Kothari describes. Part of this instability comes from the essay's non-linear chronology, and part of it comes from the meanings we attach to the differing varieties of food she describes. When responding to Kothari's essay, it may help you to consider your own experiences: Are there times where you've found yourself in a culture, group, or situation, but not knowing how the "codes" worked?

To belong is to understand the tacit codes of the people you live with.

—Michael Ignatieff, *Blood and Belonging*

I

The first time my mother and I open a can of tuna, I am nine years old. We stand in the doorway of the kitchen, in semidarkness, the can tilted toward daylight. I want to eat what the kids at school eat: bologna, hot dogs, salami—foods my parents find repugnant because they contain pork and meat byproducts, crushed bone and hair glued together by chemicals and fat. Although she had never been able to tolerate the smell of fish, my mother buys the tuna, hoping to satisfy my longing for American food.

Indians, of course, do not eat such things.

The tuna smells fishy, which surprises me because I can't remember anyone's tuna sandwich actually smelling like fish. And the tuna in those sandwiches doesn't look like this, pink and shiny, like an internal organ. In fact, this looks similar to the bad foods my mother doesn't want me to eat. She is silent, holding her face away from the can while peering into it like a half-blind bird.

"What's wrong with it?" I ask.

She has no idea. My mother does not know that the tuna everyone else's mothers made for them was tuna *salad*.

"Do you think it's botulism?"

I have never seen botulism, but I have read about it, just as I have read about but never eaten steak and kidney pie.

There is so much my parents don't know. They are not like other parents, and they disappoint me and my sister. They are supposed to help us negotiate the world outside, teach us the signs, the clues to proper behavior: what to eat and how to eat it.

We have expectations, and my parents fail to meet them, especially my mother, who works full-time. I don't understand what it means, to have a mother who works outside and inside the home; I notice only the ways in which she disappoints me. She doesn't show up for school plays. She doesn't make chocolate-frosted cupcakes for my class. At night, if I want her attention, I have to sit in the kitchen and talk to her while she cooks the evening meal, attentative to every third or fourth word I say.

We throw the tuna away. This time my mother is disappointed. I go to school with tuna eaters. I see their sandwiches, yet cannot explain the discrepancy between them and the stinking, oily fish in my mother's hand. We do not understand so many things, my mother and I.

II

On weekends, we eat fried chicken from Woolworth's on the back steps of my father's first-floor office in Murray Hill. The back steps face a small patch of garden—hedges, a couple of skinny trees, and gravel instead of grass. We can see the back window of the apartment my parents and I lived in until my sister was born. There, the doorman watched my mother, several months pregnant and wearing a sari, slip on the ice in front of the building.

My sister and I pretend we are in the country, where our American friends all have houses. We eat glazed doughnuts, also from Woolworth's, and french fries with ketchup.

III

My mother takes a catering class and learns that Miracle Whip and mustard are healthier than mayonnaise. She learns to make egg salad with chopped celery, deviled eggs dusted with paprika, a cream cheese spread with bits of fresh ginger and watercress, chicken liver pâté, and little brown-and-white checkerboard sandwiches that we have only once. She makes chicken à la king in puff pastry shells and eggplant Parmesan. She acquires smooth wooden paddles, whose purpose is never clear, two different egg slicers, several wooden spoons, icing tubes, cookie cutters, and an electric mixer.

IV

I learn to make tuna salad by watching a friend. My sister never acquires a taste for it. Instead, she craves

bologna

hot dogs

bacon

sausages

and a range of unidentifiable meat products forbidden by my parents. Their restrictions are not about sacred cows, as everyone around us assumes; in a pinch, we are allowed hamburgers, though lamb burgers are preferable. A "pinch" means choosing not to draw attention to ourselves as outsiders, impolite visitors who won't eat what their host serves. But bologna is still taboo.

V

Things my sister refuses to eat: butter, veal, anything with jeera. The babysitter tries to feed her butter sandwiches, threatens her with them, makes her cry in fear and disgust. My mother does not disappoint her; she does not believe in forcing us to eat, in using food as a weapon. In addition to pbj, my sister likes pasta and marinara sauce, bologna and Wonder Bread (when she can get it), and fried egg sandwiches with turkey, cheese, and horseradish. Her tastes, once established, are predictable.

VI

When we visit our relatives in India, food prepared outside the house is carefully monitored. In the hot, sticky monsoon months in New Delhi and Bombay, we cannot eat ice cream, salad, cold food, or any fruit that can't be peeled. Definitely no meat. People die from amoebic dysentery, unexplained fevers, strange boils on their bodies. We drink boiled water only, no ice. No sweets except for jalebi, thin fried twists of dough in dripping hot sugar syrup. If we're caught outside with nothing to drink, Fanta, Limca, Thums Up (after Coca-Cola is thrown out by Mrs. Gandhi) will do. Hot tea sweetened with sugar, served with thick creamy buffalo milk, is preferable. It should be boiled, to kill the germs on the cup.

My mother talks about "back home" as a safe place, a silk cocoon frozen in time where we are sheltered by family and friends. Back home, my sister and I do not argue about food with my parents. Home is where they know all the rules. We trust them to guide us safely through the maze of city streets for which they have no map, and we trust them to feed and take care of us, the way parents should.

Finally, though, one of us will get sick, hungry for the food we see our cousins and friends eating, too thirsty to ask for a straw, too polite to insist on properly boiled water.

At my uncle's diner in New Delhi, someone hands me a plate of aloo tikki, fried potato patties filled with mashed channa dal and served with a sweet and a sour chutney. The channa, mixed with hot chilies and spices, burns my tongue and throat. I reach for my Fanta, discard the paper straw, and gulp the sweet orange soda down, huge drafts that sting rather than soothe.

When I throw up later that day (or is it the next morning, when a stomachache wakes me from deep sleep?), I cry over the frustration of being singled out, not from the pain my mother assumes I'm feeling as she holds my hair back from my face. The taste of orange lingers in my mouth, and I remember my lips touching the cold glass of the Fanta bottle.

At that moment, more than anything, I want to be like my cousins.

VII

In New York, at the first Indian restaurant in our neighborhood, my father orders with confidence, and my sister and I play with the silverware until the steaming plates of lamb biryani arrive.

What is Indian food? my friends ask, their noses crinkling up.

Later, this restaurant is run out of business by the new Indo-Pak-Bangladeshi combinations up and down the street, which serve similar food. They use plastic cutlery and Styrofoam cups. They do not distinguish between North and South Indian cooking, or between Indian, Pakistani, and Bangladeshi cooking, and their customers do not care. The food is fast, cheap, and tasty. Dosa, a rice flour crepe stuffed with masala potato, appears on the same trays as chicken makhani.

Now my friends want to know, Do you eat curry at home?

One time my mother makes lamb vindaloo for guests. Like dosa, this is a South Indian dish, one that my Punjabi mother has to learn from a cookbook. For us, she cooks everyday food—yellow dal, rice, chapati, bhaji. Lentils, rice, bread, and vegetables. She has never referred to anything on our table as "curry" or "curried," but I know she has made chicken curry for guests. Vindaloo, she explains, is a curry too. I understand then that curry is a dish created for guests, outsiders, a food for people who eat in restaurants.

VIII

I have inherited brown eyes, black hair, a long nose with a crooked bridge, and soft teeth with thin enamel. I am in my twenties, moving to a city far from my parents, before it occurs to me that jeera, the spice my sister avoids, must have an English name. I have to learn that haldi = turmeric, methi = fenugreek. What to make with fenugreek, I do not know. My grandmother used to make methi roti for our breakfast, cornbread with fresh fenugreek leaves served with a lump of homemade butter. No one makes it now that she's gone, though once in a while my mother will get a craving for it and produce a facsimile ("The cornmeal here is wrong") that only highlights what she's really missing: the smells and tastes of her mother's house.

I will never make my grandmother's methi roti or even my mother's unsatisfactory imitation of it. I attempt chapati; it takes six hours, three phone calls home, and leaves me with an aching back. I have to write translations down: jeera = cumin. My memory is unreliable. But I have always known garam = hot.

IX

My mother learns how to make brownies and apple pie. My father makes only Indian food, except for loaves of heavy sweet brown bread that I eat with thin slices of American cheese and lettuce. The recipe is a secret, passed on to him by a woman at work. Years later, when he finally gives it to me, when I finally ask for it, I end up with three bricks of gluten that even the birds and my husband won't eat.

X

My parents send me to boarding school, outside of London. They imagine that I will overcome my shyness and find a place for myself in this all-girls' school. They have never lived in England, but as former subjects of the British Empire, they find London familiar, comfortable in a way New York— my mother's home for over twenty years by now—is not. Americans still don't know what to call us; their Indians live on reservations, not in Manhattan. Because they understand the English, my parents believe the English understand us.

I poke at my first school lunch—thin, overworked pastry in a puddle of lumpy gravy. The lumps are chewy mushrooms, maybe, or overcooked shrimp.

"What is this?" I don't want to ask, but I can't go on eating without knowing.

"Steak and kidney pie."

The girl next to me, red-haired, freckled, watches me take a bite from my plate. She has been put in charge of me, the new girl, and I follow her around all day, a foreigner at the mercy of a reluctant and angry tour guide. She is not used to explaining what is perfectly and utterly natural.

"What, you've never had steak and kidney pie? Bloody hell."

My classmates scoff, then marvel, then laugh at my ignorance. After a year, I understand what is on my plate: sausage rolls, blood pudding, Spam, roast beef in a thin, greasy gravy, all the bacon and sausage I could possibly want. My parents do not expect me to starve.

The girls at school expect conformity; it has been bred into them, through years of uniforms and strict rules about proper behavior. I am thirteen and contrary, even as I yearn for acceptance. I declare myself a vegetarian and doom myself to a diet of cauliflower cheese and baked beans on toast. The administration does not question my decision; they assume it's for vague, undefined religious reasons, although my father, the doctor, tells them it's for my health. My reasons, from this distance of many years, remain murky to me.

Perhaps I am my parents' daughter after all.

XI

When she is three, sitting on my cousin's lap in Bombay, my sister reaches for his plate and puts a chili in her mouth. She wants to be like the grownups, who dip green chilies in coarse salt and eat them like any other vegetable. She howls inconsolable animal pain for what must be hours. She doesn't have the vocabulary for the oily heat that stings her mouth and tongue, burns a trail through her small tender body. Only hot, sticky tears on my father's shoulder.

As an adult, she eats red chili paste, mango pickle, kimchee, foods that make my eyes water and my stomach gurgle. My tastes are milder. I order raita at Indian restaurants and ask for food that won't sear the roof of my mouth and scar the insides of my cheeks. The waiters nod, and their eyes shift—a slight once-over that indicates they don't believe me. I am Indian, aren't I? My father seems to agree with them. He tells me I'm asking for the impossible, as if he believes the recipes are immutable, written in stone during the passage from India to America.

XII

I look around my boyfriend's freezer one day and find meat: pork chops, ground beef, chicken pieces, Italian sausage. Ham in the refrigerator, next to the homemade bolognese sauce. Tupperware filled with chili made from ground beef and pork.

He smells different from me. Foreign. Strange.

I marry him anyway.

He has inherited blue eyes that turn gray in bad weather, light brown hair, a sharp pointy nose, and excellent teeth. He learns to make chili with ground turkey and tofu, tomato sauce with red wine and portobello mushrooms, roast chicken with rosemary and slivers of garlic under the skin.

He eats steak when we are in separate cities, roast beef at his mother's house, hamburgers at work. Sometimes I smell them on his skin. I hope he doesn't notice me turning my face, a cheek instead of my lips, my nose wrinkled at the unfamiliar, musky smell.

XIII

And then I realize I don't want to be a person who can find Indian food only in restaurants. One day my parents will be gone and I will long for the foods of my childhood, the way they long for theirs. I prepare for this day the way people on TV prepare for the end of the world. They gather canned goods they will never eat while I stockpile recipes I cannot replicate. I am frantic, disorganized, grabbing what I can, filing scribbled notes haphazardly. I regret the tastes I've forgotten, the meals I have inhaled without a thought. I worry that I've come to this realization too late.

XIV

Who told my mother about Brie? One day we were eating Velveeta, the next day Brie, Gouda, Camembert, Port Salut, Havarti with caraway, Danish fontina, string cheese made with sheep's milk. Who opened the door to these foreigners that sit on the refrigerator shelf next to last night's dal?

Back home, there is one cheese only, which comes in a tin, looks like Bakelite, and tastes best when melted.

And how do we go from Chef Boyardee to fresh pasta and homemade sauce, made with Redpack tomatoes, crushed garlic, and dried oregano? Macaroni and cheese, made with fresh cheddar and whole milk, sprinkled with bread crumbs and paprika. Fresh eggplant and ricotta ravioli, baked with marinara sauce and fresh mozzarella.

My mother will never cook beef or pork in her kitchen, and the foods she knew in her childhood are unavailable. Because the only alternative to the supermarket, with its TV dinners and canned foods, is the gourmet Italian deli across the street, by default our meals become socially acceptable.

XV

If I really want to make myself sick, I worry that my husband will one day leave me for a meat-eater, for someone familiar who doesn't sniff him suspiciously for signs of alimentary infidelity.

XVI

Indians eat lentils. I understand this as absolute, a decree from an unidentifiable authority that watches and judges me.

So what does it mean that I cannot replicate my mother's dal? She and my father show me repeatedly, in their kitchen, in my kitchen. They coach me over the phone, buy me the best cookbooks, and finally write down their secrets. Things I'm supposed to know but don't. Recipes that should be, by now, engraved on my heart.

Living far from the comfort of people who require no explanation for what I do and who I am, I crave the foods we have shared. My mother convinces me that moong is the easiest dal to prepare, and yet it fails me every time: bland, watery, a sickly greenish yellow mush. These imperfect imitations remind me only of what I'm missing.

But I have never been fond of moong dal. At my mother's table it is the last thing I reach for. Now I worry that this antipathy toward dal signals something deeper, that somehow I am not my parents' daughter, not Indian, and because I cannot bear the touch and smell of raw meat, though I can eat it cooked (charred, dry, and overdone), I am not American either.

I worry about a lifetime purgatory in Indian restaurants where I will complain that all the food looks and tastes the same because they've used the same masala.

XVII

About the tuna and her attempts to feed us, my mother laughs. She says, "You were never fussy. You ate everything I made and never complained ."

My mother is at the stove, wearing only her blouse and petticoat, her sari carefully folded and hung in the closet. She does not believe a girl's place is in the kitchen, but she expects me to know that too much hing can ruin a meal, to know without being told, without having to ask or write it down. Hing = asafetida.

She remembers the catering class. "Oh, that class. You know, I had to give it up when we got to lobster. I just couldn't stand the way it looked."

She says this apologetically, as if she has deprived us, as if she suspects that having a mother who could feed us lobster would have changed the course of our lives.

Intellectually, she understands that only certain people regularly eat lobster, people with money or those who live in Maine, or both. In her catering class there were people without jobs for whom preparing lobster was a part of their professional training as caterers. Like us, they wouldn't be eating lobster at home. For my mother, however, lobster was just another American food, like tuna—different, strange, not natural yet somehow essential to belonging.

I learned how to prepare and eat lobster from the same girl who taught me tuna salad. I ate bacon at her house too. And one day this girl, with her houses in the country and Martha's Vineyard, asked me how my uncle was going to pick me up from the airport in Bombay. In 1973, she was surprised to hear that he used a car, not an elephant. At home, my parents and I laughed, and though I never knew for sure if she was making fun of me, I still wanted her friendship.

My parents were afraid my sister and I would learn to despise the foods they loved, replace them with bologna and bacon and lose our taste for masala. For my mother, giving up her disgust of lobster, with its hard exterior and foreign smell, would mean renouncing some essential difference. It would mean becoming, decidedly, definitely, American—unafraid of meat in all its forms, able to consume large quantities of protein at any given meal. My willingness to toss a living being into boiling water and then get past its ugly appearance to the rich meat inside must mean to my mother that I am somehow someone she is not.

But I haven't eaten lobster in years. In my kitchen cupboards, there is a thirteen-pound bag of basmati rice, jars of lime pickle, mango pickle, and ghee, cans of tuna and anchovies, canned soups, coconut milk, and tomatoes, rice noodles, several kinds of pasta, dried mushrooms, and unlabeled bottles of spices: haldi, jeera, hing. When my husband tries to help me cook, he cannot identify all the spices. He gets confused when I forget their English names and remarks that my expectations of him are unreasonable.

I am my parents' daughter. Like them, I expect knowledge to pass from me to my husband without one word of explanation or translation. I want him to know what I know, see what I see, without having to tell him exactly what it is. I want to believe that recipes never change.

James McBride

What Color Is Jesus?

James McBride is a musician, freelance writer, and self-described "mu-latto" son of an African-American father and Polish mother. In "What Color Is Jesus?" McBride explores his own abiding determination si-multaneously to escape and to answer the nagging question "am I black or white?" As you read this highly personal narrative, consider the wider questions about identity and race it raises. Examine the particular private as well as social conditions prompting McBride's childhood question and his adult answer. Then think about the weav-ing of cultural, ethnic, and religious strands in your own heritage: how much of your own "self" is lost, captured, or perhaps even created when you check the racial identity box on a census form or college application? Finally, if we see how, by imposing socially contrived meanings onto the range of human complexions, society turns "color" into "race," McBride's story may invite us to regard ourselves as texts of sorts, formed in the reading as much as the seeing.

Just before I quit my last job in Washington, I drove down into Virginia to see my stepfather's grave for the first time. He was buried in a little country graveyard in Henrico County, near Richmond, about a hundred yards from the schoolhouse where he learned to read. It's one of those old "colored" graveyards, a lonely, remote backwoods place where the wind blows through the trees and the graves are marked by lopsided tombstones. It was so re-mote I couldn't find it by myself. I had to get my aunt Maggie to show me where it was. We drove down a dirt road and then parked and walked down a little dusty path the rest of the way. Once we found his grave, I stood over it for a long time.

I was fourteen when my stepfather died. One minute he was there, the next—boom—gone. A stroke. Back then I thought a stroke was something you got from the sun. I didn't know it could kill you. His funeral was the first I had ever attended. I didn't know they opened coffins at funerals. When the funeral director, a woman with white gloves, unlatched the coffin, I was horrified. I couldn't believe she was going to open it up. I begged her in my mind not to open it up—please—but she did, and there he was. The whole place broke up. Even the funeral director cried. I thought I would lose my mind.

Afterward, they took him out of the church, put him in a car, and flew him down to Virginia. My mother and older brother and little sister went, but I'd seen enough. I didn't want to see him anymore. As a kid growing up in New York, I'd been embarrassed by him because he wasn't like the other guys' fathers, who drove hot rods, flew model airplanes with their sons, and talked about the Mets and civil rights. My father was solitary, gruff, busy. He worked as a furnace fireman for the New York City Housing Authority for thirty-six years, fixing oil burners and shoveling coal into big furnaces that heated the housing projects where my family lived. He drove a Pontiac, a solid, clean, quiet car. He liked to dress dapper and drink Rheingold beer and play pool with his brother Walter and their old-timey friends who wore fedoras and smoked filterless Pall Malls and called liquor "likka" and called me "boy." They were weathered Southern black men, quiet and humorous and never bitter about white people, which was out of my line completely. I was a modern-day black man who didn't like the white man too much, even if the white man was my mother.

My mother was born Jewish in Poland, the eldest daughter of an Orthodox rabbi. She married my natural father, a black man, in 1941. He died in 1957, at forty-eight, while she was pregnant with me. She married my stepfather, Hunter L. Jordan, Sr., when I was about a year old. He raised me and my seven brothers and sisters as his own—we considered him to be our father—and he and my mother added four more kids to the bunch to make it an even twelve.

My parents were unique. As unique as any parents I have known, which I suppose makes their children unique. However, being unique can spin you off in strange directions. For years I searched for a kind of peace. I vacillated between being the black part of me that I accept and the white part of me that I could not accept. Part writer, part musician, part black man, part white man. Running, running, always running. Even professionally I sprinted, from jazz musician to reporter and back again. Bounding from one life to the other—the safety and prestige of a journalism job to the poverty and fulfillment of the musician's life.

Standing over my stepfather's grave, thinking about quitting my gig to move back to New York to be a musician and freelance writer, I was nervous. He would never approve of this jive. He would say: "You got a good job and you quit that? For what? To play jazz? To write? Write what? You need a job." Those were almost the exact words my mother always used.

My aunt Maggie, who's about seventy-two, was standing there as I waged this war in my mind. She came up behind me and said, "He was a good man. I know y'all miss him so much."

"Yep," I said, but as we walked up the dusty little path to my car to go to the florist to get flowers, I was thinking, "Man, I'm sure glad he's not here to see me now."

I'm a black man and I've been running all my life. Sometimes I feel like my soul just wants to jump out of my skin and run off, things get that mixed up. But it doesn't matter, because what's inside is there to stay no matter how fast you sprint. Being mixed feels like that tingly feeling you have in your nose when you have to sneeze—you're hanging on there waiting for it to happen, but it never does. You feel completely misunderstood by the rest of the world, which is probably how any sixteen-year-old feels, except that if you're brown-skinned like me, the feeling lasts for the rest of your life. "Don't you sometime feel like just beating up the white man?" a white guy at work once asked me. I hate it when people see my brown skin and assume that all I care about is gospel music and fried chicken and beating up the white man. I could care less. I'm too busy trying to live.

Once a mulatto, always a mulatto, is what I say, and you have to be happy with what you have, though in this world some places are more conducive to the survival of a black white man like me than others. Europe is okay, Philly works, and in New York you can at least run and hide and get lost in the sauce; but Washington is a town split straight down the middle—between white and black, haves and have-nots, light-skinned and dark-skinned—and full of jive-talkers of both colors. The blacks are embittered and expect you to love Marion Barry unconditionally. The whites expect you to be either grateful for their liberal sensibilities or a raging militant. There's no middle ground. No place for a guy like me to stand. Your politics is in the color of your face, and nothing else counts in Washington, which is why I had to get out of there.

All of my brothers and sisters—six boys, five girls, wildly successful by conventional standards (doctors, teachers, professors, musicians)—have had to learn to plow the middle ground. Music is my escape, because when I pick up the saxophone and play, the horn doesn't care what color I am. Whatever's inside comes out, and I feel free.

My family was big, private, close, poor, fun, and always slightly confused. We were fueled by the race question and also befuddled by it. Everyone sought their own private means of escape. When he was little, my older brother Richie, a better sax player than I and the guy from whom I took all my cues, decided he was neither black nor white, but green, like the comic book character the Hulk. His imagination went wild with it, and he would sometimes lie on our bed facedown and make me bounce on him until he turned green.

"Do I look green yet?" he'd ask.

"Naw…"

"Jump some more."

I'd bounce some more.

"How about now?"

"Well, a little bit."

"RRRrrrrr…I'm the Hulk!" And he'd rise to attack me like a zombie.

Richard had a lot of heart. One morning in Sunday school, he raised his hand and asked our Sunday school teacher, Reverend Owens, "Is Jesus white?"

Reverend Owens said no.

"Then why is he white in this picture?" and he held up our Sunday school Bible.

Reverend Owens said, "Well, Jesus is all colors."

"Then why is he white? This looks like a white man to me." Richie held up the picture high so everyone in the class could see it. "Don't he look white to you?" he asked. Nobody said anything.

Reverend Owens was a nice man and also a barber who tore my head up about once a month. But he wasn't that sharp. I could read better than he could, and I was only twelve.

So he kind of stood there, wiping his face with his handkerchief and making the same noise he made when he preached. "Well…ahhh… well…ahhh…"

I was embarrassed. The rest of the kids stared at Richie like he was crazy. "Richie, forget it," I mumbled.

"Naw. If they put Jesus in this picture here, and he ain't white, and he ain't black, they should make him gray. Jesus should be gray."

Richie stopped going to Sunday School after that, although he never stopped believing in God. My mother tried to make him go back, but he wouldn't.

When we were little, we used to make fun of our mother singing in church. My mother can't sing a lick. She makes a shrill kind of sound, a cross between a fire engine and Curly of the Three Stooges. Every Sunday morning, she'd stand in church, as she does today, the only white person there, and the whole congregation going, "Leaannnnning, ohhh, leaaning on the crossss, ohhhhh Laaawwwd!" and her going, "Leeeeeaaannnning, ohhhh, clank! bang! @*%$@*!," rattling happily along like an old Maytag washer. She wasn't born with the gift for gospel music, I suppose.

My mother, Ruth McBride Jordan, who today lives near Trenton, is the best movie I've ever seen. She's seventy-six, pretty, about five three, bowlegged, with curly dark hair and pretty dark eyes. She and my father and step-father raised twelve children and sent them to college and graduate school, and at age sixty-five she obtained her own college degree in social welfare from Temple University. She's a whirlwind, so it's better to test the wind before you fly the kite. When I began writing my book about her, she said, "Ask me anything. I'll help you as much as I can." Then I asked her a few questions and she snapped: "Don't be so nosy. Don't tell all your business. If you work too much, your mind will be like a brick. My pot's burning on the stove. I gotta go."

When we were growing up, she never discussed race. When we asked whether we were black or white, she'd say, "You're a human being. Educate your mind!" She insisted on excellent grades and privacy. She didn't encourage us to mingle with others of any color too much. We were taught to mind our own business, and the less people knew about us, the better.

When we'd ask if she was white, she'd say, "I'm light-skinned," and change the subject. But we knew she was white, and I was embarrassed by her. I was ten years old when Martin Luther King, Jr., was killed, and I feared for her life because it seemed like all of New York was going to burn. She worked as a night clerk-typist at a Manhattan bank and got home every night about 2 A.M. My father would often be unavailable, and one of the older kids would meet her at the bus stop while the rest of us lay awake, waiting for the sound of the door to open. Black militants scared me. So did the Ku Klux Klan. I thought either group might try to kill her.

I always knew my mother was different, knew my siblings and I were different. My mother hid the truth from her children as long as she could. I was a grown man before I knew where she was born.

She was born Ruchele Dwajra Sylska in a town called Dobryn, near Gdansk, Poland. Her father was an Orthodox rabbi who lived in Russia. He escaped the Red Army by sneaking over the border into Poland. He married my grandmother, Hudis, in what my mother says was an arranged marriage, emigrated to America in the early 1920s, changed his name, and sent for his family. My mother landed on Ellis Island like thousands of other European immigrants.

The family settled in Suffolk, Virginia, and operated a grocery store on the black side of town. Her father also ran a local synagogue. Theirs was the only store in town open on Sundays.

He was feared within the family, my mother says. His wife, who suffered from polio, was close to her three children—a son and two daughters—but could not keep the tyranny of the father from driving them off. The oldest child, my mother's brother, left home early, joined the army, and was killed in World War II. The remaining two girls worked from sunup to sundown in the store. "My only freedom was to go out and buy little romance novels," my mother recalls. "They cost a dime." In school, they called her "Jew-baby."

When she was seventeen, she went to New York to visit relatives for the summer and worked in a Bronx factory owned by her aunt. At the factory, there was a young black employee named Andrew McBride, from High Point, North Carolina. They struck up a friendship and a romance. "He was the first man who was ever kind to me," my mother says. "I didn't care what color he was."

Her father did, though. When she returned home to finish her senior year of high school, her father arranged for her to marry a Jewish man after graduation. She had other plans. The day after she graduated, she packed her bags and left. After floating between New York and Suffolk for a while, she finally decided to marry my father in New York City. Her father caught up to her at the bus station the last time she left home. He knew that she was in love with a black man. The year was 1941.

"If you leave now, don't ever come back," he said.

"I won't," she said.

She gave up Judaism, married Andrew McBride, and moved to a one-room flat in Harlem where she proceeded to have baby after baby. Her husband later became a minister, and together they started New Brown Memorial Baptist Church in Red Hook, Brooklyn, which still exists. The mixed marriage caused them a lot of trouble—they got chased up Eighth Avenue by a group of whites and endured blacks murmuring under their breath, and she was pushed around in the hallway of the Harlem building by a black woman one day. But she never went home. She tried to see her mother after she married, when she found out her mother was ill and dying. When she called, she was told the family had sat shiva for her, as if she had died. "You've been out; stay out," she was told. She always carried that guilt in her heart, that she left her mother with her cruel father and never saw her again.

In 1957, Andrew McBride, Sr., died of cancer. My mother was thirty-six at the time, distraught after visiting him in the hospital, where doctors stared and the nurses snickered. At the time, she was living in the Red Hook project in Brooklyn with seven small kids. She was pregnant with me. In desperation, she searched out her aunt, who was living in Manhattan. She went to her aunt's house and knocked on the door. Her aunt opened the door, then slammed it in her face.

She told me that story only once, a few years ago. It made me sick to hear it, and I said so.

"Leave them alone," she said, waving her hand. "You don't understand Orthodox Jews. I'm happy. I'm a Christian. I'm free. Listen to me: When I got home from your daddy's funeral, I opened our mailbox, and it was full of checks. People dropped off boxes of food—oranges, meat, chickens. Our friends, Daddy's relatives, the people from the church, the people you never go see, they gave us so much money. I'll never forget that for as long as I live. And don't you forget it, either."

A number of years ago, after I had bugged her for months about details of her early life, my mother sat down and drew me a map of where she had lived in Suffolk. She talked as she drew: "The highway goes here, and the jailhouse is down this road, and the slaughterhouse is over here...."

I drove several hours straight, and was tired and hungry once I hit Suffolk, so I parked myself in a local McDonald's and unfolded the little map. I checked it, looked out the window, then checked it again, looked out the window again. I was sitting right where the store used to be.

I went outside and looked around. There was an old house behind the McDonald's. I knocked on the door, and an old black man answered.

"Excuse me..." and I told him my story: Mother used to live here. Her father was a rabbi. Jews. A little store. He fingered his glasses and looked at me for a long time. Then he said, "C'mon in here."

He sat me down and brought me a soda. Then he asked me to tell my story one more time. So I did.

He nodded and listened closely. Then his face broke into a smile. "That means you the ol' rabbi's grandson?"

"Yep."

First he chuckled, then he laughed. Then he laughed some more. He tried to control his laughing, but he couldn't, so he stopped, took off his glasses, and wiped his eyes. I started to get angry, so he apologized. His name was Eddie Thompson. He was sixty-six. He had lived in that house all his life. It took him a minute to get himself together.

"I knew your mother," he said. "We used to call her Rachel."

I had never heard that name before. Her name is Ruth, but he knew her as Rachel, which was close to Ruchele, the Yiddish name her family called her.

"I knew that whole family," Thompson said. "The ol' rabbi, boy, he was something. Rachel was the nice one. She was kindhearted. Everybody liked her. She used to walk right up and down the road here with her mother. The mother used to limp. They would say hello to the people, y'know? Old man, though ..." and he shrugged. "Well, personally, I never had no problem with him."

He talked for a long time, chuckling, disbelieving. "Rachel just left one day. I'm telling you she left, and we thought she was dead. That whole family is long gone. We didn't think we'd ever see none of them again till we got to the other side. And now you pop up. Lord knows it's a great day."

He asked if we could call her. I picked up the phone and dialed Philadelphia, got my mother on the line, and told her I had somebody who wanted to talk to her. I handed the phone to him.

"Rachel? Yeah. Rachel. This is Eddie Thompson. From down in Suffolk. Remember me? We used to live right be—yeaaaaah, that's right." Pause. "No, I was one of the little ones. Well, I'll be! The Lord touched me today.

"Rachel!? That ain't you crying now, is it? This is old Eddie Thompson. You remember me? Don't cry now."

I went and got some flowers for my stepfather's grave and laid them across it. My mother wanted me to make sure the new tombstone she got him was in place, and it was. It said OUR BELOVED DADDY, HUNTER L. JORDAN, AUGUST 11, 1900, TO MAY 14, 1972.

He was old when he died and a relatively old fifty-eight when he married my mother. They met in a courtyard of the Red Hook housing project where we lived, while she was selling church dinners on a Saturday to help make ends meet. He strolled by and bought some ribs, came back the next Saturday and bought some more. He ended up buying the whole nine yards—eight kids and a wife. He used to joke that he had enough for a baseball team.

I never heard him complain about it, and it never even occurred to me to ask him how he felt about white and black. He was quiet and busy. He dealt with solid things. Cars. Plumbing. Tricycles. Work. He used to joke about how he had run away from Richmond when he was a young man because Jim Crow was tough; but racism to him was a detail that you stepped over, like you'd step over a crack in the sidewalk. He worked in the stockyards in Chicago for a while, then in a barbershop in Detroit, where, among other things, he shined Henry Ford's shoes. He went to New York in the 1920s. He never told me those things; his brother Walter did. He didn't find those kinds of facts interesting. All he wanted to talk about was my grades.

He was strong for his age, full and robust, with brown eyes and handsome American Indian features. One night, he had a headache, and the next day he was in the hospital with a stroke. After a couple of weeks, he came home. Then two days later, he asked me to come out to the garage with him. I was one of the older kids living at home; most were away at college or already living on their own. He could barely walk and had difficulty speaking, but we went out there, and we got inside his Pontiac. "I was thinking of maybe driving home one more time," he said. He was talking about Henrico County, where we spent summer vacations.

He started the engine, then shut if off. He was too weak to drive. So he sat there, staring out the windshield, looking at the garage wall, his hand on the steering wheel. He was wearing his old-timey cap and his peacoat, though it was May and warm outside. Sitting there, staring straight ahead, he started talking, and I listened closely because he never gave speeches.

He said he had some money saved up and a little land in Virginia, but it wasn't enough. He was worried about my mother and his children. He said I should always mind her and look out for my younger brothers and sisters, because we were special. "Special people," he said. "And just so special to me." It was the only time I ever heard him refer to race, however vaguely, but it didn't matter because right then I knew he was going to die, and I had to blink back my tears. Two days later, he was gone.

Standing over his grave—it seemed so lonely and cold, with the wind blowing through the trees—part of me wanted to throw myself on the ground to cover and warm him. We arranged the flowers. Plastic ones, because, as Aunt Maggie said, they lasted longer. I took one last look and thought, Maybe he would understand me now. Maybe not. I turned and left.

I suppose I didn't look too happy, because as I started up the little road toward my car, Aunt Maggie put her arm in mine. I'd known her since I was a boy, just like I'd known these woods as a boy when he took us down here, but I'd blanked her and these woods out of my mind over the years, just like you'd blank out the words of a book by covering them with a piece of paper. She didn't judge me, which is what I always appreciated most about our friends and relatives over the years, the white and the black. They never judged, just accepted us as we were. Maybe that's what a black white man has to do. Maybe a black white man will never be content. Maybe a black white man will never fit. But a black white man can't judge anybody.

I remember when I was ten years old, when I pondered my own race and asked my mother, as she was attempting to fix our dinner table that had deteriorated to three-legged status, whether I was white or black. She paused a moment, then responded thoughtfully: "Pliers."

"Huh?"

"Hand me the pliers out of the kitchen drawer."

I handed her the pliers and she promptly went to work on the kitchen table, hammering the legs and top until dents and gouges appeared on all sides. When the table finally stood shakily on all fours, she set the pliers down, stood up and said, "Pliers can fix anything."

"What about me being black?" I asked.

"What about it?" she said. "Forget about black. You are a human being."

"But what do I check on the form at school that says White, Black, Other?"

"Don't check nothing. Get a hundred on your school tests and they won't care what color you are."

"But they do care."

"I don't," she said, and off she went.

Perturbed, I picked up the pliers and sought out my father, hammering at the fuel pump of his 1969 Pontiac. "Am I black or white?" I asked.

"Where'd you get my pliers?" he asked.

"I got 'em from Ma."

"I been looking for 'em all day." He took them and immediately put them to work.

"Am I black or white, Daddy?"

He grabbed a hose in his hand and said, "Hold this." I held it. He went inside the car and cranked the engine. Fuel shot out of the line and spilled all over me. "You all right?" he asked. I shook my head. He took me inside, cleaned me up, put the hose in the car, and took me out for ice cream. I forgot about my color for a while.

But the question plagued me for many years, even after my father's death, and I never did find out the answer because neither he nor my mother ever gave any. I was effectively on my own. I searched for years to find the truth, to find myself as a black white man. I went to Africa, got VD, came home with no answers. I went to Europe, sipped café and smoked in Paris for months, came home empty. Last year, while working on my '53 Chevy at my home in Nyack, while my four-year-old son rolled around in the leaves and ate mud, it hit me. I asked him to hand me the pliers, and as he did so, he asked me, "What color is Grandma?"

"She's white," I said.

"Why isn't she like me?"

"She is like you, she's just whiter."

"Why is she whiter?"

"I don't know. God made her that way."

"Why?"

"I don't know. Would you like her better if she looked more like you?"

"No. I like her the way she is."

It occurred to me then that I was not put on this earth to become a leader of mixed-race people, wielding my race like a baseball bat, determined to force white people to accept me as I am. I realized then that I did not want to be known as Mr. Mulatto, whose children try to be every race in the world, proudly proclaiming Indian blood, African blood, Jewish blood, singing Peter, Paul, and Mary songs at phony private schools where yuppie parents arrive each morning hopping out of Chevy Suburban tanks with bumper stickers that read "Question Authority." I want the same thing every parent wants—a good home for my wife and children, good schools, peace and quiet, a good set of wrenches, and a son big enough to hand them to me. And when he gets big enough to have his own tools and work on his own car, maybe he will understand that you can't change someone's opinion about you no matter how many boxes you check, no matter how many focus groups you join, no matter how much legislation you pass, no matter how much consciousness raising you do. It's a real simple answer. Give 'em God. Give 'em pliers. Give 'em math. Give 'em discipline. Give 'em love, and let the chips fall where they may. Pontificating about it is okay. Passing laws is important, but I never once in my life woke up not knowing whether I should eat matzo ball or fried chicken. I never once felt I'd be able to play the sax better if my mom had been black, or that I'd have been better at math if my father were Jewish. I like me, and I like me because my parents liked me.

Mark Crispin Miller

Deride and Conquer

Mark Crispin Miller teaches media studies at New York University. In "Deride & Conquer" Miller claims that television no longer offers the endless choice that once defined the myth of America—the promise of an affluent society, gleaming cars, full houses, as much food as one could desire, an inexhaustible multitude of images, sounds, and rhythms night after night. Miller suggests that television has become increasingly self-conscious and self-referential. It celebrates our total lack of choices as both consumers and citizens. He argues that TV has adopted irony as its mode of communication—giving the constant appearance of political sophistication, a world-weary understanding of power and social affairs—disarming our ability to critique it on the grounds that it is lying. Most important, irony gives television—more specifically, advertising—the appearance that it is on our side, funded not by some of the largest transnational corporations in the world but by people like yourself: skeptical, critical, unable to be taken in.

> Nobody could watch it all—and that's the point. There *is* a *choice. Your* choice. American television and you.
> —Jim Duffy, President of Communications, *ABC, in one of a series of ads promoting network television* (1986)

Every evening, TV makes a promise, and seems at once to keep it. TV's nightly promise is something like the grand old promise of America herself. Night after night, TV recalls the promise that was first extended through America's peerless landscape, with its great mountains, cliffs, and canyons, tumbling falls, gigantic woodlands, intricate bayous, lakes the size of seas, heavenly valleys, broiling deserts, and a network of massive rivers hurrying in all

200

directions, through a north thick with trees, through interminable plains, through multicolored tropics, through miles and miles of grass or corn or granite, clay or wheat, until those rushing waters ultimately cascade into the surrounding ocean. And throughout this astonishing land mass lie a multitude of huge and spreading cities, each distinctive and yet each itself diverse, bustling with the restless efforts of a population no less heroically varied than the land itself—white and black and brown and yellow, bespeaking the peculiarities of every creed and culture in the world, and yet all now living here, savoring the many freedoms that distinguish the United States so clearly from those other places where our citizens, or their ancestors, came from.

Here all enjoy the promise of that very opportunity, that very differentiation which they, and this great land mass, represent: the promise of unending *choice*. Here they are not ground down by party rule, church dictate, authoritarian tyranny, or the daily dangers of fanatical vendetta; and in this atmosphere of peace and plenty, they are free to work and play, have families, and contemplate, if not yet actually enjoy, the bounty of our unprecedented system.

Such is the promise of America; and TV, every evening, makes a similar sort of promise. Each night (and every day, all day), TV offers and provides us with an endless range of choices. Indeed, TV can be said to have itself incorporated the American dream of peaceful choice. This development was poignantly invoked by one of the hostages taken, in June of 1985, by the Shiite gunmen who hijacked TWA Flight 847. Back home after his captivity in Lebanon, Clint Suggs observed that "when you go to Beirut, you live war, you hear it, you smell it and it's real. It made me appreciate my freedom, the things we take for granted." In America, such freedom is available to any viewer: "When we sit here in our living room, with the sun setting, the baby sleeping, we can watch television, change channels. We have choices."

TV's promise of eternal choice arises from the whole tempting spectacle that is prime time: the full breasts, the gleaming cars, the glistening peaks of ice cream, mounds of candy, long clean highways, colossal frosted drinks, endless laughter, bands of dedicated friends, majestic houses, and cheeseburgers. The inexhaustible multitude of TV's images, sounds, and rhythms, like the dense catalog on every page of *TV Guide*, reassures us again and again that TV points to everything we might ever want or need. Nor is this promise merely implicit. The commercials, perhaps the quintessential components of TV's nonstop display, not only reconfirm our sense of privilege with millions of alluring images, but refer explicitly and often to this extensive "choice" of ours: AT&T offers us "The Right Choice," electricity, we are told, grants us "The Power of Choice," Wendy's reminds us that "There Is No Better Choice," McDonald's is "America's Choice," Coke is "The Real Choice," "In copiers, the choice is Canon," Taster's Choice is "The Choice for Taste"—

all such assurances, and the delicious images that bolster them, combining to enhance even further TV's rich, ongoing paean to its own unimaginable abundances. And yet, consider carefully just one of those innumerable commercials that seem to celebrate "choice."

A white van parks on a hot beach crowded with young people. Unnoticed by these joggers and sunbathers, the driver jumps from the front seat and quickly hoists himself inside the van's rear compartment—a complete broadcasting facility. Seated at the console, with a sly look on his boyish face, he puts on a pair of headphones and flips a switch. Two white speakers rise out of the van's roof. He then picks up a cold bottle of Pepsi-Cola, tilts it toward the microphone before him, and opens it. The enticing *pop* and *whoosh* reverberate across the beach. A young woman, lying as if unconscious on a beach chair, suddenly comes to, turning her face automatically toward the speakers. The hubbub starts to die down.

Grinning now, the driver pours the Pepsi into a tall Styrofoam cup, so that everyone can hear the plash, the fizz, the wet ascending arpeggio of liquid decanted from a bottle. Inside the van, the full cup sighs and sparkles at the microphone. Outside, the air is filled with the dense crackle of carbonation. Intrigued by the sound, a dog—with a white kite draped raffishly across its head—looks to its right, toward the speakers. Intrigued, a young man shifts his gaze in exactly the same way, taking off his glasses as he does so.

Now the driver leans toward his microphone and drinks the Pepsi noisily. At the sound of his parched gulping, the crowd falls completely still. One girl reflexively smacks her lips. His cup emptied, the driver sits back and delivers a long, convincing "aaaaaaahhh!"

The crowd snaps out of its collective daze. There is an atmosphere of stampede. Now ringed by customers, the driver stands behind his van, its rear doors opened wide, revealing a solid wall of fresh six-packs, each bearing the familiar Pepsi logo. He puts on a Pepsi vendor's cap and chirps, "Okay! Who's first?" Each customer immediately raises one arm high, and all clamor for a Pepsi, as the camera zooms far back to show that the driver's victory is total. All those beach-goers have suddenly converged on the white van like houseflies descending on a fallen Popsicle. Except for that tight throng of consumers in the distance, the beach is a wide wasteland of deserted towels. In this depopulated space, a single figure wanders, the only one who has not (yet) succumbed to Pepsi—a man equipped with a metal detector, presumably searching for loose change, and so protected, by his earphones, from the driver's irresistible sound effects. Finally, there is this signature, printed over the final image and solemnly intoned by Martin Sheen: "Pepsi. The Choice of a New Generation."

Thus, this ad leaves us with the same vague conviction that all advertising, and TV in general, continually reconfirm: that we are bold, experienced, fully self-aware, and therefore able to pick out what's best from the enormous range of new sensations now available. Like most ads, then, this one seems to salute its viewers for their powers of discrimination, their advanced ability to choose; and yet, like most ads, this one contradicts its own celebration of "choice" by making choice itself seem inconceivable.

Within the little beach universe devised for Pepsico by BBDO, "choice" is nothing but a quaint illusion. The members of this "new generation" succumb at once to the driver's expert Pavlovian technique, like so many rats responding to any systematic stimulus. This easy mass surrender is no "choice," nor are these Pepsi drinkers capable of exercising "choice," since they are the mere tanned particles of a summer mob—transient, pretty, easygoing and interchangeable. To belong to such a "generation" is not to derive one's own identity from that multitude of peers, but to give up all identity, to dissolve into a single reactive mass, and become a thing lightweight and indefinite, like so much flotsam. In such a primal group, dog and man are indeed equals, the dog trying, just like a man, to beat the heat by covering its head, the man removing his glasses, as if to be more like a dog, the two of them responding identically to the sound of Pepsi streaming from a bottle.

In place of those capacities that might distinguish man from dog, here it is merely Pepsi that fills up every heart and mind, just as it fills that Styrofoam cup. No one thus saturated could make choices. Although not, it seems, as malleable as his customers, the driver himself is no less driven by Pepsi, blitzing his territory on behalf of himself and the company combined. And even the sole survivor of the pitch, temporarily deaf to those delicious noises, escapes only by cutting himself off. His solitary project, moreover, does not really distinguish him from all the rest, since there is apparently nothing he can do, having scrounged those dimes and pennies from the sand, but spend his income on a Pepsi.

So it cannot matter, in this beach universe, that there is no one capable of choosing, because there isn't anything to choose. Here there is nothing but Pepsi, and the mass compulsion to absorb it. As soon as the sound of Pepsi fills the air, all the pleasures of the afternoon evaporate, so that this full beach, with its sunny fraternizing, its soporific heat, its quiet surf returning and returning, becomes, in an instant, nothing more than a sandy area where you crave a certain beverage. Despite the ad's salute to "choice," what triumphs over all the free and various possibilities of that summer day is an eternal monad: Pepsi, whose taste, sound, and logo you will always recognize, and always "choose," whether you want to or not.

It is not "choice," then, that this ad is celebrating, but the total negation of choice and choices. Indeed, the product itself is finally incidental to the pitch. The ad does not so much extol Pepsi per se as recommend it by implying that a lot of people have been fooled into buying it. In other words, the point of this successful bit of advertising is that Pepsi has been advertised successfully. The ad's hero is himself an adman, a fictitious downscale version of the dozens of professionals who collaborated to produce him. He, like them, moves fast, works too hard (there are faint dark circles under his eyes), and gets his kicks by manipulating others en masse for the sake of a corporate entity. It is his power—the power of advertising—that is the subject of this powerful advertisment, whose crucial image reveals the driver surrounded by his sudden customers, who face him eagerly, each raising one arm high, as if to hail the salesman who has so skillfully distracted them.

This ad, in short, is perfectly self-referential; and that self-reflection serves to immunize the ad against the sort of easy charges often leveled against advertising. This commercial cannot, for example, be said to tell a lie, since it works precisely by acknowledging the truth about itself: it is a clever ad meant to sell Pepsi, which people buy because it's advertised so cleverly. It would be equally pointless to complain that this ad manipulates its viewers, since the ad wittily exults in its own process of manipulation. To object to the ad at all, in fact, is to sound priggish, because the ad not only admits everything, but also seems to take itself so lightly, offering up its mini-narrative of mass capitulation in a spirit of sophisticated humor, as if to say, "Sure, this is what we do. Funny, huh?"

In the purity of its self-reference, this ad is entirely modern. Before the eighties, an ad for Pepsi, or for some comparable item, would have worked differently—by enticing its viewers toward a paradise radiating from the product, thereby offering an illusory escape from the market and its unrelenting pressures. In such an ad, the Pepsi would (presumably) admit its drinker to some pastoral retreat, which would not then—like that beach—lose all of its delightfulness to the product, but would retain its otherworldly charms. In this way, advertising, until fairly recently, proffered some sort of transcendence over the world of work, trying to conceal the hard economic character of its suasive project with various "humane" appeals—to family feeling, hunger, romantic fantasy, patriotism, envy, fear of ostracism, the urge to travel, and dozens of other "noncommercial" longings and anxieties. Of course, there are ads out now that attempt to make this dated offer, but nowhere near as often, or as convincingly, as the advertising of the past. Like this Pepsi commercial, more and more of today's mass advertisements offer no alternative to or respite from the marketplace but the marketplace itself, which (in the world as advertising represents it) appears at last to have permeated every one of the erstwhile havens in its midst. Now products are presented as desirable not because they offer to release you from the daily grind, but because they'll pull you under, take you in.

— ✦ —

As advertising has become more self-referential, it has also become harder to distinguish from the various other features of our media culture. This coalescence has resulted in part from the meticulous efforts of the advertising industry, whose aim is to have the ads each look like an appealing aspect of what they once seemed to deface or interrupt. In the world of print, this tendency toward "nonadvertising advertising" (as it has been termed within the industry) has resulted, for example, in the "advertorial," a magazine ad disguised as editorial content, and in the "magalogue," a direct-mail catalog as slick and startling in its graphics as any fashion magazine. The standard items of print advertising reflect the same aesthetic pretension, the same widespread effort to make advertising seem the primary and most attractive feature of contemporary journalism. According to one adman, the major advertisers in today's magazines "are making great impressions on intelligent audiences that find the ads a bonus—not an intrusion."

But in this society, TV is the main attraction; and so it is on TV that advertisers strive most inventively, and at the greatest cost, to merge their messages with the ostensible "nonadvertising." The agencies, as one executive at Foote, Cone and Belding puts it, "have a much greater concern to get the viewer to like the advertising." The real object of this "concern," to put it in the boyish parlance of the industry, is to prevent the viewer from "zapping," or skipping past, the commercials, an evasive action now made possible by the VCR; and those without VCRs can also zap the ads, by turning down the volume with remote control devices. Aspiring to zap-proof status, "commercials," says the executive, "are becoming more like entertaining films," adorned with stunning cinematic gimmicks. Timex, for instance, entered the 1984 Christmas season with a two-minute commercial, broadcast in prime time. "Although its ad is all sell," reported the *Wall Street Journal*, "Timex believes viewers will stay tuned for the special effects that show giant watches doubling as beach chairs and racketball courts." Alternately, the advertiser will append his message to, or embed it in, a long, diversionary bit of pseudoprogramming. Such tactics are especially prevalent on cable TV. Corporations are now using cable as "a sort of laboratory where they can experiment with long commercials, creative techniques, and 'infomercials,' which are a blend of advertising and practical advice." If such "experiments" prove satisfactory to their sponsors, the ads on network TV will rely more and more on the sort of camouflage now widespread on cable: "The General Foods subsidiary of Philip Morris shoehorns its ads in the middle of two-minute recipe spots, Campbell Soup Co. recently produced a music video for teens about exercise and nutrition, and Procter & Gamble is running Crest toothpaste infomercials on Nickelodeon, a children's cable channel."

Such efforts are not new. Advertisers have long sought to disguise their messages as news items or feature stories. The current coalescence is significant not because of its novelty, but because such practices have come to represent the ideal type of TV advertising; and this development cannot be wholly explained by pointing to the admen's various ploys. For the conscious tactics of advertisers, however sly, finally matter less than the objective process that has made them possible. In order for TV's ads to seem "a bonus—not an intrusion," the rest of television first had to change in many subtle ways, imperceptibly taking on the quality of the commercials, just as the commercials have had to begin looking "more like entertaining films." This mutual approximation works to the distinct advantage of the advertisers, whose messages are today no longer overshadowed, contradicted, or otherwise threatened by programming that is too noticeably different from the ads.

Two pieces of advertising news, one from TV's early days and one quite recent, illuminate this shift. In 1955, Philip Morris gave up its sponsorship of *I Love Lucy*, then TV's top-rated show, in part because the company's sales had dropped steeply despite the show's popularity. "There are those at PM and its agency (Biow-Biern-Togo) who subscribe to the idea," *Tide* magazine reported, "that an extremely good show might never sell products. Reason: you tend to talk about the program during the commercials." Others at Philip Morris felt that this painful rift between the show and the commercials ought to have been ameliorated by the commercials themselves: "Certainly, little was done [by the agency] to merchandise Philip Morris with Lucy, as Chesterfield, for example, does with Jack Webb and Perry Como."

There are such stories from the fifties, of programming not bland enough to offset the intermittent sales pitch, stories that suggest a common wisdom, back then, on the need to maintain, for profit's sake, a certain vacuity throughout TV. Some of TV's insiders have confirmed that this imperative did not lose its force after the fifties. "Program makers," wrote an ABC executive in 1976, must "attract mass audiences" without "too deeply moving them emotionally," since such disturbance "will interfere with their ability to receive, recall, and respond to the commercial message. This programming reality is the unwritten, unspoken *Gemeinschaft* of all professional members of the television fraternity." And Todd Gitlin, describing the TV industry of the early 1980s, reports that the TV writers' "product is designed to go down easy. It has to be compatible with commercials. Advertising executives like to say that television shows are the meat in a commercial sandwich."

Whereas *I Love Lucy* was evidently too exciting to complement the ads, some of the latest research now suggests that when the viewer is happily absorbed in some enthralling program, he or she will enjoy the commercials equally, and even trust them all the more. "Television viewers," a consulting outfit claimed to have discovered in 1984, "generally find commercials more memorable, likable, credible, and persuasive when placed in programs they find involving [*sic*]." In order to arrive at this conclusion, its authors first developed a "Program Impact Index," which "measures the degree of intellectual and emotional stimulation a program provides its viewers." Their subsequent researches led them to conclude that the "commercial message" is more memorable, more believable, and more successful when the program that contains it seems especially engrossing.

These recent findings, conveyed with all the drabness of contemporary social science, seem to contradict, even disprove, the casual intuitions of those unnamed executives at Philip Morris. If, however, we regard both TV and its audience as changeable and increasingly commingled, we can recognize the truth of both those intuitions and these findings. For as TV has undergone vast changes since 1955, so has its audience changed with it, and because of it.

It is not enough to conclude, however accurately, that a rousing TV show will always complement its advertising, because that conclusion fails to take into account the historical character of the relationship. What seemed exciting to TV's audience in 1955 differs immeasurably from what might seem "involving" to us nowadays—a subtle shift in taste that has had everything to do with the gradual triumph of advertising, which today is no longer despised as it was in the fifties. Much faster and more gorgeous than ever, the commercials now seem not to interrupt, abrasively, a given TV narrative, but rather to set the pace for it. The experience of televisual "excitement," in fact, has been closely linked in the last decade to advertising's rise in status and its advances in technique. In other words, TV's managers, through their continuing efforts to create a televisual atmosphere hospitable to the commercials, have surely succeeded, after all these years, in altering their public's expectations: *I Love Lucy*, if it were made today, would seem continuous with its ads, and would therefore probably pay off in ways that would have satisfied those executives at Philip Morris.

Whenever the networks' representatives, or their hired consultants, or the advertising experts tell us what "the people" want or like, they assume that they themselves have had no hand in forming, or deforming, those desires. And yet we must confront the possibility that commercial TV has itself created its appropriate audience. As ads and shows continue to converge, our unvoiced collective standards of "intellectual and emotional stimulation" are also changing, which is to say that those vague standards are descending; and this descent makes any reversal or renewal more and more unlikely. "To the bulk of the audience," Grant Tinker recently worried aloud, "bad programming may not be a problem." Thus, when we speak about the decline of TV's programming as inextricable from the ascent of TV's ads, we have necessarily raised the possibility of a concomitant stupefaction of the American audience—a mass regression that is continuous with TV's advanced development as an advertising medium. As Tinker put it: "The audience has changed some—and not for the better. I don't know why. It has something to do with the maturing of the medium."

This uneasy statement offers us a dismal truth: TV has finally come into its own, and yet neither TV nor its audience has been improved by this "maturing of the medium." How, then, has TV "matured"? Certainly, it has fulfilled none of its documentary or dramatic possibilities, a failure that explains the character of TV's recent consummation. For in order to "bring you the world," whether through reportage or drama, TV would have to point beyond itself. Yet "the maturing of the medium" consists precisely in TV's near-perfect inability to make any such outward gesture. TV tends now to bring us nothing but TV. Like the Pepsi ad, TV today purports to offer us a world of "choices," but refers us only to itself.

The commercialization of TV has now reached a new level. Since the mid-fifties, TV's programs have sold consumption openly, insistently, and garishly. Commodities have been promoted through continuous mention, constant presentation in the foreground or as background, and even through the very look of TV's personnel—the attractive "guest" and "host," the game show MC and his slim manikins, the stars and starlets of the soaps, the animated warriors, all of whom have not only helped to push goods outright, but who have themselves been compact and implicit ads for everything it takes to look almost as telegenic as they do: skin cream, sun block, toothpaste, shaving cream, a blow dryer, dandruff shampoo, hair conditioner, hair dye (if not a wig), tweezers, scissors, blushers, mascara, lipstick (if not plastic surgery), lip balm, exercise equipment, aerobics classes, various diet plans, a new wardrobe, Woolite, eye drops, contact lenses, cold cream, and sleeping pills.

However, it is not just by envisioning a universe crammed with new products that TV now demonstrates its maturity. For TV has gone beyond the explicit celebration of commodities to the implicit reinforcement of that spectatorial posture which TV requires of us. Now it is not enough just to proffer an infinitude of goods; TV must also try to get its viewers to prefer the passive, hungry watching of those goods, must lead us to believe that our spectatorial inaction is the only sort of action possible. Appropriately, TV pursues this project through some automatic strategies of modern advertising.

First of all, TV now exalts TV spectatorship by preserving a hermetic vision that is uniformly televisual. Like advertising, which no longer tends to evoke realities at variance with the martket, TV today shows almost nothing that might somehow clash with its own busy, monolithic style. This new stylistic near integrity is the product of a long process whereby TV has eliminated or subverted whichever of its older styles have threatened to impede the sale of goods; that is, styles that might once have encouraged some nontelevisual type of spectatorship. Despite the rampant commodity emphasis on TV since the mid-fifties, there were still several valuable rifts in its surface, contrasts that could still enable a critical view of TV's enterprise.

For instance, there was for years a stark contrast between the naturalistic gray of TV's "public interest" programming (the news and "educational television") and the bright, speedy images surrounding it—a contrast that sustained, however vaguely, the recognition of a world beyond the ads and game shows. That difference is gone now that the news has been turned into a mere extension of prime time, relying on the same techniques and rhetoric that define the ads. Similarly, there was once a visible distinction, on TV, between the televisual and the cinematic, sustained by the frequent broadcast of "old movies," each a grandiose reminder of the theater, of "the stars," of narrative—possibilities quite alien to the process of network TV, which has since obliterated the distinction. Now *The Late Night Movie* will turn out to be a rerun of *Barney Miller*, and the first broadcast of the latest telefilm is called "A World Premiere."

Through such gradual exclusions, TV has almost purified itself, aspiring to a spectacle that can remind us of no prior or extrinsic vision. As a result, the full-time viewer has become more likely to accept whatever TV sells, since that selling process seems to be the only process in existence. Yet it would be wrong to argue that TV treats its audience like a mass of wide-eyed bumpkins, approaching them as easy marks; for such a claim would underestimate the subtlety of TV's self-promotion. TV does not solicit our rapt absorption or hearty agreement, but—like the ads that subsidize it—actually flatters us for the very boredom and distrust which it inspires in us. TV solicits each viewer's allegiance by reflecting back his/her own automatic skepticism toward TV. Thus, TV protects itself from criticism or rejection by incorporating our very animus against the spectacle into the spectacle itself.

◄┈ ═◆═ ┈►

Like the Pepsi ad, with its cool and knowing tone, TV is pervasively ironic, forever flattering the viewer with a sense of his/her own enlightenment. Even at its most self-important, TV is also charged with this seductive irony. On the news, for instance, the anchorman or correspondent is often simultaneously pompous and smirky, as if to let us know that he, like us, cannot be taken in. When covering politicians or world leaders, newsmen like Chris Wallace, David Brinkley, Harry Reasoner, Roger Mudd, and Sam Donaldson seem to jeer at the very news they report, evincing an iconoclastic savvy that makes them seem like dissidents despite their ever-readiness to fall in line. The object of the telejournalistic smirk is usually an easy target like "Congress" or "the Democrats," or a foreign leader backed by the Soviets, or an allied dictator who is about to lose his grip. Seldom does the newsman raise a serious question about the policies or values of the multinationals, the CIA, the State Department, or the president. Rather, the TV news tends to "raise doubts" about the administration by playing up the PR problems of its members (PR problems which the TV news thereby creates): Can David Stockman be muzzled? Can Pat Buchanan get along with Donald Regan? Can George Bush alter the perception that he doesn't know what he's saying? Through such trivialities, the TV news actually conceals what goes on at the top and in the world, enhancing its own authority while preserving the authority of those in power, their ideology, their institutions.

Nevertheless, the telejournalists' subversive air can often seem like the exertion of a mighty democratic force. Certainly, TV's newsmen like to think that a jaundiced view is somehow expressive of a popular sympathy with all the rest of us; and, of course, if we glance back through TV's history since the sixties, we will recall a number of thrilling confrontations between some potentate and a reporter bold enough to question him: Frank Reynolds putting it to Richard Nixon, Dan Rather talking back to Richard Nixon, Sam Donaldson hectoring Jimmy Carter or Ronald Reagan. Each time Ted Koppel sits before someone like Ferdinand Marcos, each time Mike Wallace interrogates some well-dressed hireling whose desk cannot protect him from that cool scrutiny, we sense a moment of modern heroism, as the newsman, with his level gaze and no-nonsense queries, seems about to topple one more bad authority for the sake of a vast, diverse, and righteous public—or republic, for there is something in this routine televisual agon that seems quintessentially American. We are, the TV news seems always to be telling us, a young and truth-loving nation, founded upon the vigorous rejection of the old European priests and kings, and still distrustful of all pompous father figures; and so those boyish skeptics who face down the aging crook or tyrant thereby act out a venerable ideal of American innocence.

⊶ ⥳♦⥲ ⊷

Miller states that TV increasingly exalts its passive, ironic viewers: "It is, in short, TV's own full-time viewer" that TV now "reflects and celebrates" in sitcoms and other shows. Miller gives several examples and continues...

TV today is almost unified by its self-reflection. The contemptuous underling who rolls her eyes behind the back of her ex-husband, mother, daughter, boss, or closest friend has analogues throughout the other genres. The talk show host, for instance, is a figure of the ideal viewer. As we watch TV's images, so does he sit and look on at his parade of guests, evincing a boyish wryness against which all too-demonstrative behavior seems comic, especially when he glances our way with a look that says, "Can you believe this?" He is a festive version of the anchorman, with an air of detached superiority that is enabled by his permanent youthfulness, and by his middle-American calm and plainness. Johnny Carson of Iowa, like his heir apparent, that supreme ironist, David Letterman of Indiana, always seems somehow above the excesses of either coast, even as he brings them to us....

TV's heroics are now also reflective of the viewers who cannot help but watch them. This has been evidenced in a negative way by the extinction of the TV Western, whose heroes were too self-sufficient, its locales too spare and natural, to survive in an ad-saturated atmosphere. TV now permits the Western only in the form of burlesque, whether as sitcoms like *Best of the West* or in parodic commercials. Today, the solemnity of the old TV cowboys has evolved into the spectatorial cool of the new TV Cop: Sonny Crockett is at once the descendant and the antithesis of Davy Crockett. An exemplary voyeur, the TV cop demonstrates his righteousness through the hip judgmental stare with which he eyes the many hookers/pimps/drug dealers/hit men/Mafia dons/psychotic killers/oily lawyers who flash and leer so colorfully before him. The history of TV's cops, in fact, is a history of disguised looks, from the outraged glower of *Dragnet's* Sergeant Friday to the more laid-back jeering gazes of the cops today—the casual smirk of Detective Hunter, the sarcastic glances that create the sense of solidarity at Hill Street Station, the deadpan looks of incredulity exchanged by Cagney and Lacey. Like us, the TV cop seems to deplore the bad guys even as he keeps on watching them; and TV's latest cop-hero is not only an adept voyeur, but is himself also a slick visual object, derived from the imagery of advertising. Indeed, his "heroism" is entirely (tele)visual and consumeristic. We see him as "the good" because he knows how to shop for clothes. The eponymous bodyguard of *The Equalizer* is a well-armed and contemptuous onlooker, as stately and impassive as the connoisseur in an ad for scotch, and routinely angered by the many scummy types who, ill-dressed and misbehaving, cross his sight.

TV's reflection on the knowing viewer is a cynical appeal not only to the weakest part of each of us, but to the weakest and least experienced among us. It is therefore not surprising that this reflection has transformed the children's shows along with the rest of TV. Today the slow and beaming parent figures of the past—Fran Allison, Captain Kangaroo, Miss Frances, Mr. Wizard—recur to us like lame old jokes. TV now urges its younger viewers to adopt the same contemptuous and passive attitude that TV recommends to grown-ups. The child who sits awed by He-Man, the GoBots, the Thundercats, or G.I. Joe is not encouraged to pretend or sing or make experiments, but is merely hypnotized by those speedy images; and in this trance he learns only how to jeer. The superheroes wage interminable war, and yet it is not belligerence per se that these shows celebrate, but the particular belligerence that TV incites toward all that seems nontelevisual. The villains are always frenzied and extremely ugly, whereas the good guys are well built, smooth, and faceless, like the computers that are programmed to animate them. Empowered by this contrast, they attack their freaky enemies not just with swords and guns, but with an endless stream of witless personal insults— "bonehead," "fur-face," "long-legged creep," and on and on. Like TV's ads, these shows suggest that nothing could be worse than seeming different; but TV now teaches the same smug derisiveness even on those children's shows without commercials. For example, *Sesame Street*—despite its long-standing reputation as a pedagogical triumph—has become merely one more exhibition of contagious jeering. The puppets often come across as manic little fools, while the hosting grown-ups come across as wise and cool—a marked superiority which they express through the usual bewildered exasperated looks. Thus, the program's little viewers learn how to behave themselves— i.e., as viewers only. They are invited not to share the puppet's crazed exuberance, but only to look down on it; and so they practice that ironic posture which the show advises just as unrelentingly as it repeats the primary numbers and the letters of the alphabet.

As this flattery of the viewer now nearly unifies TV, so has it, necessarily, all but unified the culture which TV has pervaded. Throughout TV, these figures of cool irony recur seductively as our embattled fellow viewers; and yet these seeming dissidents only serve to bolster a corporate system that would make all dissidence impossible. Of course, through their commercials, these corporations too pretend to take our side (while taking sides against us), defusing our rebelliousness by seeming to mimic it: AT&T advises us, through the soft-spoken Cliff Robertson, to reject its big, impersonal competitors, as if AT&T were a plucky little mom-and-pop enterprise; Apple likens IBM to a totalitarian state, as if Apple Computer Inc. were a cell of anarchists; GE depicts a world of regimented silence, its citizens oppressed and robotized, until the place is gloriously liberated by a hip quartet bearing powerful GE tape players, as if that corporation were a hedonistic sect and not a major manufacturer of microwave ovens, refrigerators and—primarily—weapons systems.

•—• ⊫◆⊨ •—•

TV is suffused with the enlightened irony of the common man, "the little guy," or—to use a less dated epithet—the smart shopper. Thus, TV has absorbed for its own purposes an ancient comic stance that has, throughout the history of the West, hinted at the possibility of freedom. Countless old scenes and stories have assured us that aggressive power cannot withstand the wry gaze and witty comment of the observant ironist, whose very weakness thereby seems the source of a latent revolutionary strength. Through such a stance, Diogenes embarrassed Alexander, Jesus discomfited the Pharisees; and in scores of comedies from Plautus through the Restoration and beyond, in hundreds of satires from Juvenal well into the eighteenth century, the servile fop or lumbering bully seems to be deflated by the sharp asides of an independent-minded onlooker.

Such spectatorial subversion of the powerful, or of those who have clearly given in to power, recurs throughout the European literary canon—but it was in America that this device became especially widespread, as the familiar comic weapon of a nation of iconoclasts. Here the spectatorial irony took on an overtly democratic force through the writings and performances of our most celebrated humorists: Artemus Ward, Josh Billings, Mr. Dooley, "Honest Abe," Mark Twain, Will Rogers. Through mastery of the native idiom, and by otherwise projecting "an uncommon common sense," such ironists were each adept at seeming to see through, on behalf of decent fellows everywhere, all pomp, hypocrisy, convention, and whatever else might seem to stink of tyranny.

The history of this subversive irony has reached its terminus, for now the irony consists in nothing but an easy jeering gaze that TV uses not to question the exalted, but to perpetuate its own hegemony. Over and over, the spectator recurs within the spectacle, which thereby shields itself from his/her boredom, rage, or cynicism. TV deflects these (potentially) critical responses onto its own figments of the unenlightened Other, and therefore seems itself to be enlightened, a force of progress and relentless skepticism. Yet the televisual irony now contravenes the very values which the older irony was once used to defend.

TV's irony functions, persistently if indirectly, to promote consumption as a way of life. Whereas the native humorists spoke out from an ideology of individualism, TV's cool tots appear to us as well-dressed hostages, branded with the logos of Benetton, Adidas, Calvin Klein. The self is an embarrassment on TV, an odd encumbrance, like a hatbox or a watch fob. TV's irony at once discredits any sign of an incipient selfhood, so that the only possible defense against the threat of ridicule would be to have no self at all. In order not to turn into a joke, then, one must make an inward effort to become like either—or both—of those supernal entities that dominate TV: the commodity and the corporation. These alone are never ironized on TV, because these alone can never lapse into the laughable condition of mortality. The corporation is, by definition, disembodied; the commodity-as-advertised, a sleek and luminous portent of nonhumanity. Both seem to gaze back at us from within the distant future, having evolved far beyond our weaknesses and fear: TV's irony derives from that contemptuous gaze, which threatens even the most blasé actors, the most knowing spectators. Through its irony, in short, TV advises us not just to buy its products, but to emulate them, so as to vanish into them.

Thus, the most derisive viewer is also the most dependent: "Students do not take *General Hospital* seriously," writes Mark Harris in *TV Guide*. "They know it's not life; they say it's a 'soporific'; they feel superior to it. But *General Hospital* is also necessary, indispensable." In short, our jeering hurts TV's commercial project not at all. Everybody knows that TV is mostly false and stupid, that almost no one pays that much attention to it—and yet it's on for over seven hours a day in the average household, and it sells innumerable products. In other words, TV manages to do its job even as it only yammers in the background, despised by those who keep it going.

And it certainly is despised. Everybody watches it, but no one really likes it. This is the open secret of TV today. Its only champions are its own executives, the advertisers who exploit it, and a compromised network of academic boosters. Otherwise, TV has no spontaneous defenders, because there is almost nothing in it to defend. In many ways at once, TV negates the very "choices" that it now promotes with rising desperation. It promises an unimpeded vision of the whole known universe, and yet it shows us nothing but the laughable reflection of our own unhappy faces. It seems to offer us a fresh, "irreverent" view of the oppressive past, and yet that very gesture of rebelliousness turns out to be a ploy by those in power. Night after night, TV displays a bright infinitude of goods, employs a multitude of shocks and teases; and the only purpose of that spectacle is to promote the habit of spectatorship. It celebrates unending "choice" while trying to keep a jeering audience all strung out. TV begins by offering us a beautiful hallucination of diversity, but it is finally like a drug whose high is only the conviction that its user is too cool to be addicted.

Walker Percy
The Loss of the Creature

Walker Percy started his career as a doctor, and at the age of 26 he contracted tuberculosis while on the job. During his long convalescence, he read extensively, becoming particularly interested in Existentialist philosophy and the problems of authenticity, perception, and meaning in everyday life. He built his work as a writer (of both fiction and nonfiction) upon these interests, and has often been characterized as a "philosophical novelist." In this essay, Percy thinks through some of the problems of human perception—the way that we look at and take in our surroundings. In what ways do you think Percy's thoughts on tourism point to larger issues involving the ways in which we live, perceive, and understand? What kind of "traveler" do you think you are?

I

Every explorer names his island Formosa, beautiful. To him it is beautiful because, being first, he has access to it and can see it for what it is. But to no one else is it ever as beautiful—except the rare man who manages to recover it, who knows that it has to be recovered.

Garcia López de Cárdenas discovered the Grand Canyon and was amazed at the sight. It can be imagined: One crosses miles of desert, breaks through the mesquite, and there it is at one's feet. Later the government set the place aside as a national park, hoping to pass along to millions the experience of Cárdenas. Does not one see the same sight from the Bright Angel Lodge that Cárdenas saw?

The assumption is that the Grand Canyon is a remarkably interesting and beautiful place and that if it had a certain value P for Cárdenas, the same value *P* may be transmitted to any number of sightseers—just as Banting's discovery of insulin can be transmitted to any number of diabetics. A counterinfluence is at work, however, and it would be nearer the truth to say that if the place is seen by a million sightseers, a single sightseer does not receive value *P* but a millionth part of value *P*.

It is assumed that since the Grand Canyon has the fixed interest value *P*, tours can be organized for any number of people. A man in Boston decides to spend his vacation at the Grand Canyon. He visits his travel bureau, looks at the folder, signs up for a two-week tour. He and his family take the tour, see the Grand Canyon, and return to Boston. May we say that this man has seen the Grand Canyon? Possibly he has. But it is more likely that what he has done is the one sure way not to see the canyon.

Why is it almost impossible to gaze directly at the Grand Canyon under these circumstances and see it for what it is—as one picks up a strange object from one's backyard and gazes directly at it? It is almost impossible because the Grand Canyon, the thing as it is, has been appropriated by the symbolic complex which has already been formed in the sightseer's mind. Seeing the canyon under approved circumstances is seeing the symbolic complex head on. The thing is no longer the thing as it confronted the Spaniard; it is rather that which has already been formulated—by picture postcard, geography book, tourist folders, and the words *Grand Canyon*. As a result of this preformulation, the source of the sightseer's pleasure undergoes a shift. Where the wonder and delight of the Spaniard arose from his penetration of the thing itself, from a progressive discovery of depths, patterns, colors, shadow, etc., now the sightseer measures his satisfaction *by the degree to which the canyon conforms to the preformed complex*. If it does so, if it looks just like the postcard, he is pleased; he might even say, "Why it is every bit as beautiful as a picture postcard!" He feels he has not been cheated. But if it does not conform, if the colors are somber, he will not be able to see it directly; he will only be conscious of the disparity between what it is and what it is supposed to be. He will say later that he was unlucky in not being there at the right time. The highest point, the term of the sightseer's satisfaction, is not the sovereign discovery of the thing before him; it is rather the measuring up of the thing to the criterion of the preformed symbolic complex.

Seeing the canyon is made even more difficult by what the sightseer does when the moment arrives, when sovereign knower confronts the thing to be known. Instead of looking at it, he photographs it. There is no confrontation at all. At the end of forty years of preformulation and with the Grand Canyon yawning at his feet, what does he do? He waives his right of seeing and knowing and records symbols for the next forty years. For him there is no present; there is only the past of what has been formulated and seen and the future of what has been formulated and not seen. The present is surrendered to the past and the future.

The sightseer may be aware that something is wrong. He may simply be bored; or he may be conscious of the difficulty: that the great thing yawning at his feet somehow eludes him. The harder he looks at it, the less he can see. It eludes everybody. The tourist cannot see it; the bellboy at the Bright Angel Lodge cannot see it: for him it is only one side of the space he lives in, like one wall of a room; to the ranger it is a tissue of everyday signs relevant to his own prospects—the blue haze down there means that he will probably get rained on during the donkey ride.

How can the sightseer recover the Grand Canyon? He can recover it in any number of ways, all sharing in common the stratagem of avoiding the approved confrontation of the tour and the Park Service.

It may be recovered by leaving the beaten track. The tourist leaves the tour, camps in the back country. He arises before dawn and approaches the South Rim through a wild terrain where there are no trails and no railed-in lookout points. In other words, he sees the canyon by avoiding all the facilities for seeing the canyon. If the benevolent Park Service hears about this fellow and thinks he has a good idea and places the following notice in the Bright Angel Lodge: *Consult ranger for information on getting off the beaten track*—the end result will only be the closing of another access to the canyon.

It may be recovered by a dialectical movement which brings one back to the beaten track but at a level above it. For example, after a lifetime of avoiding the beaten track and guided tours, a man may deliberately seek out the most beaten track of all, the most commonplace tour imaginable: he may visit the canyon by a Greyhoud tour in the company of a party from Terre Haute—just as a man who has lived in New York all his life may visit the Statue of Liberty. (Such dialectical savorings of the familiar as the familiar are, of course, a favorite stratagem of the *The New Yorker* magazine.) The thing is recovered from familiarity by means of an exercise in familiarity. Our complex friend stands behind his fellow tourists at the Bright Angel Lodge and sees the canyon through them and their predicament, their picture taking and busy disregard. In a sense, he exploits his fellow tourist; he stands on their shoulders to see the canyon.

Such a man is far more advanced in the dialectic than the sightseer who is trying to get off the beaten track—getting up at dawn and approaching the canyon through the mesquite. This stratagem is, in fact, for our complex man the weariest, most beaten track of all.

It may be recovered as a consequence of a breakdown of the symbolic machinery by which the experts present the experience to the consumer. A family visits the canyon in the usual way. But shortly after their arrival, the park is closed by an outbreak of typhus in the south. They have the canyon to themselves. What do they mean when they tell the home folks of their good luck: "We had the whole place to ourselves"? How does one see the thing better when the others are absent? Is looking like sucking: the more lookers, the less there is to see? They could hardly answer, but by saying this they testify to a state of affairs which is considerably more complex than the simple statement of the schoolbook about the Spaniard and the millions who followed him. It is a state in which there is a complex distribution of sovereignty, of zoning.

It may be recovered in a time of national disaster. The Bright Angel Lodge is converted into a rest home, a function that has nothing to do with the canyon a few yards away. A wounded man is brought in. He regains consciousness; there outside his window is the canyon.

The most extreme case of access by privilege conferred by disaster is the Huxleyan novel of the adventures of the surviving remnant after the great wars of the twentieth century. An expedition from Australia lands in Southern California and heads east. They stumble across the Bright Angel Lodge, now fallen into ruins. The trails are grown over, the guard rails fallen away, the dime telescope at Batttleship Point rusted. But there is the canyon, exposed at last. Exposed by what? By the decay of those facilities which were designed to help the sightseer.

This dialectic of sightseeing cannot be taken into account by planners, for the object of the dialectic is nothing other than the subversion of the effort of the planners.

This dialectic is not known to objective theorists, psychologists, and the like. Yet it is quite well known in the fantasy-consciousnness of the popular arts. The devices by which the museum exhibit, the Grand Canyon, the ordinary thing, is recovered have long since been stumbled upon. A movie shows a man visiting the Grand Canyon. But the moviemaker knows something the planner does not know. He knows that one cannot take the sight frontally. The canyon must be approached by the stratagems we have mentioned: the Inside Track, the Familiar Revisited, the Accidental Encounter. Who is the stranger at the Bright Angel Lodge? Is he that ordinary tourist from Terre Haute that he makes himself out to be? He is not. He has another objective in mind, to revenge his wronged brother, counterespionage, etc. By virtue of the fact that he has other fish to fry, he may take a stroll along the rim after supper and then we can see the canyon through him. The movie accomplishes its purpose by concealing it. Overtly the characters (the American family marooned by typhus) and we the onlookers experience pity for the sufferers, and the family experience anxiety for themselves; covertly and in truth they are the happiest of people and we are happy through them, for we have the canyon to ourselves. The movie cashes in on the recovery of sovereignty through disaster. Not only is the canyon now accessible to the remnant: the members of the remnant are now accessible to each other, a whole new ensemble of relations becomes possible—friendship, love, hatred, clandestine sexual adventures. In a movie when a man sits next to a woman on a bus, it is necessary either that the bus break down or that the woman lose her memory. (The question occurs to one: Do you imagine there are sightseers who see sights just as they are supposed to? a family who live in Terre Haute, who decide to take the canyon tour, who go there, see it, enjoy it immensely, and go home content? A family who are entirely innocent of all the barriers, zones, losses of sovereignty I have been talking about? Wouldn't most people be sorry if Battleship Point fell into the canyon, carrying all one's fellow passengers to their death, leaving one alone on the South Rim? I cannot answer this. Perhaps there are such people. Certainly a great many American families would swear they had no such problems, that they came, saw, and went away happy. Yet it is just these families who would be happiest if they had gotten the Inside Track and been among the surviving remnant.)

It is now apparent that as between the many measures which may be taken to overcome the opacity, the boredom, of the direct confrontation of the thing or creature in its citadel of symbolic investiture, some are less authentic than others. That is to say, some stratagems obviously serve other purposes than that of providing access to being—for example various unconscious motivations which it is not necessary to go into here.

Let us take an example in which the recovery of being is ambiguous, where it may under the same circumstances contain both authentic and unauthentic components. An American couple, we will say, drives down into Mexico. They see the usual sights and have a fair time of it. Yet they are never without the sense of missing something. Although Taxco and Cuernavaca are interesting and picturesque as advertised, they fall short of "it." What do the couple have in mind by "it"? What do they really hope for? What sort of experience could they have in Mexico so that upon their return, they would feel that "it" had happened? We have a clue: Their hope has something to do with their own role as tourists in a foreign country and the way in which they conceive this role. It has something to do with other American tourists. Certainly they feel that they are very far from "it" when, after traveling five thousand miles, they arrive at the plaza in Guanajuato only to find themselves surrounded by a dozen other couples from the Midwest.

Already we may distinguish authentic and unauthentic elements. First, we see the problem the couple faces and we understand their efforts to surmount it. The problem is to find an "unspoiled" place. "Unspoiled" does not mean only that a place is left physically intact; it means also that it is not encrusted by renown and by the familiar (as in Taxco), that it has not been discovered by others. We understand that the couple really want to get at the place and enjoy it. Yet at the same time we wonder if there is not something wrong in their dislike of their compatriots. Does access to the place require the exclusion of others?

Let us see what happens.

The couple decide to drive from Guanajuato to Mexico City. On the way they get lost. After hours on a rocky mountain road, they find themselves in a tiny valley not even marked on the map. There they discover an Indian village. Some sort of religious festival is going on. It is apparently a corn dance in supplication of the rain god.

The couple know at once that this is "it." They are entranced. They spend several days in the village, observing the Indians and being themselves observed with friendly curiosity.

Now may we not say that the sightseers have at last come face to face with an authentic sight, a sight which is charming, quaint, picturesque, unspoiled, and that they see the sight and come away rewarded? Possibly this may occur. Yet it is more likely that what happens is a far cry indeed from an immediate encounter with being, that the experience, while masquerading as such, is in truth a rather desperate impersonation. I use the word *desperate* advisedly to signify an actual loss of hope.

The clue to the spuriousness of their enjoyment of the village and the festival is a certain restiveness in the sightseers themselves. It is given expression by their repeated exclamations that "this is too good to be true," and by their anxiety that it may not prove to be so perfect, and finally by their downright relief at leaving the valley and having the experience in the bag, so to speak—that is, safely embalmed in memory and movie film.

What is the source of their anxiety during the visit? Does it not mean that the couple are looking at the place with a certain standard of performance in mind? Are they like Fabre, who gazed at the world about him with wonder, letting it be what it is; or are they not like the overanxious mother who sees her child as one performing, now doing badly, now doing well? The village is their child and their love for it is an anxious love because they are afraid that at any moment it might fail them.

We have another clue in their subsequent remark to an ethnologist friend. "How we wished you had been there with us! What a perfect goldmine of folkways! Every minute we would say to each other, if only you were here! You must return with us." This surely testifies to a generosity of spirit, a willingness to share their experience with others, not at all like their feelings toward their fellow Iowans on the plaza at Guanajuato!

I am afraid this is not the case at all. It is true that they longed for their ethnologist friend, but it was for an entirely different reason. They wanted him, not to share their experience, but to certify their experience as genuine.

"This is it" and "Now we are really living" do not necessarily refer to the sovereign encounter of the person with the sight that enlivens the mind and gladdens the heart. It means that now at last we are having the acceptable experience. The present experience is always measured by a prototype, the "it" of their dreams. "Now I am really living" means that now I am filling the role of sightseer and the sight is living up to the prototype of sights. This quaint and picturesque village is measured by a Platonic ideal of the Quaint and the Picturesque.

Hence their anxiety during the encounter. For at any minute something could go wrong. A fellow Iowan might emerge from an adobe hut; the chief might show them his Sears catalog. (If the failures are "wrong" enough, as these are, they might still be turned to account as rueful conversation pieces. "There we were expecting the chief to bring us a churinga and he shows up with a Sears catalog!") They have snatched victory from disaster, but their experience always runs the danger of failure.

They need the ethnologist to certify their experience as genuine. This is borne out by their behavior when the three of them return for the next corn dance. During the dance, the couple do not watch the goings-on; instead they watch the ethnologist! Their highest hope is that their friend should find the dance interesting. And if he should show signs of true absorption, an interest in the goings-on so powerful that he becomes oblivious of his friends—then their cup is full. "Didn't we tell you?" they say at last. What they want from him is not ethnological explanations; all they want is his approval.

What has taken place is a radical loss of sovereignty over that which is as much theirs as it is the ethnologist's. The fault does not lie with the ethnologist. He has no wish to stake a claim to the village; in fact, he desires the opposite: he will bore his friends to death by telling them about the village and the meaning of the folkways. A degree of sovereignty has been surrendered by the couple. It is the nature of the loss, moreover, that they are not aware of the loss, beyond a certain uneasiness. (Even if they read this and admitted it, it would be very difficult for them to bridge the gap in their confrontation of the world. Their consciousness of the corn dance cannot escape their consciousness of their consciousness, so that with the onset of the first direct enjoyment, their higher consciousness pounces and certifies: "Now you are doing it! Now you are really living!" and, in certifying the experience, sets it at nought.)

Their basic placement in the world is such that they recognize a priority of title of the expert over his particular department of being. The whole horizon of being is staked out by "them," the experts. The highest satisfaction of the sightseer (not merely the tourist but any layman seer of sights) is that his sight should be certified as genuine. The worst of this impoverishment is that there is no sense of impoverishment. The surrender of title is so complete that it never even occurs to one to reassert title. A poor man may envy the rich man, but the sightseer does not envy the expert. When a caste system becomes absolute, envy disappears. Yet the caste of layman-expert is not the fault of the expert. It is due altogether to the eager surrender of sovereignty by the layman so that he may take on the role not of the person but of the consumer.

I do not refer only to the special relation of layman to theorist. I refer to the general situation in which sovereignty is surrendered to a class of privileged knowers, whether these be theorists or artists. A reader may surrender sovereignty over that which has been theorized about. The consumer is content to receive an experience just as it has been written about, just as a consumer may surrender sovereignty over a thing which has been presented to him by theorists and planners. The reader may also be content to judge life by whether it has or has not been formulated by those who know and write about life. A young man goes to France. He too has a fair time of it, sees the sights, enjoys the food. On his last day, in fact as he sits in a restaurant in Le Havre waiting for his boat, something happens. A group of French students in the restaurant get into an impassioned argument over a recent play. A riot takes place. Madame la concierge joins in, swinging her mop at the rioters. Our young American is transported. This is "it." And he had almost left France without seeing "it"!

But the young man's delight is ambiguous. On the one hand, it is a pleasure for him to encounter the same Gallic temperament he had heard about from Puccini and Rolland. But on the other hand, the source of his pleasure testifies to a certain alienation. For the young man is actually barred from a direct encounter with anything French excepting only that which has been set forth, authenticated by Puccini and Rolland—those who know. If he had encountered the restaurant scene without reading Hemingway, without knowing that the performance was so typically, charmingly French, he would not have been delighted. He would only have been anxious at seeing things get so out of hand. The source of his delight is the sanction of those who know.

This loss of sovereignty is not a marginal process, as might appear from my example of estranged sightseers. It is a generalized surrender of the horizon to those experts within whose competence a particular segment of the horizon is thought to lie. Kwakiutls are surrendered to Franz Boas; decaying Southern mansions are surrendered to Faulkner and Tennessee Williams. So that, although it is by no means the intention of the expert to expropriate sovereignty—in fact he would not even know what sovereignty meant in this context—the danger of theory and consumption is a seduction and deprivation of the consumer.

In the New Mexico desert, natives occasionally come across strange-looking artifacts which have fallen from the skies and which are stenciled: *Return to U.S. Experimental Project, Alamogordo. Reward.* The finder returns the object and is rewarded. He knows nothing of the nature of the object he has found and does not care to know. The sole role of the native, the highest role he can play, is that of finder and returner of the mysterious equipment.

The same is true of the laymen's relation to *natural* objects in a modern, technical society. No matter what the object or event is, whether it is a star, a swallow, a Kwakiutl, a "psychological phenomenon," the layman who confronts it does not confront it as a sovereign person, as Crusoe confronts a seashell he finds on the beach. The highest role he can conceive himself as playing is to be able to recognize the title of the object, to return it to the appropriate expert and have it certified as a genuine find. He does not even permit himself to see the thing—as Gerard Hopkins could see a rock or a cloud or a field. If anyone asks him why he doesn't look, he may reply that he didn't take that subject in college (or he hasn't read Faulkner).

This loss of sovereignty extends even to oneself. There is the neurotic who asks nothing more of his doctor than that his symptoms should prove interesting. When all else fails, the poor fellow has nothing to offer but his own neurosis. But even this is sufficient if only the doctor will show interest when he says, "Last night I had a curious sort of dream; perhaps it will be significant to one who knows about such things. It seems I was standing in a sort of alley—" (I have nothing else to offer you but my own unhappiness. Please say that it, at least, measures up, that it is a *proper* sort of unhappiness.)

II

A young Falkland Islander walking along a beach and spying a dead dogfish and going to work on it with his jackknife has, in a fashion wholly unprovided in modern educational theory, a great advantage over the Scarsdale high-school pupil who finds the dogfish on his laboratory desk. Similarly the citizen of Huxley's *Brave New World* who stumbles across a volume of Shakespeare in some vine-grown ruins and squats on a potsherd to read it is in a fairer way of getting at a sonnet than the Harvard sophomore taking English Poetry II.

The educator whose business it is to teach students biology or poetry is unaware of a whole ensemble of relations which exist between the student and the dogfish and between the student and the Shakespeare sonnet. To put it bluntly: A student who has the desire to get at a dogfish or a Shakespeare sonnet may have the greatest difficulty in salvaging the creature itself from the educational package in which it is presented. The great difficulty is that he is not aware that there is a difficulty; surely, he thinks, in such a fine classroom, with such a fine textbook, the sonnet must come across! What's wrong with me?

The sonnet and the dogfish are obscured by two different processes. The sonnet is obscured by the symbolic package which is formulated not by the sonnet itself but by the *media* through which the sonnet is transmitted, the media which the educators believe for some reason to be transparent. The new textbook, the type, the smell of the page, the classroom, the aluminum windows and the winter sky, the personality of Miss Hawkins—these media which are supposed to transmit the sonnet may only succeed in transmitting themselves. It is only the hardiest and cleverest of students who can salvage the sonnet from this many-tissued package. It is only the rarest student who knows that the sonnet must be salvaged from the package. (The educator is well aware that something is wrong, that there is a fatal gap between the student's learning and the student's life: the student reads the poem, appears to understand it, and gives all the answers. But what does he recall if he should happen to read a Shakespeare sonnet twenty years later? Does he recall the poem or does he recall the smell of the page and the smell of Miss Hawkins?)

One might object, pointing out that Huxley's citizen reading his sonnet in the ruins and the Falkland Islander looking at his dogfish on the beach also receive them in a certain package. Yes, but the difference lies in the fundamental placement of the student in the world, a placement which makes it possible to extract the thing from the package. The pupil at Scarsdale High sees himself placed as a consumer receiving an experience-package; but the Falkland Islander exploring his dogfish is a person exercising the sovereign right of a person in his lordship and mastery of creation. He too could use an instructor and a book and a technique, but he would use them as his subordinates, just as he uses his jackknife. The biology student does not use his scalpel as an instrument, he uses it as a magic wand! Since it is a "scientific instrument," it should do "scientific things."

The dogfish is concealed in the same symbolic package as the sonnet. But the dogfish suffers an additional loss. As a consequence of this double deprivation, the Sarah Lawrence student who scores A in zoology is apt to know very little about a dogfish. She is twice removed from the dogfish, once by the symbolic complex by which the dogfish is concealed, once again by the spoliation of the dogfish by theory which renders it invisible. Through no fault of zoology instructors, it is nevertheless a fact that the zoology laboratory at Sarah Lawrence College is one of the few places in the world where it is all but impossible to see a dogfish.

The dogfish, the tree, the seashell, the American Negro, the dream, are rendered invisible by a shift of reality from concrete thing to theory which Whitehead has called the fallacy of misplaced concreteness. It is the mistaking of an idea, a principle, an abstraction, for the real. As a consequence of the shift, the "specimen" is seen as less real than the theory of the specimen. As Kierkegaard said, once a person is seen as a specimen of a race or a species, at that very moment he ceases to be an individual. Then there are no more individuals but only specimens.

To illustrate: A student enters a laboratory which, in the pragmatic view, offers the student the optimum conditions under which an educational experience may be had. In the existential view, however—that view of the student in which he is regarded not as a receptacle of experience but as a knowing being whose peculiar property is to see himself as being in a certain situation—the modern laboratory could not have been more effectively designed to conceal the dogfish forever.

The student comes to his desk. On it, neatly arranged by his instructor, he finds his laboratory manual, a dissecting board, instruments, and a mimeographed list:

Exercise 22: Materials

1 dissecting board

1 scalpel

1 forceps

1 probe

1 bottle india ink and syringe

1 specimen of *Squalus acanthias*

The clue of the situation in which the student finds himself is to be found in the last item: 1 specimen of *Squalus acanthias*.

The phrase *specimen of* expresses in the most succinct way imaginable the radical character of the loss of being which has occurred under his very nose. To refer to the dogfish, the unique concrete existent before him, as a "specimen of *Squalus acanthias*" reveals by its grammar the spoliation of the dogfish by the theoretical method. This phrase, *specimen of*, example of, instance of, indicates the ontological status of the individual creature in the eyes of the theorist. The dogfish itself is seen as a rather shabby expression of an ideal reality, the species *Squalus acanthias*. The result is the radical devaluation of the individual dogfish. (The *reductio ad absurdum* of Whitehead's shift is Toynbee's employment of it in his historical method. If a gram of NaCl is referred to by the chemist as a "sample of" NaCl, one may think of it as such and not much is missed by the oversight of the act of being of this particular pinch of salt, but when the Jews and the Jewish religion are understood as—in Toynbee's favorite phrase—a "classical example of" such and such a kind of *Voelkerwanderung*, we begin to suspect that something is being left out.)

If we look into the ways in which the student can recover the dogfish (or the sonnet), we will see that they have in common the stratagem of avoiding the educator's direct presentation of the object as a lesson to be learned and restoring access to sonnet and dogfish as beings to be known, reasserting the sovereignty of knower over known.

In truth, the biography of scientists and poets is usually the story of the discovery of the indirect approach, the circumvention of the educator's presentation—the young man who was sent to the *Technikum* and on his way fell into the habit of loitering in book stores and reading poetry; or the young man dutifully attending law school who on the way became curious about the comings and goings of ants. One remembers the scene in *The Heart is a Lonely Hunter* where the girl hides in the bushes to hear the Capehart in the big house play Beethoven. Perhaps she was the lucky one after all. Think of the unhappy souls inside, who see the record, worry about scratches, and most of all worry about whether they are *getting it*, whether they are bona fide music lovers. What is the best way to hear Beethoven: sitting in a proper silence around the Capehart or eavesdropping from an azalea bush?

However it may come about, we notice two traits of the second situation: (1) an openness of the thing before one—instead of being an exercise to be learned according to an approved mode, it is a garden of delights which beckons to one; (2) a sovereignty of the knower—instead of being a consumer of a prepared experience, I am a sovereign wayfarer, a wanderer in the neighborhood of being who stumbles into the garden.

One can think of two sorts of circumstances through which the thing may be restored to the person. (There is always, of course, the direct recovery: A student may simply be strong enough, brave enough, clever enough to take the dogfish and the sonnet by storm, to wrest control of it from the educators and the educational package.) First by ordeal: The Bomb falls; when the young man recovers consciousness in the shambles of the biology laboratory, there not ten inches from his nose lies the dogfish. Now all at once he can see it directly and without let, just as the exile or the prisoner or the sick man sees the sparrow at his window in all its inexhaustibility; just as the commuter who has had a heart attack sees his own hand for the first time. In these cases, the simulacrum of everydayness and of consumption has been destroyed by disaster; in the case of the bomb, literally destroyed. Secondly, by apprenticeship to a great man: one day a great biologist walks into the laboratory; he stops in front of our student's desk; he leans over, picks up the dogfish, and, ignoring instruments and procedure, probes with a broken fingernail into the little carcass. "Now here is a curious business," he says, ignoring also the proper jargon of the specialty. "Look here how this little duct reverses its direction and drops into the pelvis. Now if you would look into a coelacanth, you would see that it—" And all at once the student can see. The technician and the sophomore who loves his textbooks are always offended by the genuine research man because the latter is usually a little vague and always humble before the thing; he doesn't have much use for the equipment or the jargon. Whereas the technician is never vague and never humble before the thing; he holds the thing disposed of by the principle, the formula, the textbook outline; and he thinks a great deal of equipment and jargon.

But since neither of these methods of recovering the dogfish is pedagogically feasible—perhaps the great man even less so than the Bomb—I wish to propose the following educational technique which should prove equally effective for Harvard and Shreveport High School. I propose that English poetry and biology should be taught as usual, but that at irregular intervals, poetry students should find dogfishes on their desks and biology students should find Shakespeare sonnets on their dissection boards. I am serious in declaring that a Sarah Lawrence English major who began poking about in a dogfish with a bobby pin would learn more in thirty minutes than a biology major in a whole semester; and that the latter upon reading on her dissecting board

> That time of year Thou may'st in me behold
> When yellow leaves, or none, or few, do hang
> Upon those boughs which shake against the cold—
> Bare ruin'd choirs where late the sweet birds sang

might catch fire at the beauty of it.

The situation of the tourist at the Grand Canyon and the biology student are special cases of a predicament in which everyone finds himself in a modern technical society—a society, that is, in which there is a division between expert and layman, planner and consumer, in which experts and planners take special measures to teach and edify the consumer. The measures taken are measures appropriate to the consumer: the expert and the planner *know* and *plan*, but the consumer *needs* and *experiences*.

There is a double deprivation. First, the thing is lost through its packaging. The very means by which the thing is presented for consumption, the very techniques by which the thing is made available as an item of need-satisfaction, these very means operate to remove the thing from the sovereignty of the knower. A loss of title occurs. The measures which the museum curator takes to present the thing to the public are self-liquidating. The up-shot of the curator's efforts are not that everyone can see the exhibit but that no one can see it. The curator protests: why are they so indifferent? Why do they even deface the exhibit? Don't they know it is theirs? But it is not theirs. It is his, the curator's. By the most exclusive sort of zoning, the museum ex-hibit, the park oak tree, is part of an ensemble, a package, which is almost impenetrable to them. The archaeologist who puts his find in a museum so that everyone can see it accomplishes the reverse of his expectations. The re-sult of his action is that no one can see it now but the archaeologist. He would have done better to keep it in his pocket and show it now and then to strangers.

The tourist who carves his initials in a public place, which is theoreti-cally "his" in the first place, has good reasons for doing so, reasons which the exhibitor and planner know nothing about. He does so because in his role of consumer of an experience (a "recreational experience" to satisfy a "recreational need") he knows that he is disinherited. He is deprived of his title over being. He knows very well that he is in a very special sort of zone in which his only rights are the rights of a consumer. He moves like a ghost through schoolroom, city streets, trains, parks, movies. He carves his initials as a last desperate measure to escape his ghostly role of consumer. He is say-ing in effect: I am not a ghost at all; I am a sovereign person. And he estab-lishes title the only way remaining to him, by staking his claim over one square inch of wood or stone.

Does this mean that we should get rid of museums? No, but it means that the sightseer should be prepared to enter into a struggle to recover a sight from a museum.

The second loss is the spoliation of the thing, the tree, the rock, the swal-low, by the layman's misunderstanding of scientific theory. He believes that the thing is *disposed of* by theory, that it stands in the Platonic relation of being a *specimen of* such and such an underlying principle. In the transmis-sion of scientific theory from theorist to layman, the expectation of the the-orist is reversed. Instead of the marvels of the universe being made available to the public, the universe is disposed of by theory. The loss of sovereignty takes this form: as a result of the science of botany, trees are not made avail-able to every man. On the contrary. The tree loses its proper density and mystery as a concrete existent and, as merely another *specimen of* a species, becomes itself nugatory.

Does this mean that there is no use taking biology at Harvard and Shreveport High? No, but it means that the student should know what a fight he has on his hands to rescue the specimen from the educational pack-age. The educator is only partly to blame. For there is nothing the educator can do to provide for this need of the student. Everything the educator does only succeeds in becoming, for the student, part of the educational package. The highest role of the educator is the maieutic role of Socrates: to help the student come to himself not as a consumer of experience but as a sovereign individual.

The thing is twice lost to the consumer. First, sovereignty is lost: it is theirs, not his. Second, it is radically devalued by theory. This is a loss which has been brought about by science but through no fault of the scientist and through no fault of scientific theory. The loss has come about as a consequence of the seduction of the layman by science. The layman will be seduced as long as he regards beings as consumer items to be experienced rather than prizes to be won, and as long as he waives his sovereign rights as a person and accepts his role of consumer as the highest estate to which the layman can aspire.

As Mounier said, the person is not something one can study and provide for; he is something one struggles for. But unless he also struggles for himself, unless he knows that there is a struggle, he is going to be just what the planners think he is.

Debra Seagal

Tales from the
Cutting-Room Floor

The reality of "reality-based" television

Debra Seagal's essay deals with her brief career as a story analyst for the "reality TV" show *American Detective.* The producer of *American Detective* tells Seagal, "You empathize with the wrong people." When reading this essay, whom do you empathize with? Seagal's essay was written in 1993; since then, "reality TV" has grown explosively, which makes it even more relevant when she asks, "Why the national obsession with this sort of voyeuristic entertainment?" Voyeurism is certainly one aspect of reality television and Seagal's essay about it, but the essay opens several topics, including notions of authenticity and reality and edited "reality," and in a way becomes its own subject. Seagal writes, "Evidently the 'reality' of a given episode is subject to enhancement" and the same thing may be said of her diary account. She watches, and we watch her watching— supposedly. But what does Seagal herself leave out? What does she play up? And why? How does the way reality is shaped or edited in the essay affect your sympathies? Finally you might ask yourself, How authentic or enhanced is the "reality" you represent in your own writing?

May 6, 1992

Yesterday I applied for a job as a "story analyst" at *American Detective,* a prime-time "reality-based" cop show on ABC that I've never seen. The interview took place in Malibu at the program's production office, in a plain building next door to a bodybuilding gym. I walked past rows of bronzed people working out on Nautilus equipment and into a dingy array of padded dark rooms crowded with people peering into television screens. Busy people ran up and down the halls. I was greeted by the "story department" manager, who explained that every day the show has camera crews in four different cities trailing detectives as they break into every type of home and location to search, confiscate, interrogate, and arrest. (The crews have the right to do this, he told me, because they have been "deputized" by the local police department. What exactly this means I was not told.) They shoot huge amounts of videotape and it arrives every day, rushed to Malibu by Federal Express. Assistants tag and time-code each video before turning it over to the story department.

After talking about the job, the story-department manager sat me in front of a monitor and gave me two hours to "analyze" a video. I watched the camera pan through a dilapidated trailer while a detective searched for incriminating evidence. He found money in a small yellow suitcase, discovered a knife under a sofa, and plucked a tiny, twisted marijuana butt from a swan-shaped ashtray. I typed each act into a computer. It took me forty-five minutes to make what seemed a meaningless record. When I got home this afternoon there was a message on my phone machine from the story-department manager congratulating me on a job well done and welcoming me to *American Detective*. I am pleased.

May 18, 1992

Although we're officially called story analysts, in-house we're referred to as "the loggers." Each of us has a computer/VCR/print monitor/TV screen/headphone console looming in front of us like a colossal dashboard. Settling into my chair is like squeezing into a small cockpit. The camera crews seem to go everywhere: Detroit, New York, Miami, Las Vegas, Pittsburgh, Phoenix, Portland, Santa Cruz, Indianapolis, San Jose. They join up with local police teams and apparently get access to everything the cops do. They even wear blue jackets with POLICE in yellow letters on the back. The loggers scrutinize each hour-long tape second by second, and make a running log of every visual and auditory element that can be used to "create" a story. On an average day the other three loggers and I look at twenty to forty tapes, and in any given week we analyze from 6,000 to 12, 000 minutes—or up to 720,000 seconds of film.

The footage comes from handheld "main" and "secondary" cameras as well as tiny, wirelike "lock-down" cameras taped to anything that might provide a view of the scene: car doors, window visors, and even on one occasion—in order to record drug deals inside an undercover vehicle—a gear-shift handle. Once a videotape is viewed, the logger creates a highlight reel—a fifteen-minute distillation of the overall "bust" or "case." The tapes and scripts are then handed over to the supervising producer, who in turn works with technical editors to create an episode of the show, each of which begins with this message on the screen: "What you are about to see is real. There are no re-creations. Everything was filmed while it actually happened."

There are, I've learned, quite a few of these reality and "fact-based" shows now, with names like *Cops, Top Cops,* and *FBI: The Untold Stories.* Why the national obsession with this sort of voyeuristic entertainment? Perhaps we want to believe the cops are still in control. The preponderance of these shows is also related to the bottom line: they are extremely inexpensive to produce. After all, why create an elaborate car-chase sequence costing tens of thousands of dollars a minute when a crew with a couple of video cameras can ride around with the cops and get the "real" thing? Why engage a group of talented writers and producers to make intelligent and exciting TV when it's more profitable to dip into the endless pool of human grief?

I've just participated in my first "story meeting" with the supervising producer. He occupies a dark little room filled with prerecorded sound of police banter, queer voice-over loops, segments of the *American Detective* theme song, and sound bites of angry drug-busting screams ("Stop! Police! Put your hands up, you motherfucker!"). A perpetual cold wind blows from a faulty air duct above his desk. He is tall, lanky, in his fifties; his ambition once was to be a serious actor. His job is to determine what images will be resurrected as prime-time, Monday-night entertainment. He doesn't look miserable but I suspect he is.

There are six of us in the story meeting, the producer, four loggers, and the story-department manager. Each logger plays highlight reels and pitches stories, most of which are rejected by the producer for being "not hot enough," "not sexy." Occasionally, I learned today, a highlight reel is made of a case that is still in progress, such as a stakeout. Our cameramen then call us on-site from their cellular phones during our story meeting and update us on what has been filmed that day, sometimes that very hour. The footage arrives the next morning and then is built into the evolving story. This process continues in a flurry of calls and Federal Express deliveries while the real drama unfolds elsewhere—Pittsburgh or San Jose or wherever. We are to hope for a naturally dramatic climax. But if it doesn't happen, I understand, we'll "work one out."

May 26, 1992

I'm learning the job. Among other tasks, we're responsible for compelling stock-footage books—volumes of miscellaneous images containing every conceivable example of guns, drugs, money, scenics, street signs, appliances, and interior house shots. This compendium is used to embellish stories when certain images or sounds have not been picked up by a main or secondary camera: a close-up of a suspect's tightly cuffed wrists missed in a rush, a scream muffled by background traffic noise. Or, most frequently, the shouts of the cops on a raid ("POLICE! Open the door! Now!") in an otherwise unexciting ramrod affair. Evidently the "reality" of a given episode is subject to enhancement.

Today the story-department manager gave me several videotapes from secondary and lock-down cameras at an undercover mission in Indianapolis. I've never been to Indianapolis, and I figured that, if nothing else, I'd get to see the city.

I was wrong. What I saw and heard was a procession of close-up crotch shots, nose-picking, and farting in surveillance vans where a few detectives waited, perspiring under the weight of nylon-mesh raid gear and semiautomatic rifles. Searching for the scraps of usable footage was like combing a beach for a lost contact lens. The actual bust—a sad affair that featured an accountant getting arrested for buying pot in an empty shoe-store parking lot—was perhaps 1 percent of everything I looked at. In the logic of the story department, we are to deplore these small-time drug busts not because we are concerned that the big drugs are still on the street but because a small bust means an uninteresting show. A dud.

Just before going home today, I noticed a little list that someone tacked up on our bulletin boards to remind us what we are looking for:

Death

Stab

Shoot

Strangulation

Club

Suicide

June 3, 1992

Today was the first day I got to log Lieutenant Bunnell, which is considered a great honor in the office. Lieutenant Bunnell is the show's mascot, the venerated spokesperson. Only two years ago he was an ordinary narcotics detective in Oregon. Today he has a six-figure income, an agent, fans all over the country, and the best voice coach in Hollywood. He's so famous now that he's even stalked by his fans, such as the strange woman who walked into our office a few days ago wearing hole-pocked spandex tights, worn-down spike-heeled back-less pumps, and a see-through purse. She'd been on his trail from Florida to California and wanted his home phone number. She was quietly escorted out the door to her dilapidated pickup truck.

At the beginning of each episode, Lieutenant Bunnell sets the scene for the viewer (much like Jack Webb on *Dragnet*), painting a picture of the crime at hand and describing the challenges the detectives face. He also participates in many of these raids, since he is, after all, still a police lieutenant. The standard fare: Act I, Bunnell's suspenseful introduction; Act II, Bunnell leads his team on a raid; Act III, Bunnell captures the bad suspect and throws him in the squad car, etc. The format of each drama must fit into an eleven-minute segment. So it is that although *American Detective* and its competitors seem a long way from *Dragnet, The Mod Squad, The Rookies,* et al.—all the famous old cop shows—they follow the same formula, the same dramatic arc, because this is what the viewers and advertisers have come to expect.

June 10, 1992

The producers are pleased with my work and have assigned me my own beat to log—Santa Cruz in northern California. Having spent several summers there as a teenager, I remember its forests, its eucalyptus and apple orchards. But today, two decades later, I strap on earphones, flip on the equipment, and meet three detectives on the Santa Cruz County Narcotic Enforcement Team. Dressed in full SWAT-team regalia, they are Brooks, an overweight commander; Gravitt, his shark-faced colleague; and Cooper, a detective underling. The first image is an intersection in Santa Cruz's commercial district. While an undercover pal negotiates with a drug dealer across the street, the three detectives survey an unsuspecting woman from behind their van's tinted windows. It begins like this:

> [*Interior of van. Mid-range shot of Commander Brooks, Special Agent Gravitt, and Dectective Cooper*]
>
> COOPER: Check out those volumptuous [*sic*] breasts and that volumptuous [*sic*] ass.
> BROOKS: Think she takes it in the butt?
> COOPER: Yep. It sticks out just enough so you can pull the cheeks apart and really plummet it. [*Long pause*] I believe that she's not beyond fellatio either.
> [*Zoom to close-up of Cooper*]
> COOPER: You don't have true domination over a woman until you spit on 'em and they don't say nothing.
> [*Zoom to close-up of Gravitt*]

GRAVITT: I know a hooker who will let you spit on her for twenty bucks…[*Direct appeal to camera*] Can one of you guys edit this thing and make a big lump in my pants for me?
[*Zoom to close-up of Gravitt's crotch, walkie-talkie between his legs*]

June 15, 1992

I'm developing a perverse fascination with the magic exercised in our TV production sweatshop. Once our supervising producer has picked the cases that might work for the show, the "stories" are turned over to an editor. Within a few weeks the finished videos emerge from the editing room with "problems" fixed, chronologies reshuffled, and, when necessary, images and sound bites clipped and replace by old filler footage from unrelated cases.

By the time our 9 million viewers flip on their tubes, we've reduced fifty or sixty hours of mundane and compromising video into short, action-packed segments of tantalizing, crack-filled, dope-dealing, junkie-busting cop culture. How easily we downplay the pathos of the suspect; how cleverly we breeze past the complexities that cast doubt on the very system that has produced the criminal activity in the first place. How effortlessly we smooth out the indiscretions of the lumpen detectives and casually make them appear as pistol-flailing heroes rushing across the screen. Watching a finished episode of *American Detective*, one easily forgets that the detectives are, for the most part, men whose lives are overburdened with formalities and paperwork. They ambush one downtrodden suspect after another in search of marijuana, and then, after a long Sisyphean day, retire into red-vinyl bars where they guzzle down beers among a clientele that, to no small degree, resembles the very people they have just ambushed.

June 23, 1992

The executive producer is a tiny man with excessively coiffed, shoulder-length blond hair. He is given to wearing stone-washed jeans, a buttoned-to-the-collar shirt, and enormous cowboy boots; he also frequently wears a police badge on his belt loop. As I log away, I see his face on the screen flashing in the background like a subliminal advertisement for a new line of L.A.P.D. fashion coordinates. He sits in on interrogations, preens the detectives' hair, prompts them to "say something pithy for the camera." He gets phone calls in surveillance vans and in detective briefing rooms. With a cellular phone flat against his ear, he even has conversations with his L.A. entourage—Lorimar executives, ABC executives, other producers—while he runs in his police jacket behind the cops through ghettos and barrios.

I am beginning to wonder how he has gained access to hundreds of cop cars from California to New Jersey. Clearly the cops don't fear they will be compromised; I see the bonding that takes place between them and the executive producer, who, after a successful raid, presents them with *American Detective* plaques that feature their own faces. Their camaraderie is picked up continuously by the cameras. One of my colleagues has a photograph of our executive producer and Lieutenant Bunnell with their arms around a topless go-go dancer somewhere in Las Vegas; underneath it is a handwritten caption that reads, "The Unbearable Lightness of Being a Cop."

June 25, 1992

Today I logged in several hours of one detective sitting behind a steering wheel doing absolutely nothing. How a man could remain practically immobile for so long is beyond by comprehension. He sat and stared out the window, forgetting that the tiny lock-down camera under his window visor was rolling. After an hour, it seemed as though *I* had become the surveillance camera, receiving his every twitch and breath through the intravenous-like circuitry that connects me to my machine and my machine to his image. There was, finally, a moment when he shifted and looked directly at the camera. For a second our eyes met, and, flustered, I averted my gaze.

June 26, 1992

Today would have been inconsequential had not the supervising producer emerged from his air-conditioned nightmare and leaned over my desk. "We'll have a crew covering Detroit over the weekend," he said. "Maybe we'll get a good homicide for you to work on." I was speechless. I've never seen a homicide, and I have no interest in seeing one. But I'm working in a place where a grisly homicide is actually welcomed. I am supposed to look forward to this. After work, I prayed for benevolence, goodwill, and peace in Detroit.

June 29, 1992

My prayers must have worked—no Detroit homicide case came in today. That doesn't mean, however, that I'm any less complicit in what is clearly a sordid enterprise. This afternoon I analyzed a tape that features detectives busting a motley assortment of small-time pot dealers and getting them to "flip" on their connections. The freshly cuffed "crook" then becomes a C.I. (confidential informant). Rigged with hidden wires and cameras, the C.I. works for the detectives by setting up his friends in drug busts that lead up the ladder. In exchange for this, the C.I. is promised a more lenient sentence when his day comes up in court. Some of the C.I.'s have been busted so many times before that they are essentially professional informants. Ironically, some have actually learned how the game is played by watching reality-based cop shows. This is the case with a nervous teenage first-time pot seller who gets set up and busted in a bar for selling half an ounce of pot. When the undercover cop flashes his badge and whips out his cuffs, a look of thrilled recognition brightens the suspect's face. "Hey, I know you!" he gasps. "You're what's-his-name on *American Detective*, aren't you? I watch your show every week! I know exactly what you want me to do!"

The cops are flattered by the recognition, even if it comes from a teenage crook caught selling pot. They seem to become pals with the C.I.'s. Sometimes, however, they have to muscle the guy. The tape I saw today involves a soft-spoken, thirtysomething white male named Michael who gets busted for selling pot out of his ramshackle abode in the Santa Cruz mountains. He's been set up by a friend who himself was originally resistant to cooperating with the detectives. Michael has never been arrested and doesn't understand the mechanics of becoming a C.I. He has only one request: to see a lawyer. By law, after such a request the detectives are required to stop any form of interrogation immediately and make a lawyer available. In this case, however, Commander Brooks knows that if he can get Michael to flip, they'll be able to keep busting up the ladder and, of course, we'll be able to crank out a good show.

So what happens? Hunched in front of my equipment in the office in Malibu, this is what I see, in minute after minute of raw footage:

[*Michael is pulled out of bed after midnight. Two of our cameras are rolling and a group of cops surround him. He is entirely confused when Brooks explains how to work with them and become a confidential informant.*]

MICHAEL: Can I have a lawyer?...I don't know what's going on. I'd rather talk to a lawyer. This is not my expertise at all, as it is yours. I feel way outnumbered. I don't know what's going on....

BROOKS: Here's where we're at. You've got a lot of marijuana. Marijuana's still a felony in the state of California, despite whatever you may think about it.

MICHAEL: I understand.

BROOKS: The amount of marijuana you have here is gonna send you to state prison....That's our job, to try to put you in state prison, quite frankly, unless you do something to help yourself. Unless you do something to assist us....

MICHAEL: I'm innocent until proven guilty, correct?

BROOKS: I'm telling you the way it is in the real world....What we're asking you to do is cooperate...to act as our agent and help us buy larger amounts of marijuana. Tell us where you get your marijuana....

MICHAEL: I don't understand. You know, you guys could have me do something and I could get in even more trouble.

BROOKS: Obviously, if you're acting as our agent, you can't get in trouble....

MICHAEL: I'm taking your word for that?...

BROOKS: Here's what I'm telling you. If you don't want to cooperate, you're going to prison.

MICHAEL: Sir, I do want to cooperate—

BROOKS: Now, I'm saying if you don't cooperate right today, now, here, this minute, you're going to prison. We're gonna asset-seize your property. We're gonna asset-seize your vehicles. We're gonna asset-seize your money. We're gonna send your girlfriend to prison and we're gonna send your kid to the Child Protective Services. That's what I'm saying.

MICHAEL: If I get a lawyer, all that stuff happens to me?

BROOKS: If you get a lawyer, we're not in a position to wanna cooperate with you tomorrow. We're in a position to cooperate with you right now. Today. Right now. Today...

MICHAEL: I'm under too much stress to make a decision like that. I want to talk to a lawyer. I really do. That's the bottom line.

[*Commander Brooks continues to push Michael but doesn't get far*]

MICHAEL: I'm just getting confused. I've got ten guys standing around me....

BROOKS: We're not holding a gun to you.

MICHAEL: Every one of you guys has a gun?

BROOKS: How old is your child?

MICHAEL: She'll be three on Tuesday.

BROOKS: Well, children need a father at home. You can't be much of a father when you're in jail.

MICHAEL: Sir!

BROOKS: That's not a scare tactic, that's a reality.

MICHAEL: That is a scare tactic.

BROOKS: No, it isn't. That's reality....And the reality is , I'm sending you to prison unless you do something to help yourself out....

MICHAEL: Well, ain't I also innocent until proven guilty in a court of law?...You know what guys? I really just want to talk to a lawyer. That's really all I want to do.

BROOKS: How much money did you put down on this property?…Do you own that truck over there?
MICHAEL: Buddy, does all this need to be done to get arrested?…
BROOKS: Yeah. I'm curious—do you own that truck there?
MICHAEL: You guys know all that.
BROOKS: I hope so, 'cause I'd look good in that truck
MICHAEL: Is this Mexico?
BROOKS: No. I'll just take it. Asset-seizure. And you know what? The county would look good taking the equity out of this house.
MICHAEL: Lots of luck.

[*Commander Brooks continues to work on Michael for several minutes.*]

MICHAEL: I feel like you're poking at me.
BROOKS: I *am* poking at you.
MICHAEL: So now I really want to talk to a lawyer now.
BROOKS: That's fine. We're done.

[*Brooks huffs off, mission unaccomplished. He walks over to his pals and shakes his head.*]

BROOKS: That's the first white guy I ever felt like beating the fucking shit out of.

If Michael's case becomes an episode of the show, Michael will be made a part of a criminal element that stalks backyards and threatens children. Commander Brooks will become a gentle, persuasive cop who's keeping our streets safe at night.

July 1, 1992

Today I got a video to analyze that involves a car chase. It includes the three Santa Cruz cops and a few other officers following two Hispanic suspects at top speed through a brussels-sprouts field in the Central Valley. Our cameramen, wearing police jackets, are in one of their undercover vans during the pursuit. (One of them has his camera in one hand and a pistol held high in the other. The police don't seem to care about his blurred role.) When the suspects stop their car and emerge with their arms held high, the detectives bound out of their vans screaming in a shrill chorus ("Get on the ground, cocksucker!" "I'll blow your motherfucking head off.") I watch. Within seconds, the suspects are pinned to the ground and held immobile while cops kick them in the stomach and the face. Cooper is particularly angry because his van has bounced into a ditch during the pursuit. He looks down at one of the suspects. "You bashed my car," he complains. "I just got it painted, you motherfucker." With that he kicks the suspect in the head. Our main cameraman focuses on the detectives ambling around their fallen prey like hunters after a wild-game safari; a lot of vainglorious, congratulatory back-slapping ensues. Our secondary cameraman holds a long, extreme close-up of a suspect while his mouth bleeds into the dirt. "I feel like I'm dying," he wheezes, and turns his head away from the camera. I watch.

This afternoon, in the office, the video drew a crowd. One producer shook his head at the violence. "Too bad," he said. "Too bad we can't use that footage." This was clearly a case of too much reality for reality-based TV. I couldn't help but wonder what the producers would do if these two suspects were beaten so badly that they later died. Would they have jeopardized their own livelihoods by turning over the video to the "authorities"?

September 21, 1992

I'm losing interest in the footage of detectives; now it is the "little people" who interest me, the people whose stories never make it past a highlight reel. I am strangely devoted to them. There is "the steak-knife lady" who waves her rusty weapon in front of a housing project in Detroit. I replay her over and over again. There is something about her: her hysteria, her insistence on her right to privacy, and her flagrant indignation at the cameras ("Get those cameras outta my face, you assholes!"); the way she flails her broken knife in self-defense at a drunk neighbor while her gigantic curlers unravel; the way she consoles her children, who watch with gaping mouths. This woman is *pissed*. She is *real*. Little does she know I'm going to be watching her in Malibu, California, while I sip my morning cappuccino, manipulating her image for my highlight reel. I feel like I'm in the old Sixties movie *Jason and the Argonauts*, in which Zeus and Hera survey the little humans below them through a heavenly pool of water that looks, oddly enough, like a TV screen.

And there is a skinny, mentally disturbed redhead who took in a boyfriend because she was lonely and friendless. Unknown to her, he is selling heroin out of her apartment. But in the eyes of the law she is considered an accomplice. When the cops interrogate her, all she can say about her boyfriend is, "I love him. I took him in because I love him. He's a little bit retarded or something. I took him in." Later she breaks down sobbing. She is terrified that her father will throw her into a mental institution. "I need love. Can't you understand that?" she cries to the policeman who is trying to explain to her why they are arresting her boyfriend. "I need love. That's all I need, sir."

There are, too, the hapless Hispanic families living in poverty, stashing marijuana behind tapestries of the Virgin Mary and selling it to some of the same white middle-class couch potatoes who watch reality-based cop shows. There are the emotionally disturbed, unemployed Vietnam veterans selling liquid morphine because their SSI checks aren't enough to cover the rent. And there are AIDS patients who get busted, their dwellings ransacked, for smoking small quantities of pot to alleviate the side effects of their medication.

In our office the stories of people like these collect dust on shelves stacked with *Hollywood Reporters,* cast aside because they are too dark, too much like real life. I feel overwhelmed by my ability to freeze-frame their images in time-coded close-ups. I can peer into their private lives with the precision of a lab technician, replaying painful and sordid moments. I am troubled that something of their humanity is stored indefinitely in our supervising producer's refrigerated video asylum. Some of their faces have even entered my dreamworld. This afternoon when I suggest that such unfortunates might be the real stars of our show, my boss snapped, "You empathize with the wrong people."

September 28, 1992

This morning I realized that watching hour after hour of vice has begun to affect me. After a raid, when the detectives begin to search for drugs, money, and weapons while our cameras keep rolling, I find myself watching with the intensity of a child foraging through a grassy backyard for an exquisitely luminous Easter egg. The camera moves through rooms of the unknown suspect as the detectives poke through bedrooms with overturned mattresses and rumpled, stained sheets, through underwear drawers and soiled hampers; into the dewy, tiled grottoes of bathrooms, past soap-streaked shower doors and odd hairs stuck to bathtub walls, clattering through rows of bottles, creams, tubes, and toothbrushes, their bristles splayed with wear. The exploration continues in kitchens, past half-eaten meals, where forks were dropped in surprise moments earlier, past grime-laden refrigerators and grease-pitted ovens, past cats hunched frozen in shock, and onward, sometimes past the body of a dog that has recently been shot by the police, now stiffening in the first moments of rigor mortis.

In the midst of this disarray the police sometimes find what they are so frantically looking for: abundant stacks of $100 bills stuffed in boots, behind secret panels and trap doors; heroin vials sealed in jars of cornmeal stashed in the dank corners of ant-infested cupboards; white powders in plastic Baggies concealed behind moldy bookshelves; discarded hypodermic needles in empty, economy-size laundry-detergent boxes; and thin, spindly marijuana plants blooming in tomato gardens and poppy fields. And, finally, on a lucky day, the guns: the magnums, automatics, shotguns, machine guns, and in one case, assault rifles leaned against walls, their barrels pointed upward.

I feel as though my brain is lined with a stratum of images of human debris. Sitting at home in my small bungalow, I have begun to wonder what lurks behind the goodwill of my neighbors' gestures, what they are doing behind their porches and patios.

September 30, 1992

Today was stock-footage day. I spent ten hours finding, cutting, and filing still-shots of semiautomatic rifles and hypodermic needles. I am starting to notice signs that I am dispirited and restless. I spend long moments mulling over camera shots of unknown faces. Today I took my lunch break on the Malibu pier, where I sat transfixed by the glassy swells, the kelp beds, and minnows under the jetty. I know I can't go on much longer, but I need to pay the rent.

October 1, 1992

I've just worked through a series of videos of the Las Vegas vice squad as they go on a prostitute rampage with our cameramen and producers. Pulling down all-nighters in cheesy motel rooms, the detectives go undercover as our camera crew, our producers, and some of the detectives sit in an adjacent room, watching the live action through a hidden camera. It is, essentially, a voyeur's paradise, and definitely X-rated. The undercover cops' trick is to get the call girls into a position where they are clearly about to accept money for sexual acts. The scam goes something like this: "Hi, I'm John. Me and my buddies here are passing through town. Thought you gals might be able to show us a good time…"

"What did you have in mind?" they ask. The detectives respond with the usual requests for blow jobs. Maybe the undercover cops ask the girls to do a little dancing before getting down to real business. They sit back and enjoy the show. Sometimes they even strip, get into the motel's vibrating, king-size bed, and wait for just the right incriminating moment before the closet door busts open and the unsuspecting woman is overwhelmed by a swarm of detectives and cameramen.

"He's my boyfriend!" many insist as they hysterically scramble for their clothes.

"What's his name?" the cops respond while they snap on the cuffs.

"Bill. Bob. Uh, John..."

It doesn't matter. The police get their suspect. The camera crew gets it footage. The cameras keep on rolling. And what I see, what the viewer will never see, is the women—disheveled, shocked, their clothes still scattered on musty hotel carpets—telling their stories to the amused officers and producers. Some of them sob uncontrollably. Three kids at home. An ex who hasn't paid child support in five years. Welfare. Food stamps. Some are so entrenched in the world of poverty and pimps that they are completely numb, fearing only the retribution they'll suffer if their pimps get busted as a result of their cooperation with the cops. Others work a nine-to-five job during the day that barely pays the rent and then become prostitutes at night to put food on the table. Though their faces are fatigued, they still manage a certain dignity. They look, in fact, very much like the girl next door.

I can't help but see how each piece of the drama fits neatly into the other: one woman's misery is another man's pleasure; one man's pleasure is another man's crime; one man's crime is another man's beat; one man's beat is another man's TV show. And all of these pieces of the drama become one big paycheck for the executive producer.

October 5, 1992

Today the executive producer—in the flesh, not on tape—walked into the office and smiled at me. I smiled back. But I was thinking: one false move and I'll blow your head off.

October 9, 1992

It would seemed that there could not be any further strangeness to everything that I've seen, but, in fact, there is: almost all of the suspects we film, including the prostitutes, sign releases permitting us to put them on TV. Why would they actually want to be on TV even when they've been, literally, caught with their pants down? Could it be because of TV's ability to seemingly give a nobody a certain fleeting, cheap celebrity? Or is it that only by participating in the non-reality of TV can these people feel *more* real, more alive? I asked around to understand how the release process happens.

Usually a production coordinator—an aspiring TV producer fresh out of college—is assigned the task of pushing the legal release into the faces of overwhelmed and tightly cuffed suspects who are often at such peak stress levels that some can't recognize their own faces on their driver's license. "We'll show your side of the story," the production coordinator might say. Sometimes it is the police themselves who ask people to sign, suggesting that the cameras are part of a training film and that signing the form is the least of their present concerns. And to anyone in such a situation this seems plausible, since the entire camera crew is outfitted with police jackets, including the executive producer, who, with his "belt badge," could easily be mistaken for a cop in civilian attire. And, clearly, many of those arrested feel that signing anything will help them in court. In the rare event that a suspect is reluctant to sign the release, especially when his or her case might make for a good show, the *American Detective* officials offer money; but more frequently, it seems, the suspect signing the release form simply doesn't adequately read or speak English. Whatever the underlying motive, almost all of the arrested "criminals" willingly sign their releases, and thus are poised—consciously or not—to participate in their own degradation before the American viewing public.

October 16, 1992

Today I saw something that convinced me I may be lost in the netherworld of videotape; I did, finally, get a homicide. The victim lived in Oregon and planned to save up to attend Reed College. She was a stripper who dabbled in prostitution to make ends meet. On the tape the cops find her on her bed clutching a stuffed animal, her skull bludgeoned open with a baseball bat. A stream of blood stains the wall in a red arc, marking her descent just three hours earlier.

The guy who killed her was a neighbor—blond, blue-eyed, wore a baseball cap, the kind of guy you'd imagine as the head of a Little League team, or a swim coach. He has that particularly American blend of affability, eagerness, and naiveté. When the cops ask him why he bludgeoned her repeatedly after clubbing her unconscious with the first stroke, he replies, "I don't know. I don't really know."

She was Asian, but you would never have known it from what was left of her. What one sees on the tape is that bloody red stain on the wall. We never know why he killed her. We never really know who she was. But it doesn't really matter. She is "just another prostitute." And she will be very good for the show's ratings.

October 19, 1992

This morning I explained my feelings to my boss. I said I "didn't feel good" about the work and had decided to quit. He understood, he said, for he'd once had certain ideals but had eventually resigned himself to the job.

Before departing, I asked a colleague if he was affected by the grief and vice on our monitors. "They're only characters to me," he replied. I noted this quietly to myself, and, with barely a good-bye to my other co-conspirators, I slipped out of the *American Detective* offices into the noon blaze of the California sun, hoping to recover what it is I've lost.

Susan Sontag

Against Interpretation

Susan Sontag went to North Hollywood High School, and from there went to the University of Chicago. At the height of her popularity, she was admired for both her intellectual credibility—if Susan Susan Sontag was talking about it, you knew it was cool—and for serving as American intellectualism's respondent to what many people thought of as the impenetrable difficulty of many European critics and authors. Her writings were a way for many readers to feel they could get a handle on and talk back to some of the most obscure and esoteric ideas of the time.

Still, "Against Interpretation" may seem forbidding in a number of ways: its challenging vocabulary (*incantatory, mimesis, trompe l'oeil, hermeneutics, philistinism, hegemony*), its assumptions regarding the reader's knowledge of the history of art and philosophy (Lascaux, Altamira, Niaux; Plato, Aristotle, the Stoics; Nietzsche, Marx, Freud), and its references to literature and cinema (Kafka, Beckett, Rilke; Bergman, Truffaut, Antonioni). How can we reply to what she's saying if we don't know what she's referring to? One useful strategy with Sontag might be to try to apply what she's saying—about how people think about paintings, books, and movies—to more familiar or contemporary aspects of culture. Think about books you've read, movies you've seen: is Sontag right? As well, it may be helpful to recognize that, like John Berger, Sontag was profoundly influenced by the thinking and life of Walter Benjamin. For more detail, see the brief profile of Berger earlier in this set of readings.

> *Content is a glimpse of something, an encounter like a flash. It's very tiny—very tiny, content.*
> Willem De Kooning, *in an interview*

It is only shallow people who do not judge by appearance. The mystery of the world is the visible, not the invisible.

Oscar Wilde, *in a letter*

I

The earliest experience of art must have been that it was incantatory, magical; art was an instrument of ritual. (Cf. the paintings in the caves at Lascaux, Altamira, Niaux, La Pasiega, etc.) The earliest *theory* of art, that of the Greek philosophers, proposed that art was mimesis, imitation of reality.

It is at this point that the peculiar question of the value of art arose. For the mimetic theory, by its very terms, challenges art to justify itself.

Plato, who proposed the theory, seems to have done so in order to rule that the value of art is dubious. Since he considered ordinary material things as themselves mimetic objects, imitations of transcendent forms or structures, even the best painting of a bed would be only an "imitation of an imitation." For Plato, art is neither particularly useful (the painting of a bed is no good to sleep on) nor, in the strict sense, true. And Aristotle's arguments in defense of art do not really challenge Plato's view that all art is an elaborate *trompe l'oeil*, and therefore a lie. But he does dispute Plato's idea that art is useless. Lie or no, art has a certain value according to Aristotle because it is a form of therapy. Art is useful, after all, Aristotle counters, medicinally useful in that it arouses and purges dangerous emotions.

In Plato and Aristotle, the mimetic theory of art goes hand in hand with the assumption that art is always figurative. But advocates of the mimetic theory need not close their eyes to decorative and abstract art. The fallacy that art is necessarily a "realism" can be modified or scrapped without ever moving outside the problems delimited by the mimetic theory.

The fact is, all Western consciousness of and reflection upon art have remained within the confines staked out by the Greek theory of art as mimesis or representation. It is through this theory that art as such—above and beyond given works of art—becomes problematic, in need of defense. And it is the defense of art which gives birth to the odd vision by which something we have learned to call "form" is separated off from something we have learned to call "content," and to the well-intentioned move which makes content essential and form accessory.

Even in modern times, when most artists and critics have discarded the theory of art as representation of an outer reality in favor of the theory of art as subjective expression, the main feature of the mimetic theory persists. Whether we conceive of the work of art on the model of a picture (art as a picture of reality) or on the model of a statement (art as the statement of the artist), content still comes first. The content may have changed. It may now be less figurative, less lucidly realistic. But it is still assumed that a work of art *is* its content. Or, as it's usually put today, that a work of art by definition says something. ("What X is saying is…" "What X is trying to say is…" "What X said is …" etc., etc.)

II

None of us can ever retrieve that innocence before all theory when art knew no need to justify itself, when one did not ask of a work of art what it said because one knew (or thought one knew) what it did. From now to the end of consciousness, we are stuck with the task of defending art. We can only quarrel with one or another means of defense. Indeed, we have an obligation to overthrow any means of defending and justifying art which becomes particularly obtuse or onerous or insensitive to contemporary needs and practice.

This is the case, today, with the very idea of content itself. Whatever it may have been in the past, the idea of content is today mainly a hindrance, a nuisance, a subtle or not so subtle philistinism.

Though the actual developments in many arts may seem to be leading us away from the idea that a work of art is primarily its content, the idea still exerts an extraordinary hegemony. I want to suggest that this is because the idea is now perpetuated in the guise of a certain way of encountering works of art thoroughly ingrained among most people who take any of the arts seriously. What the overemphasis on the idea of content entails is the perennial, never-consummated project of *interpretation*. And, conversely, it is the habit of approaching works of art in order to *interpret* them that sustains the fancy that there really is such a thing as the content of a work of art.

III

Of course, I don't mean interpretation in the broadest sense, the sense in which Nietzsche (rightly) says, "There are no facts, only interpretations." By interpretation, I mean here a conscious act of the mind which illustrates a certain code, certain "rules" of interpretation.

Directed to art, interpretation means plucking a set of elements (the X, the Y, the Z, and so forth) from the whole work. The task of interpretation is virtually one of translation. The interpreter says, Look, don't you see that X is really—or, really means—A? That Y is really B? That Z is really C?

What situation could prompt this curious project for transforming a text? History gives us the materials for an answer. Interpretation first appears in the culture of late classical antiquity, when the power and credibility of myth had been broken by the "realistic" view of the word introduced by scientific enlightenment. Once the question that haunts post-mythic consciousness—that of the *seemliness* of religious symbols—had been asked, the ancient texts were, in their pristine form, no longer acceptable. Then interpretation was summoned, to reconcile the ancient texts to "modern" demands. Thus, the Stoics, to accord with their view that the gods had to be moral, allegorized away the rude features of Zeus and his boisterous clan in Homer's epics. What Homer really designated by the adultery of Zeus with Leto, they explained, was the union between power and wisdom. In the same vein, Philo of Alexandria interpreted the literal historical narratives of the Hebrew Bible as spiritual paradigms. The story of the exodus from Egypt, the wandering in the desert for forty years, and the entry into the promised land, said Philo, was really an allegory of the individual soul's emancipation, tribulations, and final deliverance. Interpretation thus presupposes a discrepancy between the clear meaning of the text and the demands of (later) readers. It seeks to resolve that discrepancy. The situation is that for some reason a text has become unacceptable; yet it cannot be discarded. Interpretation is a radical strategy for conserving an old text, which is thought too precious to repudiate, by revamping it. The interpreter, without actually erasing or rewriting the text, *is* altering it. But he can't admit to doing this. He claims to be only making it intelligible, by disclosing its true meaning. However far the interpreters alter the text (another notorious example is the rabbinic and Christian "spiritual" interpretations of the clearly erotic Song of Songs), they must claim to be reading off a sense that is already there.

Interpretation in our own time, however, is even more complex. For the contemporary zeal for the project of interpretation is often prompted not by piety toward the troublesome text (which may conceal an aggression) but by an open aggressiveness, an overt contempt for appearances. The old style of interpretation was insistent, but respectful; it erected another meaning on top of the literal one. The modern style of interpretation excavates, and as it excavates, destroys; it digs "behind" the text, to find a sub-text which is the true one. The most celebrated and influential modern doctrines, those of Marx and Freud, actually amount to elaborate systems of hermeneutics, aggressive and impious theories of interpretation. All observable phenomena are bracketed, in Freud's phrase, as *manifest content*. This manifest content must be probed and pushed aside to find the true meaning—the *latent content*—beneath. For Marx, social events like revolutions and wars; for Freud, the events of individual lives (like neurotic symptoms and slips of the tongue) as well as texts (like a dream or a work of art)—all are treated as occasions for interpretation. According to Marx and Freud, these events only *seem* to be intelligible. Actually, they have no meaning without interpretation. To understand *is* to interpret. And to interpret is to restate the phenomenon, in effect to find an equivalent for it.

Thus, interpretation is not (as most people assume) an absolute value, a gesture of mind situated in some timeless realm of capabilities. Interpretation must itself be evaluated, within a historical view of human consciousness. In some cultural contexts, interpretation is a liberating act. It is a means of revising, of transvaluing, of escaping the dead past. In other cultural contexts, it is reactionary, impertinent, cowardly, stifling.

IV

Today is such a time, when the project of interpretation is largely reactionary, stifling. Like the fumes of the automobile and of heavy industry which befoul the urban atmosphere, the effusion of interpretations of art today poisons our sensibilities. In a culture whose already classical dilemma is the hypertrophy of the intellect at the expense of energy and sensual capability, interpretation is the revenge of the intellect upon art.

Even more. It is the revenge of the intellect upon the world. To interpret is to impoverish, to deplete the world—in order to set up a shadow world of "meanings." It is to turn *the* world into *this* world. ("This world"! As if there were any other.)

The world, our world, is depleted, impoverished enough. Away with all duplicates of it, until we again experience more immediately what we have.

V

In most modern instances, interpretation amounts to the philistine refusal to leave the work of art alone. Real art has the capacity to make us nervous. By reducing the work of art to its content and then interpreting *that*, one tames the work of art. Interpretation makes art manageable, comfortable.

This philistinism of interpretation is more rife in literature than in any other art. For decades now, literary critics have understood it to be their task to translate the elements of the poem or play or novel or story into something else. Sometimes a writer will be so uneasy before the naked power of his art that he will install within the work itself—albeit with a little shyness, a touch of the good taste of irony—the clear and explicit interpretation of it. Thomas Mann is an example of such an overcooperative author. In the case of more stubborn authors, the critic is only too happy to perform the job.

The work of Kafka, for example, has been subjected to a mass ravishment by no less than three armies of interpreters. Those who read Kafka as a social allegory see case studies of the frustrations and insanity of modern bureaucracy and its ultimate issuance in the totalitarian state. Those who read Kafka as a psychoanalytic allegory see desperate revelations of Kafka's fear of his father, his castration anxieties, his sense of his own impotence, his thralldom to his dreams. Those who read Kafka as a religious allegory explain that K. in *The Castle* is trying to gain access to heaven, that Joseph K. in *The Trial* is being judged by the inexorable and mysterious justice of God...Another body of work that has attracted interpreters like leeches is that of Samuel Beckett. Beckett's delicate dramas of the withdrawn consciousness—pared down to essentials, cut off, often represented as physically immobilized—are read as a statement about modern man's alienation from meaning or from God, or as an allegory of psychopathology.

Proust, Joyce, Faulkner, Rilke, Lawrence, Gide...one could go on citing author after author; the list is endless of those around whom thick encrustations of interpretation have taken hold. But it should be noted that interpretation is not simply the compliment that mediocrity pays to genius. It is, indeed, the modern way of understanding something, and is applied to works of every quality. Thus, in the notes that Elia Kazan published on his production of *A Streetcar Named Desire*, it becomes clear that, in order to direct the play, Kazan had to discover that Stanley Kowalski represented the sensual and vengeful barbarism that was engulfing our culture, while Blanche DuBois was Western civilization, poetry, delicate apparel, dim lighting, refined feelings and all, though a little the worse for wear, to be sure. Tennessee Williams's forceful psychological melodrama now became intelligible: it was about something, about the decline of Western civilization. Apparently, were it to go on being a play about a handsome brute named Stanley Kowalski and a faded mangy belle named Blanche DuBois, it would not be manageable.

VI

It doesn't matter whether artists intend, or don't intend, for their works to be interpreted. Perhaps Tennessee Williams thinks *Streetcar* is about what Kazan thinks it to be about. It may be that Cocteau in *The Blood of a Poet* and in *Orpheus* wanted the elaborate readings which have been given these films, in terms of Freudian symbolism and social critique. But the merit of these works certainly lies elsewhere than in their "meanings." Indeed, it is precisely to the extent that Williams's plays and Cocteau's films do suggest these portentous meanings that they are defective, false, contrived, lacking in conviction.

From interviews, it appears that Resnais and Robbe-Grillet consciously designed *Last Year at Marienbad* to accommodate a multiplicity of equally plausible interpretations. But the temptation to interpret *Marienbad* should be resisted. What matters in *Marienbad* is the pure, untranslatable, sensuous immediacy of some of its images, and its rigorous if narrow solutions to certain problems of cinematic form.

Again, Ingmar Bergman may have meant the tank rumbling down the empty night street in *The Silence* as a phallic symbol. But if he did, it was a foolish thought. ("Never trust the teller, trust the tale," said Lawrence.) Taken as a brute object, as an immediate sensory equivalent for the mysterious abrupt armored happenings going on inside the hotel, that sequence with the tank is the most striking moment in the film. Those who reach for a Freudian interpretation of the tank are only expressing their lack of response to what is there on the screen.

It is always the case that interpretation of this type indicates a dissatisfaction (conscious or unconscious) with the work, a wish to replace it by something else.

Interpretation, based on the highly dubious theory that a work of art is composed of items of content, violates art. It makes art into an article for use, for arrangement into a mental scheme of categories.

VII

Interpretation does not, of course, always prevail. In fact, a great deal of today's art may be understood as motivated by a flight from interpretation. To avoid interpretation, art may become parody. Or it may become abstract. Or it may become ("merely") decorative. Or it may become non-art.

The flight from interpretation seems particularly a feature of modern painting. Abstract painting is the attempt to have, in the ordinary sense, no content; since there is no content, there can be no interpretation. Pop Art works by the opposite means to the same result; using a content so blatant, so "what it is," it, too, ends by being uninterpretable.

A great deal of modern poetry as well, starting from the great experiments of French poetry (including the movement that is misleadingly called Symbolism) to put silence into poems and to reinstate the *magic* of the word, has escaped from the rough grip of interpretation. The most recent revolution in contemporary taste in poetry—the revolution that has deposed Eliot and elevated Pound—represents a turning away from content in poetry in the old sense, an impatience with what made modern poetry prey to the zeal of interpreters.

I am speaking mainly of the situation in America, of course. Interpretation runs rampant here in those arts with a feeble and negligible avant-garde: fiction and the drama. Most American novelists and playwrights are really either journalists or gentlemen sociologists and psychologists. They are writing the literary equivalent of program music. And so rudimentary, uninspired, and stagnant has been the sense of what might be done with form in fiction and drama that even when the content isn't simply information, news, it is still peculiarly visible, handier, more exposed. To the extent that novels and plays (in America), unlike poetry and painting and music, don't reflect any interesting concern with changes in their form, these arts remain prone to assault by interpretation.

But programmatic avant-gardism—which has meant, mostly, experiments with form at the expense of content—is not the only defense against the infestation of art by interpretations. At least, I hope not. For this would be to commit art to being perpetually on the run.(It also perpetuates the very distinction between form and content which is, ultimately, an illusion.) Ideally, it is possible to elude the interpreters in another way, by making works of art whose surface is so unified and clean, whose momentum is so rapid, whose address is so direct that the work can be …just what it is. Is this possible now? It does happen in films, I believe. This is why cinema is the most alive, the most exciting, the most important of all art forms right now. Perhaps the way one tells how alive a particular art form is is by the latitude it gives for making mistakes in it and still being good. For example, a few of the films of Bergman—though crammed with lame messages about the modern spirit, thereby inviting interpretations—still triumph over the pretentious intentions of their director. In *Winter Light* and *The Silence*, the beauty and visual sophistication of the images subvert before our eyes the callow pseudo-intellectuality of the story and some of the dialogue. (The most remarkable instance of this sort of discrepancy is the work of D. W. Griffith.) In good films, there is always a directness that entirely frees us from the itch to interpret. Many old Hollywood films, like those of Cukor, Walsh, Hawks, and countless other directors, have this liberating antisymbolic quality, no less than the best work of the new European directors, like Truffaut's *Shoot the Piano Player* and *Jules and Jim*, Godard's *Breathless* and *Vivre sa Vie*, Antonioni's *L'Avventura*, and Olmi's *The Fiancés*.

The fact that films have not been overrun by interpreters is in part due simply to the newness of cinema as an art. It also owes to the happy accident that films for such a long time were just movies; in other words, that they were understood to be part of mass, as opposed to high, culture, and were left alone by most people with minds. Then, too, there is always something other than content in the cinema to grab hold of, for those who want to analyze. For the cinema, unlike the novel, possesses a vocabulary of forms—the explicit, complex, and discussable technology of camera movements, cutting, and composition of the frame that goes into the making of a film.

VIII

What kind of criticism, of commentary on the arts, is desirable today? For I am not saying that works of art are ineffable, that they cannot be described or paraphrased. They can be. The question is how. What would criticism look like that would serve the work of art, not usurp its place?

What is needed, first, is more attention to form in art. If excessive stress on *content* provokes the arrogance of interpretation, more extended and more thorough descriptions of *form* would silence. What is needed is a vocabulary—a descriptive, rather than prescriptive, vocabulary—for forms.* The best criticism, and it is uncommon, is of this sort that dissolves considerations of content into those of form. On film, drama, and painting respectively, I can think of Erwin Panofsky's essay "Style and Medium in the Motion Pictures," Northrop Frye's essay "A Conspectus of Dramatic Genres," Pierre Francastel's essay "The Destruction of a Plastic Space." Roland Barthes's book *On Racine* and his two essays on Robbe-Grillet are examples of formal analysis applied to the work of a single author. (The best essays in Erich Auerback's *Mimesis*, like "The Scar of Odysseus," are also of this type.) An example of formal analysis applied simultaneously to genre and author is Walter Benjamin's essay "The Storyteller: Reflections on the Works of Nicolai Leskov."

Equally valuable would be acts of criticism which would supply a really accurate, sharp, loving description of the appearance of a work of art. This seems even harder to do than formal analysis. Some of Manny Farber's film criticism, Dorothy Van Ghent's essay "The Dickens World: A View from Todgers'," Randall Jarrell's essay on Walt Whitman are among the rare examples of what I mean. These are essays which reveal the sensuous surface of art without mucking about in it.

*One of the difficulties is that our idea of form is spatial (the Greek metaphors for form are all derived from notions of space). This is why we have a more ready vocabulary of forms for the spatial than for the temporal arts. The exception among the temporal arts, of course, is the drama; perhaps this is because the drama is a narrative (i.e., temporal) form that extends itself visually and pictorially, upon a stage. What we don't have yet is a poetics of the novel, any clear notion of the forms of narration. Perhaps film criticism will be the occasion of a breakthrough here, since films are primarily a visual form, yet they are also a subdivision of literature.

IX

Transparence is the highest, most liberating value in art—and in criticism—today. Transparence means experiencing the luminousness of the thing in itself, of things being what they are. This is the greatness of, for example, the films of Bresson and Ozu and Renoir's *The Rules of the Game*.

Once upon a time (say, for Dante), it must have been a revolutionary and creative move to design works of art so that they might be experienced on several levels. Now it is not. It reinforces the principle of redundancy that is the principal affliction of modern life.

Once upon a time (a time when high art was scarce), it must have been a revolutionary and creative move to interpret works of art. Now it is not. What we decidedly do not need now is further to assimilate Art into Thought, or (worse yet) Art into Culture.

Interpretation takes the sensory experience of the work of art for granted, and proceeds from there. This cannot be taken for granted now. Think of the sheer multiplication of works of art available to every one of us, superadded to the conflicting tastes and odors and sights of the urban environment that bombard our senses. Ours is a culture based on excess, on overproduction; the result is a steady loss of sharpness in our sensory experience. All the conditions of modern life—its material plenitude, its sheer crowdedness—conjoin to dull our sensory faculties. And it is in the light of the condition of our senses, our capacities (rather than those of another age), that the task of the critic must be assessed.

What is important now is to recover our senses. We must learn to *see* more, to *hear* more, to *feel* more.

Our task is not to find the maximum amount of content in a work of art, much less to squeeze more content out of the work than is already there. Our task is to cut back content so that we can see the thing at all.

The aim of all commentary on art now should be to make works of art—and, by analogy, our own experience—more, rather than less, real to us. The function of criticism should be to show *how it is what it is,* even *that it is what it is,* rather than to show *what it means.*

X

In place of a hermeneutics we need an erotics of art.

(1964)

Preparatory Exercises

Most of all, I rewrote everything; first drafts were like the first
time you tried a new takedown—you needed to drill it, over and
over again, before you even dreamed of trying it in a match.
                         —John Irving, "The Imaginary Girlfriend"

As noted in the Introduction, reading a text is just one part of a larger communicative process that takes place between the author and you through the printed text. When you read an essay, or any text, two things happen. You *observe* the words the author has written and, in effect, listen <u>to</u> the message those words convey. You also listen <u>for</u> the text's message and actively *interpret* it. That is, you respond to the text in front of you, make your own associations with it, and apply your own judgments to it, interpreting the author's original message according to your own unique background and point of view.

A reader's capacity for interpretation is powerful. Therefore, you must use your power responsibly, recognizing that when you read a text, especially when you prepare to wrestle a text, you enter into two contracts: one with yourself and one with the author. Your contract with yourself promises that your own thoughts will not become lost, your own voice will not be silenced, in the writer's persuasive words. Your contract with the author promises, on the other hand, that your own inner voice will not overpower the writer's voice and turn your reading into misreading.

The following exercises will help you become increasingly mindful of your power as a reader, and as a writer, through the process we refer to as "close reading"—of the text, of your own reader-response, and of the interactions between the two. You will focus on *observation*—paying close attention to what the writer says and the way the writer says it, that is, to the text itself. You will also focus on *interpretation*—paying special attention to your own responses to the text. Ultimately you will bring your powers of *observation* and *interpretation* together as you forward the conversation begun by the author and contribute your own essay, your own text.

Close Reading

Adapted from a workshop by Christine Cooper, UMass Amherst Department of English, this two-part exercise implies a crucial understanding: Anything worth reading once is worth reading twice…or three times, or more.

Close reading is a self-conscious type of reading. It is almost like watching yourself read, noticing what words or phrases catch your attention and shape your sense of what a text expresses and how it means. We tend to be more familiar—hence, comfortable—with questions like "what does the writer (or text) seem to be saying?" or "what does the writer (or text) mean?" But it is equally important to consider how we come to the ideas we have about a text's meanings. In this exercise, you will examine both the ideas that a text presents and the elements in it that led you to your sense of those ideas.

You will undoubtedly find that this kind of reading takes more time. Close reading is different from merely moving through a text from the beginning to its end—reading to get the assignment done—or losing yourself in the process of reading the text. You will find, however, that close reading generates much more material with which to wrestle in your essays and in your discussions with your classmates and peers.

Part 1

I. Read through your chosen text (or an assigned passage from it), without taking notes or marking the text.

II. As soon as you've finished reading, jot down all the details you can remember from or about the text. That is, freewrite or list elements, images, and ideas you recall from the text, but be as specific as you can be. You can do this on a piece of paper or on note cards, in your journal, or in the margins of your text.

III. Look over the notes you have jotted down. See whether any patterns develop from the material you recalled. Do individual details relate to one another or have certain features in common? How might they relate to the ideas you thought the writer or text expressed? Make some more notes recording these observations.

Note: You may well find you don't have much to work with or cannot recall many specifics. That is your signal to move to Part 2, which will slow your reading down and require you to be more attentive.

Part 2

    I. Read through your chosen text again, this time marking the things that stand out to you as you go. Read slowly, just a paragraph or "chunk" of text at a time. Star, circle or underline anything that stands out: repeated words or phrases; odd or particularly pleasing or moving language patterns; moments that seem to articulate directly (or even just hint at) significant ideas; analogies, images or figures of speech that help (or hinder) your understanding; words or phrases that bother you or make you uncomfortable; or maybe just things that you underline, star, or circle simply, well, because...

    II. When you've finished this reading process, step back from the text and jot possible answers to those familiar questions mentioned at the start of this exercise: "What is the writer or text expressing?" "What does the writer or text seem to mean?" You are attempting here to summarize, to offer some conclusions, based on your general recollections of the reading.

    III. Going back now to the markings you made while reading the text, see if you can identify particular moments or details that might have led you to the conclusions you just reached or to the memory patterns you recorded after your first reading. Here your goal is to test your general ideas against the specifics of the text, enabling you to develop, or adapt, your ideas accordingly. Some questions to consider:

- Are there certain images or ideas that stayed with you and shaped your conclusions?

- Are there certain things that got lost or buried that might need more consideration?

- Did you intuitively come to conclusions that the textual details support, but that might require some refocusing or different emphases in order to capture more precisely the significance of those details?

You may find that the details you marked are not exactly what you remembered them to be when you jotted down your ideas/conclusions; some details of the text might even conflict with your conclusions. This is an opportunity not just to fine-tune your understanding of the text, but also to reflect on what it is that might have led you to think what you did. By questioning your first assumptions and reflecting on your reading process, you may come to a deeper sense of how you approach reading more generally.

What's Good for the Goose...

Adapted from a workshop by Peggy Woods, this exercise, like Christine Cooper's Close Reading, helps you move into a text and record your observations and interpretations of it. The emphasis here, however, is on marginal notes and note-taking techniques—with a twist.

You've probably been asked to respond to an early draft of a friend's or classmate's essay with some feedback and advice: When you read this, can you tell what I'm saying? Do I say anything good? Did I miss anything? Do you have any questions about what I'm trying to say? The obvious point is for you to help your friend come up with some new ideas with which to revise and usually expand the essay.

What's good for a friend's or classmate's essay is good for both a published text and your own text-wrestling essay. That is, similar questions, applied to a published text, will help you develop your conversation with it by representing the author's ideas accurately and simultaneously preparing for your addition to the dialogue.

Do this exercise right in your book. After all, you bought it. Now make it your own by entering into your dialogue with the author right there in the margin of his or her text.

As you read slowly through the essay, keep a pencil in hand—<u>not a highlighter</u>. (You can't write notes with a highlighter, and highlighters can be zombie-makers in pastel tubes: three highlighted pages later, you wake up and don't remember a word you read!) Make strong, straight lines alongside paragraphs that seem especially important or interesting. Make wavy lines alongside paragraphs that seems puzzling or problematic. Circle or box in any specialized terms or words the writer uses, especially if the writer defines them or uses them again and again.

All along the margin, also make notes—about what the writer says, what strikes you as interesting, what the writer doesn't (quite) say, what questions you have or what you just don't get.

- *Sayback*—Alongside each paragraph, summarize in your own words just what the writer is saying—not what the writer "means" to say or is "trying" to say, <u>just what s/he does say</u>. (Write small because there's more.)

- *Pointing*—When you come across something that sticks out for you, note it in the margin. And make a quick note to yourself telling why it's so striking or memorable: Is it something *observed* in the writing itself or is it something in your own *interpretive response* that makes this point stick? Does it remind you of something you've experienced? Something else you've read? (Put these observations and interpretations in parentheses or brackets: you made them—not the writer—and they may become your own contribution to the "conversation" when you draft your text-wrestling essay.)

- *Almost Says-back*—You can also make notes about what the writer *almost says* or "means" or "tries" to say, but put these *inferences* of yours in brackets or parentheses, too, in order to distinguish them from what the writer actually does say. (These inferences and amplifications may also become part of your own contribution to the "conversation" of your essay. Just keep in mind one important aim of all close reading: to sort out what the writer "almost says" or "is trying to say" from what you as reader "almost" hear.)

- *Questions*—Record any questions you have about the text right there in the margin as they come up for you. It's always impressive to ask some smart, specific questions in class. Sometimes you'll get direct and helpful answers. Just as often, however, the writer was being intentionally—or unintentionally—ambiguous or even self-contradictory. And ambiguity as well as contradiction opens any conversation to further discussion—in this case, the possible topic of your text-wrestling essay.

As soon as you've finished reading—even if you haven't yet finished reading the entire essay—review your marginal notes and then, on a separate piece of paper in your notebook or journal, do some informal writing about the comments you've made. You can do this informal writing as just some private freewriting or as the sort of "peer review" letter you would do for a classmate or friend. Summarize some of your marginal notes; amplify others or explain them in more detail; record any connections or patterns you find running through the text or through your responses to it.

It's not surprising how much more you can remember about a text, and your own reactions to it, immediately after you've read it. It is surprising, though, how much a quick post-reading review can help you remember later on, when it's time for class discussion or composing your essay. The review notes you scribble here may even reveal the beginnings of a rough draft.

Movies of the Mind

Adapted from a workshop by Peter Elbow, this exercise is really an experiment in observing an unknown object through an unknown lens. The unknown object is the text and the unknown lens is your mind. But by closely observing your reactions to and interpretations of the text-and even more, by comparing your responses to classmates'—you can probably arrive at a pretty good picture of the unknown object, the text. As a result, you can get a much better sense of what kind of lens your mind is, too.

While providing another route to close reading, this exercise works particularly well when done as a group workshop, with the teacher or another group facilitator reading aloud. Oral reading guarantees slow reading and provides the text with an embodied voice.

The exercise is simple. Rather than reading the entire text through to the end, take small steps through it, periodically stopping to freewrite (as much as possible and without worry about spelling or structure) along the way. For example, begin with just the title and the first paragraph. Stop and freewrite. Then read another two- or three-paragraph chunk of text. Stop and freewrite again. Repeat this process through to the end of the essay. As you read and freewrite, ask yourself these questions (even the same questions may bring very different answers to mind as you go along through the text).

- What is this piece about?
- What does it means so far?
- Where is the text taking me and what do I expect next?
- What thoughts, associations, memories are popping to mind?
- What am I feeling right now?
- What questions do I have at this point?

Don't leave out any "mental events," no matter how stray or irrelevant they may seem. And don't just notice and write down what you associate with English classes! You are making a movie of your own mind as you respond to the reading. And you are projecting it onto the screen of your freewriting pages. You can review and edit this film later. For now, capture as much of the mental action as you can: If it comes to mind, write it down!

As you move through the essay, it is possible to read larger chunks. Remember, however, the point is to capture as much as possible of what you are thinking as you read. Smaller chunks enable you to do that so resist the temptation to read all the way to the end.

After you've finished working your way through the text, it's very important to read back over all the freewriting you've done. It's a valuable record of the process your mind went through as it gradually constructed meaning from a text—from your first hunches and glimmers through to your final (or not so final) understanding and set of feelings. Not only will your freewriting show you how reading is a gradual process of making meaning; it's also particularly valuable as a record of how your mind works.

Look at the hunches or guesses you made as you first read through the text. Look for the places where your reactions changed. Observe places in the text where the writer met your expectations or surprised you. Notice places where you gained interest or lost it. Note any patterns that seem to develop. These "movie frames" show what you take for granted or what assumptions lie unnoticed in your mind. And such review will provide points to explore further in your writing.

It's also important to go back and read the whole text through at least once more—this time without stopping—and write about any *new* meanings, reactions, or changes that come from a second reading. (New meanings always do!)

Finally, compare your own Movies of the Mind with some of your classmates'. Their reactions and constructions may interplay in interesting ways with yours. They may also point to ways in which your mind—and all the various influences on it—contributed to the meaning you and the text together made.

Re-conceptualizing the Text—
And Taking a Breather

The next two exercises afford you some opportunity to approach reading and meaning-making from a different perspective and in a different medium—the visual, audial, or perhaps even physical.

A Cartoon

After reading your chosen text, and finding at least some meaning in it, draw a large cartoon. It might include suitcases, backpacks, or other bundles. In the cartoon, show what the <u>text</u> contained or <u>author</u> brought that contributed to meaning, and what <u>you</u> brought.

In a Different Mode

Meaning can be expressed in many ways. For example, Shakespeare's plays and characters have been reconceived as photographs, paintings, operas, musical compositions, ballets, sculptures, and even local bands [Cordelia's Dad]. Present the text you've just read or a selection from it to your class or group as if it were in a medium other than print—as if it were a TV show, rap or C&W song, MTV video, poem, photograph, collage, sports rally, theme wedding, banquet, etc. Tell (or show) how the text would be presented, with specific examples related to parts of the text.

A Voice Workshop

Contributed by Peter Elbow, this exercise is probably best carried on in the class-room. Working with others on interpretation can enhance the social aspects of reading and learning, as can hearing written texts read aloud.

You'll often find that the quickest way to understand a text and its complexities is to figure out how it ought to sound. To put it more precisely, the trick is to figure out the range of *different* ways that a text *could* sound—in order to see which ones seem better or worse at bringing out potentialities. This is the most entertaining way to do "serious work on the interpretation of texts."

Start by working in pairs or small groups. Choose an interesting or controversial passage from the essay that seems to illustrate the author's voice or one of the voices the author is using—or just choose one that seems difficult or tricky in some way. It's particularly interesting if different groups work on the same passage—in order to explore different voice possibilities lurking in the same words.

Then develop an out loud "reading" of this passage—an enactment or embodiment of the words to share with the rest of the class. This is not so much an exercise in acting or performance but rather just an attempt to make your reading sound "right." Simply try to make it sound the way you sense this passage or author ought to sound. It is important to keep in mind that there is no single right voicing or enactment of a text. Also, the voice often changes in different parts of an essay as the author's feelings or attitudes change or come out more clearly.

It is useful to develop two or three contrasting readings of the same passage: either ones that all sound "right" or else some that are kind of "pushing the envelope" and are marginal or even satirical. Marginal readings that are clearly "wrong" can often nevertheless bring out an element that's really there in the text—but only faintly there. For example in a serious essay, people might not notice traces of humor or satire that are actually "in there" till someone does a smart-aleck reading. Similarly, in a light hearted comic piece, people might not be able to hear the faint elements of anger or even sadness till someone does a reading that emphasizes such voices.

Your group's interpretations and the interpretations of other groups will provide a good way to begin wrestling with the text.

Quote-Writing

Contributed by Peggy Woods, this exercise returns you to your chosen text to examine more closely specific passages noted in your initial reading of it. It works especially well when it follows the Voice exercise previously described.

Look over the reading and your notes on it. Pull out a quotation that you marked or noted as particularly interesting or intriguing or even confusing. (Sometimes a confusing quotation is more productive to work with because this exercise will enable you to write through your confusion.)

Copy down the full quotation on a page of your notebook or journal. (Even if just a few words actually interested or confused you, quote the surrounding chunk of text so you have something substantial to work with.)

Spend about five to ten minutes writing about the quotation. What is the author saying here? How does this particular passage relate to other passages you've identified in your notes and to the essay as a whole? What exactly did you—and do you now—find interesting, intriguing or confusing about it?

When you have said everything that you can say about that particular quotation, go back to the text and select another one and write again. Once you are done, go back and review your commentary. Look for patterns. Does a common theme seem to emerge? What questions do you now have about the piece? This will provide a starting pointing for further exploration.

If you are working with more than one text, you may find it useful to address quotations by both authors, allowing one author to shed light on or provide a context for your understanding of the other.

Dialogue with an Author

Adapted from a workshop by Peter Elbow, this exercise asks you to engage in an imagined conversation with the author—not only to speak directly to the author but to imagine how he or she would respond to your questions and thoughts about the essay. The exercise also suggests a way to sequence and extend the Quote-Writing exercise just described.

A good way to begin is to go through the essay and pick out phrases and passages that you find particularly interesting. Then begin a dialogue with the author, allowing him or her to start the conversation.

You may start your dialogue by writing out a sentence or more from the reading. Then write your own response to these words. Try to let your response be only a sentence or two. (You're trying for a conversation, not extensive speech-making.) Then "get" the author to "reply" to you. If the words don't pop into your head, just think. Take a moment to see what the writer "wants" to answer. It is fine to make up words for the author, and words will come if you step sympathetically into the role. But see how often you can bring in some of the author's actual words from the essay: such practices will help you to carry on a genuine dialogue—and have some fun in your role.

Note: This exercise can be time-consuming, but it can also be rewarding. Just make sure to leave yourself time enough to transform this exercise, as you would the other exercises, into a true and finished essay.

Wrestling the Terms of the Text

Adapted from a workshop by Margaret Price, this exercise again returns you to the text, now for a closer, more detailed analysis of some of the specific terms, repeated words and phrases, or other expressions you noted during your initial reading.
    This exercise is certainly useful to do alone but may be particularly helpful when done by a small group of students who have all read the same text.

In almost every essay, an author will use terms that are specific to the text and crucial to the meaning of it. One way to enter more deeply into a text is to identify these terms and the ways the author uses them to construct meaning.

First list at least three specific terms the author uses. Then respond as fully as you can to the following questions without worrying too much, during this exploratory stage, about matters of spelling, structure, etc.

- What does each of the terms mean? Try to paraphrase and summarize what the author has written about each term.

- What does each of the terms seem to imply—that is, what tones or nuances do the terms carry? Use specific examples from the text to support your analysis of the terms.

- What do the terms mean to you? What meanings do they carry in your life? Again, use specific examples.

While remaining as true as possible to the author's words and intentions, don't worry too much about getting the "right" answer for there are no perfectly right answers to these questions. Instead, work to find responses and ideas that are interesting and lead to more questions. If you are working in a group, it is useful to note any disagreements and/or differences group members may have concerning the terms. These points of difference will lead to interesting questions and help further your understanding of the text.

Note on the Preparatory Exercises: We have presented here a variety of preparatory exercises to help you enter most any printed text and to emerge again with some thoughts toward your own text-wrestling essay. Other exercises related to specific readings in this volume can be found on our *Original Text-Wrestling Book* Web site <http://www.umass.edu/writprog/otwb.htm>, and in the Appendix for Teachers is the complete text for three workshops—A Laboratory in the Reading Process, A Voice Workshop, and A Dialogue Workshop—by Peter Elbow.

Sample Text-Wrestling Essays by Students

Five essays were selected to illustrate a range of approaches. "Seeing Our Own Individuality" by Michael Ianello briefly addresses three readings on sight and seeing, and may be regarded as a traditional academic essay. Kristina Martino's "Uncovering Reality" concentrates on a single reading. In a wide-ranging conversation, Matthew Libby's "Learning: The Uncommon Nature of a Common Experience" not only discusses selections by Walker Percy and William Gass but also brings in commentary of two classmates. Having gained insight from two readings on social justice themes, Nadine Hanna wrestles with meanings and her own conscience in "I Am an Oppressor." And last, "Notes on an Education: A Dialogue" by Kristi J. Cousins contains two voices from one student author in witty dialogue responding to Walker Percy.

Note on Spacing: Writing in MLA style uses double spacing throughout and presents a Works Cited list on a separate page after the body of the essay itself. This book deliberately deviates from MLA style in spacing.

In classrooms, students' text-wrestling essays are often collected, photocopied, and bound together as a class magazine. To save paper and photocopying costs, text-wrestling essays typically are single-spaced and begin Works Cited lists a few lines below finished essay text—not on a new page. Most examples in this reader are not shown with attention to double-spacing. The first student essay, that by Michael Ianello, does show MLA style, including double-spaced format.

Michael Ianello
Seeing Our Own Individuality

Seeing Our Own Individuality

Everyone can see. Even the blind can feel their surroundings and "see" them. "Close your eyes, move round the room and notice how the faculty of touch is like a static limited form of sight": John Berger offers us this experiment in seeing in his essay "Ways of Seeing"(52). I reiterate, everyone can see, in some form or another. Everyone can situate themselves according to their surroundings. We all can see, but the great difference that separates us is what we actually see. What I choose to see and what an eighty-year-old man chooses to see will most likely differ. What I choose to see and what my immediate family chooses to see are also very different things. What we see makes us individuals in an ocean of seers.

Annie Dillard's essay "Seeing" discusses just that, seeing. She uses past experience coupled with her vivid imagination and amazing sense of imagery to get across her point. "The secret of seeing is to sail on solar wind. Hone and spread your spirit till you yourself are a sail, whetted, translucent, broadside to the merest puff"(93). Words and phrases like these can be found throughout the essay, words and phrases that seem to overfill the mind with possibilities and images. Dillard's command of the language is equalled only by her apparent mastery of the sense of sight. She sees things a normal person would either ignore or take for granted. Instead she treats them like pennies from heaven, small gifts that alone seem insignificant but when accumulated can lead you to riches unimaginable.

Annie Dillard understands that what we see makes us individuals. She knows that those who take for granted their ability to see are trapped in a one-dimensional prison of simple black and white. She knows that once we embrace our amazing ability to see the world around us, we can finally move that much closer to it. By seeing, we actually take the world around us and put it into our heads. We remember the sights we have seen with our memory; we amass the coppers from above. Dillard knows we will never be able to see what she has seen, so she writes. Writing down her images allows her to give us the gift to see the same thing and also see something completely different. We use our imaginations to mold the sights she offers us. She is sharing her pennies so that we may start a collection of our own.

Susan Sontag writes, "As photographs give people an imaginary possession of a past that is unreal, they also help people to take possession of space in which they are insecure" (183). This statement characterizes her essay "On Photography" very well. In her essay Sontag takes a path different from Dillard's. Sontag uses the camera as a way of showing us what people see. The camera is an extension of ourselves as well as a tool that we may use to help us to take control of a situation. We use the camera as a sort of crutch, a helping hand to bring back past sights and experiences that time may have worn away from our memories. Sontag sees the faults in this method as well. Simply look in any magazine or on any television, and you will see people "limiting experience to a search for the photogenic"(Sontag 183). While photography can allow us a peek at exactly what someone else was seeing for an instant in time, it can also allow people to control and warp our own sense of what is beautiful. Should we find only skinny, young, attractive people worthy of our sight? Should we want to watch only the superior professional athletes? What about my grandmother then? What about my little cousin's wiffleball game in the backyard? Are these sights simply not worthy of my eyes and ears? This is when photography can become dangerous, when it can actually limit and even extinguish a person's idea of beauty.

Sontag goes on to discuss how the photograph makes things that would normally not even be worth looking at important images: "After the event has ended, the picture will still exist, conferring on the event a kind of immortality (and importance) it would never otherwise have enjoyed"(184). I both agree and disagree with this statement. Anything that I see has an importance and worth that far exceeds any amount of gold or silver in the world. Anything and everything I see is a gift, equally important. The beauty of a sunset is no more beautiful than studying the wrinkles of age on my grandmother's shaking hands. I admit to taking more time to study some things as opposed to others. I most certainly study a new sight with more fervor than one I have already seen or see everyday. This choice of what I get to look at is what makes everything so beautiful. Our environment is simply sitting around us, not caring if we look at it or not, not caring if we photograph it or walk on it or burn it down. It doesn't complain and it doesn't protest. It simply allows itself to be seen, and we all have front row seats and an endless supply of film.

John Berger's essay "Ways of Seeing" offered up so many good ideas but brought them to a halt with his pretentiousness and snobbery. Berger's points are all made, just simply not made well (or too well, depending on how you look at it). "An image became a record of how X had seen Y," Berger states early in his essay (53). An image, a photo, a movie, a painting, all of these do just that. They put us in the mind of the original seer and allow us to pretend we were there, if only for a few fleeting instants. They allow us to get a sense of exactly what kind of an individual the photographer, painter, and writer are. We can take a quick dip in their psyche and wiggle our toes around, testing the waters of their minds.

"The past is not for living in; it is a well of conclusions from which we draw in order to act" (Berger 54). This is true: we use past experiences, whether our own or someone else's, and apply them to present situations. Our ability to take the past and alter it to fit the present is what allows us to continue evolving. It allows our own memories to aide us in the future. By using those "pennies from heaven" and applying them to the present we can change our environment to something less menacing and fearful. We use the sights of the past to mold our reactions to the present.

Berger discusses *The Virgin and Child with St. Anne and St. John the Baptist* later in the essay: "It has acquired a new kind of impressiveness. Not because of what it shows—not because of the meaning of its image. It has become impressive, mysterious, because of its market value"(62). Berger is referring to the fact that, because someone attempted to pay a large sum of money to purchase the painting, public interest in it has skyrocketed. This is an example of how easily our idea of beauty and what is worthy of sight can be altered or warped in a few seconds. Our minds are more impressionable than a new born bird at times.

All three of these writers make good connections between seeing and individuality. They all go about it in completely different ways, too. Dillard uses her exotic everyday images, Sontag uses her impressions of photographs and photography to make her points clear, and Berger uses an air of snobbery and elitism to make his points come across, which he does do, as much as I hate to admit it. Whereas their talents can be found in different places, they are all talented and they do make a simple point. We all see, whether it is with our eyes or our ears or our hands or our noses. All of our senses can act alone or come together to form pictures in our heads. These pictures make us individuals. The infinite possibilities of what we actually can see and what we can simply imagine inside our own heads will never be measured. The fact that we can choose our own path of images through life is one of the greatest gifts given to us. Whether we use it or not is a decision we all must make, consciously or subconsciously. All three authors' essays can come together to form one point: Individuality lies within the mind's eye.

Works Cited

Berger, John. "Ways of Seeing." Curtis, et al. 50–70.

Curtis, Marcia, Benjamin Balthaser, Michael Edwards, Zan Goncalves, Robert Hazard, Noria Jablonski, Brian Jordan, and Shauna Seliy, eds. <u>The Original Text-Wrestling Book</u>. Dubuque: Kendall/Hunt, 2001.

Dillard, Annie. "Seeing." Curtis, et al. 81–94.

Sontag, Susan. "On Photography." <u>Seeing & Writing</u>. Ed. Donald McQuade and Christine McQuade. New York: Bedford, 2000. 38–47.

Kristina Martino

Uncovering Reality

The average American who sits down at night to read the paper or watch the news typically assumes that what is being presented as factual really occurred. Perhaps some people are aware of the media's way of embellishment, a hint of calligraphy to attract the eye and draw more viewers or readers. Many, however, place their trust in the news reporters and journalists who provide the world with "facts." There are even those who actually buy, read, and believe the *The National Inquirer* instead of smirking at the ridiculous headlines that attempt to draw in the audiences by advertising some celebrity's turmoil. With the recent popularity of such shows as *Big Brother*, *Survivor*, and *Temptation Island*, it seems as though America is becoming obsessed with "reality" entertainment. Perhaps we enjoy watching real people living their lives on a screen because we can relate to them more as a character if we believe their stories are real. We are oddly entertained by what we see, not realizing our intrigue becomes the vehicle for producers to snare us in and snag our cash. At the heart of reality-based television is money, not reality. While news programs tend to be more factual than entertainment programs, the main objective of media leaders is to get the ratings, and, as illustrated in the diary excerpt "Tales from the Cutting-Room Floor," producers will stop at nothing to do so.

As a story analyst for the popular show *American Detective*, Debra Seagal reveals the behind the scenes nightmare that occurs in the making of each action-packed "reality" cop show. The subtitle of the piece, "The Reality of 'Reality-based' Television," hints at the falseness of reality-based shows, at something else beyond what's being seen. Seagal offers a new perspective that exposes the truth to those who are otherwise incapable of seeing it:

> Why the national obsession with this sort of voyeuristic entertainment? Perhaps we want to believe the cops are still in control. The preponderance of these shows is also related to the bottom line: they are extremely inexpensive to produce. After all…why engage a group of talented writers and producers to make intelligent and exciting TV when it's more profitable to dip into the endless pool of human grief?(232)

This excerpt expresses the struggle the writer has with her job at *American Detective*. The producer's objective is not to present reality or a documentary; it is to use other people's misfortunes to make a profit. It is to push the extreme of violence and grittiness, gore and grief as far as television will allow in order to attract the attention of viewers. These are the words that sell: "Death, Stab, Shoot, Strangulation, Club, Suicide." Without these audience-grabbing terms and events, a show would be uninteresting: an "unsellible dud."

Ironies abound in the making of the show, such as the fact that the cops are, in some cases, worse than the criminals they reprimand. In addition to casually making racist and sexist remarks, they beat their suspects, lie to them about their rights, deny them their right to an attorney, and hire prostitutes. They stop at nothing to get the eleven-minute action-packed sequence needed to make "good" TV. The world Debra Seagal witnesses isn't protected by the Constitution, but rather by the moneymaking tactics and immoral amendments of the shows producers.

As for the realness and humanity in the people the cameras capture, the producers aren't interested:

> It doesn't matter. The Police get their suspect. The camera gets its footage. The cameras keep on rolling. And what I see, what the viewers will never see, is the women—disheveled, shocked, their clothes still scattered on the musty hotel carpets—telling their stories to the amused officers and producers. Some of them sob uncontrollably. Three kids at home. An ex who hasn't paid child support in five years.... Though their faces are fatigued, they still manage a certain dignity. They look, in fact, very much like the girl next door. (243)

On *American Detective*, no one is interested in capturing reality, only good Nielson ratings.

Seagal writes about her ability to peer into the real lives of others. She begins to become attached to these people. Not only is she able to empathize with them, she can replay the most bitter and painful moments of their lives over and over, like a powerless god. Her powerful ability to intrude on the weak becomes overwhelming and is ultimately accompanied by the inability to reach out to these people jailed within the bars of a TV screen. With this powerlessness, Seagal begins to be filled with "useless," in the eyes of the producers, empathy as well as a terrible lack of trust: "I have begun to wonder what lurks behind the goodwill of my neighbors' gestures, what they are doing behind their porches and patios" (242). Not only is the writer bringing the emptiness and privacy-invading nature of her job into her real life, her job has begun to change her own character. It makes her untrusting, timid and cynical. She is like a lab rat, testing out what reality TV does to viewers over time. It destroys empathy.

Behind the gauze of personal narrative in Debra Seagal's essay is both a fear and a plea. Why would this essay be published if not to make a statement about what America is coming to? Seagal writes—and publishes her writing—to make America aware of the distructiveness of seemingly harmless entertainment habits. These habits become obsessions that lead to cynicism and mistrust. Even the diary format of the article illustrates that we readers read the article because we are able to intrude. Of course, what we find in the article is not the candy-coated, action-packed world of entertainment expected from the producers of *American Detective*. What is found in the article is, ultimately, a plea to readers to realize the truth, stop watching reality TV, and fill the emptiness that causes our obsession: "to regain what is lost."

Debra Seagal uncovers the disturbing truth about fact-based television with "Tales from the Cutting-Room Floor." Her words are a reminder and awakening to the viewer that reality can easily be manipulated and sculpted for one's own use, rather than for the sake of what is just and true. It is up to the viewer to decide whether to keep watching so-called "reality" television, or to be content in living real life.

Work Cited

Seagal, Debra. "Tales from the Cutting-Room Floor." *The Original Text-Wrestling Book*. Ed. Marcia Curtis, et al. Dubuque: Kendall/Hunt, 2001. 230–245.

Matthew Libby

Learning: The Uncommon Nature of a Common Experience

One of the inevitable experiences that all humans encounter is the learning process. From the moment of birth, people begin to learn. The brain soaks up information like an infinitely dry sponge tossed into an infinitely wet ocean. However, despite the fact that the learning experience is shared by all, each individual person will have his or her own unique learning experience from which different thoughts and feelings will be derived. In their essays, William Gass and Walker Percy each present views on the learning process. In the essay "On Reading to Oneself," Gass shows his reader how various styles of reading can lead to different levels of enjoyment and comprehension of a literary work. Percy's essay, "The Loss of the Creature," discusses the initial learning experience and the effect that "prepackaged learning" has on the individual's ability to gain the most thorough learning experience possible. Both writers present the argument stating that it is the responsibility of the learner to look beyond the curtain and seek out the fullest experience possible, making the experience truly theirs, and thus creating a lasting impression within their minds.

To give support to his argument, Gass reflects back upon his days as a member of his high school speed-reading team. Gass tells the reader how he used to "butcher" his understanding and appreciation of literature by racing through it as though it was an unpleasant chore. Gass claims that it is important to stop and smell the roses when you are reading in order to get the most out of the work. In his untitled essay, Eric J. Ferreira comments:

> You may see a sunrise or sunset. It may be another person that you see. Whatever it is, there must be something out there that would amaze you. Life isn't just eating and sleeping and working. It's a lot more than that. There are many little thing that help to make up life, but many times people get too caught up in other things to notice them. One day, just take the time to do it.

Here, Mr. Ferreira tells his audience that it's important to notice the little things in life as well as in literature. When one learns, it is important to see the big picture. A college freshman who takes an introductory class on the history of western thought cannot claim to be a master of Kant, Marx, and Locke. Rather this student has merely opened a window to the world of western philosophers. It is now up to the student to pursue further knowledge in this area of study. His teacher will only be able to provide him with so much knowledge given the time constraints of the academic system, but the knowledge that is provided will serve as a key when the student attempts to further his understanding of the topic. Taking a survey course in a subject and claiming to know all about it is just as bad as skimming *War and Peace* in half an hour and claiming to have read it thoroughly. There cannot be any true understanding of the topic; only a general idea of what is going on will be acquired. It is required that the individual student seek out further information and a greater understanding of the topic.

Percy examines the negative influence on the learning experience from outside factors, using several examples to illustrate his thesis. One is the Spanish explorer who accidentally discovered the Grand Canyon. Percy claims that the Spaniard will get a greater amount of satisfaction from encountering the Grand Canyon than a man from Boston who visits the canyon while on vacation. The Spaniard had no preexisting expectations of what the Grand Canyon looked like. He just happened to stumble upon it while wandering through the desert. However, the man from Boston had to actively seek out the canyon and travel to it. According to Percy, the Bostonian would automatically compare the Grand Canyon to the preexisting expectations of what the canyon would be, thus lessening his enjoyment of the experience(215–16). While Percy makes a valid argument about outside influences, his logic is skewed. One cannot simply plan to encounter something unplanned. The unexpected will suddenly come upon us, and when one does encounter something, he must work to derive the full educational value from it. In many cases, this would require a further study of the subject. This further research would require the effort of the individual learner. A person could find a new type of metal while gardening, but unless she closely examined it, the significance of the discovery would be tossed aside with the weeds.

Percy furthers his argument by contrasting the experiences of two people. One is a Falkland Islander who finds a dogfish on the shore; the other is a biology student who encounters a dogfish in class during a dissection. Percy believes that the islander will get more enjoyment out of the experience because of the lack of the classroom environment. The student will be much more apt to be distracted by his focus on getting the best grade possible in the shortest amount of time, whereas the Falkland Islander is simply enjoying the educational experience(224). David Buckley misinterprets Percy:

> Percy seems to be a real tree hugging, twigs and berries type bleeding heart liberal. ….if we were to dismantle traditional education….absolutely nothing would get done…. All the benefits of scientific research, like the discovery of life saving drugs, would be destroyed.

Percy means that it takes much more than a biology class for one to become a Nobel Prize winning scientist. The experience on the beach will provide a window to further enlightenment. Instead, it takes years of learning more and more about the science itself to become proficient. In the fast-paced world of today, people want to simply get the facts and get on with life. But this isn't the way that humans learn best. It takes time to reflect on one's own interpretation of data to gain useful insights. The individual must play an active role in the educational process in order to truly learn. A parrot can sit in a classroom and sing back what the teacher has said. But only a human, only a student, can take the information provided in this classroom setting and take it to greater heights. It is this aspect of the learning process that separates the scholar from the parrot. While "traditional education" provides a nice backbone for learning, it is up to the student to wrestle with the information and make it his own.

Both Gass and Percy ask their readers to take the time to enjoy their learning experiences. They emphasize the importance of the learner taking the active role when learning. Passive behavior will not allow one to engage in the learning process in the way that is required for one to have fully experienced something. People must find a passion somewhere in life. Once that passion is found, whatever it may be, one must indulge in it—eat it, drink it, feel it, sleep it, make it become part of oneself and then take it to a higher level. That is where the true learning process takes the human form and fully embodies the human spirit that is collectively shared by all who take part in that uniquely human activity: *learning*.

Works Cited

Buckley, David. "Response to Gass." *English 112 College Writing Joint Class Magazine* May 2001: 38.

Curtis, Marcia, Benjamin Balthaser, Michael Edwards, Zan Goncalves, Robert Hazard, Noria Jablonski, Brian Jordan, and Shauna Seliy, eds. *The Original Text-Wrestling Book*. Dubuque: Kendall/Hunt, 2001.

Ferreira, Eric J. "Response to Gass." *English 112 College Writing Joint Class Magazine* May 2001: 14.

Gass, William. "On Reading to Oneself." Curtis, et al. 122–134.

Percy, Walker. "The Loss of the Creature." Curtis, et al. 215–229.

Nadine Hanna

I Am an Oppressor

When my mother blamed "those damn Cambodians" for "taking over" her area of Lowell, MA, and becoming "the problem that stands in the way of fixing Lowell," I'd poke her and tell her to be quiet, because you just don't say things like that. When my Lebanese Christian father met a Muslim or Jewish person and, immediately after leaving him, told me not to talk to him because he was bad, I would say but isn't it the same God?

I thought that I was not racist. If a debate came up in class that involved age, race, sex or class I was always the first to defend the underdog. I always told the oppressor how wrong he was for oppressing. I always told the oppressed that it was not his fault. I thought that I saw everyone as equal. When I walked down the street, everywhere I just saw people. I convinced myself that I saw people of all social classes as the same. I convinced myself that I did not see myself as above anyone.

I was wrong. When I came to this university, I still believed that I was an equal-opportunity friend, neighbor, and student. After taking a diversity course here, I slowly began seeing through someone else's eyes. Suddenly, there were people of all races and religions all around me. Where did these people come from? Better yet, why was I suddenly seeing them? Like a fan on an ember, the sneaking suspicion began to burn that it was not that I had always seen people as the same, but that I had never truly seen that anyone was different. Once someone had turned on this light inside my head, I couldn't turn it off. I tried and tried to stop myself from seeing people. Walking back from class, I was bombarded: black, white, black, Spanish, white, white, Arabian. I began to ask myself what had happened that made me see people so negatively. Why was I suddenly making these distinctions?

Then it occurred to me that these were not new distinctions to my mind, but newly admitted ones. It was not that I had suddenly developed racism, but that I had just accepted my part in it (Harro 173). Now at school as I walk to and from class, my mind is better. It sees: person, person, black, person, person, white. The distinctions are still there but are dwindling. However, now it is not that I am ignoring the different faces that pass me by, but accepting them (Hardiman and Jackson 163).

So, poof, I am cured, right? Wrong. Here on campus, I see everyone as the same. Here we are all students; we are all trying to make the money, make the friends, make the grade. We are a "we," a group of people with a common goal.

Last Friday I took two of my friends from the university back to my hometown for a day trip. As we were driving through the center of town, a young Hispanic man in an old Hyundai cut me off. Immediately, all of the thoughts associated with Hispanics in my area rushed through my head. "That damn guy, why doesn't he go back to Lawrence?" That was the big joke in my high school: go back to Lawrence if you're ethnic or poor, or even better, both. And I thought it. And I almost slammed my car into another one as I realized what had just gone through my head. Goddamnit, wasn't I supposed to be newly enlightened? Hadn't I just had these new revelations that made everything happy? Wasn't I no longer a racist?

After more thought, because there was much to come, it seemed to me that at school I could let go of my assumptions because I had intentionally added to my identity. I had made a conscious effort to see everyone as equal. It occurred to me that at home I hid behind the social veil my parents created for me (Harro 172). My parents are working-class people with rather large paychecks. I am a snob. I hide behind the hard work they put in every day, talk of how proud I am that they do it, but wish they could find someone to do it for them. I claim that it's because I love them.

I love my family. I treat everyone equally, but don't always see everyone as the same. I make assumptions about people from the clothes they wear, the cars they drive (or don't drive) and the color of their skin. Am I a racist? Yes. I am a passive racist. I find myself caught between Resisting and Redefining (Hardiman and Jackson 165). I try so hard to see things through a new perspective, but I am always catching myself ignoring instead of accepting. Will I ever shake these ideas that I grew up with? I believe that someday I will get past them; I believe that I will be able to grow and become a better person with all that I take into myself. But I also feel, even if I no longer believe these ideas, I will never forget them.

Works Cited

Curtis, Marcia, Benjamin Balthaser, Michael Edwards, Zan Goncalves, Robert Hazard, Noria Jablonski, Brian Jordan, and Shauna Seliy, eds. *The Original Text-Wrestling Book*. Dubuque: Kendall/Hunt, 2001.

Hardiman, Rita, and Bailey Jackson. "Conceptual Foundations for Social Justice Courses." Curtis, et al. 157–168.

Harro, Bobbie. "The Cycle of Socialization." Curtis, et al. 169–178.

Kristi J. Cousins

Notes on an Education:
A Dialogue

Walker Percy's essay "The Loss of Creature" discusses the downfall of modern-day education due to educational packaging. To Percy, a student who has the desire to learn more about or explore a specific subject has a very difficult time because of the classroom setting and the lesson plan. These two things, along with the instructor, constitute an obstacle the student has to overcome in order to truly learn.[1]

In order to demonstrate that packaging diminishes the learning experience, Percy uses a comparison between a Falkland Islander and a high school biology student. Both have a dogfish in front of them, except there are a couple of major differences: the Islander is on the beach alone and sees the creature in its natural environment, while the student is in a laboratory surrounded by several other students, looking at the creature out of its natural habitat. Percy states, "A student who has the desire to get at a dogfish…may have the greatest difficulty in salvaging the creature itself from the educational package in which it is presented(223–24)." This "package" is the laboratory, the instructor, and the set of directions the student is supposed to follow. These things provide a method for the high school student to adhere to and leave no room for exploration. A scalpel, forceps, and a probe can all be used by the high school student, but Percy believes that the Islander who stabs at a dogfish with his jackknife has the educational advantage over the student. He states that "…the Falkland Islander exploring his dogfish is a person exercising the sovereign right of a person in his lordship and mastery of creation(224)." In other words, he is discovering the

---

[1]You know, I started writing this piece with the idea that I do not agree with Percy and his view on educational packaging. However, after writing this intro, I am beginning to change my mind. My introduction is so formulated! Just briefly glancing at the intro, you can tell I have been brainwashed into writing in a specific manner. I have to ask myself, am I really learning about Walker Percy's views by writing in this particular way? I am not so sure.

dogfish for himself. "He too could use an instructor and a book and a tech-nique, but he would use them as subordinates...."(224) [2]

Percy's argument is wrong.[3] A high school biology student does not learn less about dogfish than the Falkland Islander. The "educational packaging" Percy speaks of is necessary for the student to learn. A high school biology instructor, along with the set of laboratory directions, is there to give the students direction and support. A teenager is not expected to know how to perform a dissection and understand the mechanics of a dogfish on his/her own. If a student were left to dissect a specimen without previous knowledge of what to do, the specimen would be mangled and the student left uneducated about how the living thing works.

The same is true for the Falkland Islander. Percy feels that the Islander's poking and prodding at the dogfish with a jackknife is the greatest learning experience. However, how much is he/she really learning? If a person were to walk along a street and come across a deceased creature lying on the sidewalk, would this person really find out what this creature is by stabbing at it with a stick? Of course not. Previous knowledge of similar creatures, a set of

[2]Now I am changing my mind again. Reading through my essay, I can't help but notice my use of Percy's quotes. Boy am I good! I almost convince myself that I am correct in my argument and that Percy is wrong. Unfortunately, I should not have to use Percy's words to help with my ideas. But that is the only way I know how to write a text-wrestling essay. In high school, I was taught the basic five-paragraph essay—brief introduction, three descriptive paragraphs, and a concluding paragraph. Of course, you also needed to include direct quotation from the article you were writing about. By the time you were finished, your own argument and feelings toward the piece had changed. Writing in such a methodical manner makes the student find *any* quote from the piece and make it fit into his/her essay. There is no room for exploring a thought. No way would a teacher let you change your mind half-way through. That is wrong! Pick one idea and stick with it or you will not get an A in the class. I think I am changing my mind about Percy once again. Maybe he is right.

[3]Is he really? Deep down I believe that he is wrong, but I also think that he is kind of right. Remembering my high school English classes really keeps me unsure on the issue. Once again, look at my essay. I just blurt out that Percy is wrong. Doesn't it seem rehearsed in a way? This essay would most likely get an excellent grade if I passed it into my previous English teachers because that is the way they want a text-wrestling essay to be. "This is the way you will need to write a paper in college," they would say. I heard this everyday from every English teacher. Personally, I think that I could do a better job if I could write this essay in the way I want to, if I could explore a new frame to work with. This is what makes me think that Percy is correct in his idea of educational packaging. I could learn more if I tried something new and unique instead of writing in the same way all the time. Andy Vogt has the right idea in his interpretation of Percy's piece. He feels that a student will have a hard time exploring something on his own "...because he will be too busy trying to please his teacher...or interpreting the way the school wants, the 'correct' way" (Vogt 85). I know I have spent four years of my high school career pleasing my teachers and writing in a specific way. Too bad it isn't the way they want us to write in college.

detailed instructions, and several dissecting tools are necessary to explore the creature and find out how it functions. A doctor does not get his/her degree without performing several dissections on various specimens prior to a human cadaver. These prior dissections also had a set of instructions to follow, since most people would not go to a doctor who had only "explored" several human beings, rather than performing numerous structured experiments.

Therefore, Percy's argument that structured learning environments distort and devalue the intellectual learning experience is incorrect. Since all new discoveries are based on previous discoveries, educational packaging does not hinder the intellectual experience. In fact, "packaging" helps the student learn more and enables him/her to explore other things on his own later on.[4]

Works Cited

Percy, Walker. "The Loss of the Creature." *The Original Text-Wrestling Book*. Ed. Marcia Curtis, et al. Dubuque: Kendall/Hunt, 2001. 215–229.

Vogt, Andy. "Comments for Walker Percy." *College Writing Joint Class Magazine* Nov. 2000: 15.

[4]Well, I believe that Percy is wrong in this context. However, getting back to my high school English classes, I agree with him. It is good that I had structured writing classes freshman and sophomore year, but I feel that as I moved on to higher grades, I should have had more freedom. I should have had time to think of unique and creative ways to get my ideas across. Now that I think of it, maybe I shouldn't say whether I agree with Percy or not. Maybe I should say I fall in the middle. Structure is needed early on in order for the student to learn the basics, but as he/she gets older, I think that a student should begin to discover for himself. It is only with prior knowledge that the student can learn in the future.

A Short Introduction to MLA Documentation Style

A Short Introduction to MLA Documentation Style

with a Sampling of Common In-Text Citations and Works Cited Entries

In-Text Citations: What

MLA style is a detailed set of rules for formatting written work and providing information about sources. If you have been worrying about what *in-text citations* (or parenthetical citations) might be, worry no more. You frequently have seen them and probably have used them, at least informally. When you write an essay containing a quotation followed by the author's name and a page number, you are giving an *in-text citation*. (For examples, turn back to the sample student essays or turn forward to boxed illustrations on the next few pages.) You *cite* the author's name and the correct page in *parentheses*, and you put the information directly within your own paragraph of *text* rather than in a footnote at the bottom of your page or end of your essay. For these reasons, the brief source information embedded in your paragraph is called a *parenthetical* or *in-text citation*.

Quoting and Citing
Your Information Sources: Why

As a participant in the "conversation" of academic writing, you need to invite your own readers to join the conversation, too. Answering certain questions helps them enter the discussion.

- Who are the other writers participating in your conversation?
- What do they have to say about your subject?

- Where did you find their comments and observations, and where can your readers find them?

Proper methods of quoting (and paraphrasing or summarizing) other writers' words, **in-text citations** within the body of your essay, and an accompanying **Works Cited** list at the end of your essay answer these important questions.

By quoting other writers—by accurately reproducing within your own essay important statements other writers have made in theirs—you allow your readers to listen into all sides of the conversation and see for themselves the various points of view on your subject. By citing the authors you quote and identifying the works in which you found these quotations, you enable your readers to find the same information you used for your paper, and to study it more fully if they choose.

As a participant in the "conversation" of academic writing, you have other important reasons for accurately quoting other writers and properly citing the sources of your quotations as well. These are the ways you distinguish your own thoughts from the thoughts of others, and give honest credit to those who have helped you advance your own ideas, whether by agreeing or disagreeing.

The world of the university is a world of knowledge and ideas expressed sometimes in speaking but more often in writing. If material possessions are the property of the outside world, ideas are the primary "intellectual property" of a university. Were you, then, to take another person's words or ideas and use them as though they belonged to you, you would be committing what amounts to an act of theft. You would be committing "plagiarism," which carries severe punishment, possibly including expulsion from college. On the other hand, proper methods of quoting and citing another person's work give you permission to use that work as a building block for your own.

So proper quoting and citing is a matter of academic honesty, but it is not only a matter of honesty. It shows that you are aware of the discussions taking place among writers and thinkers, and that you have taken part in the on-going "conversation" of university life. It is a sign of your membership in the worldwide community of academic writers.

Quoting and Citing Your Information Sources: How

Each time you use another writer's words within the body of your own essay, you must indicate to readers that you are quoting this writer either by enclosing the words **in quotation marks** or, for longer quotations, by formatting the selection as a **block quotation**. (These two methods of quoting will be described below.) Whether you quote a writer or paraphrase a writer's ideas in your own words, you must follow your entry with an **in-text citation**. The in-text citation consists of the author's last name, if you have not used the author's name when introducing the quotation, followed by the page number on which the quotation can be found. At the end of your paper, a **Works Cited** list provides readers with all the detailed information necessary—such as author, title, publishing company, place and date of publication, etc.—to find each book, journal, newspaper or Web site referred to in your in-text citations.

The specific details you include in your in-text citations and Works Cited list, as well as the format in which you arrange them, will depend upon the documentation style you are asked to use. And the style you are asked to use will depend upon the discipline in which you are working.

Most writing handbooks contain a variety of documentation styles, and when composing essays or research papers for college courses, you should follow the style suggested by your instructor. *The Everyday Writer*, for instance, provides instructions and model entries for the Modern Language Association (MLA) style of documentation, used in most courses in the arts and humanities such as art history, classics, theater, English and other language courses; the American Psychological Association (APA) style, used in psychology, sociology, anthropology and other social science courses; the Council of Science Editors (previously the Council of Biology Editors or CBE), used in the natural and physical sciences as well as mathematics; and *The Chicago Manual of Style*, often referred to as "Turabian" for Kate Turabian, editor of the Chicago style guide and preferred by some people.

Whatever style you use, it is crucial that you follow the entry models precisely, including content, capitalization, punctuation, and formatting. These conventions may be somewhat arbitrary, but so are most conventions. And the difference between a comma and a period is as crucial to documentation codes as the difference between a plus and minus sign is to mathematics, or a forward and backslash to computer language. Some general tips are offered here, but you may also refer to your handbook or to a pertinent Web site.

Signal Phrases and Short Quotations

The first time you quote an author, *introduce the quotation with a few words naming the author and the work in which the quotation appears.* These introductory words are referred to as a "signal phrase." The signal phrase usually follows or is part of a sentence integrating the author's words smoothly into your own writing. The author's words are then placed within quotation marks and followed by the page number, in parentheses, where they are found. The following paragraph offers an example:

Notice these factors

In MLA style, the page number stands alone, with <u>no</u> preceding "page" or "p."

The page number goes inside parentheses, after the quotation but <u>before</u> the period (or other punctuation mark if relevant).

> Words and names are a source as well as an expression of power and control. As the linguist Dale Spender observes in her essay "The Politics of Naming," "Naming is the means whereby we attempt to order and structure the chaos and flux of existence" (195). Spender goes on to explain that by naming phenomena around us "we impose a pattern and meaning which allows us to manipulate the world" (195).

Notice these factors

The first time Spender is quoted, her <u>full</u> name is given; the second time (and thereafter), just her <u>last</u> name is used.

When the word *that* appears in the phrase introducing a quotation, no comma is used before the quotation.

Some Often-Encountered Signal Words

As you compose, you will not only be selecting appropriate quotations and using signal phrases. You will also be gaining familiarity with many useful signal words and phrases.

According to _____	_____ considers	In the opinion of _____
_____ acknowledges	_____ describes	_____ maintains
_____ admits	_____ disagrees	_____ notes
_____ comments	_____ emphasizes	_____ points out
_____ concludes	_____ explains	_____ reports

Many options for signal words and their positions exist. Consider the meaning and placement of the following three examples.

As Berger states, "_____" (xx).

"_____," according to Berger, "_____" (xx).

"_____," Berger concludes (xx).

Quoting a Longer Passage of Four or More Lines

Longer, more substantial quotations can be an effective means to help your readers see more fully and clearly the other writer's position on a subject or the text with which you are wrestling. When you quote a longer "passage" (of four or more typed lines), the signal-phrase rule still applies. However, do not use quotation marks. Instead, format the quotation in its own separate paragraph. Then, using the same line spacing and font size used in the body of your essay, indent the left-hand margin one inch to form what is termed a **block quotation**. Consider the next example.

Notice these factors

The longer quotation is introduced by a complete "signal sentence," which could stand alone as a sentence and is therefore followed by a colon (:) instead of a comma.

The long quotation has no quotation marks around it but is instead indented.

Unlike the short quotation, the long quotation ends with a period *before* the page number citation.

In her essay "The Politics of Naming," linguist Dale Spender describes the inescapable authority of language:

> In order to live in the world we must name it. Names are essential for the construction of reality for without a name it is difficult to accept the existence of an object, an event, a feeling. Naming is the means whereby we attempt to order and structure the chaos and flux of existence which would otherwise be an undifferentiated mass. By assigning names we impose a pattern ... which allows us to manipulate the world. (195)

As Spender suggests, "naming" has a power similar to the power other writers have attributed to narrative. Like narrative story telling, Spender's "naming" gives unutterable experience a "pattern" that simultaneously determines and limits our view of the world. Whether we want to agree with this claim or not, we have all experienced times of feeling speechless or at a loss for words. At these moments, I believe, we know intuitively the power of naming.

Notice these factors

The quotation is not left hanging alone but is woven into the overall essay, first introduced and afterwards summarized in the essay-writer's own words.

The three spaced periods—the "dot dot dot" called "ellipses"—in the middle of the quotation indicate some unnecessary words have been left out.

Summarizing and Paraphrasing

Summarizing captures and condenses another writer's main idea in as few words as possible. Therefore, by its nature, a summary will be shorter than what is being summarized. **Paraphrasing**, on the other hand, recasts another writer's thoughts in full detail and in their original order but in entirely different words and phrases. Paraphrases are therefore often just as long as the passage paraphrased, sometimes longer. So while in the example above the passage from Dale Spender's "Politics of Naming" is followed by a two-sentence summary, a paraphrase would read more like this:

Notice these factors

The paraphrase reproduces all the ideas in Spender's original passage without reusing any of her original words or phrases: the paraphrase literally translates Spender's English into another set of English words and sentences.

Changing just a few of the writer's original words into your own constitutes plagiarism, even if you provide an in-text citation. So when in doubt, consider quoting.

> Human beings could not exist without language and the words, the linguistic labels, it comprises. Without the words to identify objects, emotions and occurrences, we would not recognize them or acknowledge their place in the world and in our consciousness of it. The words we apply to objects enable us to make order out of the disorder of phenomena otherwise engulfing us. Language affords us the ability to manage and control the universe of our experiences (Spender 195).

Notice these factors

An in-text citation follows the paraphrase because the ideas belong to Spender, even if the words do not.

Spender's name is included within the citation because it was not given in an introductory signal phrase. Notice that according to MLA style, no punctuation separates name from page number.

Sample MLA In-text Citations

One Author with Signal Phrase

When you have introduced the writer by name in a signal phrase, include only the page number(s) in parentheses.

As the linguist Dale Spender observes, "Naming is the means whereby we attempt to order and structure the chaos and flux of existence" (195).

One Author without Signal Phrase

When you have not identified the writer in a signal phrase, include the writer's last name, along with the page number, in parentheses—with no punctuation separating the two.

> Names are essential to human thought and life because "without a name it is difficult to accept the existence of an object, an event, a feeling" (Spender 195), or to locate ourselves among these phenomena.

Note: If the quotation falls in the middle of your sentence, do not interrupt the flow of your words with the in-text citation. Instead, place the citation before a natural pause or sentence break as close to the quotation as possible. For example:

> Names are essential to human thought and life because "without a name it is difficult to accept the existence" of surrounding phenomena (Spender 195) or to locate ourselves among these phenomena.

Two or Three Authors

When quoting from any text by two or three joint authors, name each writer (in the order originally presented) in your signal phrase or in-text citation.

> As Hardiman and Jackson remind us, during periods or stages of resistance, one may "experience an identity void and a need to redefine one's self" (22).

> By drawing an analogy between the way we read and the way we experience life generally, social scientists "made it possible to conceive of the evolution of lives and relationships in terms of the reading and writing of texts, insofar as every new reading of a text is a new interpretation of it, a different writing of it" (White and Epston 65).

Four or More Authors

If the work you are citing was written by four or more authors, it is best to name each author in a signal phrase or shorten your citation by following the first author's name with the Latin phrase et al. (meaning "and others").

> Belenky, Clinchy, Goldberger, and Tarule discovered that most high school and college courses "begin not with the student's knowledge, but with the teacher's knowledge" (198).

Most high school and college courses "begin not with the student's knowledge, but with the teacher's knowledge" (Belenky et al. 198).

Notice: The Latin word *et* means *and*. The term *al.* is the abbreviation of *alia*, meaning *others*; therefore, the period must be used.

Author Unknown

When the author is unknown—as in a newspaper or magazine article or often a Web site—use the title in place of the author's name. If the title is short, use the complete title; if it is long, you may use a shortened version as long as it is recognizable in your Works Cited list.

> The winner of this week's water polo tournament will receive, according to at least one report, "an automatic bid to the inaugural NCAA women's water polo championship at Palo Alto" ("Women's Water" 8).

Notice: The full title of this news article is "Women's Water Polo Heads to Tourney." It was appropriately shortened for an in-text citation.

Indirect (Quoted) Source

If you wish to quote the words of another writer quoted in the work you are reading, put the name of the person whose words you are quoting in a signal phrase. Within the parentheses of your in-text citation, put the author and page number of the book or article in which you found them, preceded by the abbreviation qtd. in.

> French philosopher Michel Foucault advises, "We should try to grasp subjection in its material instance as a constitution of subjects" (qtd. in White and Epston 72).

Interview

Treat a spoken interview as you would any text without page or paragraph numbers: simply follow the quotation or paraphrase with the speaker's last name in parentheses.

> When asked the key to good reading, Peter Elbow replied, "It is to be both objective and subjective at the same time, while always remaining respectful of the text and its writer" (Elbow).

Movies, Music and Art

Movies, music and works of art are best treated as you would a one-page article, that is, as a whole by giving the title in a signal phrase.

> Brian DePalma fans may try to forget *Carrie*, but the prom scene is burnt forever in our collective memory.

> Joe Cocker's rendition of "Feeling Alright" on his 1969 hit album *With a Little Help from My Friends* remains a rock-'n'-roll tour de force.

> Frans Hals's portraiture in his painting *Regents of the Old Men's Alms House* asks to be read like a Dickens narrative.

Web Site or Other Electronic Source, with or without Page Numbers

When citing an electronic source, follow the same conventions used for other print media. If the author's name is available, use it; if the name is not available, use the site title. If page numbers are visible on the screen, include the relevant number in your citation. (Do not use your own printout page numbers since these will vary from printer to printer.)

Some electronic sources provide numbered paragraphs, screens, or sections instead of page numbers. You may use the available numbering system just as you would a page number, except for these changes: 1) <u>Do</u> insert a comma and one space after the name or title; 2) use the abbreviation *par.* for a paragraph, followed by the number; 3) use *screen* for a numbered screen and its number; 4) use *sec.* for a numbered section and its number.

Many Web sites do not provide page numbers or any other visible numbering system. For these sites use just the author's name, if available, or the site title, if no author is given.

> Reading Annie Dillard is truly transporting. As one ardent fan suggests, it seems you begin reading "just another bird story, and it suddenly turns into much more — you can just feel the profound implications as she simply relates what she is seeing around her" (Elliott).

> At least one on-line travel guide establishes sightseers' expectations before they even leave home: "Grand Canyon is unmatched in the incomparable vistas it offers to visitors on the rim" (*Grand Canyon*).

Note: The Annie Dillard site is a personal Web page; the Grand Canyon site is supported by the National Park Service. You will see a difference in the two Works Cited entries: the Grand Canyon entry includes the National Park Service as the site's sponsoring organization.

The "Works Cited" List in MLA Style

The **Works Cited** list following your essay complements the in-text citations within the essay's body by providing publication information for each citation. Because you want your readers to use the same source you used and because some writers' essays have been published in a variety of media—for example, a magazine or journal, then a book, then a collection or anthology—you must include specific, detailed information about every work you have quoted from and cited. Note that unlike the traditional **bibliography**, which lists all sources used in your research whether quoted or not, the MLA-preferred **Works Cited** list contains only those works you have actually quoted or paraphrased (and therefore cited) in the body of your essay.

The overall Works Cited list is arranged in alphabetical order by the authors' last names, and individual entries are formatted as hanging indents (first line, flush left; succeeding lines, .5" indent). Arrangement and format together allow your readers to locate individual citation entries quickly and easily.

The information contained within each entry of the Works Cited list also follows a specific arrangement and format, including matters of capitalization and punctuation. Again, the rules governing these arrangements are seemingly arbitrary yet necessary conventions, similar to the conventions governing mathematical statements and computer commands. The simple mathematical expression $3X - 5 = 25^2$ is not the same as $5 + 3X = 252$. If you want to visit the Web site <http://www.well.com/user/elliotts/dillard.html> but instead type <http\www.com/user\elliotts.html>, you will not get there! Mixing up the detail elements in a Works Cited entry is similarly misleading.

The exact information contained in each entry will vary according to the medium it represents—anthology selection, book, journal article, Web site, interview, etc. Basically, however, every entry will inform your readers of the author's (or authors') full name(s), the title of the work, the title and editor of the anthology if relevant, the place of publication, publisher, date of publication, and range of pages in which the work appears.

Below is a sample Works Cited list for the essay on MLA Documentation Style you have just read. When you compose your own Works Cited list, you may use the entries as models for the various citations you have included in your essay. Or you may use the models offered in your grammar handbook. Think of all these models as providing a pattern of information, arrangement, capitalization, and punctuation to be followed as you insert your own specific details.

Entry type

Book, with more than three authors

Movie

Music

Anthology, more than one selection used

Interview

Web Site, known author

Web Site, sponsoring organization.

Work of Art: Name museum; just city if widely known.

Single Anthology Selection: two authors from anthology with multiple editors

Multiple Selections in One Anthology: Cross reference with anthology.

Unknown Author: newspaper article

Works Cited

Belenky, Mary Field, Blythe McVicker Clinchy, Nancy Rule Goldberger, and Jill Mattuck Tarule. *Women's Ways of Knowing: The Development of Self, Voice, and Mind.* New York: Basic, 1986.

Carrie. Dir. Brian DePalma. United Artists, 1976.

Cocker, Joe. "Feeling Alright." *With a Little Help from My Friends.* A&M, 1969.

Curtis, Marcia, ed. *The Composition of Ourselves.* 2nd ed. Dubuque: Kendall/Hunt, 2000.

Elbow, Peter. Personal interview. 12 Feb. 2001.

Elliott, Sandra Stahlman. *The Mysticism of Annie Dillard's Pilgrim at Tinker Creek.* 12 Feb. 2001. 5 May 2001 <http://www.well.com/user/elliotts/smse_dillard.html>.

Grand Canyon National Park. 17 May 2001. National Park Service. 22 May 2001 < http://www.nps.gov/grca/>.

Hals, Frans. *Regents of the Old Men's Alms House.* Frans Halsmuseum, Haarlem, Netherlands.

Hardiman, Rita, and Bailey Jackson. "Conceptual Foundations for Social Justice Courses." *Teaching for Diversity and Social Justice.* Ed. Maurianne Adams, et al. New York: Rutledge, 1997. 16–29.

Spender, Dale. "The Politics of Naming." Curtis 195–200.

White, Michael, and David Epston. "Story, Knowledge, and Power." Curtis 64–77.

"Women's Water Polo Heads to Tourney." *Campus Chronicle* 27 April 2001: 8.

Notice these factors

Single or first author, list last name first. Additional authors, if any, list first name first.

Titles: Book, journal, newspaper, film titles appear either underlined or in italics. Essays, songs, and other short works published within a longer work appear inside quotation marks.

Publication information (city, publishing company, copyright © year) is found on opening pages of most books. Use first city and latest date if more than one is given.

For Web site, give date created or updated, then date you accessed. (In Explorer, find date through File menu and Properties; in Netscape, use View menu and Page Info.)

Anthologies: If you cite just one selection in an anthology, do not list the anthology. List just the essay selection (See Hardiman entry). If you cite more than one selection from same anthology, do list the anthology itself. Also list the essay selections using a shortened form cross-referenced with the anthology (See Curtis, Spender, White entries).

Film Videos: When citing a movie you watched on video, include video company and date.

Carrie. Dir. Brian DePalma. Videocassette. MGM Video, 1976.

MLA Documentation Practice

Before starting this practice guide, select from your reading a short statement that interests you and a longer passage (of four or more lines). Then answer the questions and follow the directions below.

1. What is MLA style?

2. What is a signal phrase?

3. Using a signal phrase, write a sentence that includes the short statement you chose to quote and ends with an in-text citation.

4. Now quote the same statement and provide the appropriate in-text citation, this time without using a signal phrase.

5. Introduce and provide an in-text citation for the longer passage you chose using the block quotation format.

6. What are the significant differences between quoting, paraphrasing, and summarizing?

7. Paraphrase the longer passage you selected.

8. What is a key difference between a bibliography and an MLA Works Cited list?

9. What is a "hanging indent"?

10. Using the short statement and the longer passage you quoted above, make a sample Works Cited list in MLA style.

MLA Classroom Practice

This practice exercise may be especially useful when you are working to draft your own essay.

Work in a class (or group) with members who have studied and are wrestling with the same reading. Divide into small-group teams—A, B, and C.

Team A: Select two short passages from the reading. Introduce them using an appropriate signal phrase, quote exactly, and document with an in-text citation.

Team B: Select two short passages. Introduce and paraphrase them carefully.

Team C: Select two or more substantial paragraphs. Introduce and summarize them succinctly.

All teams will work in writing and show their finished products to the class for review, perhaps by putting examples on the board.

Help one another! The exercise is harder than it appears and requires attention to detail.

Some Successful Text-Wrestling Strategies from Student Essays

Contributed by Claire Schomp
Review the following effective models. They suggest that the student writers quoted in each model are close readers, indeed, and skilled writers, too. See whether you can incorporate some of the strategies illustrated into your own essay's later drafts.

Introducing the essay or summarizing its main ideas or techniques: (do this early on)
"How may one pay homage to the simplistic happiness of children? In his essay 'Snickers, Green Blobs, and Quarters: A Perfect World,' Tim Maynard...does this using rhetorical strategies such as colorful descriptions of his experiences, concrete nouns relating to childhood, and flashing back from adulthood and dreaming of childhood life" (Heather Lavigne).

Combining summary with analysis:
"[Kelly Craven's] commentary is an entertaining analysis of forwarded email, something that just about everyone receives" (Amanda Roche).

Stating your opinions clearly (and as "fact"):
"Not sure of anything except that whatever Edmundson says is wrong, Tolson stumbles her way through a grocery list of failed rebuttals inter-twined with valid points and well-thought out arguments. Overall, these inconsistencies make for any uneasy read" (James Taylor).
"The History of American Ideals Through Comic Books' is definitely an effective and well thought out essay that proves that comic books are more than just another way for children to throw away their allowances" (Eric Salgado).

Describing, responding or relating to the text on a personal level:
"Through reading Hobby-Reichstein's essay, I could identify with her emotions to a certain degree by remembering my first encounters with the subject of racism" (Melanie Leftick).

Commenting on style and effect of text:
"The honesty and openness with which the essay begins helps engage the reader in the narrative" (Caitlin Foote).

Maintaining <u>your own</u> voice and style:
"The essay is a story set up as a childhood flashback cleverly sandwiched between a first and last paragraph of the person in his adult life" (Benjamin Pease).

Setting up a quotation:
"She gets more serious, stating 'Forwarded mail has to be one of the most impersonal ways for humans to pretend like they are staying in touch with one another'" (Meghan Sullivan).

Going further: discussing the relevance of quotations or techniques:
"You can hear the contempt in these words, and it gets to the heart of what the author is upset and writing about""(Meghan Sullivan).

Noticing patterns in the writing itself:
"Interwoven throughout Maynard's essay there are references to wind, air, space, and freedom from responsibility" (Jessica Prince).

Appendix for Teachers

Three Workshops by Peter Elbow

> What is a wrestling? It is a close grappling that has some elements of fighting and some elements of embracing in it, at the same time and *in the same process*. There are both love and anger in a wrestle. In a wrestle I do not pretend my partner is the same as me—and I do not pretend I am the same as my partner. We are two; I, who I fully am; and the other, fully other.
> —Arthur I. Waskow, *Seasons of Our Joy*

In what follows, I'll describe three workshops I like to use when I teach text-wrestling essays—workshops that help people understand and improve their process of reading. These workshops grow out of the insights about the reading process that I described in the Foreword to this book.

A Laboratory in the Reading Process

The workshop is very simple. I present a text to my students one small portion at a time. I start by reading the title and the first paragraph or two. I'm trying to give them only the first small taste or bite or chunk. I want to make it blatantly obvious that when we read, our eyes can only take in one portion at a time—and our minds are chewing over every bit as it comes in. So I ask students to freewrite for a couple of minutes about what their mind is doing with this short piece of text. What meanings do they get so far? What do they sense the piece might be about or might be saying? What do they expect next? What thoughts or associations or memories come to mind? What kind of reactions are they having (frustration, attraction, agreement, disagreement, resistance, &c. &c.)?

Then I'll present another chunk: probably two or three more paragraphs; whatever seems to be a likely "next bit"; enough to get the essay somewhat "started." (It's interesting to take a more extreme approach and slow down the camera even more: present just a few *words* at a time. This is just what cognitive psychologists do in their experiments. You could conduct this kind experiment yourself.) Again, we write briefly. What do we sense the text is saying? What meanings, expectations, associations, and reactions do we get? Then a third chunk: and the same process of monitoring and recording our minds' attempts to make meaning.

Unless the piece is very short, we can't get through it all in one class. But before class ends, I make sure to have some time for students to *share* these movies of their minds-in-action in pairs or small groups. It's helpful and interesting to see where people agree or had similar reactions—and where they differ. Some texts invite more divergent reactions than others, and some groups of people contain more difference in the histories of their experiences with the same words. The unpredictability makes it interesting.

I encourage my students not to leave out mental events that might seem stray or irrelevant. "Don't just notice and write down what you associate with English classes," I say. "Don't leave out odd memories and associations or even daydreams. These seemingly 'irrelevant' mental events will often show you some interesting things about the text." My point is not to worry about the relevance or usefulness of the reaction: if it comes to mind, write it down.

Homework

I ask students to continue with this reading-and-writing process of recording their reactions. They can take somewhat larger chunks as they continue along. I ask them to write at greater length when they finally get to the end; but it's also important to go back and read the whole thing at least once more—probably without stopping—and write about any *new* meanings, reactions, or changes that usually come from a second reading. It's also important to try to note what happens in their minds on the basis of having heard other people's reactions and constructions.

The homework assignment, then, is a long "first draft" that consists of nothing but all this writing out of movies of the mind gradually constructing meaning from a text. This is an unusually long draft—but one that didn't take much struggle to create. I'm happy to emphasize and dignify this writing as a "draft" of an essay because I care so much about students learning this precious skill of articulating what goes on in their minds as they read. For one thing, this ability to monitor your own reactions ("meta-discourse") leads to richer deeper thinking; but in addition, these "movies of the reader's mind" are probably the most useful form of feedback that a reader can give to a writer.

What Do I Hope to Accomplish with this Workshop?

This workshop helps us see what usually goes undetected: the gradual process by which we gradually actively *construct* the meaning from a text. If we see only the first few lines or paragraphs of a text and we take the trouble to articulate what reactions and meanings occurred in us, we have created a guess or hypothesis of what the text is saying; and we have usually created expectations about what will come next. When we repeat the process with succeeding chunks of the text, we notice that later chunks of text often force us to adjust or even change our earlier reactions and interpretations. Unless we go through this admittedly artificial, slow motion exercise, we often forget those earlier meanings, reactions, and expectations because we revised them so quickly. In normal reading, those earlier responses were often completely subliminal.

With this workshop I'm trying to take a scientific, empirical approach to the activity of learning to study and interpret a text. In effect, I'm teaching people to train a slow-motion camera on their reading process—or to dip test-tubes periodically into their brains and bring out timed samples. I am trying to get people out of the normal agenda in school reading: *try to figure out the correct answer*. I think I can help people's skill in reading best by taking some emphasis away from the traditional question of *what's right* and putting more emphasis on the empirical question of *what happens*. Eventually—after people have shared and discussed their reactions, and as they are in the process of writing drafts of their individual essays—we can talk about…well, not exactly about right and wrong but rather about which interpretations are more plausible or persuasive. For I'm not, with this workshop, trying to argue that all reactions and interpretations are equally valid. But the process is all about *noticing* reactions rather than *judging* them: learning to *pay better attention*—attention to the text and attention to one's own mental events.

I'm trying to show that if we look closely enough, we can see that the human mind is never stupid or random. That is, *every* reaction, response, and interpretation that comes to anyone's mind makes perfect sense—*given everything else that person has experienced*, as well as not experienced. All reactions make sense—given everything else in one's mind or not in one's mind—even if those reactions turn out to be "misreadings" or bad fits with the text. (Really "wrong" or "stupid"-seeming responses usually come from a lack of certain experiences with words—or from emotional static that is jamming the works.)

Sometimes people object to this workshop by saying, "But this activity doesn't give an accurate, scientific picture of my reading. I never read in such a peculiar artificial way. This workshop makes me think of things in reac-

tion to the text that I never would have thought of if I'd read it normally."
But this is an easy objection to answer. "Think a little further about all those
things that you said would never have normally come to mind," I say.

> Did I or my exercise *put* anything in your head that wasn't already there?
> Nobody *added* anything to your mind except for what you got out of the
> text—or rather brought *to* the text. Any of these allegedly "new" or "odd"
> reactions, thoughts, feelings, or memories were *already* in your mind.
> The only thing I did was to interrupt you and make you pause and write.
> I did nothing but create more opportunity for what was already in your
> mind to come to conscious awareness. All these things were already in
> your mind—and already influencing your "normal" fast reading—but
> influencing it in ways that are usually below your level of awareness. The
> only thing new was your heightened consciousness.

This workshop helps me enrich discussions of texts. The workshop gives
enormous particularity to responses and gets us beyond *global* responses
such as "I like/hate it" or "I think it means X/Y" or "It was beautiful/sad/iron-
ic." For students having to write their papers, there's a big practical payoff:
the process gives them *too much* to talk about in their essays rather than too
little. It helps students and the class become awash in very particulate textual data.

Some people also object that I am promoting intellectual laziness when
I emphasize *what happens* rather than what's the right or best interpretation.
But notice that I'm not saying, "Just see what happens when you relax lazi-
ly with a text." Rather I'm saying, "Notice what happens when you pay good
attention and work hard at trying to figure out meanings." I sometimes have
to remind students to keep reading: "Read it again. See what happens when
you read it again."

"But don't forget," I emphasize, "part of the discipline here is to pay attention to *everything* going on in you, not just the most academic or proper
things." That is, I'm trying to persuade students not to go into a special
"school gear" or "academic gear" when reading for a school essay—not to
push away all their "regular" thinking and reacting. Our regular "street thinking" is often smarter than our "school thinking."

It's often the less experienced or school-savvy students who need this
nudge not to narrow their thinking. I like to look at the movies of the mind
of the most experienced and skilled readers as they try to make sense of hard
texts. (I don't mean "good students" in the limited sense of mere skill at
playing the school game; I mean genuinely good readers who look closely
but think creatively.) Such readers tend to make *more* hypotheses at any given
moment; they tend to be *more* playful and flexible about changing their ear-

lier ideas on the basis of later input. You could even say that skilled readers usually have more "wrong answers." That is, they start off with more associations and reactions—in effect, more hypotheses—and therefore end up having to *throw away* more. And it's palpably obvious that when skilled readers engage a text, they do not enter some "other" "literary" world or "artificial space." They use all the parts of their minds. They often consider feelings and reactions and memories that less experienced readers push away as "inappropriate" for school.

I like the way this empirical process of monitoring the movies of our minds can lead to interesting discussions about cultural issues. When students pay better attention to their actual responses at the micro level, they can see more vividly the various powerful forces and cultural assumptions that tend to shape their minds: media, family, religion, gender, class, race, and sexual orientation.

A Few Notes to Teachers

The "purest" way to present a text in pieces is actually to cut it up and hand out one scrap of paper at a time (or to fold the first few pages in such a way that students can see only one part at a time). This gives us the most scientific "movie" of students alone with a text. If I read the text out loud, I am, in a sense, already providing a bit of interpretation.

Nevertheless, I often do present the text out loud—stopping periodically for students to write out what is happening in their minds as they try to process the text. For one thing, reading out loud is logistically easier. And I also prefer this method if I think the text is difficult and I fear that too many students will spend too much time simply working out the literal meaning. I don't want their main reaction to be mere frustration or annoyance at the difficulty. I'm not so interested, in this workshop, in the process of figuring out merely the literal meaning of sentences as the larger meaning and interpretation across sentences. And I've found that I don't shape or bias their interpretation too much if I read out loud slowly and deliberately. I try to put literal meaning and clarity into my rendering—but not much "expression" or character. This way, I can get them "started" on a difficult essay that they'll take home and finish on their own.

Sharing

When is it best for students to share their reactions or movies with each other (usually in pairs or very small groups at first)? If I want to increase the social nature of the process, I start this process after only a couple of fragments. And this helps less practiced readers to feel more secure as they start off. And whether or not the text is hard, it's interesting for people to notice how different minds understand and react differently to the same few words. But more often than not, I hold off the sharing till towards the end of that first session—after they've reacted on their own to four or more fragments.

I find it helpful sometimes to go through this process with a text that *I* haven't yet seen. I ask a student or small group to choose a text, divide it into sections, and bring in copies for all of us to work on. Then I can share my written movies, and students can see me having initial reactions, responses, and interpretations, and then adjusting and changing my mind as I realize that these initial reactions were inappropriate or plain wrong.

A Voice Workshop

I look for a passage in the essay that is interesting or even controversial in what it says, but most of all, one that seems to illustrate the author's voice— or *one* of the voices the writer uses. Then I ask students to work in small groups to develop an out-loud "reading" of this passage—an enactment or embodiment of the words. "This is not an exercise in acting or performance," I say. "Just try to get it to *sound right*. Try to make it sound somehow the way this writer ought to sound, or like this writer, or how these words want to sound." Then we hear two or three or four enactments or voicings.

In this workshop, my goal is to get students to *hear* a voice in any passage of writing. I want them to sense a *person* in there—even in hard or scholarly texts. I want them to get over the feeling that important authoritative texts are written by a "they" or an "it"—a disembodied authority. (Unfortunately, students have good reason for this prejudice: so much school reading is in textbooks—books in which authors deliberately try to suppress voice and achieve the quality of "it" or "they.") Hearing a voice helps us connect and engage with authoritative texts. Hearing a person in a text leads us to converse with that person. I want to increase the chances that students will listen for voices in everything they read.

My goal in setting up these group tasks is to get vocal renderings that *differ* from each other—differ in voice or character or "implied author." If the first readings are too similar, I myself will try out a very different one—and I'll overtly make the point that there is no single right reading or enactment of a text—just as there is no right performance of a Shakespeare play. If the readings are too similar or too drab, I push exaggerations or parodies. Sometimes we don't get at a certain flavor in the voice of a text till we "lay it on" too thick.

I try to alert them to the notion that a voice might significantly change over the course of an essay. A writer's attitude or feeling may only peep out clearly in certain passages—and sometimes different attitudes or moods will emerge at different places in the essay. But even though writers may change their mood, feeling, tone, or stance even in short pieces of writing—their voice—it's still the work of a single writer. So I frankly invite students to hypothesize or "construct" a single person or implied author of the *whole* essay. (Some theorists don't like this idea of a single self, but I find it only natural.)

This workshop highlights a profound theoretical and pedagogical point. It's impossible to read a passage out loud without implying at least some interpretation (unless you mumble or read in completely mechanical monotone). So many class discussions of a text are attempts to get students to articulate an interpretation. But if we get students to figure out how they think a text ought to *sound*—and give it that way—they have already produced an interpretation. Then all we need to do is articulate the interpretation that all of us have already heard.

A Dialogue Workshop

I ask each student to look through the published essay and notice a half dozen or so of their own underlinings that now strike them as interesting or important. Then I ask them to write something I admit is artificial and playful—but I insist that it is feasible if they'll just go along with me: a *dialogue* between them and the author. In particular, I push them to use passages from the essay (particularly passages they underlined) for the author's part of the dialogue. In fact this is how I tell them to get the dialogue going:

> Let the author start the conversation. That is, start off your dialogue by writing out a sentence or more from the essay. Then write your response to these words. Try to let your response be only a sentence or two. You're trying for a conversation, not two people making speeches at each other. Then "get" your author to reply to you. That is, if the words don't already pop into your head, just sit there a moment and wait to see what he or she wants to answer. It's fine to make up words for the author. Words will come if you just step into the role. But see how often you can bring in some of the author's actual words from the essay. Have fun pretending to be someone different from yourself.

I've found for myself and my students that a strong voice and lively thinking often erupt in the voice of this other person. Somehow we seem to be able to tap a certain kind of personal, intellectual energy when we are freed from having to speak as ourselves.

Then two more activities:

- Some sharing in pairs of their dialogues—or as much as they are willing to share;

- Five or ten minutes of writing at the end to stand back and write for themselves: What is this dialogue is all about? What is it telling you? Where is your thinking now?

In the next class or conference, I can try to work more on the conventions of quoting and citing. (I have already had a chance to work on this earlier in the semester, when I asked students to write an essay about a class publication—an essay in which they needed to quote from their classmates' writing).

In my comments on their midprocess drafts, I can try to push students individually where I sense they need to go: to be braver and feistier with their own thinking; or to be fairer or more accurate in their reading of the published essay; or to try to figure out a larger point that is implied in a lot of little thoughts and observations they have made.